Early Catholic Church Records in Baltimore, Maryland

1782 through 1800

Compiled by

Mary A. and Stanley G. Piet

HERITAGE BOOKS
2020

HERITAGE BOOKS
AN IMPRINT OF HERITAGE BOOKS, INC.

Books, CDs, and more—Worldwide

For our listing of thousands of titles see our website
at
www.HeritageBooks.com

Published 2020 by
HERITAGE BOOKS, INC.
Publishing Division
5810 Ruatan Street
Berwyn Heights, Md. 20740

Copyright © 1989, 1991 Willow Bend Books

All rights reserved. No part of this book may be reproduced or transmitted in any form or by any means, electronic or mechanical, including photocopying, recording or by any information storage and retrieval system without written permission from the author, except for the inclusion of brief quotations in a review.

International Standard Book Number
Paperbound: 978-1-58549-142-1

INTRODUCTION

St. Peter's Catholic Church was founded by the Jesuit Fathers to meet the needs of the French Acadian refugees and the Irish immigrants of Baltimore City. It was the first building erected as a Catholic Church in the city. Construction began in 1770 and was ended in 1783

St. Peter's Church was a plain brick building of modest dimensions (25 by 30 feet), and built very much unlike a church building as the Catholic Church was still under suppression by an act of the legislature. It was located near what is now known as the Basilica of the Assumption at Cathedral & Mulberry Streets in Baltimore. As the Parish grew an addition was made to the original building and a cemetery was added.

Its records are part of the Baltimore Cathedral Archives and contain the only Catholic parish records up to the year 1806, when the records of St. Patrick's Church, Fells Point, began to be preserved.

With the establishment of the See of Baltimore in 1789 and the appointment of the Rev. John Carroll as its first Bishop, Baltimore became the primary see of the new Republic and St. Peter's became his seat of authority. At this time another addition was made to the church. It existed as such until the Cathedral (now Basilica) of the Assumption was completed and put into service about 1821. Old St. Peter's was demolished around 1840 and later the Church of St. Peter the Apostle was erected in a different location. There is no connection between the two St. Peter's Churches. The records of the original St. Peter's are part of the Cathedral Archives. St. Peters the Apostle Church has its own archives.

This book contains baptismal, burial and marriage data as transcribed from the original records from the first entry in 1782 through the year 1800 inclusive.

The compilers experienced the usual difficulties in interpreting some of the handwriting of the various persons who made entries in the journals, and where data were missing, tried to fill it in from other sources, notably marriage license records, if such were available.

The researcher using this collection should be aware that in many instances the names are often spelled phonetically and inconsistently. In no instance have the compilers attempted to alter the spelling of any names, given or proper, or alter the spelling of any physical location.

Abbreviations Used

bn. - date of birth
bpt. - date of baptism
bur. - date of burial
da. - days
died - date of death
dau. of - daughter of
hsb. of - husband of

inh. of - inhabitant of
mo. - months
nat. of - native of
sps. - sponsor(s)
wf. of - wife of
wks. - weeks
yrs. - years

In the case of slaves lacking a last name, the compilers have taken the liberty of inserting the owner's last name in parentheses as an aid to the researcher. Free born children of slaves are listed under the name of the owner their parents.

INTRODUCTION

Beginning in June 1789, the names of parents began to appear in the records of baptisms. Prior to that time the names of the sponsors were recorded but not the parents' names.

The list begins with persons with given names only.

NOTE

For a complete history of old St. Peter's Church, see Old St. Peter's, or the Beginning of Catholicity in Baltimore by Rev. J. A. Fredericks, a copy of which is in the library of the Maryland Historical Society in Baltimore.

1790 Married

July 26	John Dunn to Eleanor Fitzgerald	P
31	George Hotch to Catherine Green	L
Sep. 4	William Merrick to Catherine Desmond	L
	Daniel Donoghue to Brigit Helnan	P
26	John Baptist Peat to Peggy Chemeau	L
21	Job Logsdon to Patience Helms	L
October 6	Peter Crisall to Margaret Richards	P
12	James Flornes to Magdalene Babin	L
20	Matthew Taylor to Mary Smith	L
20	Patrick Herrick to Ann Hamilton	L
30	Richard Gore to Lettice Montgomery	P
Nov. 1	William Layde to Mary Walsh	P
1	Peter Lick to Rosanna Willis	P
7	John Hammond to Frances Clifford	P
11	John Garland to Mary Ann Lyston	L
20	Nicholas Corbeley to Hannah Yreals	L
23	Peter Haily to Margaret Leary	L
Xer. 9	Daniel Leary to Mary McBride	L
27	Redmond Berry to Johanna Kanney	L
28	John Madden to Elizabeth Yost	P
28	Thomas Mullet to Nancy Fewshou	L

1791

Jan. 4	John Friday to Elizabeth Boughan	P
25	Joseph Hook to Sarah Johnson	P
30	Peter Blossom to Mary Magdalene La Blanc	L
Feb. 1	Matthew Harding to Mary Davis	L
	John Peck to Eleanor Piper	L P
March 3	Martin Waters to Diana Harriman	P
5	Nathaniel Carven to Eleanor Freeman	L
29	John McCan to Ann Egan	

A page from the register of marriages. The letter appearing in the right column indicates License (L) or Publication of Banns (P)

HAGERS-TOWN GAZETTE

Michael LOWMAN, Jun., has lost a white woolen cloth of 7 1/2 yards; leave at COFFROTH's store in Greencastle or Mr. M'ILHENNYS store in Hagers-Town.

255. Dec 22 1812
Daniel GEHR, living at the plantation of John BEARD, Wash Co, has taken up a stray bull calf.
Sale of tavern stand in Williams-Port, now in tenure of Mr. MUIR - Benjamin YOE.

CONTENTS

Introduction iii

A page from the Register of Marriages v

Baptisms 1

Marriages - by Groom 126

Marriages - by Bride 146

Burials 159

BAPTISMS

Achilles; bpt. Nov 11, 1793; dau. of Adrienne, Mulatress
Albert; bpt. Aug 31, 1794; Mulatto child; son of Angelica of St. Domingo
Ann; bpt. Jul 25, 1794; 8 months; dau. of Mary Magdalen, free Negress
Ann; bpt. Nov 3, 1799; 6 months; dau. of Pompey, slave of James Sloan & Nancy, free Negro
Antoinette; bpt. Oct 21, 1798; 6 weeks; dau. of Nancy, free Negro
Augustin; bpt. May 25, 1797; 18 months; son of Jeannite, free Negro
Bartholomew Felix; bn. Apr 2, 1794; bpt. May 9, 1794; son of Amilia, free Mulatress
Basil; bpt. Aug 1, 1797; 5 months; son of Justine, free French Negro
Basil; bpt. Jan 19, 1800; 2 months; son of Henny, free Negro
Bertrand Simon Judah; bn. Mar 29, 1796; bpt. Apr 23, 1796; son of Marie Franciose Lorette, Mulatto, Cp. Francois
Catharine; bpt. May 27, 1798; 1 month; dau. of Mary Jane, free Negress of St. Domingo; child declared free
Catharine Augustine George; bpt. Nov 22, 1798; 2 months; dau. of Eugenie, free Multress, St. Domingo
Catharine Josephine Delphina; bpt. Aug 23, 1794; 5 years old; dau. of Catharine Gadra, called Rozette, Mulatress of St. Domingo
Charles; bpt. Dec 24, 1797; 6 months; son of Mary, free French Negro
Charles; bn. Oct 20, 1799; bpt. Nov 24, 1799; son of Marie Claire, French Mulatress
Charlotte; bn. May 20, 1785; bpt. Sep 17, 1785; sps. Nancy Gutterau
Cyrus; bn. Jan 17, 1787; bpt. Mar 7, 1787; sps. Joanna Hawkins
Edmund William; bpt. Sep 11, 1797; Mulatto; 5 months; parents unknown; sps. Edmund Liuse & Jane Victoria Cartier, a Mulatto of St. Domingo
Edward; bn. Nov ?, 1797; bpt. Jan 14, 1798; son of John, slave & Phyllis, free woman
Eleanora; bpt. Jul 17, 1796; 6 1/2 years old; Mulatto; dau. of Julie, free Negro, nat. of Africa
Elizabeth; bpt. Aug 15, 1796; 14 1/2 months; dau. of Elizabeth, free Mulatto
Elizabeth; bpt. Aug 30, 1796; dau. of Stephen & Hetty, free Negroes
Elizabeth; bn. Dec 23, 1796; bpt. Jan 1, 1797; dau. of Mary Frances, free Mulatto
Elizabeth; bn. Jun ?, 1796; bpt. Jan 7, 1797; dau. of Jany, free Mulatto
Elizabeth; bpt. Aug 31, 1800; 30 years old; called Marie Jeanne; slave of Mulatto Jean Baptiste
Emilie; bpt. Nov 19, 1796; 7 months; dau. of Marie Louise, free Mulatto
Frances; bn. Aug 8, 1796; bpt. Sep 22, 1796; dau. of Rosine Jeannette, free Mulatto
Frances Elizabeth; bpt. Mar 4, 1798; 7 years old; dau. of Frances
Gaspar; bn. Mar 7, 1797; bpt. Jun 5, 1797; son of Eulalie, French Mulatto

BAPTISMS

Gaspar; bpt. Jul 15, 1798; 10 months; son of Elizabeth, free
    French Mulatto
George; bn. Jun 12, 1797; bpt. Jul 28, 1798; son of Mary
    Magdalen, free Mulatto
Hanna; bpt. Dec 2, 1787; Negro
Hannah; bpt. Jun 22, 1800; 3 weeks; dau. of Phoebe, free Negro
Harina; bn. Dec 18, 1791; bpt. Feb 22, 1792; Negro
Harriet; bpt. Mar 3, 1792; Negro; 4 weeks
Henrietta; bpt. Apr 8, 1798; 3 months; dau. of Resette
Henrietta Maria; bpt. Nov 27, 1791
Henrietta Mary Theresa; bn. Oct 12, 1794; bpt. Oct 18, 1794; dau.
    of Mary Rose
Henry; bn. May 22, 1784; bpt. Jun 20, 1784; Negro; sps. Elizabeth
Henry; bpt. Jun 29, 1788; Negro; 8 weeks; sps. Jack & Peg
Henry; bpt. Jul 3, 1791; Mulattoe; 5 months
Henry; bn. Dec 10, 1792; bpt. Dec 23, 1792; Negro; son of Leonard
    & Beth
Irene Adelle; bpt. Mar 24, 1799; 6 weeks; Mulatto, dau. of
    Jeannot Justine, free French Mulatress
James; bpt. Sep 28, 1785; Negro; born a few days ago; sps. Nace &
    Nance
James; bpt. Jul 8, 1787; Negro; 4 months; sps. Margaret Love
James; bpt. Oct 29, 1792; Negro; 2 weeks
James; bpt. Jun 2, 1799; 5 months; Mulatto; son of Elizabeth,
    free Negro
Jeanne Marie; bpt. Sep 2, 1798; dau. of Sophie, French Mulatto
John; bn. Dec 31, 1785; bpt. Apr 16, 1786; Negro; sps. Ruth
John; bpt. Apr 6, 1788; Negro; about 4 months; sps. Clare
John; bn. Oct 20, 1788; bpt. May 30, 1789; son of Milly
John; bn. Oct 24, 1791; bpt. Dec 1, 1791; son of Dick & Henny
John; bn. Jun 2, 1795; bpt. Feb 25, 1796; son of Mary
John; bn. Jun 24, 1796; bpt. Jun 26, 1796; sps. Francis Faguere &
    Mary Teresa Marsan
John; bpt. Jul 18, 1796; 13 months; Mulatto; son of Jane, free
    Mulatress, St. Domingo
John; bpt. Jun 4, 1797; 1 month; son of Countess, slave of Mamie,
    free Mulatto
John; bn. Dec 22, 1798; bpt. Apr 10, 1799; Mulatto; son of
    Bretet, free French Mulatto & Suky, free Negro
John; bn. May 18, 1800; bpt. Jul 13, 1800; son of Rachel, free
    Negro
John; bpt. Aug 3, 1800; 5 months; son of Nancy, free Negro
John Anthony; bn. Nov 1, 1797; bpt. Mar 19, 1798; free Mulatto;
    son of Emilia, Mulatress of St. Domingo
John Baptist; bpt. Aug 9, 1787; 8 days; son of Mary; sps. Peter
    Gerard & Ann Butler
John Baptist; bpt. Jun 24, 1796; 10 months; son of Emelie, free
    Negro, St. Domingo
John Baptist; bpt. Sep 23, 1796; 5 weeks; son of Mary Magdalen,
    free Negro
John Baptist; bpt. Jun 2, 1799; 3 weeks; son of Comptesse, slave
    of Mamie, French Mulatress
John Bartholomew; bpt. Aug 11, 1799; 1 month; son of Catharine,
    free French woman

BAPTISMS

John Charles; bn. Sep 28, 1797; bpt. Jan 8, 1798; son of Mary Jane, an Indian woman

John Lewis; bpt. Sep 21, 1794; 10 or 11 years old; free Negro from St. Domingo

John Lewis; bpt. Jul 24, 1796; 2 years old; free Negro; son of Camille; declared free by Mr. Desnoutieres

John Lewis; bpt. Jul 9, 1797; 1 month; son of Francoise Collette, slave of Therese, French Mulatto

John Mary; bn. Oct 12, 1794; bpt. Jun 22, 1795; son of Mary Elizabeth (called Victorine)

John Peter Theodore; bn. Dec 19, 1794; bpt. May 31, 1795; son of Jeanne Louise, Mulattoe

John Peter; bpt. Jun 24, 1796; 7 months; son of Mary Catharine, free Negro, St. Domingo

John Stephen; bpt. Aug 10, 1794; 7 years; son of Mary Louisa, free Negress of St. Domingo

John Valentin; bn. Feb 22, 1795; bpt. Mar 8, 1795; son of Luts & Appolonia

Joseph; bpt. Aug 19, 1794; 18 months; son of Mary Catharine, free Negress of St. Domingo

Joseph; bpt. Dec 25, 1794; son of Victoire, slave from St. Domingo

Joseph; bpt. Apr 5, 1795; son of Mary Magdalen, free Negress

Joseph; bn. Apr 26, 1796; bpt. Jun 12, 1796; son of Collette, slave of Terese, French Mulatto, St. Domingo

Joseph; bpt. Dec 19, 1797; 2 1/2 years old; son of Mary, Negro

Justina; bpt. Sep 21, 1795; 3 years old; dau. of Mary Frances, free French Mulattoe

Lewis; bpt. Sep 10, 1795; 2 years old; son of Mimie, free Mulatress

Lewis; bpt. Nov 6, 1798; 5 weeks; son of Catharine, free Multress

Lewis; bpt. Dec 14, 1800; son of Louise

Lewis Marc; bpt. Apr 26, 1795; son of Justina, Mulattress

Louisa; bn. Jul 6, 1797; bpt. Oct 25, 1797; dau. of Louise Nicole, Negro of St. Domingo

Louise; bpt. Nov 14, 1798; 4 months; dau. of Magdalen, free Multress

Louise; bpt. Mar 2, 1800; a foundling, about a fortnight old; sps. Mary Ann, free Negro

Margaret; bpt. Jun 5, 1797; 7 months; dau. of Mary Magdalen, free Mulatto

Margaret; bpt. Jul 31, 1797; 3 weeks; dau. of Thomas & Mary, French Negroes

Margaret Elizabeth; bn. Apr 1, 1798; bpt. Aug 16, 1798; dau. of Sophie, free Mulatto, St. Domingo

Margaret Mary Ann; bn. May 22, 1800; bpt. Jun 22, 1800; dau. of Susanna, free Negro & William, Negro slave

Margarite Adelaide; bpt. Apr 15, 1794; 7 weeks; dau. of Frances, Negro slave (deceased)

Maria Stone; bpt. Aug 29, 1798; 1 month; a foundling, parents unknown

Marie Sophie; bpt. May 4, 1793; adult

Mary; bn. Jan 9, 1790; bpt. Jan 24, 1790; Negro; dau. of Regis & Harriette

Mary; bpt. Oct 6, 1793; Negro; about 5 years old

BAPTISMS

Mary; bn. Oct 10, 1795; bpt. Dec 19, 1795; dau. of Henrietta, Negro
Mary; bpt. Feb 11, 1798; 3 months; dau. of Mary Ann
Mary; bn. Aug 27, 1798; bpt. Aug 28, 1798; a foundling, parents unknown
Mary Antoinette; bpt. Nov 5, 1794; 14 months; dau. of Ann, free Mulatress
Mary Charlotte; bn. Jan 23, 1786; bpt. Feb 4, 1786; sps. John Nachez & Margaret Wells
Mary Charlotte; bpt. Mar 4, 1798; 5 years old; dau. of Frances
Mary Frances; bn. Dec 1, 1793; bpt. Dec 29, 1793; Negro; dau. of Mary Frances
Mary Frances; bn. Jan 26, 1793; bpt. Jun 9, 1795; dau. of Julie, free Negro
Mary Frances; bpt. Jul 27, 1797; 1 year old; dau. of Julie
Mary Frances; bpt. Apr 8, 1798; Mulatto; 16 years old
Mary Gabriel; bpt. May 31, 1797; 7 years old; Mulatto; dau. of Lurencia of St. Domingo
Mary Jane; bn. Jul 21, 1799; bpt. Jan 14, 1800; dau. of Ulalie, free Mulatto
Mary Joseph; bpt. Dec 15, 1799; 1 month; dau. of James Antony & Mary Magdalea, both free
Mary Louise; bpt. Jul 3, 1796; 5 months; dau. of Emanuel & Sophia, free Negroes
Mary Magdalen; bpt. Nov 5, 1794; 2 years old; dau. of Ann, free Mulatress
Mary Rose; bpt. Nov 12, 1797; 5 months; Mulatto; dau. of Sally, free Negro
Mary Virginia; bpt. Jul 17, 1796; 18 months; Mulatto; dau. of Julie, free Negro, nat. of Africa
Milly; bn. Dec 4, 1784; bpt. Jun 17, 1788; Negro; sps. Francis Snowden & Susanna Pierce
Moses; bpt. Jul 12, 1789; 3 weeks; son of Anastatia
Moses; bpt. Jun 4, 1798; adult free Negro
Nancy; bpt. Sep 1, 1799; 1 week; dau. of Regis & Harriet, both free
Noel; bpt. Feb 11, 1798; 5 months; son of Mary Magdalen
Paul; bn. Jan 3, 1795; bpt. Oct 21, 1795; son of Victoire, free Negress, St. Domingo
Paul Ferdinand; bpt. May 5, 1800; Mulatto; son of Emily, free Negress
Peter; bpt. Nov 27, 1791; Negro; 5 weeks; son of Regis & Harriet; sps. Nace & Appollina
Peter; bpt. Jul 7, 1796; 2 months; Mulatto, son of Sophia, free Negro
Peter; bpt. Sep 14, 1800; 3 months; son of Marie, slave
Peter Joseph; bn. Aug 3, 1795; bpt. Nov 8, 1795; son of Mary Jane, free Mulatress, St. Domingo
Peter Lewis; bpt. Jul 6, 1800; 2 months; son of Betsy, free Mulatto
Prince; bpt. Jan 1, 1788; Negro man
Priscilla; bn. Aug 9, 1800; bpt. Sep 28, 1800; dau. of John & Eleanor, free Negroes
Rachel; bpt. Oct 13, 1799; 2 years old; dau. of Paul & Betty
Richard; bpt. Apr 4, 1790; Negro; 10 weeks

BAPTISMS

Rosa; bpt. Oct 19, 1794; 3 months; dau. of Amata Rose
Rose; bpt. May 31, 1797; 5 years old; dau. of Lurencia of St. Domingo
Sophie; bpt. Nov 19, 1797; 8 months; dau. of Sally, free Negro
Stephen; bn. May 2, 1795; bpt. Jun 8, 1795; unknown parents; sps. James Gormly & Neal McKinley
Susanna; bn. Oct 5, 1794; bpt. Oct 9, 1794; dau. of Samuel, free Negro & Apollina, free Mulatress
Terese; bpt. Apr 14, 1799; 11 months; Mulatto; dau. of Adelaide, free Mulatress
Theophile; bpt. Dec 14, 1800; son of Eur--
Thomas; bn. Jun 28, 1794; bpt. Jul 11, 1794; son of Nancy, free Negro
Thomas; bn. Aug 15, 1793; bpt. Dec 14, 1794; son of Luke & Rakel
Thomas; bpt. Mar 22, 1798; Mulatto; child of unknown parents
Victoire Elizabeth; bpt. Oct 18, 1795; 18 months; dau. of Rosette, French Negro, St. Domingo
Will; bn. Apr 11, 1784; bpt. May 23, 1784; Negro; sps. Beth
William; bpt. Aug 9, 1798; 4 months; a foundling, parents unknown
William; bn. Sep 15, 1799; bpt. Oct 20, 1799; Mulatto; son of Abraham & Ally, free Mulattoes
ADDESON, Charles; bpt. Jul 12, 1789; son of Joseph & Sara
ADONE, Andrew Maurice; bn. Jul 8, 1800; bpt. Nov 2, 1800; son of Peter & Catharine
ADONE, Julia Susanna; bn. Jun 23, 1798; bpt. Jul 2, 1798; dau. of Peter & Catharine Estave
(ADOU), Eustace; bpt. Jul 20, 1794; 16 years old; slave of Adou, planter of St. Domingo
ALCORN, Mary; bn. Oct 22, 1797; bpt. Oct 14, 1799; dau. of James (deceased) & Jane
ALCORN, William; bn. Oct 22, 1797; bpt. Oct 14, 1799; son of James (deceased) & Jane
ALFRED, James; bn. Feb 5, 1794; bpt. Feb 12, 1794; son of Charles & Rose
ALLAIN, Lewis Thomas; bn. Aug 2, 1797; bpt. Nov 7, 1797; son of Lewis & Ann Boisson
ALLEN, James; bn. Jul 20, 1793; bpt. Sep 1, 1793; son of Patrick & Elizabeth
ALLEN, John; bn. Aug 22, 1797; bpt. Mar 11, 1798; son of Patrick & Elizabeth
ALLEN, Mary; bn. Apr 24, 1791; bpt. May 22, 1791; dau. of Patrick & Elizabeth
ALLEN, Thomas; bn. Mar 23, 1800; bpt. Apr 17, 1800; son of Patrick (deceased) & Elizabeth
ALLGIER, George; bn. Oct 6, 1787; bpt. Nov 1, 1787; sps. George Rozensteel & Susanna Rozensteel
ALLGIER, Joseph; bn. Dec 23, 1783; bpt. Dec 28, 1783; sps. Peter Plum & Elizabeth Plum
ALLGIER, Peter; bn. Oct 23, 1785; bpt. Oct 30, 1785; sps. Peter & Elizabeth Plum
ALLRIDGE, James; bn. Jun 22, 1792; bpt. Jun 26, 1792; son of John & Peggy
ALTHOFF, Henry William; bn. Nov 25, 1791; bpt. Feb 12, 1792; son of Benjamin & Anna Catherina

BAPTISMS

AMBROSE, John Prendergast; bn. Aug 10, 1799; bpt. Aug 23, 1799; son of John & Elizabeth

AMI, Armand; bn. Apr 5, 1796; bpt. Oct 6, 1796; son of Peter & Sophia

AMIE, John Baptist Balthasar Edward; bn. Feb 12, 1799; bpt. Apr 27, 1799; son of John Baptist Joseph Amable & Mary Helen Frances

AMPHOUSE, Catharine Virginia; bn. Oct 13, 1794; bpt. Dec 11, 1795; dau. of Francis & Teresa

ANDERSON, Arthur; bn. Jan 10, 1796; bpt. Aug 5, 1796; son of Thomas & Rebecca

ANDERSON, Daniel; bn. Sep 2, 1779; bpt. Apr 3, 1796; son of Daniel & Mary

ANDERSON, Jane; bn. May 23, 1790; bpt. Oct 22, 1798; dau. of Thomas & Rebecca

ANDERSON, Margaret; bpt. Aug 31, 1794; 13 years old; dau. of Daniel & Mary

ANDERSON, Mary; bn. Aug 4, 1784; bpt. Aug 8, 1784; sps. Mark Jones & Joanna Jones

ANDERSON, Rebecca; bn. Dec 19, 1779; bpt. Nov 19, 1796; dau. of Thomas & Rebecca

ANDERSON, Rebecca; bpt. Oct 22, 1798; adult, widow of Thomas Anderson

ANDERSON, Recard; bn. Feb 10, 1793; bpt. Oct 22, 1798; son of Thomas & Rebecca

ANDREWS, Elizabeth; bn. Apr 10, 1800; bpt. Sep 7, 1800; dau. of Pres & Julia

ANDREWS, Margaret; bn. Feb 25, 1796; bpt. Mar 5, 1796; dau. of Robert & Eleanor

ANDREWS, Mary Ann; bn. Apr 8, 1799; bpt. May 5, 1799; dau. of George & Elizabeth

ANGER, Eleanor; bpt. Jun 6, 1790; 6 months; son of James & Sally Roberts

ANSY, Ann; bpt. Aug 18, 1794; dau. of Richard & Grace

ANSY, Eleanor; bpt. Aug 18, 1794; dau. of Richard & Grace

(ANTICHAMP), John Gabriel; bpt. Aug 27, 1797; 6 months; son of Sophie, slave of Mr. Antichamp

ANTICHAN, Louise Sophie; bn. Feb 19, 1795; bpt. May 2, 1795; dau. of Anthony of Bordeaux & Elizabeth St. Martin

APELIN, Marie; bn. Dec 9, 1792; bpt. Dec 26, 1792; dau. of Pierre Michel & Demoiselle Francoise Elizabeth LaFarge

APPOLONIA, Mary; bn. Sep 11, 1787; bpt. Sep 16, 1787; sps. Jacob Laurence & Sarah Laurence

ARCHDEAKEN, James; bn. Oct 22, 1788; bpt. Jan 4, 1789; sps. William Merrick & Catharine Desmond

ARIEU, Gabriel August; bn. Jun 6, 1800; bpt. Jun 29, 1800; son of Charles & Elizabeth Lasschanal

ARMAND, John; bn. Oct 22, 1797; bpt. Feb 11, 1798; son of Francis & Margaret

ARMAND, John Peter; bn. Jul 20, 1796; bpt. Aug 11, 1796; son of Francis & Margaret

ARMAND, Margaret; bn. Aug 9, 1794; bpt. Aug 15, 1794; dau. of Anthony & Margaret

ARMAND, Mary; bn. Jul 20, 1796; bpt. Jul 29, 1796; dau. of Francis & Margaret

BAPTISMS

ARMOUR, Anna Marie; bn. Mar 17, 1794; bpt. Apr 13, 1794; dau. of
    David & Mary
ARMOUR, David; bn. Sep 29, 1795; bpt. Nov 2, 1795; son of David &
    Mary
(ARMOUR), Priscilla; bpt. Nov 20, 1796; 5 years old; slave of
    David Armour
ARMOUR, Solomon; bn. Oct 18, 1796; bpt. Nov 20, 1796; son of
    David & Mary
ARMOUR, William; bpt. Apr 21, 1799; son of David & Mary
ARMSBY, Catharine; bn. Jan 24, 1800; bpt. Jan 25, 1800; dau. of
    John & Unity
ARMSBY, Mary; bpt. Jul 25, 1798; dau. of John & Unity
ARMSTRONG, Harriette; bn. Feb 20, 1793; bpt. Feb 24, 1793; dau.
    of Michael & Mary
ARMSTRONG, Mary; bn. Feb ?, 1790; bpt. May 23, 1790; dau. of
    Michael & Mary
ARMSTRONG, Patrick; bn. Jun 18, 1787; bpt. Sep 9, 1787; sps. John
    Frean & Mary Nelson
ARMSTRONG, William; bn. Jan 16, 1796; bpt. May 15, 1796; son of
    William & Esther
ARNOLD, Catharine; bn. Apr 1, 1783; bpt. May 4, 1783; sps.
    William Haden & Catharine Haden
ASHMORE, Jane; bn. Apr 1, 1797; bpt. Feb 10, 1799; dau. of Thomas
    & Margaret
ASKMORE, Sarah; bpt. Jul 21, 1799; dau. of Thomas & Margaret
(ASSELIN), John Baptist; bn. May 12, 1796; bpt. Jun 12, 1796; son
    of Acemia, slave of Mrs. Asselin, St. Domingo
ATTRIDGE, Mary Ann; bn. Nov 12, 1795; bpt. Dec 22, 1795; dau. of
    James & Mary
ATTRIDGE, Thomas; bn. Apr 12, 1794; bpt. Apr 22, 1794; son of
    James & Mary
AUTICHAN, Anne; bn. Jul 30, 1796; bpt. Oct 6, 1796; dau. of
    Antony & Belon
AYZIC, John; bn. Jun 22, 1796; bpt. Jun 26, 1796; son of Rachel
BABIN, Charles; bn. Apr 27, 1793; bpt. Aug 18, 1793; son of
    Charles & Mary
BABIN, Elizabeth; bn. Jun 18, 1791; bpt. Sep 18, 1791; dau. of
    Charles & Mary
BABIN, John Baptist; bn. Jun 7, 1784; bpt. Jun 14, 1784; sps.
    Antoine Fauleanet & Margaret Mangee
BABIN, Joseph; bpt. May 3, 1788; 6 weeks; sps. Bishop Carroll
BACKSTER, Rachael; bpt. Feb 8, 1789; adult
BADION, Elizabeth; bn. Jul 23, 1799; bpt. Sep 1, 1799; dau. of
    Peter & Mary
BAESS, Mary; bn. Mar 9, 1789; bpt. Apr 6, 1789; sps. Mary Bride
(BAILLE), John Lewis; bpt. Apr 8, 1798; 3 months; son of
    Fleurice, slave of Mr. Baille
BAILY, Margaret; bpt. Jun 29, 1792; 5 weeks; dau. of Thomas &
    Katy
BAISS, Claudius Etienne; bn. Sep 27, 1785; bpt. Nov 18, 1785;
    sps. Stephen Zacharie & Polly Bride
BAISS, Mary Elizabeth; bn. Mar 15, 1787; bpt. Apr 23, 1787; sps.
    Francis Coopman & Mary Nochez
BAKER, Anthony; bn. Sep 28, 1800; bpt. Oct 26, 1800; son of Adam
    & Mary

7

BAPTISMS

BAKER, Catharine; bn. Feb 18, 1797; bpt. Feb 24, 1797; dau. of Mathias & Mary

BAKER, Elizabeth; bn. Jan 8, 1800; bpt. Jan 11, 1800; dau. of Mathias (deceased) & Magdalen

BAKER, Peter; bn. Jan 8, 1800; bpt. Jan 11, 1800; son of Mathias (deceased) & Magdalen

BALDERY, John; bn. Mar 6, 1800; bpt. Apr 7, 1800; son of John & Elizabeth

BALSER, Mary Magdalen; bn. Aug 14, 1791; bpt. Sep 17, 1791; dau. of George & Christina

BANFIELD, Mary; bpt. Sep 19, 1784; 8 years old; sps. Charles O'Brian & Mary Perkins

BARBARIN, Joseph; bn. Aug 7, 1792; bpt. Aug 17, 1792; son of Lewis & Mary

BARBARIN, Lewis Stephen; bn. Dec 26, 1793; bpt. Jan 1, 1794; son of Lewis & Mary Calbert

BARBARIN, Maria Teresia; bn. Apr 20, 1790; bpt. May 16, 1790; dau. of Lewis & Mary

(BARBENCOUR), John; bpt. Sep 19, 1796; 5 weeks; son of Clair, slave of Mr. Barbencour

BARCKMAN, Bartholomew; bn. Jun 18, 1796; bpt. Jun 22, 1796; son of Anthony & Ann

BARCKMAN, Elizabeth; bn. Aug 18, 1798; bpt. Sep 3, 1798; dau. of Anthony & Ann

BARGE, Susanna; bpt. Oct 16, 1795; 1 week; foundling, parents unknown; sps. Ann Dugan

BARICKMAN, Catharine; bn. Nov 12, 1793; bpt. Nov 17, 1793; dau. of Joseph & Catharine

BARICKMAN, Mary; bn. Jan 4, 1795; bpt. Feb 1, 1795; dau. of Joseph & Catharine

BARKLEY, Catharine; bn. Feb 10, 1798; bpt. Apr 26, 1798; dau. of Phoebe Barkley

BARLY, John; bn. May 30, 1800; bpt. Jul 23, 1800; son of George & Catharine

BARNEY, William Moses; bn. Jul 22, 1800; bpt. Aug 8, 1800; son of Samuel & Eve

BAROUX, Augustine; bn. Feb 26, 1796; bpt. Apr 3, 1796; son of James Michael & Mary

BAROUX, Charles Anthony; bn. Aug 15, 1800; bpt. Dec 4, 1800; son of James Michael & Mary Deagle

BAROUX, John Charles; bn. Apr 22, 1798; bpt. May 23, 1798; son of James Michael & Mary

BARRATON, John Joseph; bpt. May 7, 1798; 3 years old; son of Justine Barraton, St. Domingo

BARRAULT, Elizabeth; bn. Sep 10, 1794; bpt. Sep 28, 1794; dau. of Michael & Mary

BARRET, Eliza; bpt. Jul 1, 1792; 4 weeks; dau. of Edward & Eleanor

BARRY, Edward Ward; bn. Aug 14, 1799; bpt. Sep 8, 1799; son of Michael & Elizabeth

BARRY, John; bn. Jan 6, 1792; bpt. Jan 13, 1793; son of John & Mary

(BARRY), John; bn. Oct 8, 1800; bpt. Nov 24, 1800; Mulatto; son of Nancy, slave of Redmond Barry

BAPTISMS

BARRY, Mary; bn. Aug 29, 1792; bpt. Sep 4, 1792; dau. of William & Eleanor Barret
BARRY, Mary Ann; bn. Sep ?, 1800; bpt. Nov 9, 1800; dau. of Michael & Elizabeth
(BARTHELEMI), Jeanne; bpt. May 4, 1794; dau. of Rona, slave of Mr. Barthelemi
(BARTHELENIE), John Joseph; bpt. Aug 27, 1797; 13 months; son of Ronne, slave of Mrs. Barthelenie
BARTHOLOMEE, Charlotte; bn. Jul 6, 1799; bpt. May 24, 1800; dau. of Philip Joseph & Renee Olive Moriss
BARTLEY, Elizabeth; bn. Jan 28, 1796; bpt. Apr 15, 1796; dau. of Elizabeth Bartley, free Mulatto
BARTOLS, Rosalia Bertholin; bn. Aug 20, 1788; bpt. Oct 26, 1788; sps. Simon Renau & Elizabeth Deagle
BASTARD, John; bn. Jul 28, 1795; bpt. Aug 2, 1795; son of John & Louisa
BATCHFORD, Elizabeth; bpt. Apr 8, 1790; conditional
BATTLE, Mary; bpt. Jul 18, 1798; 17 days; dau. of Francis & Mary
BAXLEY, Phoebe; bpt. Jun 24, 1796; 18 years old; dau. of William & Mary
(BAYOT), Elizabeth; bpt. Nov 13, 1795; 14 years old; slave of Boujot Bayot
BAYTHORNE, Mary; bpt. Dec 22, 1792; adult; conditional; dau. of James & Catharine
BEANDU, Lewis; bn. Apr 25, 1797; bpt. Dec 8, 1797; son of William & Mary Ann Hubon
BEARD, Alexander; bn. Jan 16, 1794; bpt. Jan 27, 1794; son of Alexander & Mary
BEARD, Henry Claudius Bride; bn. May 1, 1796; bpt. May 31, 1796; son of Alexander & Mary
BEARD, Isabella; bn. Jul 9, 1791; bpt. Sep 5, 1791; dau. of Alexander & Mary
BEARD, Mary Ann; bn. Jul 19, 1799; bpt. Aug 17, 1799; dau. of Alexander & Mary
BEAUCHAMP, Elizabeth; bn. Nov 21, 1793; bpt. Aug 31, 1794; dau. of John & Mary
BEAUCHAMP, Thomas; bn. Oct 17, 1796; bpt. Nov 13, 1796; son of John & Mary
BEAUCHAMP, William; bn. Dec 3, 1798; bpt. Mar 24, 1799; son of John & Mary
BEAUDU, James Joseph; bn. Feb 19, 1800; bpt. Jul 19, 1800; son of William & Mary Ann Hubon
BEAVER, Elizabeth; bn. Mar 31, 1789; bpt. Jun 21, 1789; dau. of Adam & Susanna
BEEVEN, Elizabeth; bn. Oct 15, 1785; bpt. Mar 2, 1786; sps. Priscilla Harrison
BEEVEN, Mary; bpt. Oct 28, 1787; 5 years; sps. Margaret Cusick
BEHNER, Susanna; bpt. Feb 13, 1799; dau. of William & Elizabeth
BELL, Margaret Susanna; bn. Jun 11, 1789; bpt. Oct 11, 1789; dau. of Christopher & Ann
BELL, William Brooks; bn. Jan 28, 1791; bpt. Apr 24, 1791; son of Christopher & Ann
BENAU, Mary; bn. Apr 30, 1790; bpt. May 9, 1790; dau. of Matthew & Nancy

BAPTISMS

BENER, Henry; bn. Aug 20, 1795; bpt. Aug 28, 1795; son of William
    & Bessy
BENER, Mary; bn. Mar 20, 1794; bpt. Mar 30, 1794; dau. of William
    & Becky
BENNAN, Ann; bn. Jun 2, 1787; bpt. Jun 7, 1787; sps. Joseph
    Pinchand & Mary Cataron
BENNER, Catharine; bn. Nov 3, 1794; bpt. Nov 9, 1794; dau. of
    Henry & Elizabeth
(BENNET), Jane; bpt. Sep 20, 1789; 1 month; slave of Pat Bennet;
    dau. of Jube & Taymur
(BENNET), Maria; bpt. May 6, 1792; 10 months; dau. of Alicia,
    slave of Patric Bennet
(BENNET), Mary Araminta; bn. Feb ?, 1793; bpt. Mar 6, 1796;
    Mulatto; dau. of Esther, slave of Patrick Bennet
(BENNETT), Samuel; bpt. Sep 1, 1793; 4 weeks; son of Alicia,
    slave of Mr. Patrick Bennett
(BENTALOE), William; bn. Sep 8, 1795; bpt. Oct 18, 1795; son of
    Edward & Milky, slave of Paul Bentaloe
BENTLEY, Mary; bpt. Mar 4, 1798; 2 weeks; dau. of Dorothy Bentley
BERBINE, Margaret; bn. Jun 27, 1798; bpt. Jul 29, 1798; dau. of
    Charles & Mary
BERCHMAN, Susanna; bn. Nov 16, 1800; bpt. Nov 30, 1800; dau. of
    Joseph & Catharine
BERGER, Claudius; bpt. Dec 10, 1793; 2 1/2 months; son of
    Claudius & Mary Anne
BERGER, Jane; bpt. Dec 10, 1793; 15 months; dau. of Claudius &
    Mary Anne
BERGERMAN, Mary Anne; bn. Sep 12, 1794; bpt. Sep 21, 1794; dau.
    of Antony & Ann
BERGIN, John; bn. Mar 1, 1791; bpt. Jun 12, 1791; son of John &
    Catharine
BERGMAN, Anna Elizabeth Catherina; bn. May 2, 1784; bpt. May 9,
    1784; sps. John Sheuler & Elizabeth Sheuler
BERGMAN, Antony; bn. Apr 30, 1786; bpt. Apr 30, 1786; sps. Jacob
    & Sarah Laurence
BERGMAN, Antony; bn. Jan 17, 1792; bpt. Jan 22, 1792; son of
    Antony & Christina
BERGMAN, Elizabeth; bn. Apr 12, 1792; bpt. Apr 22, 1792; dau. of
    Joseph & Katy
BERGMAN, George; bn. Nov 7, 1790; bpt. Nov 21, 1790; son of
    Joseph & Catharine
BERGMAN, Henry; bn. Jun 3, 1796; bpt. Jun 19, 1796; son of Joseph
    & Catharine
BERGMAN, Jacob; bn. Jul 8, 1787; bpt. Jul 8, 1787; sps. Ferdinand
    Laurence & Sally Laurence
BERGMAN, John; bn. Feb 13, 1789; bpt. Feb 15, 1789; sps. John
    Steiger & Elizabeth Steiger
BERGMAN, John; bn. Jun 27, 1790; bpt. Aug 1, 1790; son of Antony
    & Christina
BERGMAN, John; bn. Aug 22, 1798; bpt. Aug 26, 1798; son of Joseph
    & Catharine
BERGMAN, Joseph; bn. Sep 6, 1787; bpt. Sep 16, 1787; sps. Joseph
    Sindall & Mary Bertheim
BERKLEY, James; bn. Aug 14, 1800; bpt. Sep 12, 1800; son of
    Elizabeth Berkley

BAPTISMS

BERKLEY, John; bn. Dec 11, 1797; bpt. Mar 5, 1798; son of
    Elizabeth Berkley, Mulatto
BERMAN, Matthew; bn. Nov 3, 1784; bpt. Nov 14, 1784; sps. Stephen
    Burke & Margaret LaTar
BERNABEU, Carlos Marcellinos; bn. Apr 28, 1799; bpt. May 2, 1799;
    son of Don John Baptist & Donna Marie Bethsabee
(BERNABEU), Elizabeth; bpt. Feb 22, 1796; adult, slave of Mr.
    Bernabeu
BERNABEU, Josepha Joanna Matilda; bn. Oct 7, 1796; bpt. Nov 23,
    1796; dau. of Dr. John Baptist & Donna Marie Bethsabee
BERNABEU, M. L. Josepha; bn. Nov 16, 1800; bpt. Dec 14, 1800;
    dau. of Don Juan Baptista & --
BERNARD, Elizabeth; bn. Jun 25, 1783; bpt. Jul 6, 1783; sps.
    Arnold Newton & Ann Overton
BERNARD, John Charles; bn. Jun 24, 1787; bpt. Jul 25, 1787; son
    of Charles & Mary; sps. Patrick LeMoine & Martha Gold
BERNARD, Joseph; bn. Aug 27, 1788; bpt. Sep 11, 1789; son of
    Archibald & Elizabeth
BERNARD, Lewis; bn. Jul 13, 1789; bpt. Jul 26, 1789; son of Lewis
    & Mary
BERNARD, Louis; bn. Jul 12, 1784; bpt. Aug 7, 1784; sps.
    Bartholomy Bertholin & Peggy Murry
BERNARD, Margaret; bn. Feb 2, 1783; bpt. Mar 1, 1783; sps.
    Francis Purry & Elizabeth King
BERRAGE, Susannah; bn. Nov 13, 1793; bpt. May 13, 1794; dau. of
    William & Ann
BERRIGAN, Michael; bn. Oct 3, 1792; bpt. Aug 4, 1794; son of John
    & Catharine
BERRIGE, George; bn. Nov 26, 1796; bpt. Aug 9, 1797; son of
    William & Ann
BERRY, Anne; bn. Oct 23, 1791; bpt. Dec 4, 1791; dau. of John &
    Mary
BERRY, James; bn. Dec 1, 1796; bpt. Dec 25, 1796; son of Regis &
    Harriot
BERRY, Sarah; bn. Jul 2, 1798; bpt. Jul 7, 1798; dau. of Regis &
    Harriot
BERRY, William; bn. Nov ?, 1793; bpt. Jun 22, 1794; son of
    Patrick & Mary
BERTHOLIN, Felix; bn. Oct 24, 1797; bpt. Mar 18, 1798; son of
    Joseph & Eve
BERTHOLIN, Francis Xavier; bn. Feb 10, 1793; bpt. Mar 17, 1793;
    son of Joseph & Eve
BERTHOLIN, Joseph Hepolite; bn. Mar 18, 1787; bpt. May 27, 1787;
    sps. John Levan & Mary Bernard
BERTHOLIN, Teresia Mary; bn. Oct 29, 1790; bpt. Jan 23, 1791;
    dau. of Joseph & Eve
BERTIN, Jane; bn. Nov 14, 1793; bpt. Nov 17, 1793; dau. of James
    & Ann Chirot
BERTING, Catharine; bn. Oct 25, 1799; bpt. Dec 1, 1799; dau. of
    Peter & Mary
BERTOULIN, Louisa; bn. Aug 4, 1795; bpt. Oct 25, 1795; dau. of
    Joseph & Eve
BERTRAN, Simon Jude; bpt. May 2, 1794; 3 months; son of Louisa
    Bourgeois, Mulatto

BAPTISMS

BERTRAND, Cecily; bn. May 23, 1793; bpt. Jul 18, 1793; dau. of
    Peter & Mary Ann; born at Cape Francois
(BERTRAND), Mary Rose; bpt. Nov 1, 1794; 3 months; dau. of
    Princess, slave of Peter Bertrand
BERTRAND, Peter Amadeus Victor; bn. Jun 19, 1796; bpt. Jul 16,
    1796; son of John Peter & Armande Victoire Sophie Vatinel
BERTRUX, Catharine; bn. Dec 15, 1788; bpt. Dec 23, 1788; sps.
    Lewis Bethune & Margaret Rusheld
(BERTWILLE), Lewis Paul; bpt. Jul 27, 1800; 3 months; son of
    Marie Jeanne, slave of John Baptist Bertwille
BESSE, Alexander; bn. Jun 18, 1800; bpt. Jul 9, 1800; son of
    Claudius & Margaret
BESSE, Henry Barthlet; bn. Jan 22, 1790; bpt. Jun 3, 1790; son of
    Captain Besse & wife
BESSE, John; bn. Jun 18, 1794; bpt. Jul 7, 1794; son of Claudius
    & Margaret
BESSE, Peter; bn. Apr 20, 1791; bpt. May 25, 1791; son of Capt.
    Claude & Margaret
BESSE, Simon Alexander Bunbury; bn. Apr 28, 1796; bpt. May 31,
    1796; son of Claudius & Margaret
BESSE, John Claudius; bn. Jan 29, 1798; bpt. Jun 5, 1798; son of
    Claudius & Margaret
BESSON, Mary Louisa; bn. Dec 28, 1794; bpt. Feb 3, 1795; dau. of
    Lewis Renatus & Ann Boilen
BETHUNE, Mary Ann; bn. Jul 4, 1793; bpt. Jul 7, 1793; dau. of
    Lewis & Ann
BETSEN, George; bn. Mar 19, 1799; bpt. May 12, 1799; son of John
    & Rachel
BICHOU, Peter; bn. Mar 20, 1798; bpt. Nov 21, 1799; son of
    Felicity Bichou, Mulatress
BIDAUT, Mary Louise; bn. Aug 13, 1794; bpt. Aug 1, 1795; dau. of
    John & Marguerite Tonry
BIDET, John Mary Daniel; bn. Apr 27, 1791; bpt. May 6, 1794; at
    St. Domingo; son of Peter Daniel & Mary Frances Jane LaRoque
BIDOT, Adelina; bn. Sep 12, 1795; bpt. Oct 8, 1795; dau. of John
    Peter, St. Domingo & Margaret
BIDOT, John Baptist; bn. Oct 26, 1792; bpt. Dec 3, 1792; son of
    John Peter of St. Domingo & Margaret
BIGGENSTAFFER, John; bn. Feb 5, 1797; bpt. Feb 13, 1797; son of
    Elizabeth Biggenstaffer
BIGHY, Matthew; bn. Jun 13, 1793; bpt. Jun 16, 1793; son of
    Emmanuel & Anna Marie
(BIJAU), John; bn. Sep 8, 1789; bpt. Sep 13, 1789; slave of Mrs.
    Bijau; son of Jack & Peg
(BIJOU), Mary Helen; bn. Mar 31, 1794; bpt. Apr 28, 1794; dau. of
    Magarite, Mulattoe, slave of Mrs. Bijou
(BINTIER), Mary Therese; bn. Aug 19, 1797; bpt. Dec 19, 1797;
    dau. of Rosalia, slave of Widow Bintier
BIRON, Martin; bn. Nov 23, 1792; bpt. Dec 30, 1792; son of
    Patrick & Ann
BISHOP, Mary; bn. Feb 19, 1798; bpt. Jun 5, 1798; dau. of Richard
    & Elizabeth
BITSIN, Joseph; bn. Oct 5, 1795; bpt. Nov 22, 1795; son of John &
    Rachel

BAPTISMS

BIZOURD, Anne Simeon Adel; bn. Jul 11, 1795; bpt. Aug 31, 1795; dau. of Joseph Yves & Renee Margueriette Paterson

BLACK, Barbara; bn. Mar 26, 1793; bpt. Mar 31, 1793; dau. of John & Barbara

BLACK, James; bn. Jun 29, 1788; bpt. Jul 4, 1788; sps. Winefride Star

BLACK, Nicholas; bn. Nov 22, 1797; bpt. Dec 10, 1797; son of John & Barbara

BLACK, Peter; bn. Oct 2, 1799; bpt. Oct 13, 1799; son of John & Barbara

BLAIR, John; bn. Mar 20, 1798; bpt. Apr 1, 1798; son of John & Catharine

BLAKE, Ann; bn. Oct 2, 1795; bpt. Oct 11, 1795; dau. of John & Mary

BLAKE, Mary; bpt. Feb 4, 1792; 10 days; dau. of Philip Towson & Catharine Blake

BLANC, Joseph; bn. Oct 30, 1793; bpt. Sep 17, 1794; son of Lewis Bartholomy & Magdalen Somniot

(BLANC), Mary Victor; bpt. Feb 24, 1794; son of Pauline, slave of Peter Joseph Blanc

BLANCHARD, Mary; bn. Dec 27, 1781; bpt. Mar 23, 1784; sps. Bartholomy Toutems & Louise De Bombos

BLANEY, Harriet; bn. Jan 12, 1800; bpt. Mar 13, 1800; dau. of Thomas & Sarah

BLANEY, Mary; bpt. Mar 13, 1800; 2 years old; dau. of Thomas & Sarah

BLOOM, Cecilia; bn. Feb 17, 1783; bpt. Feb 27, 1783; sps. John Ehrmond & wife

BLOOMER, Mary; bn. Feb 1, 1783; bpt. Apr 28, 1783; sps. Rose Blossom

BOCOX, William; bn. Dec 3, 1797; bpt. Jan 1, 1798; son of John & Mary

BOHNER, John; bn. Feb 19, 1797; bpt. Feb 26, 1797; son of William & Elizabeth

BOISLANDRY, Bernadine Josephine Laure; bn. Jun 20, 1799; bpt. Nov 5, 1799; dau. of Robert Charles Lelgrande & Louise Francoise Buscaille

(BOISLANDRY), Mary Joseph; bpt. Oct 12, 1800; 8 months; son of Mary Michael, slave of Mr. Boislandry

BOISLANDRY, Orpheus Arthur; bn. Jun 23, 1797; bpt. Sep 23, 1797; son of Robert Charles LeGrand & Louisa Frances Busville

(BOISSARD), Margaret; bn. May 6, 1796; bpt. Jul 7, 1796; dau. of Mary Jane, slave of Augustine Boissard, St. Domingo; free

BOISSERE, Mary Charlotte; bn. Sep 27, 1798; bpt. Jun 30, 1799;

(BOISSON), John; bpt. Jul 1, 1797; 3 months; son of Adelaide, slave of Miss Mary Boisson

BOISSONET, Marie; bn. Sep 10, 1794; bpt. Oct 1, 1795; dau. of Magdalen Boissonet, free Mulattoe

BONA, Barbara Theresia; bn. Nov 12, 1796; bpt. Dec 4, 1796; dau. of Joseph & Ann

BONA, Catharine; bn. Aug 28, 1796; bpt. Dec 4, 1796; dau. of Philip & Magdalen

BONAN, George; bn. May 3, 1783; bpt. May 10, 1793; son of Dennis & Ann

BAPTISMS

BOND, Jenny; bn. Jul 6, 1787; bpt. Sep 5, 1787; sps. Olidia Star & Mary Nelson

BOND, Sarah; bn. Apr 3, 1785; bpt. Apr 8, 1785; sps. Obidia Star & Winefrieda Star

BONER, Margaret; bn. Sep 7, 1800; bpt. Sep 9, 1800; dau. of William & Bridget

BONIER, Sophie Adelaide; bn. Jun 30, 1795; bpt. Dec 29, 1795; dau. of Anthony & Adelaide Rainquenoir

BONN, Anthony; bn. Oct 24, 1798; bpt. Jan 6, 1799; son of Joseph & Ann

BONN, Catharine; bn. Dec 12, 1799; bpt. Jan 5, 1800; dau. of Philip & Mary Magdalen Helmeling

BONN, Mary Ann; bn. Oct 14, 1800; bpt. Nov 9, 1800; dau. of Joseph & Ann

BONN, Mary Cecily; bn. Dec 28, 1797; bpt. Jan 14, 1798; dau. of Joseph & Ann

BONNE, Elizabeth; bn. Mar 9, 1798; bpt. Mar 25, 1798; dau. of Philip & ---

(BONNET), Adele; bn. Oct ?, 1795; bpt. Dec 6, 1795; dau. of Athalie, slave of Mr. Bonnet

(BONNET), Henrietta; bpt. Jul 30, 1797; 1 month; dau. of Elizabeth, slave of Mrs. Bonnet

(BONNET), Peter; bn. Jul 29, 1799; bpt. Aug 25, 1799; son of Athalie, slave of Mr. Bonnet

BONOT, Frances Elizabeth; bn. Aug 2, 1796; bpt. Nov 6, 1796; dau. of Rene & Mary Catharine Tetu

BORDENAVE, John Baptist; bn. Jul ?, 1793; bpt. Sep 29, 1794; son of John & Mary Louisa Princess

BORGLET, Anna; bn. Jul 14, 1793; bpt. Aug 4, 1793; dau. of John & Mary

BORIE, Elizabeth; bn. Jun 23, 1795; bpt. Jul 29, 1795; dau. of Joseph & Margaret Borie

BOUCHER, Bartholomew; bn. Jul 3, 1796; bpt. Jul 10, 1796; son of Bartholomew & Elizabeth

BOUCHER, Catharine; bn. Feb 28, 1791; bpt. Mar 13, 1791; dau. of Archer & Mary English

BOUCHER, Mary; bn. Nov 5, 1791; bpt. Feb 19, 1792; dau. of Arthur & Frances

BOUDERAU, Ann; bn. Apr 21, 1789; bpt. Apr 26, 1789; sps. William Boyle & Elizabeth Grainger

BOUDRAU, John Francis; bn. Sep 29, 1786; bpt. Oct 2, 1786; sps. Francis Pechey & Elizabeth Fellen

BOUDRAU, Rosalia; bn. Nov 4, 1787; bpt. Nov 4, 1787; sps. Peter Gerard & Peggy LaBatte

BOULDEN, Charles Daniel; bn. Jun 6, 1797; bpt. Jun 9, 1799;

BOULDIN, Richard; bpt. Aug 8, 1787; 2 months; son of Richard & Rebecca

BOULDINS, Henry; bn. Jun 2, 1795; bpt. Jul 13, 1795; son of Richard & Rebecca

BOWEN, Mary Ann; bn. Jun 7, 1790; bpt. May 1, 1791; dau. of James & Margaret

BOWERS, John; bn. Jan 4, 1792; bpt. Jan 29, 1792; son of John & Anna Maria

BOWING, Richard; bn. Aug 25, 1788; bpt. Oct 5, 1788; sps. Anthony Fox & Eleanor Cunningham

BAPTISMS

BOWLDIN, Ann; bpt. Nov 27, 1785; 2 months; sps. George S.
    Douglass & Elizabeth Jones
BOWLDIN, Edwin; bpt. Oct 17, 1790; 5 months old; son of Richard &
    Rebecca
BOWLDIN, Owing Sewall; bpt. Nov 27, 1785; 2 years old; sps.
    George S. Douglass & Elizabeth Jones
BOWLDIN, Sara; bpt. Nov 27, 1785; 6 years old; sps. George S.
    Douglass & Elizabeth Jones
BOWLIN, Alexander; bpt. Aug 16, 1792; 9 weeks; son of Richard &
    Rebecca
BOYD, William; bn. Jul 9, 1796; bpt. Sep 1, 1796; son of Ann
(BOYER), John Francis; bpt. Dec 19, 1798; 6 weeks; son of
    Adelaide (since deceased) slave of Mrs. Boyer
BOYLE, Ann; bn. Sep 25, 1789; bpt. Oct 1, 1789; dau. of William &
    Mary
BOYLE, Mary; bpt. May 8, 1791; 6 months; dau. of William & Mary
BOYLE, Rosanna; bn. Nov 4, 1793; bpt. Dec 8, 1793; dau. of John &
    Margaret
BOYLE, Sarah; bn. Mar 18, 1798; bpt. May 6, 1798; dau. of James &
    Ann
BOYREAU, Anne Frances; bn. Jun 17, 1794; bpt. Sep 25, 1794; dau.
    of John Joseph & Mary Marzial of St. Domingo
BOYREAU, Elizabeth; bn. Jun 14, 1798; bpt. Dec 4, 1798; dau. of
    John Joseph & Mary Marzial
BOYREAU, Magdalaine Elizabeth; bn. Apr 17, 1793; bpt. Oct 3,
    1793; dau. of Jean Joseph & Marie Marzial
BRADLEY, John Columbus; bn. Nov 15, 1798; bpt. Dec 19, 1798; son
    of Thomas & Ann
BRADLEY, Mary; bn. Sep 9, 1795; bpt. Aug 1, 1797; dau. of John &
    Mary
BRADLEY, William; bpt. Apr 23, 1799; 8 years old
BRADSHAW, Ann; bn. Dec 10, 1797; bpt. Dec 31, 1797; dau. of
    William & Catharine
BRADSHAW, James; bn. Oct 3, 1783; bpt. Nov 9, 1783; sps. Joseph
    Bertholin & Magdalene Babin
BRADY, Ann; bn. Mar 23, 1800; bpt. May 10, 1800; dau. of John &
    Elizabeth
BRADY, Catharine; bn. Jan 29, 1798; bpt. Feb 19, 1798; dau. of
    John & Elizabeth
BRADY, Eleanor; bpt. Nov 16, 1800; dau. of John & Mary
BRADY, Elizabeth; bpt. Oct 5, 1796; dau. of John & Elizabeth
BRADY, Francis Trael; bpt. Jan 19, 1794; 10 months old; son of
    Sylvester & Susanna Moore
BRADY, James; bn. Sep 1, 1793; bpt. Oct 27, 1793; son of John &
    Elizabeth
BRADY, John; bn. Jan 23, 1792; bpt. May 13, 1792; son of John &
    Elizabeth
BRADY, Mary; bn. Nov 7, 1794; bpt. Dec 26, 1794; dau. of John &
    Elizabeth
BRADY, Mary; bn. Jan 5, 1798; bpt. Feb 18, 1798; dau. of John &
    Mary
BRADY, Thomas; bn. Jul 26, 1794; bpt. Aug 24, 1794; son of John &
    Mary
BRAG, George; bn. Aug 11, 1784; bpt. Aug 22, 1784; sps. George
    Coffey & Sara Boyle

BAPTISMS

BRANEGHEN, John; bn. May 25, 1783; bpt. Jul 30, 1785; sps. Sara Boyde

BRANNAN, Rebecca; bn. Oct 23, 1793; bpt. Jun 8, 1794; dau. of Thomas & Mary

BRAY, Joseph; bn. Mar 16, 1783; bpt. Apr 20, 1783; sps. Patrick Lynch & Charity Hammer

BRAZIER, Peter; bn. Feb 26, 1800; bpt. Mar 23, 1800; son of John & Eleanor

BRAZIER, Robert; bn. Oct 31, 1797; bpt. Nov 12, 1797; son of John & Eleanor

BRAZIER, Thomas; bn. Jan 2, 1799; bpt. Feb 3, 1799; son of John & Eleanor

BREAND, Stephen Anne Robert Nante; bn. Sep 12, 1793; bpt. Sep 19, 1793; son of Michael Agustus & Sophia Frances Delore

BREMONT, Quiterre Marie; bn. Aug 16, 1795; bpt. Sep 6, 1795; dau. of John & Frances Elizabeth de Lesfauries

BREMONT, Zoe Josephine; bn. Sep 15, 1797; bpt. Nov 6, 1797; dau. of John & Frances Elizabeth Lesfauries

(BRESARD), Augustus; bpt. Apr 30, 1799; son of Eleanor, slave of Mde. Bresard

BRETON, Benedict; bn. Jul 8, 1783; bpt. Aug 3, 1783; sps. John Gallee & Magdalene Babin

BRIEDENBAUGH, Maria; bn. Nov 18, 1799; bpt. Jan 12, 1800; dau. of John & Ann

BRIEN, John; bn. Dec 16, 1792; bpt. Dec 25, 1792; son of Michael & Margaret

BRIEN, Juliana; bn. Feb 25, 1791; bpt. May 16, 1791; dau. of Charles & Margaret

BRIEN, Sara; bpt. Jul 4, 1790; adult

(BRISARD), John Baptist; bpt. Aug 15, 1800; 4 weeks; son of Bonne, slave of Mr. Brisard

BRISLERE, Daniel; bn. Aug 16, 1800; bpt. Dec 25, 1800; dau. of Jeremiah & Sarah

BRITTON, William; bn. Jan 13, 1793; bpt. Mar 21, 1793; son of John & Ann

BRITTS, Elizabeth; bpt. Jul 1, 1797; 5 years old; dau. of Rachel Britts

BROOK, Henry; bn. Mar 31, 1795; bpt. Apr 9, 1795; son of Henry & Priscilla

BROOKE, Mary Smith; bn. Aug 4, 1788; bpt. Apr 5, 1789; sps. Elizabeth Brooke

BROOKS, Mary; bn. Nov 5, 1773; bpt. Aug ?, 1784; sps. Judith Leeson

BROOM, Daniel; bn. Oct 5, 1787; bpt. Sep 28, 1788; sps. Joanna Wolloshan & Sally Mack

BROOM, Hanna; bn. Dec 13, 1780; bpt. Sep 28, 1788; sps. Joanna Wolloshan & Sally Mack

BROOM, Henry; bn. Dec 9, 1774; bpt. Sep 28, 1788; sps. Joanna Wolloshan & Sally Mack

BROOM, James; bn. Jan ?, 1776; bpt. Sep 28, 1788; sps. Joanna Wolloshan & Sally Mack

BROOM, John; bn. Oct 19, 1782; bpt. Sep 28, 1788; sps. Joanna Wolloshan & Sally Mack

BROOM, Peggy; bn. Oct 11, 1778; bpt. Sep 28, 1788; sps. Joanna Wolloshan & Sally Mack

BAPTISMS

BROOM, Thomas; bn. Oct 8, 1784; bpt. Sep 28, 1788; sps. Joanna Wolloshan & Sally Mack
BROOM, William; bn. Mar 8, 1792; bpt. Dec 8, 1794; son of James & Martha
(BROSSARD), John Baptist; bpt. Oct 7, 1798; 2 weeks; son of Horsense, slave of Mr. Brossard
BROWN, Ann; bn. Aug 4, 1796; bpt. Aug 29, 1796; dau. of John & Helena
BROWN, Ann Maria Frederica; bn. Dec 19, 1798; bpt. Dec 30, 1798; dau. of Joseph Simon & ---
BROWN, Catharine; bn. Jul 24, 1794; bpt. Jul 27, 1794; dau. of James & Mary
BROWN, Honor; bn. Oct 21, 1793; bpt. Aug 27, 1794; dau. of Joshua & Honor
BROWN, Jacob; bn. Aug 17, 1793; bpt. Jun 28, 1794; son of Jacob & Sarah
BROWN, James; bn. Aug 29, 1795; bpt. Aug 31, 1795; son of James & Mary
BROWN, John; bn. Feb 22, 1785; bpt. Apr 10, 1785; sps. John Hannon & Elizabeth Flattery
BROWN, John; bn. Nov 20, 1789; bpt. Dec 26, 1791; son of James & Mary
BROWN, Maria; bn. Sep 25, 1799; bpt. Oct 20, 1799; dau. of John & Mary
BROWN, Mary; bn. Mar 18, 1789; bpt. Mar 24, 1789; sps. Andrew Henwright & Hanna Berkley
BROWN, Mary; bn. Aug 29, 1795; bpt. Aug 31, 1795; dau. of James & Mary
BROWN, Mary; bn. May 2, 1799; bpt. Jun 2, 1799; dau. of Jacob & Sarah
(BROWN), Robert; bpt. Apr 9, 1798; 2 years old; son of Mable, slave of Aquila Brown
BROWN, Sarah; bn. Oct 17, 1794; bpt. Nov 23, 1794; dau. of James & Hannah
BROWN, Sarah; bn. Jan 31, 1798; bpt. Feb 18, 1798; dau. of John & Mary
BROWN, William; bn. Apr 11, 1783; bpt. Jun 8, 1783; sps. John Linden & Catharine Herring
BROWN, William; bpt. Nov 7, 1790; 18 years old; conditional
BROWNE, Henry John; bn. Dec 27, 1798; bpt. Apr 22, 1799; son of Henry & Henrietta
BROWNE, Latitia; bn. Nov 17, 1795; bpt. Feb 25, 1796; dau. of Henry & Hannah
BROWNE, Thomas; bn. Oct 15, 1797; bpt. Nov 19, 1797; son of James & Mary
(BRUNLOT), John Baptist; bpt. Jul 6, 1800; 2 1/2 years old; son of Katy, slave of Mr. Brunlot
(BRUSLE), Remy; bpt. May 18, 1795; 20 months; son of Mary Louisa, slave of Widow Brusle
BRUSNAHAM, Margaret; bn. Jun 8, 1791; bpt. Jul 9, 1791; dau. of James & Eleanor
BRYAN, Rosanna; bn. Dec 23, 1783; bpt. Feb 4, 1784; sps. Bartelomy Antoine & Rose Mongee
BRYSON, Bennet; bn. Nov 12, 1787; bpt. Nov 19, 1787; sps. James Green & Mary Green

BAPTISMS

BUCHEN, Barbara; bn. Nov 3, 1798; bpt. Nov 11, 1798; dau. of
    Engelhart & Magdalen
BUCHEN, Christina; bn. Oct 22, 1796; bpt. Oct 29, 1796; dau. of
    Engelhart & Mary Magdalen
BUCHEN, Elizabeth; bn. Dec 5, 1793; bpt. Dec 8, 1793; dau. of
    John & Mary
BUCHEN, James; bn. Jul 18, 1800; bpt. Jul 21, 1800; son of
    Engelhard & Magdalen
BUCHEN, John; bn. Feb 13, 1796; bpt. Feb 21, 1796; son of John &
    Eleanor
BUCHEN, John James; bn. Jan 14, 1799; bpt. Jan 20, 1799; son of
    Eleanor Buchen
BUCHEN, Mary; bn. Jan 6, 1795; bpt. Jan 8, 1795; dau. of
    Engelhart & Mary Magdalen
BUCHMAN, Joseph; bn. Jul 17, 1797; bpt. Jul 23, 1797; son of
    George & Barbara
BUCHMAN, Margaret; bn. Jan 23, 1800; bpt. Jan 26, 1800; dau. of
    George & Barbara
BUCHOLTZ, Catharine; bn. Sep 15, 1799; bpt. Sep 29, 1799; dau. of
    George & Elizabeth
BUMBURY, Hannah Elizabeth Wentworth; bn. May 17, 1799; bpt. May
    23, 1799; dau. of John & Ann
BUMBURY, Henry Alexander; bn. Mar 11, 1797; bpt. May 25, 1797;
    son of Monsieur Sims & Ann Bumbury
BURALL, John Baptist; bn. Jan 17, 1796; bpt. Aug 23, 1796; son of
    John Baptist & Elizabeth
BURAU, Lewis; bn. Jul 18, 1786; bpt. Jul 23, 1786; sps. Nancy
    Bernau
BURDEN, Mary; bpt. Apr 5, 1792; 12 years old; dau. of John & Mary
BURGOON, Jemima; bn. Nov 9, 1788; bpt. Nov 16, 1788; sps. Hellen
    Ireland
BURK, Leonard; bn. Dec 16, 1795; bpt. Dec 20, 1795; son of
    Leonard Burk, free Negro & Elizabeth, slave of Mr. Henry
BURK, Mary; bn. Nov 12, 1793; bpt. Jan 26, 1794; dau. of Edward &
    Naky
BURKE, Catharine; bpt. Mar 16, 1788; 2 weeks; sps. John Ehrmond &
    Mrs. Murphy
BURKE, John; bn. Oct 18, 1787; bpt. Nov 25, 1787; sps. Laurence
    Whelan & Elizabeth Wiliams
BURKE, Mary; bpt. Oct 1, 1795; 4 years old; dau. of John & Hannah
BURKE, Matthew; bn. Aug 19, 1798; bpt. Aug 21, 1798; son of
    Leonard Burke, free Negro & Elizabeth, slave of Mrs.
    Elizabeth Henry
BURKE, Sophia; bpt. Jan 5, 1800; 5 weeks; dau. of Edward Burke,
    free Negro & Harriot, slave of Mr. Compario
BURKE, Walter; bn. Jul 25, 1784; bpt. Sep 19, 1784; sps. Robert
    Conway & Mary Regland
BURKE, William; bn. Nov 15, 1785; bpt. Dec 5, 1785; sps. William
    Collins & Catharine Leary
(BURKET), Elizabeth; bpt. Apr 1, 1798; 16 months; dau. of
    Halloday, slave of Mr. Burket & Rosanna, slave of David
    Willson
BURNER, Eleanor; bn. Sep 21, 1794; bpt. Oct 6, 1794; dau. of
    Jacob & Mary

BAPTISMS

BURNS, Mary; bn. Apr 24, 1795; bpt. Jun 21, 1795; dau. of Samuel
    & Mary
BURRAGE, Thomas; bn. Dec 21, 1791; bpt. Sep 11, 1792; son of
    William & Ann
BUTLER, Abraham; bpt. Nov 26, 1800; 7 years old; son of William &
    Sarah
BUTLER, Ann; bpt. Feb 15, 1788; 8 years old; sps. Obedia Star &
    Winefride Star
BUTLER, Ann; bpt. Feb 10, 1799; 5 weeks; dau. of Clare Butler,
    free Mulatress
BUTLER, Anne; bpt. Nov 26, 1800; 21 months; dau. of William &
    Sarah
BUTLER, Charity; bpt. Aug 23, 1799; 5 months; dau. of Josias &
    Sally
BUTLER, David; bpt. Apr 13, 1797; 1 month; son of Nancy Butler,
    free Mulatto
BUTLER, Edmund; bpt. Oct 7, 1787; 8 months; sps. James Mullvanny
    & Mary Roach
BUTLER, Eleanor Helpin; bn. Feb 16, 1793; bpt. Apr 1, 1793; dau.
    of John & Margaret Helpin
BUTLER, Eleanor; bn. Jul 28, 1798; bpt. Aug 5, 1798; dau. of
    Nelly Butler, free Negro
BUTLER, Elizabeth; bn. Oct ?, 1783; bpt. Nov 2, 1783; sps. Simon
    Deagle & Elizabeth Bodhill
BUTLER, Elizabeth; bn. Jun 11, 1798; bpt. Jun 15, 1798; dau. of
    Lucy Butler, free Mulatto
BUTLER, Elizabeth; bpt. Oct 26, 1800; 1 month; dau. of Mathias &
    Sarah
BUTLER, Henry; bpt. Jun 9, 1799; 5 weeks; son of Nelly Butler
BUTLER, Henry; bpt. Nov 16, 1799; 2 months; son of Lucy Butler,
    free Mulatto
BUTLER, James; bn. Apr 10, 1789; bpt. Nov 8, 1789; son of John &
    Eleanor
BUTLER, Jane; bpt. Nov 8, 1789
BUTLER, Jane; bpt. May 21, 1797; 6 months; dau. of Clare Butler,
    free Mulatto
BUTLER, John; bpt. May 6, 1785; 7 weeks; sps. John & Hanna Keller
BUTLER, John; bpt. Nov 20, 1785; 16 months; sps. Dennis Sullivan
    & Mary Walsh
BUTLER, John; bn. Mar 4, 1792; bpt. Jan 6, 1793; son of Walter &
    Eliza
BUTLER, John; bn. Mar 18, 1793; bpt. Jun 22, 1794; son of John &
    Eleanor
BUTLER, John; bn. Sep 21, 1798; bpt. Nov 11, 1798; son of Nat,
    slave & Monica Butler, free
BUTLER, John; bn. Aug 18, 1799; bpt. Aug 25, 1799; son of Minty
BUTLER, Joseph Alexander; bn. May 2, 1799; bpt. Jul 16, 1799; son
    of Joseph & Mary
BUTLER, Julia; bn. Nov 22, 1788; bpt. Dec 19, 1788; sps. John
    Baptist Fellen & Mary Deagle
BUTLER, Margaret; bn. Mar 8, 1791; bpt. Apr 17, 1791; dau. of
    Joseph & Mary
BUTLER, Mary; bn. Apr 4, 1787; bpt. Sep 4, 1787; sps. Robert
    Walsh & Peggy Tonery

BAPTISMS

BUTLER, Mary Ann; bn. Mar 10, 1797; bpt. May 7, 1797; dau. of
    Christian Johns, slave of Jonathan Wilmer & Teresa Butler,
    free Negro
BUTLER, William; bn. Aug 6, 1797; bpt. Aug 15, 1797; son of
    Henry, slave of Robert Walsh & Joanna Butler, free Mulatto
BUTTLE, Eleanor; bn. Jul 7, 1792; bpt. Sep 9, 1792; dau. of John
    & Margaret
BUTTON, William; bpt. Jan 27, 1800; 5 months; son of Sally Button
BYRNE, Columbus John; bn. Nov 9, 1800; bpt. Nov 10, 1800; son of
    Columbus John & Margaret
BYRNE, William; bn. Jul 31, 1798; bpt. Aug 12, 1798; son of
    Edward & Mary
BYRON, Thomas; bn. Nov 17, 1790; bpt. Dec 12, 1790; son of
    Patrick & Ann
CABRERA, Anna; bpt. Sep 22, 1799; 3 months; dau. of John & Mary
CAHILL, Peter; bn. Feb 28, 1794; bpt. Mar 30, 1794; son of George
    & Eleanor
CAIN, Alexander; bn. Oct 18, 1790; bpt. Aug 10, 1793; son of
    Henry & Rosanna
CALAHAN, Cornelius; bn. Apr 7, 1794; bpt. Apr 12, 1794; son of
    Matthew & Mary
CALDRON, John; bn. May 19, 1791; bpt. Jun 21, 1791; son of
    Francis & Mary
CALDRON, John Baptist; bn. Sep 7, 1793; bpt. Sep 10, 1793; son of
    Francis & Mary
CALDRON, Mary; bn. Sep 26, 1783; bpt. Oct 10, 1783; sps. Laurence
    Gidon & Ann Duliar
CALDRON, Peter; bn. Nov 2, 1788; bpt. Nov 4, 1788; son of Francis
    & Mary; sps. Peter Albert & Polly Leary
CALDWELL, Joseph; bn. Oct 25, 1794; bpt. Dec 3, 1794; son of
    Joseph & Margaret
CALLAGHAN, Alice; bpt. Sep 5, 1793; about 9 years old; dau. of
    Michael & Mary
CALLAGHAN, Ann; bn. Jun 18, 1784; bpt. Aug 22, 1784; sps.
    Alexander Duff & Margaret Savage
(CALMAN), Alice; bpt. May 14, 1797; 6 months; dau. of Esther,
    slave of Monsieur Calman
(CAMMEL), John; bpt. Mar 2, 1794; 7 months; son of Mary, slave of
    Mr. Cammel
CAMPBELL, Benjamin; bn. Sep 22, 1796; bpt. Sep 30, 1796; son of
    --- (now dead) & Anne
CAMPBELL, Bridget; bn. Aug 31, 1800; bpt. Sep 13, 1800; dau. of
    Patrick & Jane
CAMPBELL, George; bn. Jul 21, 1797; bpt. Jul 26, 1797; son of
    John & Bridget
CAMPBELL, Jane; bn. May 19, 1798; bpt. May 27, 1798; dau. of
    Patrick & Jane
(CAMPBELL), Mary; bn. Feb 16, 1800; bpt. Apr 27, 1800; dau. of
    Peggy (deceased), slave of Archibald Campbell, Esq.
CAMPBELL, Mary Ann; bn. Aug ?, 1799; bpt. Sep 22, 1799; dau. of
    Matthew & Jane
CAMPBELL, Mary Anne; bn. Dec 12, 1797; bpt. Dec 20, 1797; dau. of
    Matthew & Jane
CANCHI, Mary Joseph; bn. May 1, 1796; bpt. Jun 19, 1796; dau. of
    Mary Rose Ann Canchi

BAPTISMS

CANCHI, Peter Gabriel; bn. Feb 11, 1798; bpt. Apr 14, 1798; son of Mary Rose Ann Canchi
CANNON, Obediah; bn. Nov 19, 1791; bpt. Nov 27, 1791; son of Cornelius & Eleanor
CANTWELL, John Smith; bn. Dec 8, 1796; bpt. May 6, 1797; son of Thomas & Elizabeth
CANTWELL, Mary; bpt. Dec 25, 1796; 6 weeks; dau. of Thomas & Mary
(CAPAN), Mary Ann; bpt. May 20, 1798; about 30 years;
CAPELL, Mary; bn. Dec 15, 1794; bpt. Dec 28, 1794; dau. of Francis & Mary
(CAPPEAU), Joseph; bn. Mar 7, 1796; bpt. Aug 5, 1796; Mulatto; son of Tamora, slave of Mr. Cappeau, St. Domingo
(CAPPEAU), Josephine; bn. Sep 16, 1795; bpt. Aug 5, 1796; free Negro; dau. of Sophie, slave of Mr. Cappeau, St. Domingo
(CAPPEAU), Mary Magdalen; bn. Dec 14, 1796; bpt. Sep 17, 1797; Mulatto; dau. of Therese, slave of Mr. Cappeau
CAREY, Betsey; bn. May 21, 1795; bpt. Jun 7, 1795; dau. of Dennis & Marguerite
CAREY, Catharine; bn. Oct 14, 1799; bpt. Nov 3, 1799; dau. of Dennis & Judith
CAREY, John; bn. Jun 13, 1794; bpt. Jun 22, 1794; son of Denis & Margaret
CAREY, John; bn. Jul 9, 1796; bpt. Jul 22, 1796; son of John & Eleanor
CAREY, John; bn. May 9, 1800; bpt. Jun 8, 1800; son of John & Eleanor
CAREY, Timothy; bn. Mar 1, 1798; bpt. Apr 1, 1798; son of John & Eleanor
CARNEY, Eleanor; bn. Jun 5, 1790; bpt. Aug 27, 1790; dau. of James & Margaret
CARR, Jane; bn. Aug 17, 1798; bpt. Aug 21, 1798; dau. of John & Eleanor
CARRE, Mary Magdalen; bn. Aug 4, 1794; bpt. Aug 7, 1794; dau. of Joseph & Magdalen
CARRERE, Elizabeth; bn. Mar 4, 1796; bpt. Apr 10, 1796; dau. of John & Mary
CARRERE, John; bn. Jul 22, 1797; bpt. Aug 2, 1797; son of John & Mary
CARRERE, Mary; bn. Sep 4, 1798; bpt. Sep 12, 1798; dau. of John & Mary
CARRERE, Robert; bn. Apr 28, 1800; bpt. May 8, 1800; son of John & Mary
CARRERE, Teresa; bn. Apr 5, 1794; bpt. May 1, 1794; dau. of John & Mary
CARRICK, Richard; bn. Dec 1, 1799; bpt. Dec 19, 1799; son of Daniel & Bridget
CARRICK, Rose; bn. Aug 9, 1797; bpt. Aug 13, 1797; dau. of Daniel & Bridget
(CARROLL), Charles; bn. Jul 19, 1794; bpt. Jul 27, 1794; son of Tom & Kate, slave of Charles Carroll of Carrollton
CARROLL, Cornelius; bn. Apr 21, 1790; bpt. May 16, 1790; son of Edward & Mary
CARROLL, Daniel; bn. Jul 31, 1797; bpt. Aug 6, 1797; son of John & Isabella

BAPTISMS

CARROLL, David; bn. Jul 9, 1795; bpt. Aug 12, 1796; son of John & Isabella
CARROLL, Elizabeth; bn. Mar 11, 1786; bpt. Nov 28, 1786; sps. John Kirnan & Mary Kirnan
(CARROLL), Elizabeth; bn. Jun 22, 1794; bpt. Jul 27, 1794; dau. of Jack & Mary, slave of Charles Carroll of Carrollton
(CARROLL), Elizabeth; bn. Jun 3, 1794; bpt. Jul 27, 1794; dau. of Harry & Lucy, slave of Charles Carroll of Carrollton
(CARROLL), Elizabeth; bpt. Feb 22, 1795; 1 month; dau. of Reason & Flavia, slave of Charles Carroll of Carrollton
CARROLL, Fanny; bn. Oct ?, 1784; bpt. Jun 1, 1785; sps. Daniel Carroll & Elizabeth Carroll
(CARROLL), Frances; bn. Jun 13, 1794; bpt. Jun 22, 1794; dau. of Dick & Kate, slave of Charles Carroll of Carrollton
CARROLL, Henry; bn. Aug 23, 1796; bpt. Apr 19, 1797; son of Henry & Sarah
(CARROLL), Jacob; bn. Dec ?, 1794; bpt. Sep 26, 1796; son of Samuel & Judith, slave of Daniel Carroll
(CARROLL), John; bn. Jul 30, 1794; bpt. Aug 24, 1794; son of Timothy & Hetty, slave of Charles Carroll of Carrollton
(CARROLL), Kate; bn. Jan ?, 1791; bpt. Jul 31, 1791; slave of D. Carroll
(CARROLL), Lia; bpt. Jun 3, 1798; 3 years old; dau. of Philip, slave of Mrs. Carroll & Priscilla, slave of Anthony Hook
(CARROLL), Lucy; bpt. Dec 29, 1793; 4 months; dau. of Bob & Barbara, slave of Charles Carroll of Carrollton, Esq.
(CARROLL), Margaret; bpt. Jul 27, 1794; 1 month; dau. of Nace & Latitia, slave of Charles Carroll of Carrollton
CARROLL, Mary; bn. Nov 2, 1798; bpt. Dec 16, 1798; dau. of Thomas & Mary
(CARROLL), Patrick; bpt. Nov 23, 1794; son of Joe & Sally, slave of Charles Carroll of Carrollton
CARROLL, Thomas; bn. ?, 1786; bpt. Jun 4, 1786; sps. Timothy Herrin & Katy Reed
(CARROLL), Valentine; bn. Nov ?, 1794; bpt. Sep 26, 1796; son of Susanna, free Negro & John, slave of Daniel Carroll
CARSON, George Washington; bn. Oct 19, 1798; bpt. Nov 10, 1799; son of Nathaniel & Eleanor
CARSON, Joan Goulding; bn. Dec 13, 1795; bpt. Oct 3, 1797; dau. of Nathaniel & Eleanor
CARSON, Juliet; bn. Jan 20, 1797; bpt. Apr 27, 1797; dau. of Nathaniel & Eleanor
CARSON, Maria Isabella; bn. Nov 28, 1791; bpt. May 9, 1793; dau. of Nathaniel & Eleanor
CARSON, Mary Eleanor; bn. May 8, 1800; bpt. Jun 8, 1800; dau. of Nathaniel & Eleanor
CARTER, Margaret; bn. May 8, 1784; bpt. Jun 15, 1784; sps. Ann Harrison
CARTER, Margaret; bn. Mar 24, 1786; bpt. Apr 9, 1786; sps. Bartholomy Raymond & Catharine Laurence
CARTERON, John Mary; bn. Jul 24, 1793; bpt. Oct 16, 1793; son of Rosette, Mulatress
CARTY, Bridget; bn. Nov 27, 1796; bpt. Jan 2, 1797; dau. of Michael & Eleanor

BAPTISMS

CARTY, James; bpt. Dec 14, 1794; 12 days; son of Michael & Nely O'Brian
CARTY, Mary; bpt. Dec 14, 1794; 12 days; dau. of Michael & Nely O'Brian
CASEY, Cornelius; bn. Oct 11, 1786; bpt. Oct 23, 1786; sps. Roger Conway & Nancy Malone
CASKY, Harriot; bn. Jan 11, 1792; bpt. Jan 11, 1795; dau. of Samuel & Mary Casky
CASKY, Margaret; bn. Dec 20, 1793; bpt. Dec 25, 1793; dau. of Samuel & Mary
CASSAGNE, Clare; bn. Dec 12, 1798; bpt. Apr 14, 1799; dau. of Silvain & Terese Fauconnet
CASSAGNE, Peter Silvain; bn. Apr 27, 1796; bpt. Sep 27, 1796; born in Wilmington; son of Silvain & Theresia Fanconnet of San Domingo
CASSEDY, John; bpt. Jun 10, 1787; 6 years old; sps. Mary Duffy
CASSEDY, Mark; bpt. Jun 10, 1787; 3 years old; sps. Peter Leiner & Mary Duffy
CASSEDY, Mary; bpt. Jun 10, 1787; 5 years old; sps. Peter Leiner & Mary Duffy
CASSEDY, Patrick; bpt. Jun 10, 1787; 5 weeks; sps. Peter Leiner & Mary Duffy
CASSIN, Francis; bn. Aug 24, 1793; bpt. Sep 3, 1793; son of John & Rachel
CASTAING, John Joseph; bn. Apr 1, 1798; bpt. Aug 19, 1798; son of Bennet & Mary Rose LaBarthe
CASTILE, Elizabeth; bn. Oct 24, 1796; bpt. Dec 27, 1796; dau. of Francis & Hannah
CASTON, Mary; bn. Jul 25, 1794; bpt. Jul 26, 1794; dau. of Betsy Trainer
CASTRING, Rose Marthe; bn. Sep 29, 1795; bpt. Apr 5, 1796; dau. of Benne, nat. of D'Agen & Mary Rose Labothe, nat. of Rochelle
CATON, Elizabeth; bn. May 30, 1787; bpt. Jul 10, 1787; sps. John Hindes & Mary Hindes
CATON, James; bpt. Oct 15, 1785; 2 years old; sps. Edward & Eleanor Galleghar
CATON, James; bn. May 24, 1797; bpt. Jun 11, 1797; son of Honor Caton
CATON, John; bn. Jun 2, 1789; bpt. Jul 12, 1789; son of Nan Caton
CATON, John; bn. Jan 2, 1799; bpt. Mar 10, 1799; son of Matthew & Elizabeth
(CATON), Mary; bn. Dec 8, 1796; bpt. Jan 1, 1797; dau. of Augustin & Mary, slave of Richard Caton
CATON, Mary Ann; bn. Aug 18, 1788; bpt. Sep 21, 1788; sps. Charles Carroll of Carrollton, Esq.
(CATON), Philip; bn. May 20, 1793; bpt. Aug 14, 1793; son of Philip & Clare, slave of Mr. Caton
(CATON), Thomas; bn. Jul 11, 1791; bpt. Jun 10, 1792; slave of William Caton
CAVANAUGH, George; bn. May 14, 1793; bpt. Aug 18, 1794; son of George & Ann
CAVAROE, Barbara; bn. Jun 4, 1798; bpt. Aug 1, 1798; dau. of Francis & Mary

BAPTISMS

CAVAROE, John Baptist; bn. Jul 10, 1796; bpt. Jul 12, 1796; son of Francis & Mary

CAVAROE, Mary; bn. Aug 28, 1794; bpt. Sep 6, 1794; dau. of Francois & Mary

CAWLE, Mary; bpt. Dec 14, 1787; 3 weeks; sps. Polly Fragett

CAYOL, Eugene Joseph L'Ami; bn. Aug 20, 1800; bpt. Sep 23, 1800; son of Anthony & Mary Ann Magdalen Modeste Tardieu

CEBRON, Ann Frances; bn. Jul 22, 1795; bpt. Aug 5, 1795; dau. of Oliver & Mary Jane Trouve

CHAMPAGNE, George William Henry; bn. Nov 26, 1794; bpt. Dec 3, 1794; son of John Royer & Mary Ann Second

CHAMPAYNE, William; bn. Aug 20, 1797; bpt. Dec 28, 1797; son of John Royer & Mary Ann Legond

CHANCE, Elizabeth; bn. Aug 17, 1799; bpt. Sep 18, 1800; dau. of John & Catharine

CHANCE, John Mary Joseph; bn. Oct 4, 1795; bpt. Aug 13, 1796; son of John & Catharine Provost

CHANCE, Marcellina; bn. Nov 16, 1797; bpt. Mar 20, 1798; dau. of John of Cp. Francois & Catharine Provot

(CHANCE), Peter; bn. Apr 9, 1795; bpt. May 3, 1795; son of Clementia, slave of Mr. Chanche of St. Domingo

(CHANCHE), John; bpt. Nov 9, 1800; 7 weeks; son of Clemence, slave of Mr. Chanche

(CHANCHE), John Didier; bpt. Apr 27, 1794; son of Louise, slave of Mrs. Chanche

CHANCHE, John Francis; bn. Sep 28, 1793; bpt. Oct 29, 1793; son of John & Catharine Provot

(CHANCHE), Lewis; bpt. Jul 15, 1798; 1 month; son of Clemence, slave of Mr. Chanche

CHANCHE, Lewis Paul; bn. Oct 7, 1793; bpt. May 2, 1794; son of John & Catharine Provost

CHANGEUR, Martha Leon Peter; bn. Jul 7, 1796; bpt. Aug 8, 1796; dau. of Leon & Joanna Josephine Gripiera

(CHAPEAU), Basil; bpt. Nov 10, 1799; 3 months; son of Mary, slave of Mr. Chapeau

CHAPIUS, Simeon; bn. Oct 1, 1796; bpt. Oct 9, 1796; son of Simeon & Mary

CHAPMAN, Elias; bpt. Oct 6, 1793; 20 years old; sps. Ignatius, slave of Rev. Francis Beeston

CHAPUY, Elizabeth; bn. Jun 5, 1799; bpt. Jun 30, 1799; dau. of Samuel & Mary

CHAPUY, Philip; bn. Nov 30, 1797; bpt. Dec 3, 1797; son of Simon & Mary

CHARLES, Peter; bn. Jul 3, 1785; bpt. Jul 31, 1785; sps. Blass Pimenta & Nance

CHARTREUX, Julian; bn. Oct 11, 1800; bpt. Nov 2, 1800; son of John & Elizabeth

(CHASE), Edward; bpt. Dec 25, 1798; 4 months; son of Edward, slave of Mr. Chase & Hannah, slave of Mr. John Thompson

(CHASE), Mary; bpt. Sep 25, 1796; 1 month; dau. of Nathaniel, slave of Mr. Chase & Anne, slave of Mr LeDuc

CHATEAU, Mary Teresa; bn. Feb 4, 1795; bpt. Feb 7, 1795; dau. of Louisa Chateau, Mulatress of St. Domingo

BAPTISMS

CHATEAUDUN, Louisa Margaret Raynaud; bn. Sep 10, 1796; bpt. Oct 5, 1796; dau. of John Baptist Raynaud & Margaret Louisa Charpenher
CHAUVET, John Bartholomew Philip; bn. Feb 14, 1792; bpt. Feb 17, 1794; son of Joseph Germez & Elizabeth
(CHEFFINTAINE), John Baptist; bpt. Jun 9, 1799; 1 month; son of Eustasie, slave of Mr. Cheffintaine
CHENE, Ann Marie; bn. Apr 30, 1784; bpt. Jun 19, 1784; sps. Simon, Baron of Du Puis
CHENEE, Elizabeth; bn. Oct 7, 1785; bpt. Nov 7, 1785; sps. Sebastian Fleur & Magdalen Sapin
CHEVALIER, Maria Teresa; bn. Jan 22, 1793; bpt. Jul 1, 1793; dau. of Claude Elizabeth & Mary Wallace
CHILCUT, Mary; bn. Apr 3, 1799; bpt. Jun 16, 1799; dau. of William & Juliana
CHILLCUT, Ann; bn. Jan 31, 1797; bpt. Mar 13, 1797; dau. of William & Juliana
CICERON, Francis Cumming; bn. Oct 9, 1797; bpt. Nov 6, 1797; son of Anthony & Mary
CICERON, Teline; bn. Oct 9, 1797; bpt. Nov 6, 1797; dau. of Anthony & Mary
CLANCY, Eleanor; bn. Sep 23, 1799; bpt. Apr 26, 1800; dau. of Roger & Lydia
CLANCY, Samuel; bpt. May 4, 1800; 6 weeks; son of Patrick & Ann
CLARE, Anna Marie; bn. Jun 15, 1794; bpt. Jun 29, 1794; dau. of Patric & Sara
CLARK, Alban; bn. Oct 28, 1789; bpt. Dec 13, 1789; son of William & Mary Ann
CLARK, Ann; bn. Aug 15, 1784; bpt. Aug 29, 1784; sps. Ann Wilson
CLARK, James; bn. Jul 3, 1794; bpt. Aug 17, 1794; son of Francis & Susanna
CLARK, Jane; bn. Sep 7, 1795; bpt. Feb 12, 1796; dau. of John & Jane of Bladensburg
CLARK, John; bn. Jul 16, 1787; bpt. Aug 19, 1787; sps. John Tiegler & Mary Cecil
CLARK, John; bpt. Aug 18, 1798; 3 months; son of William & Julia
CLARK, Peter William; bn. Nov 18, 1794; bpt. Dec 15, 1794; son of David & Elizabeth
CLARK, Samuel; bn. Oct 27, 1789; bpt. Feb 28, 1790; son of Ralph & Mary
CLARKE, John; bn. Jun 11, 1797; bpt. Jul 9, 1797; son of Patrick & Sarah
CLARKE, Margaret; bn. Dec 22, 1799; bpt. Mar 23, 1800; dau. of Patrick & Sarah
CLAUS, Peter; bpt. Apr 8, 1799; 6 weeks; son of Stephen & Rosina
CLEMENTS, James McSherry; bn. Apr 2, 1797; bpt. May 23, 1797; son of Josias & Sarah; sps. Fr. Beeston & Catharine McSherry
CLIFFORD, James; bn. Aug 9, 1785; bpt. Sep 18, 1785; sps. Nelly Gafny
CLIFFORD, William; bpt. Feb ?, 1787; 8 weeks; sps. Brigit Waters
CLONEY, Thomas; bn. Sep 6, 1800; bpt. Sep 7, 1800; son of James & Bridget
CLOSET, William; bpt. May 11, 1797; 18 months; son of Judith
CLOUGHERTY, Bartholomew; bn. Aug 1, 1797; bpt. Aug 6, 1797; son of Martin & Mary

BAPTISMS

CLOUGHERTY, Honor; bn. Mar 19, 1799; bpt. Mar 21, 1799; dau. of John & Mary
CLOUGHERTY, John; bn. Jan 24, 1800; bpt. Jan 27, 1800; son of Martin & Mary
CLOUGHERTY, Mary; bn. Sep 2, 1796; bpt. Sep 7, 1796; dau. of Patrick & Honor
COALE, Elizabeth; bn. Jan 12, 1783; bpt. Mar 2, 1783; sps. Hickol Perry & Mary Celestine
CODY, John; bn. Jun 3, 1795; bpt. Jul 26, 1795; son of David & Joannah
CODY, Mary; bn. Dec 22, 1792; bpt. Oct 17, 1793; dau. of David & Joannah
COFFEY, Catharine; bn. Aug 5, 1787; bpt. Aug 2, 1788; sps. Eleanor Smith
COLE, Jane; bn. Aug 1, 1797; bpt. Apr 9, 1798; dau. of Henry & Minta
COLE, John Baptist Pierre; bpt. Nov 30, 1800; 7 weeks; son of Charles & Baccha
COLGHAN, Lydia; bn. Jun 7, 1789; bpt. Jun 10, 1789; dau. of Michael & Mary
COLLINS, Elizabeth; bpt. Jul 13, 1794; 6 months; dau. of Thomas & Sarah
COLLINS, George; bn. May 31, 1785; bpt. Oct 15, 1785; sps. Thomas Towel
COLLINS, James; bn. May 22, 1784; bpt. Jun 20, 1784; sps. John Kenady & Margaret Savage
COLLINS, Jeremia; bn. Jul 10, 1796; bpt. Aug 30, 1796; dau. of Thomas & Sarah
COLLINS, John Bannister; bn. May ?, 1790; bpt. Sep 14, 1791; son of Thomas & Sarah
COLLINS, John; bn. Jan 9, 1795; bpt. Jul 13, 1795; son of Patrick & Mary
COLLINS, John Carly; bn. Nov 1, 1784; bpt. Jul 17, 1785; sps. Augustin Delatte
COLLINS, Lydia; bn. Aug 28, 1788; bpt. Apr 22, 1789; sps. Ann Collins
COLLINS, Margaret; bn. Jul 13, 1800; bpt. Jul 27, 1800; dau. of James & Catharine
COLLINS, Nancy; bn. Oct 20, 1790; bpt. Jul 12, 1791; dau. of John Baptist & Elizabeth
COLLINS, Sa---; bn. Mar 23, 1788; bpt. Oct 29, 1788; sps. Thomas Towel & Mary Towel
COLLINS, Susanna; bpt. Sep 4, 1788; 4 months; sps. Susanna Jub
COLOUR, George; bn. Dec 27, 1798; bpt. Jan 5, 1799; son of Mary
COLOUR, John; bn. Nov 3, 1799; bpt. Nov 10, 1799; son of George & Mary
COLVIN, Rachel; bpt. Sep 6, 1795; 7 years old; dau. of Walter & --
COMBS, James; bpt. Nov 17, 1800; adult; son of Coleman & Mary
COMPANIO, John; bn. Aug 15, 1784; bpt. Feb 21, 1785; sps. Bernard LaBorde & Modeste Landry
COMPARIO, Ann Eimee; bn. Feb 7, 1793; bpt. Feb 23, 1793; dau. of John & Maria Margaret
COMPARIO, Elizabeth; bn. Mar 13, 1797; bpt. Apr 9, 1797; dau. of John & Margaret

BAPTISMS

COMPARIO, Henrietta; bn. Apr 22, 1799; bpt. Jun 17, 1799; dau. of
   John & Mary
COMPARIO, James Peter; bn. Jul 5, 1794; bpt. Aug 14, 1794; son of
   John & Margaret
COMPARIO, Magdalen Julia; bn. Oct 13, 1788; bpt. Oct 18, 1788;
   sps. Peter DeLivet & Magdalene Landry
COMPARIO, Mary; bn. Mar 9, 1791; bpt. Apr 12, 1791; dau. of John
   & Margaret
COMTE, Augustus Lewis Charles; bn. Oct 7, 1795; bpt. Oct 7, 1796;
   son of Stephen Julian & Jeanne Gabrielle Claudine Bataille
   Dela Garet
(COMTE), Elizabeth; bpt. Sep 26, 1793; adult
COMTE, Elizabeth Claudine; bn. Mar 10, 1799; bpt. Mar 15, 1799;
   dau. of Stephen Julian & Jane Claudine Gabrielle Bataille
   DelaGaret
COMTE, Jean Baptiste Louis Gui; bn. Jan 6, 1792; bpt. Sep 6,
   1792; son of Etienne Julien & Denniselle Jeanne Claudine
   Gabrielle Bataille
(COMTE), John; bpt. Apr 20, 1794; son of Ann, slave of Mr. Comte
COMTE, Jules Joseph Etienne; bn. Oct 26, 1790; bpt. Sep 6, 1792;
   son of Etienne Julien & Denniselle Jeanne Claudine Gabrielle
   Bataille
(COMTE), Mary Louisa; bpt. Sep 26, 1793; dau. of Ann, slave of
   Mr. Comte
(COMTE), Mary Teresa Irene; bn. Oct ?, 1795; bpt. Dec 13, 1795;
   dau. of Mary Elizabeth, slave of Mr. Comte of St. Domingo
CONDEN, Edward; bn. Jun 8, 1800; bpt. Jun 22, 1800; son of Edward
   & Margaret
CONET, Philip; bn. May 17, 1799; bpt. Apr 27, 1800; son of
   Anthony & Eve
CONNELLY, Bridget; bpt. Nov 23, 1794; 8 weeks; dau. of Patrick &
   Judith
CONNELLY, Catharine; bn. May 23, 1784; bpt. May 29, 1784; sps.
   John Cockles & Mary Dealy
CONNELLY, John; bn. Jul 11, 1792; bpt. Jul 22, 1792; son of --- &
   Betsy Connelly
CONNELLY, Margaret; bn. Mar 15, 1795; bpt. Mar 15, 1795; dau. of
   Michael & Margaret
CONNELLY, Mary; bn. Aug 11, 1787; bpt. Dec 17, 1788; sps. John
   Hurley & Catharine Heffy
CONNELLY, Mary; bpt. Jul 2, 1790; 7 months; dau. of John & Mary
CONNER, John; bn. Jan 21, 1789; bpt. Jan 30, 1789; sps. James
   Carroll & Margaret Einson
CONNOR, John Coppinger; bpt. Feb 16, 1800; son of Daniel &
   Rebecca
CONNOR, John Allen; bn. Jun 9, 1800; bpt. Jul 6, 1800; son of
   John & Mary
CONNOR, Mary; bn. Nov 3, 1796; bpt. Nov 6, 1796; dau. of Thomas &
   Judith
CONNOR, Mary; bpt. Aug 13, 1800; adult, wf. of William Connor
CONNOR, Rebecca; bpt. Aug 13, 1800; dau. of William & Mary
CONOLY, William; bn. Nov 21, 1796; bpt. Jul 30, 1797; son of
   Michael & Margaret
CONROY, Andrew; bn. Apr 30, 1782; bpt. Jul 20, 1783; sps. Henry
   Philips

BAPTISMS

CONROY, Elizabeth; bn. Mar 2, 1789; bpt. Apr 19, 1789; sps. John Jore & Eleanor Ireland
CONSTABLE, Margaret; bn. Nov 11, 1792; bpt. Dec 5, 1792; dau. of William & Priscilla
CONSTABLE, Priscilla; bpt. Apr 27, 1792; adult
CONSTABLE, William; bpt. Apr 27, 1792; adult; conditional
CONTE, Francis Charles Thomas; bn. Aug 19, 1793; bpt. Sep 26, 1793; son of Stephen Julian & Jane Claudine Gabrielle Bastaille de la Garet of St. Domingo
CONWAY, Mary; bn. Jul 4, 1784; bpt. Aug 29, 1784; sps. Henry Philips & Honor Roach
CONWAY, Robert; bn. Jan 16, 1786; bpt. Feb 26, 1786; sps. Michael Shreagh & Catharine Conway
COOK, George; bn. Oct 30, 1794; bpt. Nov 6, 1794; son of Michael & Honor
COOKE, Henry; bpt. Jul 26, 1794; 13 months; son of Jane Cooke
COONEY, John; bn. Oct 13, 1793; bpt. Oct 18, 1793; son of Thomas & Sarah
COOPER, Mary; bn. Jul 2, 1798; bpt. Aug 1, 1798; dau. of John & Bridget
CORBET, Catharine; bn. Jun 11, 1797; bpt. Jul 18, 1797; dau. of William & Catharine
CORBET, Margaret; bn. Jan 25, 1795; bpt. Feb 8, 1795; dau. of William & Catharine
CORKERIN, Rosanna; bn. Jan 27, 1783; bpt. Apr 6, 1783; sps. John Dougherty & Ann Dougherty
CORMINS, James; bn. May 2, 1785; bpt. Jul 2, 1785; sps. Sara Boyde
CORNBROBST, Joseph; bn. Mar 16, 1796; bpt. Mar 20, 1796; son of Ignatius & Catharine
CORNBROBST, Joseph; bn. Jan 6, 1800; bpt. Mar 9, 1800; son of Joseph & Mary
CORNBROPST, Bernard; bn. Jul 7, 1791; bpt. Aug 28, 1791; son of Ignatius & Catharina
CORNBURY, Jemima; bpt. Mar 28, 1792; adult; conditional
CORNBURY, Richard; bn. Apr 18, 1792; bpt. May 6, 1792; son of James & Jemima
CORNET, Elizabeth Desiree; bn. Nov 15, 1795; bpt. Jul 8, 1798; dau. of John Baptist Arnaud & Mary Perine Hyacinthe LePere Champigny
CORNPROBST, Mary; bn. Mar 27, 1797; bpt. Jul 23, 1797; dau. of Joseph & Mary
CORREJOLLES, Francis; bpt. Feb 7, 1797; 2 years old; son of Adelaide Correjolles, an Indian of Ft. Dauphin
(CORSEALE), Mary Teresa; bn. Oct 1, 1798; bpt. Oct 14, 1798; dau. of Louise, slave of Mr. Corseale
COSKERY, Bennet; bn. Jan 30, 1800; bpt. Feb 6, 1800; son of Bernard & Anastasia
COSKERY, Catharine; bn. Sep 14, 1797; bpt. Sep 16, 1797; dau. of Bernard & Anastasia
COSKERY, Francis; bn. Feb 8, 1788; bpt. Jul 31, 1788; sps. Patrick Bennet & Martha Coskery

BAPTISMS

COSTELLOE, Henry; bpt. Aug 18, 1797; 6 months; dau. of Henry & Catharine
COSTELO, Catharine; bn. Apr 28, 1800; bpt. May 15, 1800; dau. of Henry & Catharine
COTTER, Juliana; bpt. Aug 16, 1794; 2 years old; dau. of Thomas & Elizabeth
COTTINEAU, Julia Eliza; bn. Jun 2, 1792; bpt. Aug 7, 1792; dau. of Denis Nicholas, nat. of Nantes & Dame Lule Moquet, nat. of Bouquet, St. Domingo
COTTREL, Peter; bn. Jun 23, 1794; bpt. Jul 3, 1794; son of Thomas, Rennes in Britanny & Mary Levassor, Plaisance, St. Domingo
(COUREGES), John Joseph; bpt. Jan 20, 1799; 8 weeks; son of Griffette, slave of Mr. Coureges
COURGEOLLE, Marie Antoinette; bpt. May 27, 1799; 3 1/2 months; dau. of Adelaide Courgeolle
COUTIER, Gabriel; bn. May 8, 1795; bpt. May 19, 1795; son of John Anthony & Mary Bouvier
COX, Jane; bpt. Jan 29, 1790; adult
COX, Mary Ann; bn. Sep 30, 1799; bpt. Apr 6, 1800; dau. of Peter & Jane
COY, Robert; bn. May 17, 1793; bpt. Jul 22, 1793; son of Patrick & Ann
CRAIN, Mary; bpt. Sep 30, 1787; 6 weeks; sps. Matthew Leeson & Katy Kelly
CRANDEL, William; bpt. Apr 16, 1786; 3 months, 17 days; sps. Martin Waters & Margaret Poiet
CRAWLEY, Elizabeth; bn. Mar 27, 1783; bpt. Apr 27, 1783; sps. John Verdelet & Saffia Verdelet
CREAGH, John; bn. Nov 14, 1799; bpt. Dec 29, 1799; son of John & Mary
CREAGH, Mary; bn. Jun 16, 1798; bpt. Jun 17, 1798; dau. of John & Mary
CREMER, Edward; bpt. Dec 29, 1799; 2 weeks; son of Edward & Mary
CREMER, Eleanor; bn. Nov 1, 1796; bpt. Jan 13, 1797; dau. of Edward & Mary
CREMER, Robert; bn. Jul 10, 1795; bpt. Jul 26, 1795; son of Edward & Mary
CRESSOL, Elizabeth; bn. Feb 28, 1794; bpt. Mar 1, 1794; dau. of Peter & Margaret
CRISALL, Maria; bn. Feb 22, 1796; bpt. Feb 24, 1796; dau. of Peter & Mary
CRISALL, Peter; bn. Jan 19, 1792; bpt. Jan 20, 1792; son of Peter & Peggy
CRISSALL, John; bn. Jan 28, 1799; bpt. Mar 25, 1799; son of Peter & Margaret
CROGHAN, Elizabeth; bn. Jul 24, 1791; bpt. Jul 25, 1791; dau. of James & Elizabeth
CROGHEN, Ann; bn. Aug 5, 1789; bpt. Sep 6, 1789; dau. of James & Elizabeth
CROINE, Catharine; bpt. Jun 25, 1786; 11 months; sps. George Garner & Priscilla Harrison
CROSS, Elizabeth; bn. May 2, 1794; bpt. Jun 22, 1794; dau. of John & Mary

BAPTISMS

CROSS, Mathias; bn. Dec 19, 1795; bpt. Dec 21, 1795; son of Joshua & Hannah
CROSS, Sarah; bn. Jun 4, 1794; bpt. Aug 16, 1794; dau. of Elizabeth Cross
CROUDER, Mary; bn. Jun 3, 1799; bpt. Dec 1, 1799; dau. of Joseph & Judith
CROW, Elizabeth; bn. Mar 28, 1796; bpt. Mar 26, 1798; dau. of John (deceased) & Mary
CULLASON, George; bn. Sep 30, 1795; bpt. Oct 12, 1795; son of George & Mary
CULLISON, John; bn. Oct 14, 1796; bpt. Nov 13, 1796; son of George & Mary
CULVERSON, Richard; bn. Feb 18, 1795; bpt. Apr 10, 1796; son of Richard & Mary
CUMBERLAND, Philip; bpt. May 26, 1799; 5 months; son of James & Sarah
CUMMINGHAM, Owen; bn. Sep 13, 1800; bpt. Oct 9, 1800; son of Martin & Bridget
CURRY, Ben; bn. Jul 18, 1789; bpt. Aug 9, 1789; Negro; son of John Curry & Barbara
CURRY, Hannah; bn. Jul 21, 1798; bpt. Jan 18, 1799; dau. of Unity Curry
CURTIS, John Washington; bn. Dec 15, 1794; bpt. Feb 1, 1795; son of William Puntney & Mary
CURTIS, William; bn. Aug 28, 1798; bpt. Sep 2, 1798; son of William & Mary
CURTIS, William; bn. Sep 10, 1799; bpt. Sep 15, 1799; son of William & Mary
CUSICK, Elizabeth; bn. Sep 19, 1793; bpt. Dec 26, 1793; dau. of John & Mary
CUSICK, Hannah; bn. Nov 20, 1795; bpt. Nov 24, 1795; dau. of John & Mary
CUSICK, William; bn. Feb 13, 1798; bpt. Oct 22, 1799; son of John & Mary
(DAFORD), William; bpt. Apr 26, 1795; son of Melky, slave of Daniel Daford
DALAMAS, John Henry Edmund; bn. Jul 11, 1797; bpt. Jul 18, 1797; son of Peter Francis & Helena
DALIQUET, Ann Mary; bn. Nov 28, 1795; bpt. Dec 27, 1795; dau. of John Baptist & Elizabeth
DALIQUET, Anne Louisa; bpt. Mar 12, 1800; 2 months; dau. of Elizabeth Daliquet
DALMAS, Peter Isadore; bpt. Jan 22, 1796; 10 days; son of Peter Francis & Helen
(DALMAS), Theotide; bn. Mar 15, 1798; bpt. Apr 24, 1798; son of Mary Jane, slave of Mr. Dalmas
DALTON, Anna Marie; bn. Dec 2, 1798; bpt. Dec 20, 1798; dau. of George & Catharine
DALY, Ann; bn. Jun 7, 1799; bpt. May 25, 1800; dau. of James & Catharine
DALY, Eleanor; bn. Jul 26, 1797; bpt. Aug 2, 1797; dau. of Timothy & Catharine
DALY, James; bn. Apr 19, 1795; bpt. Mar 20, 1796; son of James & Catharine

BAPTISMS

DALY, Margaret; bn. Oct 14, 1794; bpt. Feb 21, 1796; dau. of Timothy & Catharine

DALY, Patrick; bn. Nov 24, 1796; bpt. Nov 30, 1796; son of Sybil Daly

DALY, William; bn. Nov 11, 1796; bpt. Jul 7, 1797; son of James & Catharine

DAN, John Anthony; bn. May 15, 1797; bpt. May 14, 1798; son of Jane Rose Dan, St. Domingo

DANE, Charles; bn. Sep 7, 1788; bpt. Oct 19, 1788; sps. Edward Hagthrop & Eleanor Hagthrop

DANFOSSY, John Maurice Lewis Eugene; bn. Jul 18, 1800; bpt. Oct 16, 1800; son of Maurice & Catharine Mareno

DANFOSSY, Margaret Amala Eugenia; bn. Jan 23, 1799; bpt. Apr 27, 1799; dau. of Balthasar Maurice & Margaret Catharine Eugenia

DANICOURT, James Francis; bn. Jan 10, 1800; bpt. Jun 25, 1800; son of James Bernard & Sarah Evans

DANICOURT, Jeanne Bonne Henriette; bn. Jan 24, 1798; bpt. Oct 20, 1798; dau. of James Bernard & Sarah Evans

DANNEBERG, Julia; bn. Jul 23, 1794; bpt. Mar 22, 1795; dau. of Frederic & Cathartine Fry

DANNEBERG, William; bn. Jun 27, 1789; bpt. Mar 22, 1795; son of Frederic & Catharine Fry

DARKEY, Charles; bpt. Aug 19, 1798; 4 years old; son of Ann Darkey, free Indian, lately deceased

DARMAN, James; bn. Jul 25, 1785; bpt. Jun 3, 1787; sps. John Coady

DARMAN, Susanna; bn. Feb 17, 1787; bpt. Jun 3, 1787; sps. Thomas Cochran

DAVAN, Augustin; bn. Feb 15, 1794; bpt. Mar 31, 1794; son of John & Margaret Luce

DAVAN, John; bn. Jun 30, 1798; bpt. Aug 4, 1799; son of John Lewis & Margaret Elizabeth Lutz

DAVANNE, Philip Henry; bn. Aug 1, 1795; bpt. Oct 11, 1795; son of John Lewis & Margaret Elizabeth Lentz, both of Paris

DAVERIN, Margaret; bn. Aug 14, 1795; bpt. Sep 30, 1795; dau. of William & Honor

DAVID, Peter; bpt. Sep 13, 1800; son of John & Catharine Durand

DAVID, Peter Elias; bn. Aug 3, 1797; bpt. Sep 13, 1800; son of John & Catharine Durand

DAVIES, Ann Elizabeth; bn. Apr 30, 1798; bpt. Jun 14, 1798; dau. of Peter & Ann

DAVIES, Harriot; bn. Aug 7, 1794; bpt. Nov 23, 1794; dau. of Ambrose & Elizabeth

DAVIES, Samuel; bn. Sep 21, 1795; bpt. Oct 4, 1795; son of Peter & Ann

DAVIES, Thomas; bn. Sep 6, 1795; bpt. Jun 23, 1796; son of William & Mary

DAVIS, Amelia; bn. Jun 22, 1794; bpt. Aug 23, 1795; son of John Stork & Polly Davis

DAVIS, Caleb; bn. Mar 7, 1792; bpt. Jul 27, 1794; son of Sarah

DAVIS, Charles; bn. Jan 31, 1787; bpt. Mar 25, 1787; sps. John Renau & Polly White

DAVIS, Elizabeth; bn. Mar 17, 1789; bpt. Jul 12, 1789; dau. of Ambrose & Elizabeth

BAPTISMS

DAVIS, John; bn. Oct 24, 1785; bpt. Nov 7, 1785; sps. William & Elizabeth Fellen
DAVIS, Julia; bn. Oct 24, 1785; bpt. Nov 7, 1785; sps. Joseph Minion & Elizabeth King
DAVIS, Margaret; bn. Oct 14, 1790; bpt. Nov 7, 1790; dau. of Francis & Catharine
DAVIS, Mary; bn. Nov 16, 1784; bpt. Dec 12, 1784; sps. Henry Rigdale & Madalen Richardson
DAVIS, Mary Elizabeth; bn. Nov 13, 1789; bpt. Jan 24, 1790; dau. of Peter & Ann
DAVIS, Thomas; bn. May 25, 1788; bpt. May 30, 1788; sps. Peter Gold & Mrs. Loyne
DAVIS, Thomas; bn. Dec 25, 1788; bpt. Apr 19, 1789; sps. Matthew Harden & Mary Davis
DAVIS, Thomas; bn. Dec 30, 1798; bpt. Feb 1, 1799; son of Thomas & Mary
DAVIS, Walter; bn. Nov ?, 1788; bpt. Oct 11, 1789; son of Robert & Susanna
DAWSON, Mary; bn. Aug 6, 1795; bpt. Aug 13, 1795; dau. of Elizabeth Dawson
DAY, Elizabeth; bn. Mar 1, 1788; bpt. Jun 25, 1788; sps. Henry Tomalty
DAY, Frances Julia; bn. Sep 20, 1799; bpt. Aug 5, 1800; dau. of Jeanne Rose Day
DEADY, Anna Maria; bn. Dec 23, 1788; bpt. Jan 4, 1789; sps. Charles Sewall & Henrietta Williamson
DEADY, Elizabeth; bn. Jun 20, 1785; bpt. Jun 26, 1785; sps. James Ryan & Elizabeth Clemens
DEADY, Francis; bpt. Sep 28, 1791; 1 month; son of Daniel & Winefrida
(DEADY), John; bn. Jan 30, 1794; bpt. Feb 12, 1794; son of Lucy, slave of Daniel Deady
DEAGLE, Elizabeth; bpt. Sep 23, 1792; 2 weeks; dau. of Simon & Elizabeth
DEAGLE, Hannah; bn. Oct 22, 1797; bpt. Oct 23, 1797; dau. of Simon & Elizabeth
DEAGLE, Julia; bn. Dec 22, 1788; bpt. Dec 22, 1788; sps. John Renau & Clare Brien
DEAGLE, Margaret; bn. Jul 30, 1795; bpt. Jul 30, 1795; dau. of Simon & Elizabeth
DEAGLE, Matthew; bpt. Nov 16, 1800; son of Simon & Elizabeth
DEAGLE, Simon; bn. Aug 17, 1799; bpt. Aug 17, 1799; son of Simon & Elizabeth
DEAL, Henry; bn. Sep 23, 1800; bpt. Oct 19, 1800; son of Jacob & Susanna
DEALE, Andrew; bn. Aug 22, 1796; bpt. Sep 11, 1796; son of Henry & Mary
DEALE, Elizabeth; bn. Oct 11, 1790; bpt. Oct 31, 1790; dau. of Henry & Mary
DEALE, Frederic; bn. Nov 14, 1788; bpt. Nov 30, 1788; sps. William Fouss & Catharine Fouss
DEALE, John; bn. Feb 4, 1784; bpt. Mar 7, 1784; sps. William Fouss & Catharine Fouss
DEALE, John; bn. Aug 28, 1785; bpt. Sep 18, 1785; sps. Henry Philips & wife

BAPTISMS

DEALE, Peter; bn. Mar 21, 1787; bpt. Apr 8, 1787; sps. Henry
    Tomalty & Elizabeth Tomalty
DEALE, Teresa; bn. Apr 18, 1794; bpt. May 11, 1794; dau. of Henry
    & Mary
DEALY, Fanny; bn. Feb 25, 1790; bpt. Mar 24, 1790; dau. of
    Timothy & Catharine
DEALY, James; bn. Apr 24, 1792; bpt. Jun 2, 1792; son of Timothy
    & Catharine
DEAN, James; bn. May 18, 1790; bpt. Jul 11, 1790; son of James &
    Mary
DEAN, Mary Debora; bn. Mar 9, 1789; bpt. Apr 12, 1789; sps.
    Joseph Laurence & Dorothy Laurence
DEAN, Robert Ramsay; bn. Mar 13, 1796; bpt. Jun 5, 1796; son of
    James & Mary
DEANE, Felix; bn. Dec 1, 1791; bpt. Sep 16, 1792; son of James &
    Mary
DEANE, James; bn. Mar 7, 1787; bpt. May 6, 1787; sps. Richard
    Gore & Ann Prendwell
(DEBONDOIRE), Lewis Ann Constance; bn. Apr 23, 1796; bpt. May 13,
    1796; dau. of Aimee, Mulatto slave of Mr. DeBondoire, of
    Guadaloupe
(DEBOS), Mary Teresa; bn. Jul 4, 1796; bpt. Jul 31, 1796; dau. of
    Mary, slave of Madame Debos, widow Montbuisson
DEBOYSARE, Charles; bn. Jan 16, 1798; bpt. Apr 1, 1798; son of
    Charles & Terese DeBrabander
DEBOYSERE, Mary Teresa Carolina; bn. Dec 23, 1796; bpt. Dec 26,
    1796; dau. of Charles John James & Thersia Joseph Joanna
    DeBrabander
DEBRUNET, Joseph Nicholas; bn. Jun 12, 1792; bpt. May 12, 1794;
    born at Cp. Francois; son of Paul Joseph Alexander & Marie
    Radigonde DeVernis
DEBUTTS, Joseph John James; bn. Aug 5, 1799; bpt. Aug 21, 1799;
    son of Elias & Mary
DECHEFFONTAINES, Jonathas Charlotte George; bn. Jan 5, 1794; bpt.
    Jan 8, 1794; dau. of Ambrose Joseph Stephen Mary de
    Penfentenio & Mary Henrietta Creuze
DECREUZBOURG, John Joseph William Hiram; bn. Mar 15, 1794; bpt.
    Mar 24, 1794; son of Simon & Adelaide Kirsen
DEDERICH, George; bpt. Sep 5, 1800; 4 months; son of Godfrey &
    Catharine
DEGAN, Charles; bpt. Jun 19, 1797; 3 weeks; son of Catharine
DEGAN, Charlotte; bn. Jun ?, 1800; bpt. Oct 31, 1800; dau. of
    Catharine
DEGAN, Mary Ann; bpt. Apr 1, 1799; 4 weeks; dau. of Catharine
DEGILIVAN, John; bpt. Jun 17, 1787; 5 weeks; sps. Timothy Duffy &
    Ann Murry
DEIRING, John; bn. Sep 22, 1799; bpt. Sep 22, 1799; son of John
    Nicholas & Waltera
DELANY/HARVEY, Mary; bpt. Nov 10, 1793; dau. of John Delany &
    Charlotte Harvey
DELAPRADE, Marie Anne Sebastienne; bn. Aug 22, 1799; bpt. Nov 2,
    1799; dau. of John Francis Cabannes & Ann Joseph St. Martin
    DuFoureq
DELARUE, Ann Frances Uranie; bn. Aug 3, 1793; bpt. Oct 11, 1796;
    dau. of Francis Lewis & Ann Margaret Teline Daulede

BAPTISMS

DELAUET, Juliet; bn. Jul 14, 1787; bpt. Aug 14, 1787; sps. William Boyler & Mary Boyler

(DELAVETT), Adam; bpt. Jan 17, 1787; slave of Capt. deLavett; sps. deLavett & Mrs. Marshall

DELEYRITZ, Alexis Joseph Ambrose; bn. Apr 7, 1799; bpt. Jun 9, 1799; son of Alexis Lewis & Louisa Rese Gouin

DELIGMIER, Joseph Gambard; bpt. Apr 26, 1800; 9 months; son of Cecile Victoire Gambard Deligmier

DELILE, Charles Antony; bn. Apr 19, 1790; bpt. Jun 13, 1791; son of John Baptist & Mary

DELILE, Elizabeth Ann; bn. Sep 5, 1786; bpt. Jun 13, 1791; dau. of John Baptist & Mary

DELILE, Julia; bn. Dec 24, 1785; bpt. Jan 23, 1786; sps. John Renau & Mary Coulon

DELINOTTE, Mary Frances; bn. Nov 17, 1792; bpt. Dec 12, 1793; dau. of Charles, nat. of Dunkirk & Halie

(DELISLE), Louise Augustine; bpt. Jun 1, 1796; dau. of Mary Adelaide, called Venus; sl; John Baptist Godart DeLisle

DELISLE, Rosetta Eleanor; bn. Aug 2, 1800; bpt. Aug 15, 1800; dau. of Richard Rambaud & Elizabeth

DELISLE, Sophia Juliana; bn. Jan 24, 1796; bpt. Jun 1, 1796; dau. of John Baptist Godart & Sophia Pontoir

(DELONGUE), Mary Catharine; bpt. Feb 17, 1794; dau. of Rose, slave of Mr. DeLongue of St. Domingo

DELOUBERT, Louise Henriette Felicite; bn. Sep 24, 1795; bpt. Jun 24, 1797; dau. of Francis Lewis & Magdalen Victoire DeLaRue

DELOUBERT, Louise Antoniette Euphrasie; bn. Feb 20, 1798; bpt. Jun 10, 1798; dau. of Francis Lewis & Magdalen Victoire DelaRue

DEMANGIN, Anthony; bn. Nov 9, 1798; bpt. Jun 18, 1799; son of Charles & Ruth Coldwell

DEMANGIN, Margaret; bn. Jul 31, 1797; bpt. Jun 24, 1798; dau. of Charles & Ruth

DEMANQUIN, Mary Ann; bn. Sep 28, 1795; bpt. Oct 25, 1795; sps. John LaBatte & Mary Celestin

DEMPSEY, Ann; bn. Dec 25, 1786; bpt. Jul 27, 1794; dau. of John & Frances

DEMPSEY, Eleanor; bpt. May 5, 1800; adult; conditional

DEMPSEY, Frances; bn. Jul 24, 1789; bpt. Jul 27, 1794; dau. of John & Frances

DEMPSEY, Frederick; bn. Jun 29, 1791; bpt. Jul 27, 1794; son of John & Frances

DEMPSEY, Helena; bpt. Aug 14, 1800; 2 months; dau. of John & Mary

DEMPSEY, Jane; bn. Sep 14, 1795; bpt. Oct 11, 1795; dau. of John & Elizabeth

DEMPSEY, John; bpt. Oct 14, 1798; 8 months; son of Patrick & Elizabeth

DEMPSEY, Thomas; bn. Nov 3, 1794; bpt. Nov 23, 1794; son of John & Frances

DEMSEN, Diana; bn. Aug 5, 1793; bpt. Aug 5, 1793; dau. of John & Elizabeth

DENIS, Alexander Hilarion Joseph; bn. Sep 17, 1793; bpt. Jul 9, 1796; born in St. Mark, St. Domingo; son of John Peter & Mary Magdalen Cherpy, nat. of Marseilles, parish of St. Martin

BAPTISMS

(DENNIS), Francis; bpt. Feb 7, 1797; 9 weeks; son of Emilie, slave of Mr. Benjamin Dennis
(DENNIS), Mary Martha; bpt. Mar 25, 1799; 2 weeks; Mulatto; dau. of Gertrude, slave of Mde. Dennis
DENNY, Thomas; bn. Dec 5, 1799; bpt. Jan 12, 1800; son of Cornelius & Rebecca
DENNY, William; bn. Oct 28, 1797; bpt. Mar 11, 1798; son of Neil & Rebecca
(DENOTIERE), Jane; bpt. Mar 26, 1797; 1 month; dau. of Camille, slave of Mr. Pageot DeNotiere
DENTS, James Benjamin; bn. Apr 18, 1798; bpt. Jul 27, 1798; son of James Stephen & Mary Jones
DENYS, Susanna; bn. Aug 18, 1799; bpt. Dec 1, 1799; dau. of James Stephen & Mary Jones
DEPABLES, Etienne Nicholas Laurent Apelin; bn. Dec 22, 1792; bpt. Dec 26, 1792; son of Charles Apelin & Marie Joseph LaFarge
DERIDON, Mary Frances; bpt. May 2, 1797; 8 years old; dau. of John & Mary Martin
DERIVARDI, Mariana Amelia; bn. Nov 29, 1794; bpt. Jul 9, 1795; born Norfolk, Va.; dau. of John James Leopold Ulrich, nat. of Berne & Mary, nat. of Vienna
DERUET, Lewis; bn. Oct 3, 1790; bpt. Oct 24, 1790; son of Godfred & Flora
DESAUBRY, Mary Joseph Hilaire; bn. Oct 10, 1789; bpt. Mar 27, 1794; son of Hilaire Felix & Frances Abelard
DESAUGON, Louisa Victoria Mary; bn. Nov 20, 1793; bpt. May 6, 1794; dau. of Francis Charert & Perine Elizabeth de Gournay
DESBORDES, Stephen Charlotte Teresa Landrieve; bn. Oct 12, 1796; bpt. Jul 27, 1797; dau. of Anthony Giles Landrieve & Mary Clare Legardeur DeTilly
DESERMETE, Francis Charles; bn. Apr 4, 1793; bpt. Mar 1, 1794; son of Joseph Victor Cabanel & Rene Margueritte Paterson
DESGRANGES, Leo Stephen Paul; bn. Jun 23, 1795; bpt. Jun 19, 1798; son of Paul Francis Leroy D'Howal & Leonine Louise Massean LaCroise
DESGRANGES, Stephen Amadeus D'Hewal; bn. Jul 20, 1798; bpt. Oct 11, 1798; son of Francis Leroy (deceased) & Leonitte D'Hewal
DESHIELD, Juliana; bn. Aug 10, 1788; bpt. Sep 14, 1788; sps. Peirce Brignall & Polly Lockerman
DESHIELDS, Ann; bn. Dec 10, 1790; bpt. Dec 14, 1790; dau. of Francis & Magdalen
DESHIELDS, John; bn. Aug 13, 1784; bpt. Dec 11, 1784; sps. Jac LaTouche & Mary Celestin
DESHIELDS, Joseph Alexander; bn. Nov 1, 1799; bpt. Nov 9, 1799; son of Joseph & Mary
(DESIR), John Baptist; bpt. Mar 19, 1797; 6 months; slave of M'selle Desir
DESIR, Joseph; bn. Nov 26, 1796; bpt. Jan 6, 1797; son of Jacques Antoine & Mary Magdalen
DESPALLIERES, James Paul Aime; bn. May 4, 1794; bpt. May 31, 1795; son of Bernard Charles Elizabeth Martin & Margaret Felicity Rivery
DESPALLIERES, Jean Marie Ange; bn. Apr 8, 1793; bpt. Nov 11, 1793; son of Bernard Charles Elizabeth Martin & Marguerite Felicite Rivery

BAPTISMS

(DESPALLIERES), Mary Rose; bpt. Apr 5, 1795; dau. of Josephine, slave of Mde. DesPallieres
DESPOT, Anthony; bn. Apr 4, 1797; bpt. Apr 17, 1797; son of Joseph & Frances Demange
DESPOT, Bertrand; bn. Dec 17, 1798; bpt. Feb 14, 1799; son of Joseph & Frances Desmange
DESPOT, Joseph; bn. May 27, 1795; bpt. Jan 10, 1796; son of Joseph & Frances
(DESRAMEAUX), Margaret; bn. Oct 20, 1794; bpt. Oct 28, 1794; dau. of Pelagie, slave of widow DesRameaux
DESRAMEAUX, Mary; bn. Dec 20, 1790; bpt. Jul 17, 1791; dau. of Rose & Appolline
(DESSABLE), Mary Elizabeth; bpt. Jun 26, 1796; dau. of LaRose, slave of Mr. Asselin Dessable
DESSABLES, Elizabeth; bn. Mar 2, 1795; bpt. May 4, 1796; dau. of Charles Asselin of St. Domingo & Mary Joseph LaFarge
(DESSABLES), John Gabriel; bpt. Apr 2, 1797; 6 weeks; son of Marinette, French Negro slave of Mrs. Asselin Dessables
DESTAN, William; bpt. Oct 6, 1799; 6 or 7 days; son of William, free Negro & Elizabeth, since dead
DEVALCOURT, Alexander Joseph; bn. May 20, 1795; bpt. Jun 20, 1795; son of Alexander & Margaret
DEVALCOURT, Theodore John; bn. Oct 23, 1796; bpt. Aug 16, 1797; son of Alexander & Margaret Gold
DEVISE, Henrietta Margaret; bn. Jun 17, 1799; bpt. Nov 10, 1799; dau. of John & Margaret
DEVOY, Ann Rigby Wood; bn. Aug 7, 1787; bpt. Aug 12, 1787; sps. Joseph Petotoit & Elizabeth Noulin
DEVOY, Mary; bn. Feb 15, 1789; bpt. Aug 16, 1789; dau. of Michael & Ann
DEVY, Peter; bn. Feb 15, 1792; bpt. Feb 24, 1792; son of Peter & Nancy
DICKEY, Catharine; bpt. Oct 18, 1799; 9 months; dau. of John & Mary
DIDIER, Clare Rosa; bn. Sep 17, 1786; bpt. Apr 21, 1787; sps. Charles Didier & Rosa Pierson
DIDIER, John Fresier; bn. Aug 18, 1790; bpt. Oct 19, 1790; son of Henry & Margaret
DIFFENTHAAL, Sarah; bn. Mar 3, 1800; bpt. May 28, 1800; dau. of Samuel & Anna Marie
DILLON, Margaret; bn. Jan 5, 1797; bpt. Jan 26, 1797; dau. of Bridget Dillon
DILLON, William; bn. Aug 14, 1792; bpt. Sep 30, 1792; son of John & Cecilia
DISMAN, Elizabeth; bn. Mar 29, 1790; bpt. Jul 25, 1790; dau. of William & Honor
(DISPAN), Mary; bpt. Dec 19, 1796; 3 weeks; dau. of Sophie, slave of Mrs. Dispan
DISTANCE, Elizabeth; bn. Oct 12, 1796; bpt. Nov 30, 1796; dau. of William Distance, free Negro & Elizabeth, slave of J. B. Bernabeu
DITTO, Catharine; bn. Dec 20, 1787; bpt. Jan 1, 1788; sps. John Krauss & Catharine Krauss
DIXON, William; bpt. Feb 22, 1796; adult, free Negro; sps. John Baptist & Bethsheda Bernabeu

BAPTISMS

DIZABEAU, Ann Margaret; bn. Nov 21, 1798; bpt. Dec 2, 1798; dau. of John & Magdalen
DIZABEAU, Edward Valentine; bn. Feb 14, 1800; bpt. Feb 24, 1800; son of John Baptist & Margaret
DOGHERTY, Bridget; bpt. Sep 1, 1799; 2 weeks; dau. of Neill & Mary
DOLONGHERY, James; bn. Apr 10, 1798; bpt. Jun 4, 1798; son of John & Catharine
DOLOUGHERY, Mary; bn. Oct 13, 1800; bpt. Nov 23, 1800; dau. of John & Catharine
DONAHOE, Dennis; bn. Aug 2, 1791; bpt. Aug 7, 1791; son of Daniel & Brigit
DONALDSON, Charles Rogers; bn. Dec 1, 1798; bpt. Jan 22, 1799; son of James & Elizabeth
DONALDSON, James William; bpt. Nov 17, 1794; 6 months; son of James & Elizabeth
DONALDSON, John; bn. Oct 12, 1796; bpt. Dec 9, 1796; son of James & Elizabeth
DONNELL, Catharine; bn. Jun 1, 1799; bpt. Jun 16, 1799; dau. of James & Mary
DONNELLY, James; bn. Nov 4, 1800; bpt. Nov 9, 1800; son of Simon & Eleanor
DONNELLY, Margaret; bn. Sep 20, 1799; bpt. Sep 29, 1799; dau. of Simon & Eleanor
DONNELSON, Jane; bn. Jun 7, 1792; bpt. Sep 9, 1792; dau. of James & Elizabeth
DONOVAN, Eleanor; bn. Apr 4, 1791; bpt. May 23, 1791; dau. of Jeremia & Henny
DONOVAN, Mary; bn. Aug 2, 1797; bpt. Aug 3, 1797; dau. of John & Mitchill
DONOVAN, Mary; bn. Oct 10, 1797; bpt. Jan 3, 1798; dau. of Bartholomew & Sarah
DONOVAN, Sarah; bpt. Mar 4, 1797; adult
DONOVAN, Sarah; bn. Aug 2, 1797; bpt. Aug 3, 1797; dau. of John & Mitchill
DOOGAN, Antony; bpt. Aug 12, 1787; sps. Anthony Bergman & Christina Bergman
DOOGEN, Mary; bn. Mar 8, 1785; bpt. Apr 17, 1785; sps. Nancy Herrin
DOPP, Eve; bn. Dec 26, 1799; bpt. Mar 9, 1800; dau. of Henry & Mary
DORLIN, Margaret; bn. Jun 26, 1787; bpt. Jun 28, 1787; sps. Emanuel Sanchez & Mary Caloran
DORNEY, Elizabeth; bn. Mar 5, 1799; bpt. Apr 14, 1799; dau. of John & Jane
DORNEY, John; bn. Sep 2, 1797; bpt. Oct 8, 1797; son of William & Elizabeth
DORNEY, Martha; bn. Sep 5, 1797; bpt. Oct 8, 1797; dau. of John & Jane
DORNEY, Mary; bn. Nov 26, 1799; bpt. Jan 5, 1800; dau. of William & Elizabeth
DORSENS, Anthony; bn. Sep 17, 1782; bpt. Jul 20, 1783; sps. Richard Dorsey & Catharine Gomer
DORSEY, Betsy; bpt. Apr 14, 1793; dau. of Antony & Mary

BAPTISMS

DORSEY, James; bpt. May 6, 1787; 7 months; sps. James Conner & Honor Reed
DORSEY, James Ireland; bn. Oct 7, 1788; bpt. Nov 16, 1788; sps. William Sherret & Elizabeth Ireland
DORSEY, James; bn. May 25, 1796; bpt. May 31, 1796; son of James & Catharine
DORSEY, James; bn. Jun 26, 1797; bpt. Jun 27, 1797; son of James & Catharine
DORSEY, Michael; bpt. Mar 25, 1799; 10 weeks; son of James & Catharine
DORSEY, Samuel; bn. Nov 4, 1794; bpt. Nov 24, 1794; son of Vechel & Clementina
DORSEY, William; bpt. Apr 12, 1784; 6 weeks; sps. George Hall & Judith Herrin
DOUGHERTY, Catharine; bn. Mar 20, 1786; bpt. Mar 20, 1786; sps. Peter Walter & wife
DOUGHERTY, Hugh; bn. Jan 13, 1794; bpt. Sep 25, 1794; son of Edward & Christina
DOUGHERTY, James; bn. Feb 21, 1792; bpt. Mar 28, 1792; son of Hugh & Susanna
DOUGHERTY, John; bn. Sep 10, 1794; bpt. Oct 3, 1795; son of Hugh & Susanna
DOUGHERTY, Joseph; bn. Jan 21, 1799; bpt. Apr 20, 1800; son of Neil & Mary
DOUGHERTY, Mary; bn. Oct 31, 1793; bpt. Dec 25, 1793; dau. of Hugh & Susanna
(DOUGHERTY), Mary; bpt. May 13, 1798; 1 1/2 years old; Mulatto; dau. of Rachel, slave of Fanny Dougherty
DOUGLAS, Joseph John; bn. Apr 14, 1799; bpt. Jun 29, 1800; son of Cantwell & Ann
DOWD, Francis; bn. Mar ?, 1775; bpt. Nov 25, 1784; sps. Sara Boyle
DOWD, John; bpt. Jul 30, 1786; 9 months; sps. Peggy Wooden
DOWD, Margaret; bpt. Aug 20, 1784; 10 months; sps. Joanna Paterson
DOWLAN, Patrick; bn. Feb ?, 1789; bpt. Feb 4, 1789; sps. Jeremia Horgan & Elizabeth Horgan
DOWNEY, John; bn. Feb 6, 1795; bpt. Mar 1, 1795; son of John & Mary
DOWNY, Edmund; bn. Apr 10, 1789; bpt. Apr 26, 1789; sps. Daniel O'Brien & Mary Lynch
DOWYER, Daniel; bn. Oct 17, 1789; bpt. Nov 1, 1789; son of Edward & Margaret
DOYLE, John; bn. Sep 30, 1800; bpt. Oct 7, 1800; son of Martin & Susanna
DOYLE, Margaret; bpt. Jan 27, 1789; 7 months; dau. of Mary Doyle
DOYLE, Mary; bn. Feb 6, 1796; bpt. Feb 28, 1796; dau. of James & Eleanor
DOYLE, Mary; bn. Sep 5, 1795; bpt. Apr 24, 1796; dau. of Nicholas & Ann
DOYLE, Mary Ann; bn. Jun 7, 1791; bpt. Jul 31, 1791; dau. of Thomas & Margaret
DOYLE, William; bn. May 9, 1785; bpt. Nov 16, 1785; sps. James Sullivan

BAPTISMS

DRAKE, Eleanor; bn. Sep 17, 1790; bpt. Oct 17, 1790; dau. of
  Francis & Ann
DRAKE, Elizabeth; bn. Sep 23, 1784; bpt. Sep 26, 1784; sps.
  Patrick Hurley & Ann Adams
DRAKE, James; bpt. Jul 30, 1786; 2 weeks; sps. Elizabeth Steiger
DRAKE, Mary; bpt. May 27, 1795; 20 years old; dau. of Francis &
  Ann
DRAKE, Thomas Garner; bn. Apr 20, 1789; bpt. Jul 12, 1789; son of
  Hanna
DREYMAN, James; bn. Jun ?, 1785; bpt. Aug 13, 1786; sps. Margaret
  Everson
DRINAN, John; bn. Dec 18, 1796; bpt. Feb 5, 1797; son of Thomas &
  Mary
DRISCOLL, Eliza Antoinette; bn. May 27, 1796; bpt. Sep 10, 1796;
  dau. of Laurence & Elizabeth
DRISCOLL, Jeremiah; bn. Mar 15, 1799; bpt. Mar 19, 1799; son of
  Terence & Elizabeth
DRISKILL, Debra; bn. Jun 12, 1793; bpt. Jun 22, 1794; dau. of
  Mark & Mary
DRISKILL, Margaret; bn. Sep 11, 1794; bpt. Feb 22, 1795; dau. of
  Mark & Mary
DROUILLARD, Mary Louisa; bn. May 2, 1796; bpt. Oct 10, 1796; dau.
  of Andres & Elizabeth Villard
DUBOURG, Mary Louisa Frances; bpt. Dec 12, 1799; 6 months; dau.
  of Peter Francis of St. Colombe & Mary Elizabeth Lauzun de
  Charette
DUCAS, Elizabeth; bn. Apr 21, 1794; bpt. Jun 29, 1794; dau. of
  Lewis & Mary
(DUCASSE), John Francis; bpt. Feb 6, 1797; 2 months; son of
  Rosalie, slave of (late) Mr. Ducasse, St. Domingo
DUCATEL, Amiee Adelaide; bn. Dec 19, 1798; bpt. Apr 15, 1799;
  dau. of Edme & Ann Catharine Pineau
DUCATEL, John Julius; bn. Jun 27, 1796; bpt. Sep 23, 1796; son of
  Edmund & Ann Catharine Pineau
(DUCHART), Milly; bn. Feb 1, 1799; bpt. Mar 17, 1799; dau. of
  Jack & Milly, slave of Mr. Duchart
DUCHEMIN, Frances Susanna; bn. Nov 11, 1798; bpt. Apr 15, 1799;
  dau. of Francis & Margaret
DUCHEMIN, Francis Augustine; bn. Jan 5, 1795; bpt. Jan 8, 1795;
  son of Francis & Margaret
DUCHEMIN, James Joseph; bn. Sep 7, 1800; bpt. Dec 4, 1800; son of
  Francis & Margaret
DUCHEMIN, Nicholas; bn. Jan 2, 1796; bpt. Jan 3, 1796; son of
  Francis & Margaret
DUCHET, Mary; bn. Apr 1, 1788; bpt. Sep 6, 1788; sps. Michael
  Mulchale & Agnes Purcel
DUFARD, Nicholas Joseph; bn. Jul 13, 1792; bpt. Aug 16, 1796; son
  of Mary Dufard, free woman of colour
DUFF, Ann; bn. May 31, 1800; bpt. Jun 15, 1800; dau. of Patrick &
  Martha
DUFF, Mary; bn. Nov 18, 1797; bpt. Jan 14, 1798; dau. of Patrick
  & Martha
DUFF, Patrick; bn. Jul 1, 1791; bpt. Jul 24, 1791; son of Patrick
  & Martha

BAPTISMS

DUFF, Thomas; bn. Aug 13, 1794; bpt. Oct 5, 1794; son of Patrick
    & Martha
DUFFY, Catharine; bn. Mar 21, 1790; bpt. Apr 25, 1790; dau. of
    Owen & Mary
DUFFY, Hugh; bn. Dec 14, 1794; bpt. Feb 1, 1795; son of Owen &
    Mary
DUFFY, Mary; bn. Oct 3, 1798; bpt. May 7, 1799; dau. of Michael &
    Mary
DUFFY, Susanna; bn. Feb 14, 1792; bpt. Apr 1, 1792; dau. of Owen
    & Mary
DUFOUR, Mary Elizabeth Louisa; bn. Jan 6, 1797; bpt. Jan 30,
    1797; dau. of Lewis & Mary Frances
(DUGAN), Abraham; bn. Feb 1, 1795; bpt. Apr 5, 1795; son of James
    & Henny, slave of Cumberland Dugan
(DUGAN), Ann; bn. Jan 4, 1799; bpt. May 5, 1799; dau. of James &
    Henny, slave of Mr. Cumberland Dugan
DUGLAMME, John; bn. Apr 17, 1796; bpt. May 8, 1796; son of John,
    mariner of Perigord, France & Mary Magdalen Bourg, St.
    Nichoas Mole, St. Domingo
DUGOS, Henrietta; bn. Apr 17, 1796; bpt. Apr 17, 1796; dau. of
    Francis & Mary Motar
DULANY, John; bpt. Jul 29, 1787; 4 months; son of Peter & Biddy
DULOHERY, Thomas; bn. Feb 7, 1793; bpt. Jun 9, 1793; son of John
    & Catharine
DUMAS, John Gustave; bn. Feb 24, 1796; bpt. Jan 16, 1797; son of
    John & Mary Magdalen Bertau
DUMAS, Magdalen Adelaide; bn. Jul 16, 1798; bpt. Jan 19, 1799;
    dau. of John & Mary Magdalen
DUMAS, Peter; bpt. Sep 29, 1793; son of John & Mary Magdalen
    Bertaux; sps. Peter Renaudet of Bordeaux & Henrietta Landry
DUMOUCHEL, Josephine Charlotte; bn. Apr 17, 1796; bpt. Dec 10,
    1796; dau. of Francis Charles & Frances
DUMPHEY, Ann; bn. Jan 10, 1800; bpt. Jan 28, 1800; dau. of
    Richard & Mary
DUNLEVY, John; bn. Oct 10, 1799; bpt. Nov 2, 1799; son of Andrew
    & Abigael
DUNN, Edward; bn. Dec 31, 1799; bpt. Jan 22, 1800; son of Daniel
    & Elizabeth
DUNN, Elizabeth; bpt. Jul 9, 1788; 3 months; sps. Tobias Shilling
    & Catharine Shilling
DUNN, Mary; bn. Jul 3, 1790; bpt. Jul 5, 1790; dau. of John &
    Eleanor Kelly
DUNN, Matthew; bpt. Dec 25, 1789; 3 weeks; son of Michael & Mary
DUNSTON, John; bn. Aug 25, 1788; bpt. Sep 29, 1788; sps. John
    Hagthrop & Margaret Britt
(DUPARC), Justina; bn. Aug 20, 1795; bpt. Oct 20, 1795; dau. of
    Cecilia, slave of Mr. Berquin duParc
(DUPEIROU), Anthony Theophile; bn. May ?, 1798; bpt. Nov 11,
    1798; son of Rosalie, slave of Mdlle. Dupeirou
(DUPERON), Mary; bpt. Jun 19, 1800; 5 months; dau. of Rosalie,
    slave of Mde. Duperon
(DUPERRON), Peter Lewis; bpt. May 17, 1795; 1 month; son of
    Rosalie, slave of Mrs. DuPerron
DUPOIS, Elizabeth; bn. Dec 6, 1796; bpt. Dec 18, 1796; dau. of
    Christopher & Mary

BAPTISMS

DUPOIX, Ann Eve; bn. Dec 25, 1798; bpt. Jan 13, 1799; dau. of
    Christopher & Mary DuPoix
DUPUIS, David; bn. Jan 1, 1798; bpt. Feb 9, 1798; son of David &
    Anna
DUPUY, Mary Jane; bn. Aug 18, 1799; bpt. Dec 1, 1799; dau. of
    Arnold David & Ann Smith
(DURAND), Henry George; bpt. Sep 16, 1799; Mulatto; 5 months; son
    of Fastine, slave of Mr. Durand
DURAND, Suzanne Augustine Caroline; bn. May 23, 1800; bpt. Jun
    18, 1800; dau. of John James & Mary Martha Renee Gastumeau
DURKEE, Eleanor; bn. Nov 12, 1800; bpt. Nov 12, 1800; dau. of
    Pearl & Mary
DURKEE, John; bn. Nov 12, 1800; bpt. Nov 12, 1800; son of Pearl &
    Mary
DURKEE, Robert; bn. Mar 20, 1798; bpt. Mar 20, 1798; son of
    Charles & Mary
DURONDEAU, Lewis; bpt. Aug 7, 1793; about 5 weeks; son of Stephen
    & ---
DUSMAN, Joanna; bn. Mar 15, 1786; bpt. Jun 4, 1786; sps. Timothy
    Hannafin & Nelly Taylor
DUSMAN, Margaret; bn. Oct 15, 1784; bpt. Feb 13, 1785; sps. John
    Connelly & Mary Marr
DUSSEUIL, Gaspar Nazarius; bn. Jun 4, 1796; bpt. Jun 29, 1797;
    son of Nazarius & Sophia Tonneau
DWYAR, Mary; bn. Mar 31, 1791; bpt. Jun 5, 1791; dau. of Edmund &
    Peggy
DWYER, Charles; bpt. Jun 8, 1796; 8 months; son of John &
    Margaret
DWYER, Elizabeth; bn. Jun 24, 1795; bpt. Aug 2, 1795; dau. of
    William & Ann
DWYER, John; bn. Jan 9, 1795; bpt. Feb 22, 1795; son of Thomas &
    Martha
DWYER, Mary; bn. Sep 26, 1797; bpt. Sep 29, 1797; dau. of John &
    Margaret
EDDE, Ann; bpt. Jul 26, 1798; adult Indian
EDEN, James; bn. Oct 14, 1797; bpt. Nov 26, 1797; son of Garrick
    & Agnes
EDMONSON, James; bn. Mar 24, 1792; bpt. May 20, 1792; son of
    James & Sarah
EDMUNSON, William Smith Brook; bn. Apr 16, 1790; bpt. Aug 27,
    1790; son of James & Sara
EDWARDS, Jane; bn. May 30, 1798; bpt. Jun 10, 1798; dau. of Paul
    & Mary
EGAN, James; bn. May 27, 1800; bpt. Jun 29, 1800; son of James &
    Catharine
EGAN, Martin; bn. Sep 25, 1797; bpt. Oct 29, 1797; son of James &
    Catharine
EGAN, Mary; bn. Mar 5, 1799; bpt. Mar 31, 1799; dau. of James &
    Catharine
EHRLACHER, Jacob; bn. Oct 17, 1793; bpt. Dec 29, 1793; son of
    Michael & Anastasia
EHRLOCHER, Francis Antony; bn. Feb 1, 1789; bpt. Jun 1, 1789; son
    of John Michael & Anastasia
EILER, Sarah; bn. Jan 2, 1785; bpt. Jan 9, 1785; sps. Christian
    Lawdecker & Mary Worthington

BAPTISMS

EISEL, Henrietta; bn. Jan 21, 1800; bpt. Jan 26, 1800; dau. of John & Mary
EISEL, Honor; bn. Aug 9, 1797; bpt. Aug 13, 1797; dau. of John & Mary
EISEL, Philip; bn. May 28, 1793; bpt. Jun 2, 1793; son of John & Mary
EISLER, Elizabeth; bn. Oct 21, 1783; bpt. Nov 2, 1783; sps. Joseph Streider & Catharine Streider
EISLER, Magdalen; bn. May 1, 1791; bpt. May 8, 1791; dau. of John & Mary
EISLER, Margaret; bn. Mar 13, 1790; bpt. Mar 21, 1790; dau. of John & Mary
EISLER, Mary; bn. Jan 30, 1795; bpt. Feb 8, 1795; dau. of John & Mary
EISLER, Susanna; bn. Oct 22, 1788; bpt. Nov 2, 1788; sps. Joseph Streider & Catharine Streider
ELLEM, Samuel; bn. Jul 24, 1793; bpt. Aug 18, 1793; son of Samuel & Margaret
ELWES, Alfred William Henry; bn. Jul 1, 1796; bpt. Aug 4, 1796; son of William & Ann Frances Bourdon
ELWES, Amelie Anne Marie; bn. Feb 3, 1799; bpt. Apr 29, 1800; dau. of William & Ann Frances Bourdon
ELWOOD, Julia; bn. Apr 9, 1798; bpt. May 6, 1798; dau. of James & Mary
(EMORY), William; bn. Dec 2, 1798; bpt. Feb 17, 1799; son of Mitus, slave of Mr. Emory & Peggy, slave of Mr. Francis J. Mitchell
ENGLISH, Mary; bn. Sep 14, 1797; bpt. Jun 3, 1800; dau. of John & Elizabeth
ENNIS, Mary Ann; bn. Mar 29, 1797; bpt. Apr 2, 1797; dau. of Philip & Elizabeth
ENRIGHT, John; bn. May 1, 1778; bpt. Nov 27, 1794; son of John & Eleanor
ENSLOW, John; bn. Dec 18, 1788; bpt. Aug 24, 1789; son of Joseph & Mary
ENSOR, Harriot; bn. Jul 23, 1797; bpt. Aug 5, 1798; dau. of John & Mary
ERLACHER, Margaret; bn. Apr 19, 1800; bpt. May 30, 1800; dau. of Michael & Anastasia
ERSKINE, John; bn. May 17, 1784; bpt. Jul 2, 1799; son of Archibald & Ruth
ESLING, George; bpt. Sep 11, 1799; 3 weeks; son of Paul & Catharine
ESMENARD, Elizabeth; bn. Apr 30, 1797; bpt. Jun 6, 1797; dau. of John & Emilia Enders
(ETTING), David; bpt. May 7, 1797; 5 months; dau. of Sarah, slave of Solomon Etting
(EUTALE), Mary Catharine; bpt. Apr 15, 1794; 5 months; dau. of Mary, slave of Mr. Eutale
EVANS, Eliza; bn. Apr 1, 1795; bpt. Aug 28, 1796; dau. of Thomas & Martha
(EVANS), Thomas; bn. Jan 30, 1797; bpt. Apr 17, 1797; Mulatto; son of Isabella, slave of William Evans
EYSLER, Eve; bn. Apr 22, 1787; bpt. Apr 29, 1787; sps. Peter Vimewell & Eve Smith

BAPTISMS

FACKNEY, Mary; bn. Nov 23, 1793; bpt. Sep 14, 1794; dau. of John & Jane
FAGEN, Benjamin; bn. Apr 6, 1784; bpt. Apr 9, 1784; sps. Dom Jordan & Thamson Fratter
FAGEN, Patrick; bn. Apr 6, 1784; bpt. Apr 9, 1784; sps. Dominick Fagen & Thamson Fratter
(FAGOLAS), Mary Louisa; bpt. Sep 16, 1799; Mulatto; 3 years old; dau. of Sophie, slave of Mr. Fagolas
FAHERTY, Thomas; bn. Aug 6, 1799; bpt. Aug 17, 1799; son of Thomas & Mary
FARHAGER, John; bn. Dec 7, 1795; bpt. Dec 15, 1795; son of John & Judith
FARHAR, Catharine; bn. Nov 16, 1800; bpt. Nov 30, 1800; dau. of John & Juliet
FARRAGHER, Ann; bn. Nov 17, 1796; bpt. Feb 2, 1797; dau. of John & Judith
FARRAHAR, Juliana; bn. May 21, 1798; bpt. May 27, 1798; dau. of John & Julia
FARREL, George; bn. Apr 15, 1788; bpt. May 12, 1788; sps. Thomas Purcil & Agnes Purcil
FARREL, George; bn. Jul 13, 1792; bpt. Nov 6, 1792; son of George & Mary
FARREL, James; bn. Jan 3, 1783; bpt. Mar 30, 1783; sps. Thomas Hillen & Catherine Logue
FARREL, James; bn. Mar 8, 1786; bpt. Apr 17, 1786; sps. John Gleeson & Elizabeth Curry
FARREL, James; bn. Jun 17, 1790; bpt. Jun 19, 1790; son of James & Rachael
FARREL, James; bn. Aug 13, 1791; bpt. Oct 9, 1791; son of James & Mary
FARREL, John; bpt. Oct 16, 1785; 3 years old; sps. Michael Lee
FARREL, John; bpt. Jul 21, 1787; 10 days; son of Richard & Margaret Dealy; sps. Thomas Fanning & Eleanor Courtney
FARREL, John; bn. Jul 25, 1790; bpt. Oct 24, 1790; son of George & Mary
FARREL, John; bn. Jun 12, 1797; bpt. Jun 25, 1797; son of James & Mary
FARREL, Robert; bn. Aug 15, 1784; bpt. Apr 10, 1785; sps. John Ryan & Lucy Caveneaugh
FARREL, Sara; bpt. Aug 8, 1788; 1 week; sps. Hugh Harkins & Dorothy Power
FARREL, Wineride; bn. Nov 6, 1789; bpt. Nov 22, 1789; dau. of James & Mary
FARRELL, Edward; bn. Dec 25, 1776; bpt. Nov 6, 1785; sps. Thomas Daniel Murphy
FARRELL, Jane; bn. Apr 9, 1796; bpt. Jul 9, 1796; dau. of George & Mary
FARRELL, Richard; bn. Nov 30, 1793; bpt. Dec 29, 1793; son of James & Mary
FARRELL, William; bn. Jun 4, 1794; bpt. Nov 20, 1794; son of George & Mary
FATHERSTON, Philip; bn. Jun 4, 1799; bpt. Sep 22, 1799; son of Henry & Mary

BAPTISMS

FAUCHER, Ann Desiree; bn. May 10, 1794; bpt. May 12, 1794; dau. of John, ship Captain & merchant of Cp. Francois & Mary Dupont
FAUCHER, John Charles; bn. Sep 26, 1795; bpt. Jun 2, 1797; son of John, ship captain & merchant, Cp. Francais & Mary DuPont
FAURIE, Ann Josephine; bn. Feb 22, 1797; bpt. May 18, 1797; dau. of Joseph & Josephine D'Alban
FAURIE, Petronilla; bn. Jan 11, 1796; bpt. Apr 21, 1796; dau. of Joseph & Ann Frances Josephine
FAURIE, Zoe; bn. Oct 15, 1798; bpt. Jun 10, 1799; dau. of Joseph & Ann Frances Joseph D'Alban
FAVIER, Caroline; bn. Oct 8, 1798; bpt. Oct 29, 1798; dau. of John & Mary
FAWNDER, Joseph; bn. Mar 22, 1790; bpt. Jun 27, 1790; son of Peter & Catharine
FENERTY, James; bn. May 15, 1791; bpt. Aug 7, 1791; son of Andrew & Mima
FENNEL, Maurice; bn. Jan 5, 1800; bpt. Feb 2, 1800; son of John & Sarah
FERGUSON, Catharine; bpt. Jul 17, 1798; 5 weeks; dau. of William Ferguson & Ann Devine
FERGUSON, Catharine; bn. Mar 15, 1799; bpt. Apr 7, 1799; dau. of Terrence & Mary
(FERRY), Elizabeth; bpt. Jan 3, 1799; dau. of Jeanne, slave of Mr. Ferry
FERRY, Lewis Francis Alexander; bn. Feb 25, 1796; bpt. Jul 28, 1798; son of Francis Rene Peyre & Frances Elizabeth Montpellier
FHEEL, Henry; bn. Aug 16, 1797; bpt. Dec 10, 1797; son of Henry & Elizabeth
FIAR, Charles George; bn. Oct 2, 1782; bpt. Apr 19, 1784; sps. Charles Bernard & Mary White
FIELDS, Ann; bn. Dec 3, 1794; bpt. Jan 1, 1795; dau. of Ambrose & Elizabeth
FIELDS, Elizabeth; bn. Sep 4, 1797; bpt. Oct 15, 1797; dau. of Ambrose & Elizabeth
FINAUGHTY, John; bn. Aug 15, 1797; bpt. Aug 20, 1797; son of James & Mary
FINERTY, Mary; bn. Jan 22, 1796; bpt. Feb 14, 1796; dau. of Andrew & Jamima
FINWRIGHT, Ann; bn. Jul 9, 1787; bpt. Jul 14, 1787; sps. Richard Gore & Eleanor Foy
FISHER, James; bn. Nov 21, 1791; bpt. Nov 27, 1791; son of James & Anne
FISHER, John; bn. Jun 30, 1788; bpt. Jul 4, 1788; sps. William Collins & Elizabeth Wells
FISHER, John Baptist Oliver; bn. Mar 18, 1797; bpt. May 30, 1797; son of James & Ann
FISHER, Margaret; bn. Dec 21, 1793; bpt. Dec 27, 1793; dau. of James & Ann
FISHER, Mary Magdalen; bn. Oct 23, 1795; bpt. Nov 2, 1795; dau. of Joseph & Mary Magdalen
FISHER, Robert; bn. Sep 28, 1789; bpt. Oct 5, 1789; son of James & Ann

BAPTISMS

FISHER, William Patrick; bn. Oct 9, 1799; bpt. Apr 21, 1800; son of James & Ann
(FISSOM), Peter Arnold Valentine; bn. Aug 4, 1794; bpt. Apr 15, 1796; son of Ann Grissonne, slave of Mrs. Fissom, St. Domingo
FITZAWGER, Thomas; bpt. Jun 21, 1790; adult Indian
FITZGERALD, Ann; bn. Feb 11, 1797; bpt. Apr 28, 1797; dau. of John & Mary
FITZGERALD, Catharine; bn. Feb 17, 1795; bpt. Apr 19, 1795; dau. of Garret & Margaret
FITZGERALD, Eleanor; bpt. Oct 13, 1797; 2 months; dau. of Edward & Mary
FITZGERALD, Eleanor; bn. Jul 4, 1798; bpt. Sep 8, 1798; dau. of Thomas & Ann
FITZGERALD, James; bpt. Sep 1, 1799; 3 months; son of John & Mary
FITZGERALD, John; bn. Oct 27, 1796; bpt. Jun 25, 1797; son of Garret & Margaret
FITZGERALD, John; bn. Sep 14, 1799; bpt. Jan 12, 1800; son of Richard & Margaret
FITZGERALD, Mary; bpt. Apr 9, 1798; dau. of Garret & Margaret
FITZGERALD, Nancy; bn. Apr 2, 1791; bpt. May 22, 1791; dau. of Thomas & Betsy
FITZGERALD, Richard; bn. Oct 4, 1786; bpt. Oct 6, 1786; sps. James Conner & Honor Reed
FITZGERALD, Sarah; bn. Apr 27, 1799; bpt. Aug 16, 1799; dau. of Garret & Margaret
FITZGIBBONS, Joanna; bn. Aug 16, 1787; bpt. Aug 18, 1787; sps. Daniel Murphy & Nancy Gorhee
FITZPATRICK, Susanna; bn. Jun 25, 1789; bpt. Jul 7, 1789; dau. of Antony & Eleanor Pye
FITZPATRICK, William; bn. Apr 30, 1794; bpt. Jun 7, 1794; son of William & Judith
FLAGHERTY, James; bn. Feb 8, 1785; bpt. Mar 6, 1785; sps. James Stewart & Eleanor Hughes
FLAGHERTY, Mary; bpt. Sep 11, 1791; 6 weeks; dau. of Philip & Sally
FLAHARTY, Francis; bn. Jun 14, 1797; bpt. Jun 23, 1797; son of Patrick & Catharine
FLAHARTY, John; bn. Jun 20, 1793; bpt. Jul 5, 1793; son of Philip & Sarah
FLAHARTY, Michael; bpt. Dec 17, 1797; 7 weeks; son of Michael & Biddy
FLAHARTY, Thomas; bpt. Dec 14, 1800; son of Bryan & Bridget
FLAHERTY, Catharine; bpt. Mar 26, 1797; 4 months; dau. of Matthew & Bridget
FLAHERTY, Sarah; bn. Aug 7, 1795; bpt. Aug 24, 1795; dau. of Pattie & Catharine
FLEET, Archibald; bpt. Oct 13, 1796; 2 months; son of Priscilla Fleet
FLETCHER, Josias; bn. Feb 4, 1797; bpt. Mar 5, 1797; son of Robert Fletcher, Mulatto slave of Christopher Johnson & Rachel, Mulatto slave of Issac Smith
FLEURY, Peggy; bn. Jan 18, 1792; bpt. Jan 20, 1792; dau. of Sebastian & Magdalene

BAPTISMS

FLEURY, Peter; bn. Nov 22, 1787; bpt. Nov 25, 1787; sps. Paul
    Marie Pulin & Mary Wells
FLEURY, Samuel Victor; bn. Oct 15, 1795; bpt. Nov 22, 1795; son
    of Paul Aime & Clare
FLEURY, Thomas; bn. Jan 9, 1790; bpt. Jan 29, 1790; son of
    Sebastian & Magdalen
FLIN, Eleanor; bn. Aug 8, 1784; bpt. Aug 22, 1784; sps. Ferdinand
    Laurence & Susanna Morres
FLIN, John; bpt. Aug 22, 1787; 2 weeks; sps. Elizabeth Walter
FLOOD, Elizabeth; bn. Nov 18, 1792; bpt. Dec 10, 1792; dau. of
    John & Elizabeth Furlong
FLOOD, John; bn. Aug 27, 1794; bpt. Aug 31, 1794; son of
    Elizabeth
FLORA, Catharine; bn. Dec 14, 1783; bpt. Dec 21, 1783; sps.
    Christian Lawdecher & Eve Smith
FLORAY, Margaret; bn. Jun 24, 1783; bpt. Jul 13, 1783; sps.
    Margaret Salvage
FLUCHARD, Rosanna; bn. Jun 1, 1785; bpt. Jun 6, 1785; sps.
    Baptiste Gallec & Rosanna Williams
FOLDWAILDER, Catharine; bn. Sep 27, 1785; bpt. Sep 28, 1785; sps.
    Francis Anthony Miller & Catharine Smith
FOLDWEILER, Magdalen; bn. Sep 15, 1787; bpt. Sep 16, 1787; sps.
    Henry Bayner & Ann Gertrude Friecy
FOLEY, Dennis; bn. Mar 9, 1799; bpt. Mar 18, 1799; son of John &
    Juliana
FOLKS, Fanny; bn. Dec 26, 1784; bpt. Mar 23, 1790; dau. of
    Richard & Christiana
FOLKS, James; bn. Jun 12, 1786; bpt. Mar 23, 1790; son of Richard
    & Christiana
FOLKS, Mary; bn. Jun 20, 1789; bpt. Jul 20, 1789; dau. of Richard
    & Christiana
FOLKS, Richard; bn. Oct 28, 1782; bpt. Mar 23, 1790; son of
    Richard & Christiana
FOLWEILER, Margaret; bn. Apr 27, 1793; bpt. May 13, 1793; dau. of
    Francis (now dead) & Magdalen
FONDER, Catharine; bn. May 16, 1788; bpt. Jun 15, 1788; sps.
    Anthony Miller & Magdalen Foldweiler
FONDER, Peter; bn. Sep 27, 1784; bpt. May 15, 1785; sps. Antony
    Bergman & Christiana Bergman
FONTER, Mary; bn. Aug 19, 1798; bpt. Sep 23, 1798; dau. of
    Barbara Fonter
FOOS, Martha; bpt. Feb 11, 1800; adult
FOOS, Philip Jacob; bpt. Sep 1, 1799; 2 weeks; son of William &
    Martha
FORBERRY, Ann; bn. Feb 28, 1790; bpt. Jun 6, 1790; dau. of George
    & Eleanor
FORD, James; bn. Sep ?, 1798; bpt. Aug 4, 1799; son of John &
    Agnes
FORD, Samuel; bn. Mar 4, 1785; bpt. Mar 4, 1785; sps. Joseph
    Gutterau & Margaret Mongee
FOREMAN, William; bn. Aug 24, 1790; bpt. Nov 7, 1790; son of
    George & Eleanor
FORESIGHT, Mary; bpt. May 10, 1789; 2 1/2 years old; sps. Daniel
    Duggan & Ann Querny

BAPTISMS

FORGE, George; bn. Nov 18, 1789; bpt. Oct 10, 1790; son of
    Raymond & Peggy
FORGE, George; bn. Aug 8, 1792; bpt. Aug 11, 1792; son of Raymond
    & Peggy
FORGE, Joseph; bn. May 24, 1787; bpt. Sep 5, 1787; sps. Peter
    Gerard & Mary Murphy
(FORQUEAU), Eugenie Sophie; bn. Mar 21, 1796; bpt. Apr 24, 1800;
    Mulatto; dau. of Mercie, slave of Mary Ann Forqueau
FORSBENDER, John; bn. May 19, 1799; bpt. May 29, 1799; son of
    Peter & Hedwigis
FORTUNEE, Marie; bn. Sep 16, 1793; bpt. Oct 20, 1793; Negro; dau.
    of Modeste of Madam Assailly
FOSBERY, Margaret; bn. Apr 16, 1792; bpt. Jan 6, 1793; dau. of
    George & Eleanor
FOSTER, James; bpt. Apr 6, 1796; 9 months; son of Hannah Foster
(FOUCON), Andrew; bpt. Aug 9, 1799; Mulatto; 1 year old; son of
    Mercie, slave of Mde. Foucon
(FOUGERE), John Baptist; bpt. Jun 11, 1797; 5 months; son of
    Zaire, slave of Mr. Fougere
FOWLER, Priscilla; bn. Jan ?, 1797; bpt. Jul 18, 1798; dau. of
    John Fowler, free Mulatto & Darkey
FOWLY, James; bn. Sep 26, 1796; bpt. Oct 1, 1796; son of Joseph &
    Mary
FOX, Claissa Ann; bn. Jun 21, 1790; bpt. Jan 26, 1791; dau. of
    Antony & Sara
FOX, Juliet Anne O'Brien; bn. Jul 30, 1797; bpt. Aug 27, 1797;
    dau. of Antony & Sarah
FOX, Margaret; bpt. Jul 27, 1788; 5 months; sps. Margaret Bowen
FOX, Samuel Washington; bn. Mar 9, 1795; bpt. Jul 14, 1796; son
    of Anthony & Sarah
FOY, James; bn. Aug 10, 1786; bpt. Aug 13, 1786; sps. James
    Fisher & Ann DeVoy
FOY, Mary; bn. Feb 18, 1787; bpt. Feb 20, 1787; sps. Barbara
    Michael
FOY, William; bn. Dec 4, 1787; bpt. Dec 6, 1787; sps. Mark Morres
    & Barbara Bahon
FRANCOIS, Stephen Joseph; bn. Mar 3, 1785; bpt. Mar 28, 1785;
    sps. Hofferman & Eleanor Jenet
FRASIER, Eleanor; bn. Mar 15, 1788; bpt. May 11, 1788; sps.
    William Collins & Eleanor Walsh
FREAN, Mary; bn. Jan 29, 1785; bpt. Feb 20, 1785; sps. Timothy
    Herrin & Hanna Reed
FREAN, William; bn. Sep 5, 1787; bpt. Sep 30, 1787; sps. James
    Fisher & Mary Wells
FREDERIC, Jane Mary; bn. Apr 5, 1784; bpt. Apr 19, 1784; sps.
    John Baptist Joseph Conlon & Mary Mongee
FREEMAN, Anna Maria Eliza; bn. Dec 23, 1797; bpt. Dec 2, 1798;
    dau. of Nicholas & Catharine
FREEMAN, Mary; bn. Aug 11, 1787; bpt. Aug 19, 1787; sps. Matthew
    Leeson & Mary Joice
FREEMAN, Thomas; bn. Sep 18, 1799; bpt. Oct 1, 1799; son of
    Thomas William & Catharine
FREEMAN, William; bn. Feb 12, 1796; bpt. Dec 26, 1796; son of
    Nicholas & Catharine

BAPTISMS

FRESSINET, John Bernard; bn. Sep 25, 1798; bpt. Jun 12, 1799; son of John & Marie Casenave
FRIBOURG, Ann; bn. Aug 30, 1788; bpt. Jan 4, 1789; dau. of John & Mary
FRIDAY, Charles; bn. Apr 13, 1795; bpt. Apr 19, 1795; son of John & Elizabeth
FRIDAY, Charles; bpt. Feb 8, 1800; son of John & Elizabeth
FRIDAY, Engelherd; bn. Jul 4, 1792; bpt. Jul 7, 1792; son of John & Betty
FRIDAY, Jacob; bn. Jan 3, 1797; bpt. Jan 8, 1797; son of John & Elizabeth
FRIDAY, John; bn. Nov 23, 1798; bpt. Dec 2, 1798; son of John & Elizabeth
FROGET, Margaret; bn. Jul 5, 1783; bpt. Aug 10, 1783; sps. Timothy Herrin & Ann Thior
FULHART, Joseph; bn. Feb 8, 1795; bpt. Apr 5, 1795; son of Jacob & Elizabeth
FULHART, Mary; bn. Jun 17, 1792; bpt. Mar 21, 1793; dau. of Jacob & Elizabeth
(FULTON), Mima; bn. Mar 16, 1799; bpt. Apr 7, 1799; dau. of Michael, slave of Mr. David Fulton & Polly, slave of Mrs. Bailey
FULWEDER, George; bn. Apr 13, 1791; bpt. Apr 14, 1791; son of Francis & Magdalen
FULWEDER, Rachel; bn. Apr 13, 1791; bpt. Apr 14, 1791; dau. of Francis & Magdalen
GABEL, John Baptist; bn. Jun 25, 1793; bpt. Oct 12, 1793; son of Paul Mathieu of Cape Francois & Marie Anne Soreby
GAILER, Mary; bn. Sep 11, 1787; bpt. Mar 16, 1788; sps. Mary Bro---
GAILER, Sara; bn. Jan 15, 1790; bpt. Apr 4, 1790; dau. of Thomas & Elizabeth
GAILER, William Brook; bn. Jan ?, 1792; bpt. May 13, 1792; son of Thomas & Elizabeth
GAINNIER, Louisa Marcelline; bn. Aug 20, 1796; bpt. Jun 1, 1799; dau. of John & Magdalen Mary Cheron
GALLAGHER, John; bn. Apr 14, 1800; bpt. Aug 10, 1800; son of John & Eleanor
GALLAGHER, Mary Sappington; bn. Sep 14, 1786; bpt. Jul 12, 1789; dau. of Mary Gallagher
GALLEGHA, Charles; bn. Nov 7, 1787; bpt. Dec 8, 1787; sps. John Harnett & Margaret Hobs
GAMMEL, Rosanna; bn. Sep 28, 1790; bpt. Nov 7, 1790; dau. of James & Ann
(GANSZES), Lewis; bpt. May 27, 1798; 5 months; son of Nancy, slave of Mr. Ganszes
GANTEAUME, Ann; bn. Jul 31, 1796; bpt. Oct 21, 1798; dau. of James & Elizabeth Casey
GANTEAUME, Clare; bn. Feb 17, 1797; bpt. Oct 21, 1798; dau. of James & Elizabeth Casey
GANVERN, Thomas; bn. Sep 9, 1782; bpt. May 4, 1783; sps. Anthony Clark & Elizabeth Clark
GARDINER, Rebecca; bn. Jul 15, 1779; bpt. Nov 12, 1785; sps. Priscilla Harrison

BAPTISMS

GARLAND, Catharine; bn. Oct 29, 1791; bpt. Dec 25, 1791; dau. of
    John & Mary Ann
GARLICK, Philip; bn. Jan 29, 1783; bpt. Mar 16, 1783; sps.
    Francis & Margaret Latar
GARRET, Antony; bpt. Jul 23, 1791; 6 months; son of Antony &
    Elizabeth
GARRET, Elizabeth; bn. Aug 1, 1785; bpt. Apr 16, 1786; sps.
    William & Catharine Martin
GARRET, James Francis; bn. Feb ?, 1789; bpt. Aug 28, 1791; son of
    James & Elizabeth
GARVEN, Elizabeth; bn. Sep 30, 1795; bpt. Jun 18, 1797; dau. of
    John & Mary
GARVEN, Susanna; bn. Feb 16, 1799; bpt. Sep 13, 1799; dau. of
    Matthew & Ann
GAVEN, Thomas; bn. Dec 5, 1796; bpt. Jun 11, 1797; son of Matthew
    & Ann
GEANTY, Felicity; bn. Jan 25, 1800; bpt. Jun 23, 1800; dau. of
    Elizabeth Geanty, Mulatress
GEANTY, Peter Lewis; bn. Mar 7, 1796; bpt. Apr 26, 1799; son of
    Lewis & Jane Helen Mary Desnoutiens Pageot
GEORGE, Jacob; bn. Nov 22, 1796; bpt. Dec 11, 1796; son of James
    & Frances
GERARD, James; bn. Jul 12, 1795; bpt. Jul 12, 1795; son of Peter
    & Magdalen
GERARD, Margaret; bn. Mar 15, 1793; bpt. Mar 16, 1793; dau. of
    Peter & Magdalen
GERARD, Mary Magdalen; bn. Nov 3, 1787; bpt. Nov 4, 1787; sps.
    John Baptist Movisse & Sally Murphy
GERARD, Rosalia; bn. Nov 19, 1785; bpt. Nov 20, 1785; sps. John
    German & Mary Murphy
GERARD, Stephen; bn. Jan 7, 1791; bpt. Jan 8, 1791; son of Peter
    & Magdalen
GERMAN, Elizabeth; bn. Aug ?, 1785; bpt. Sep 11, 1785; sps.
    Gerard & Mary Ann Lumbel
GERMAN, Patrick; bn. Jul 22, 1796; bpt. Mar 21, 1797; son of John
    & Rosette Victoria
GHEQUIERE, Anne Louisa; bn. Dec 1, 1791; bpt. Dec 2, 1791; dau.
    of Charles & Henrietta
GHEQUIERE, Baptist Charles; bn. Dec 9, 1787; bpt. Dec 16, 1787;
    son of Paul Charles Gabriel & Henrietta
GHEQUIERE, Charlotte Sophia; bn. Dec 24, 1793; bpt. Jan 5, 1794;
    dau. of Paul Charles Gabriel & Harriet
GHEQUIERE, Esther; bn. Dec 1, 1800; bpt. Dec 14, 1800; dau. of
    Charles & --
GHEQUIERE, Henrietta Maria; bn. Mar 30, 1790; bpt. Apr 18, 1790;
    dau. of Paul Charles Gabriel & Harriette
GHEQUIERE, Henry Tiernan; bn. Jun 11, 1798; bpt. Jun 28, 1798;
    son of Charles & Harriot
(GHEQUIERE), James; bpt. Jan 8, 1792; 4 months
GHEQUIERE, John Francis William; bn. Jan 6, 1786; bpt. Jan 20,
    1786; son of Paul Charles Gabriel & Harriette; sps. Francis
    Xavier Joseph Caplan & Mary Vochez
GHEQUIERE, Joseph Charles; bn. Apr 12, 1796; bpt. May 8, 1796;
    son of Charles & Harriot

BAPTISMS

(GHEQUIERE), Lewis Felix; bn. Apr 11, 1800; bpt. Sep 28, 1800;
    son of Nace, slave of Mr. Ghequiere & Catharine, slave of
    Fr. Beeston
(GHEQUIERE), Mary; bn. Sep 15, 1793; bpt. Sep 15, 1793; dau. of
    Susanna, slave of Mr. Ghequiere
(GHEQUIERE), Rachel; bn. Apr 15, 1796; bpt. Apr 17, 1796; dau. of
    Ignatius, slave of Charles Ghequiere & Catharine, slave of
    Rev. Mr. Nagot
(GHEQUIERE), William; bn. Mar 18, 1798; bpt. Apr 9, 1798; son of
    Nace, slave of Charles Ghequiere & Catharine, slave of Rev.
    Charles Nagot
GIBBONS, William; bn. Apr 20, 1795; bpt. Apr 23, 1795; son of
    James & Hannah
GIBS, John; bpt. Mar 6, 1788; 5 years old; sps. Ann Matthews
GID, Lewis; bpt. Sep 22, 1792; 6 weeks; son of Peter & Polly
    Froget
GILES, William; bpt. Aug 14, 1791; 20 years old; conditional
GILL, Mary; bpt. Mar 18, 1787; 6 weeks; sps. Jeremiah Conner &
    Mary Kelly
GILL, Mary; bn. Mar 7, 1788; bpt. Apr 18, 1788; sps. Polly Pylan
GILLASPY, John; bn. Mar 7, 1796; bpt. Mar 13, 1796; son of
    Patrick & Alice
GILLMEYER, George; bn. Oct 3, 1797; bpt. Oct 8, 1797; son of
    Francis & Catharine
GILLMEYER, Sarah; bn. Jul 29, 1795; bpt. Aug 7, 1795; dau. of
    Francis & Catharine
GILMAN, Charlotte; bpt. May 14, 1800; 1 year old; dau. of John &
    Frances
GINEVAN, Elizabeth; bn. Mar 20, 1786; bpt. May 11, 1786; sps.
    Patrick Lynch & Katy Kelly
GINNAVEN, Hanna; bn. Jul 21, 1792; bpt. Sep 2, 1792; dau. of
    Patrick & Elizabeth
GINNAVEN, Michael; bn. Jul 26, 1788; bpt. Oct 5, 1788; sps.
    Edward Lynch & Mary Lynch
GINNEVAN, Charlotte; bn. Nov 7, 1791; bpt. Apr 1, 1792; dau. of
    Patrick & Elizabeth
(GIRARD), Elizabeth; bpt. May 13, 1796; 3 weeks; dau. of Lemire,
    slave of Miss Victoire Girard
GLADIS, Peter; bn. Nov 26, 1795; bpt. Dec 4, 1796; son of Peter &
    Mary
GLAVANNY, Elizabeth Bien Amiee; bn. Feb 17, 1800; bpt. Apr 16,
    1800; dau. of Francis & Elizabeth
GLAVANY, Elizabeth Frances; bn. Dec 21, 1794; bpt. Jan 1, 1795;
    dau. of Francis Remy & Elizabeth Dashields
GLAVANY, Mary Magdalene Aglae; bn. Apr 22, 1797; bpt. May 10,
    1797; dau. of Francis Remy & Elizabeth Deschamps
GLEESON, John; bpt. Sep 19, 1790; 7 weeks; son of Morris & Mary
GLEESON, William; bn. Mar 13, 1798; bpt. Apr 1, 1798; son of
    Patrick & Catharine
GLIN, Elizabeth; bpt. Jun 21, 1789; 8 days; dau. of Thomas &
    Catharine
GLIN, Mary; bn. Feb 16, 1788; bpt. Mar 10, 1788; sps. George &
    Elizabeth Macky
GLISSAN, Thomas; bn. Aug 10, 1796; bpt. Oct 9, 1796; son of
    Thomas & Catharine

BAPTISMS

GLOTTIS, Catharine; bn. Dec 9, 1798; bpt. Dec 16, 1798; dau. of Peter & Mary
GLYNN, James; bn. Sep 2, 1791; bpt. Sep 18, 1791; son of Thomas & Catharine
GOCHY, John; bn. Feb 12, 1798; bpt. Mar 9, 1798; son of Charles & Mary
GOCHY, Joseph; bn. Nov 7, 1795; bpt. Nov 15, 1795; son of Charles & Mary
GODART, John Baptist; bn. Sep 20, 1788; bpt. Dec 25, 1788; sps. Andre Simon & Anastasia Belisle
GOLD, Joseph; bn. Dec 6, 1783; bpt. Dec 27, 1783; sps. Francis Carrera & Mary White
GOLD, Juliana; bn. Jul 14, 1798; bpt. Aug 6, 1798; dau. of Peter & Mary
GOLD, Lewis; bn. Dec 26, 1793; bpt. Feb 12, 1794; son of Paul & Sarah
GOLD, Paul; bn. May 16, 1791; bpt. May 18, 1791; son of Paul & Sally Frogett
GOLD, Paul Oliver; bn. Oct 2, 1792; bpt. Nov 1, 1792; son of Peter & Mary
GOLD, Sophia; bn. Dec 29, 1785; bpt. Aug 12, 1786; sps. Charles Bernard & Margaret Gold
GOLDING, Arabella; bn. Mar 20, 1795; bpt. Aug 5, 1799; dau. of Patric & Arabella
GOLDING, James; bn. Jun 25, 1799; bpt. Aug 5, 1799; son of Patric & Arabella
(GONEL), Mary Catharine; bpt. May 9, 1795; dau. of Angelique, slave of Mr. Gonel
GONET, Sebastian Francis Nicholas; bn. Dec 6, 1799; bpt. Dec 16, 1799; son of Marcellin & Louisa Catharine Pallon
(GONNEL), John; bn. Mar 24, 1796; bpt. Jun 13, 1796; son of Angele, Mulatto slave of Mrs. Gonnel, Cp Francais; declared free
(GONNEL), John Felix; bn. Aug 3, 1795; bpt. Jun 13, 1796; son of Victoire, slave of Mrs. Gonnel, Cp Francais; declared free
GONZAGA, Jane Francis Emilie Louis; bn. May 20, 1795; bpt. Jun 3, 1795; dau. of Elizabeth Gonzaga
GOODWIN, William; bn. May 15, 1800; bpt. Jun 29, 1800; son of James & Lydia
GORE, Frances; bn. Jun 20, 1793; bpt. Jul 7, 1793; dau. of James & Frances
(GORE), Juliana; bn. Jun 7, 1798; bpt. Jul 1, 1798; Mulatto; dau. of Nancy, slave of Richard Gore
GORMAN, Agnes; bpt. Feb 16, 1800; 3 weeks; dau. of Michael & Bridget
GORMAN, Hesther; bn. Jun 18, 1796; bpt. Jul 31, 1796; dau. of Cornelius & Margaret
GORMANLY, Mary Anne; bn. Mar 28, 1798; bpt. Apr 28, 1799; dau. of James (deceased) & Jemima
GORMLY, Elizabeth; bn. Jun 27, 1789; bpt. Jul 12, 1789; dau. of James & Jemima
GORMLY, George; bn. Apr 14, 1795; bpt. Jun 8, 1795; son of James & Jeanimah
GORMLY, Sarah; bn. Aug 6, 1797; bpt. Sep 26, 1797; dau. of Constantine & Mary

BAPTISMS

GORMLY, Wiliam; bn. Sep 17, 1799; bpt. Nov 3, 1799; son of Owen & Catharine
GOTHIER, Peter; bn. Jul 22, 1788; bpt. Aug 4, 1788; sps. James Toole & Bridget Kennedy
(GOUGH), John Peter; bpt. Jun 10, 1800; 6 weeks; son of George, slave of Mr. Gough & Milly
(GOUGH), Philip; bpt. Nov 2, 1796; 2 months; son of Philip Murray, slave of Mr. Gough & Sarah, slave of Mrs. Young
GOUIRAN, Ann Eleanor; bn. Feb 15, 1796; bpt. Jun 19, 1796; dau. of Isidore & Margaret Peter Chaillan
GOUIRAN, John Francis Joseph; bn. Sep 9, 1793; bpt. Dec 19, 1793; son of Isidore & Margaret Pierrette Chaillan
(GOUIRAN), Louise Pierrette; bn. Mar 9, 1798; bpt. May 6, 1798; dau. of Jenny, slave of Isidore Gouiran
GOUIRAN, Mary Henrietta; bn. Oct 25, 1797; bpt. May 6, 1798; dau. of Isidore & Margaret Pierrette Challan
GOUIRAN, Virginie Sophie Fanny; bn. Sep 23, 1794; bpt. May 31, 1795; dau. of Isidore & Margaret Pierrette Chaillon
GOULDING, Mary; bpt. Sep 18, 1792; 3 weeks; dau. of Thomas & Eleanor Flin
GOULDING, Mary Martha; bn. Sep 4, 1789; bpt. Sep 6, 1789; dau. of John & Martha
GOUVERNET, John Charles William; bn. Oct 9, 1800; bpt. Nov 14, 1800; son of Charles Constant & Margare
GOZELEN, Emilia; bn. Feb 25, 1797; bpt. Nov 21, 1797; dau. of John & Susanna
GRAINGER, George; bn. Jan 9, 1788; bpt. Feb 12, 1788; son of Joseph & Rose; sps. Bishop Carroll & Mary Ann Chambely
GRAINGER, Joseph; bn. Nov 8, 1785; bpt. Nov 13, 1785; sps. Ann Gutterau
GRAINGER, Margaret; bn. Jul ?, 1783; bpt. Jul 22, 1783; sps. Andrew Gibon & Margaret Latar
GRANT, John; bn. Oct 22, 1794; bpt. Nov 22, 1794; son of John & Elizabeth
(GRASSET), Catharine; bpt. May 2, 1794; 2 1/2 years old, Mulatress; dau. of Mary Michael, slave of Mr. Grasset
GRATE, George; bn. Jul 1, 1796; bpt. Jul 3, 1796; son of Jacob & Catharine
GREEN, Andrew; bn. May 23, 1795; bpt. Aug 9, 1795; son of James & Ann
GREEN, Bernard; bn. May 24, 1793; bpt. Mar 30, 1794; son of James & Anne
(GREEN), Catharine; bpt. Jun 9, 1799; 1 month; dau. of Lucy, slave of Ann Green
GREEN, James; bn. Nov 11, 1798; bpt. Jan 12, 1799; son of Bennet & Ann
(GREEN), James; bn. Jul 19, 1799; bpt. Jun 8, 1800; son of George & Rebecca, slave of Isaac Green
GREEN, Margaret; bn. Apr 9, 1791; bpt. May 1, 1791; dau. of Barry & Mary
GREEN, Oliver; bn. Jul 27, 1800; bpt. Jul 31, 1800; son of Bennet & Ann
GREGORY, Elizabeth; bn. Apr 4, 1800; bpt. Apr 27, 1800; dau. of William & Ann

BAPTISMS

GREGORY, Harriot; bn. Jul 11, 1797; bpt. Jul 16, 1797; dau. of
    William & Ann
GREGORY, Joseph; bn. Jul 11, 1797; bpt. Jul 16, 1797; son of
    William & Ann
GREHAM, Francis James; bn. Jun 26, 1790; bpt. Jul 24, 1790; son
    of James & Elizabeth
GRELLAND, Mary Frances; bn. Jan 21, 1796; bpt. Apr 28, 1797; born
    in parish of Petit Goave, St. Domingo; dau. of Henry &
    Antoinette Dollu
GRIFFIN, Catharine; bpt. Sep 4, 1797; 3 weeks; dau. of Mary
GRIFFIN, Joseph; bn. Dec 31, 1796; bpt. Jan 10, 1797; son of
    Abraham & Mary
GRIFFIN, Mary; bn. Dec 31, 1796; bpt. Jan 17, 1797; dau. of
    Abraham & Mary
GRIFFIN, Matthew; bn. Jan 30, 1800; bpt. Mar 9, 1800; son of
    Abraham & Mary
GRIFFIN, Thomas; bn. Aug 19, 1798; bpt. Sep 16, 1798; son of
    Abraham & Mary
GRIFFIN, William; bn. Sep 22, 1795; bpt. Nov 8, 1795; son of
    Abraham & Mary
GRIFFINS, Margaret; bn. May 15, 1794; bpt. Jun 9, 1794; dau. of
    Abraham & Mary
GROS, James; bn. Jul 10, 1793; bpt. Dec 19, 1793; son of Gabriel
    & Margaret Renandy
GROSS, Catharine; bn. Feb 12, 1795; bpt. Feb 15, 1795; dau. of
    Felix & Barbara
GROSS, Elizabeth; bn. Dec 26, 1792; bpt. Oct 23, 1796; dau. of
    Joshua & Hannah
GROSS, James; bn. Jul 4, 1792; bpt. Jul 10, 1792; son of James &
    Catharine
GROSS, John Ignatius; bn. Oct 21, 1796; bpt. Oct 23, 1796; son of
    Lewis & Catharine
GROSS, Mary Magdalen; bn. Aug 12, 1785; bpt. Aug 14, 1785; sps.
    Francis Anthony Miller & Mary Magdalen Weintzweiler
GROSS, Odilia; bn. Jan 24, 1790; bpt. Feb 2, 1790; dau. of Jacob
    & Catharine
GUERDIN, Mary Rose; bpt. Jun 18, 1795; 1 year old; dau. of Peter
    & Victoire Baupuy
GUMS, Lewis; bpt. Aug 3, 1783; 5 years old; sps. Anthony Gums
GUNNING, James; bn. Jan 28, 1793; bpt. Mar 17, 1793; son of James
    & Cecilia
(GUSTON), Mary Ursula; bpt. May 14, 1793; about 5 years old; nat.
    of French West India; slave of Madame Guston
GUTTERAN, Peter; bn. Jan 25, 1785; bpt. Mar 27, 1785; sps. Joseph
    Bertholin & Elizabeth Deagle
(GUTTERAN), Thomas; bpt. Jul 10, 1786; 5 months; slave of Mrs
    Gutteran; sps. Priscilla Harrison
(GUTTERAU), Eve; bpt. Jul 20, 1789; 3 weeks; slave of Joseph
    Gutterau; dau. of Hanna
GUTTERAU, George William; bpt. Dec 27, 1785; 3 months; sps.
    William LaCage & Martha Neisson
(GUTTERAU), Robert; bpt. Feb 27, 1791; 5 weeks, 2 days
GUTTRY, James; bn. Mar 23, 1784; bpt. Aug 15, 1784; sps. Henry
    Philips & Mary Philips

BAPTISMS

GUYNEMER, Martha Augustine; bn. Jul 31, 1795; bpt. Jul 31, 1795; dau. of John Augustine & Mary Jaulais

GWINN, Robert; bpt. Apr 23, 1797; 3 months; son of John & Eleanor

HABFEN, Andrew; bn. Feb 17, 1791; bpt. Aug 18, 1794; son of Andrew & Martha

HABFEN, Gerald; bn. Jan 18, 1794; bpt. Aug 18, 1794; son of Andrew & Martha

HABFEN, Mary; bn. Jun 15, 1785; bpt. Aug 18, 1794; dau. of Andrew & Martha

HABFEN, William; bn. Feb 14, 1788; bpt. Aug 18, 1794; son of Andrew & Martha

HABLESTIN, John Bartholomew; bn. Mar 3, 1797; bpt. Mar 20, 1797; son of Bartholomew & Louisa Amelia

HABLISTIN, Nazarius Celsus; bn. Jan 5, 1795; bpt. Mar 22, 1795; son of Bartholomy & Henrietta

(HACKET), Alexander; bn. Feb 2, 1796; bpt. Feb 28, 1796; son of Thomas & Rebecca, slave of Mr. John Hacket

(HACKET), Maria; bpt. Feb 28, 1796; 4 months; dau. of Ann, slave of Mr. John Hacket

(HACKET), William; bn. May 29, 1799; bpt. Jul 14, 1799; son of Thomas & Rebecca, slave of Mr. Hacket

HAGAN, James; bn. Jul 10, 1796; bpt. Jul 12, 1796; son of James & Catharine

HAGAN, James; bn. Jan 3, 1797; bpt. Jan 10, 1797; son of Matthew & Eleanor

HAGERTY, Luke; bn. Nov 26, 1796; bpt. Jun 22, 1798; son of Michael & Eleanor

HAGERTY, Matthew; bn. May 18, 1799; bpt. Aug 21, 1799; son of Matthew & Hannah

HAGERTY, Michael; bn. Oct 16, 1799; bpt. Oct 28, 1799; son of Michael & Eleanor

HAGHERTY, Catharine; bn. Feb 13, 1787; bpt. Apr 8, 1787; sps. Mark Morres & wife

HAGTHORP, Thomas; bn. May 28, 1793; bpt. Jun 23, 1793; son of Edward & Eleanor

HAGTHROP, Eleanor; bn. Nov ?, 1788; bpt. Nov 25, 1788; sps. Timothy Herrin & Ann Herrin

HAGTHROP, Mary Ann; bn. Sep 11, 1797; bpt. Sep 24, 1797; dau. of Edward & Eleanor

HAILEY, Thomas; bn. Jan 13, 1795; bpt. Jun 7, 1795; son of Peter & Betsey

HAILY, Edward; bn. Nov 5, 1791; bpt. May 20, 1792; son of Peter & Margaret

HALFPENNY, John; bn. Mar 1, 1783; bpt. Jan 5, 1786; sps. Ann Wood

HALFPENNY, Patrick; bpt. Apr 19, 1791; 4 years old next May; son of Patrick & Catharine

HALIT/WATTS, John Baptist; bn. Feb 1, 1794; bpt. Jun 9, 1794; son of Laurence Halit & Susanna Watts, Mulatto slave

HALL, John; bn. Apr 10, 1799; bpt. Apr 11, 1799; son of John & Susanna

HALL, Mary; bpt. Nov 2, 1800; 1 month; dau. of Carlos & Ann

HALL, Winefride; bn. Feb 18, 1790; bpt. Aug 2, 1790; dau. of William & Ann

HAMELTON, Sophia; bn. May ?, 1791; bpt. Jul 1, 1792; dau. of James & Eliza

BAPTISMS

HAMILTON, Ann; bn. Sep 8, 1793; bpt. Aug 16, 1794; dau. of Latitia Hamilton
HAMILTON, Eleanor Ann; bn. Apr 28, 1800; bpt. Apr 29, 1800; dau. of Pliny & Abigail
HAMILTON, Sarah; bpt. Aug 24, 1794; dau. of David Hamilton, slave of Mr. Calahan of Annapolis & Nelly, slave of Charles Carroll of Carrollton
HAMMER, Margaret; bn. Jan 26, 1783; bpt. Feb 9, 1783; sps. Anthony Hook & Mary Hook
HAMMOND, Benjamin; bn. Mar 1, 1778; bpt. Apr 27, 1788; sps. Sebastian Nurser & Susanna Burg
(HAMMOND), James; bn. Mar 22, 1798; bpt. Apr 15, 1798; son of Charles, slave of Mr. Hammond & Rachel, slave of Edward Neale
HAMMOND, Julia Ann; bpt. Nov 28, 1792; 3 months; dau. of Henry & Mary
HAMMOND, Susanna; bn. Jul ?, 1786; bpt. Jun 10, 1791; dau. of Isaac & Susanna
HANCK, Thomas; bn. Jan 19, 1787; bpt. Mar 12, 1787; sps. Antony Steel & Barbara Michel
HANDLIN, Violette; bn. Oct 26, 1786; bpt. Apr 8, 1787; sps. John Kelly & Jane Williby
HANNA, Margaret; bn. Feb 21, 1795; bpt. Jul 28, 1795; dau. of Edward & Teresa
HANNAH, John Elisha; bn. May 30, 1791; bpt. Jan 11, 1793; son of Edward & Teresia
HANNAN, Eliza; bn. Oct 18, 1796; bpt. Nov 8, 1796; dau. of James & Eliza
(HANNAN), Elizabeth; bpt. Apr 29, 1798; 10 months; dau. of Dido, slave of John Hannan
HANNAN, John; bpt. Mar 3, 1793; 3 months; son of John & Catharine McKennerly
(HANNAN), John; bpt. Apr 29, 1798; 4 years old; Mulatto slave of John Hannan
HANNAN, John Hodgkin; bn. Nov 30, 1795; bpt. Apr 21, 1796; son of John & Margaret
HANNAN, Mary; bpt. Jan 19, 1800; 2 weeks; dau. of Michael & Jane
HANNAN, Thomas; bn. Oct 26, 1800; bpt. Nov 22, 1800; son of John & Margaret
HARDEN, John Baptist; bn. Feb 16, 1788; bpt. Aug 10, 1788; sps. Robert Harden & Sara Harden
HARDEN, Teresia; bn. Nov 20, 1788; bpt. Apr 19, 1789; sps. Robert Harden & Rachael Robinson
HARDING, Joseph; bn. Feb 25, 1794; bpt. May 4, 1794; son of Matthew & Mary
HARDING, Nicholas; bn. Mar 5, 1794; bpt. May 4, 1794; son of Joseph & Dalila
HARDY, Amintha; bn. Aug 13, 1795; bpt. Aug 29, 1795; dau. of James & Mary; triplet
HARDY, Ruth; bn. Aug 13, 1795; bpt. Aug 29, 1795; dau. of James & Mary; triplet
HARDY, Sarah; bn. Aug 13, 1795; bpt. Aug 29, 1795; dau. of James & Mary; triplet
HARE, Samuel; bpt. Jan 11, 1797; 4 months; son of Patience Hare

BAPTISMS

HARIENS, Ann; bpt. Jan 6, 1792; 2 weeks; dau. of Joseph & Margaret

HARKEN, William; bn. Apr 6, 1798; bpt. May 28, 1798; son of Daniel & Bridget

HARKIN, Daniel; bn. Jul 17, 1787; bpt. Jul 17, 1787; sps. Patrick Keith

HARKIN, Elizabeth; bn. Jul 3, 1790; bpt. Jul 3, 1790; dau. of John & Elizabeth

HARKIN, Fanny; bn. Jul 17, 1787; bpt. Jul 17, 1787; sps. Patrick Keith

HARKINS, Edward; bn. Nov 6, 1800; bpt. Dec 21, 1800; son of Daniel & Bridget

HARKINS, Elizabeth; bn. Aug 25, 1788; bpt. Jul 17, 1789; dau. of John & Elizabeth

HARMAN, Mary Ann; bn. Sep 14, 1799; bpt. Oct 21, 1800; dau. of Philip & Elizabeth

HARP, Elizabeth; bn. Apr 14, 1789; bpt. Oct 11, 1789; dau. of Joshue & Eleanor

HARPER, Elizabeth; bpt. Sep 9, 1798; 10 months; dau. of Laurence & Mary

HARPER, Mary; bn. Oct 25, 1795; bpt. Sep 15, 1798; dau. of Laurence & Mary

HARPS, Elizabeth; bn. Aug 31, 1799; bpt. Oct 7, 1799; dau. of Laurence (deceased) & Mary

HARRIEN, Joseph; bn. Dec 11, 1795; bpt. Dec 16, 1795; son of Joseph & Margaret

HARRIEN, Joseph Lewis; bn. Jul 3, 1800; bpt. Aug 17, 1800; son of Joseph & Margaret

HARRIGAN, John; bn. Apr 29, 1798; bpt. Aug 5, 1798; son of Patrick & Sarah

HARRIS, Ann; bn. Oct 5, 1784; bpt. Dec 5, 1784; sps. Dominick Laurence & Sarah Connelly

HARRISON, Charles; bn. Jan 22, 1783; bpt. Oct 24, 1799; son of William & Elizabeth

HARRISON, Eleanor; bn. Jul 12, 1797; bpt. Jul 30, 1797; dau. of Joseph & Helen

HARRISON, Elizabeth; bpt. Jul 23, 1800; 2 years old; dau. of William & Elizabeth

HARRISON, Frances; bpt. Jul 23, 1800; 4 years old; dau. of William & Elizabeth

HARRISON, Francis; bpt. Jul 23, 1800; 14 years old; son of William & Elizabeth

HARRISON, Jesse; bn. Mar 17, 1794; bpt. Apr 13, 1794; son of Joseph & Eleanor

HARRISON, Joshue; bn. May 19, 1788; bpt. Jun 15, 1788; sps. Anthony Miller & Magdalen Foldweiler

HARRISON, Richard; bpt. Jul 23, 1800; 7 years old; son of William & Elizabeth

HARRISON, Samuel; bpt. Jul 23, 1800; 12 years old; son of William & Elizabeth

HARRISON, Sara Ann; bn. May 1, 1791; bpt. May 29, 1791; dau. of Joseph & Eleanor

HARTNETT, William; bn. Dec 8, 1798; bpt. Dec 10, 1798; son of John & Mary

BAPTISMS

HASHAM, Josiah; bn. Dec 6, 1794; bpt. Dec 11, 1794; son of Josiah
    & Lucy
HASHAM, Susanna; bn. Nov 29, 1796; bpt. Dec 12, 1796; dau. of
    Josias & Lucy
HATCH, Mary; bn. Feb 13, 1798; bpt. Mar 18, 1798; dau. of John &
    Margaret
HATTERING, Ann; bn. Sep 28, 1798; bpt. Oct 4, 1798; dau. of
    Thomas & Margaret
HATTIER, Mary Magdalene; bn. Mar 25, 1794; bpt. Aug 21, 1794;
    dau. of Henry of Goigny in Burgundy & Magdalene Perrone
HAUPT, Elizabeth; bn. Feb 16, 1799; bpt. Apr 14, 1799; dau. of
    Mathias & Elizabeth
HAUVET, John; bn. Jan 20, 1798; bpt. Feb 4, 1798; son of Lewis &
    Ann
HEALLY, Henry; bn. Nov 3, 1793; bpt. Nov 24, 1793; son of Dennis
    & Mary
HEALY, Dennis; bn. Jan 29, 1796; bpt. Feb 6, 1796; son of Dennis
    & Mary
HEALY, Dennis; bn. Mar 5, 1800; bpt. Mar 23, 1800; son of Dennis
    & Mary
HEALY, Mary Ann; bn. Jun 24, 1787; bpt. May 6, 1790; dau. of Isac
    & Ann
HEALY, Peter; bn. Jan 11, 1794; bpt. Jan 19, 1794; son of Thomas
    & Charlotte
HEGTHROP, Catharine; bn. Sep 13, 1786; bpt. Mar 26, 1787; sps.
    Patrick Bennett & Catharine Peters
HEGTHROP, Edward; bn. Nov 2, 1790; bpt. Dec 13, 1790; son of John
    & Margaret
HEGTHROP, Eleanor; bn. Feb 19, 1791; bpt. Mar 4, 1791; dau. of
    Edward & Eleanor
HEGTHROP, George; bn. Dec 30, 1787; bpt. Jan 20, 1788; sps.
    Edward Hegthrop & Eleanor Hegthrop
HEGTHROP, John; bn. Apr 8, 1789; bpt. Jun 1, 1789; son of Edward
    & Eleanor
HEGTHROP, William; bpt. Jan 17, 1787; a few weeks old; sps.
    Hegthrop & wife
HEIDRICH, George; bpt. Oct 6, 1790; 4 weeks old; son of John &
    Jenny
HEIMEL, Mary; bn. Oct 9, 1798; bpt. Oct 10, 1798; dau. of Jacob &
    Catharine
HEIMLER, Catharine Elizabeth; bn. May 1, 1793; bpt. May 2, 1793;
    dau. of --- & Ann Mary
HEIRICH, John; bn. Sep 21, 1790; bpt. Oct 3, 1790; son of John &
    Margaret
HELIKAR, Elizabeth; bn. Dec 17, 1788; bpt. Jul 24, 1791; dau. of
    William & Abigail
HELIKAR, Mary; bn. Aug 17, 1790; bpt. Jul 24, 1791; dau. of
    William & Abigail
HELMELIN, Elizabeth; bn. Jul 6, 1800; bpt. Oct 28, 1800; dau. of
    Joseph & Apollonia
HELMELING, ; bn. Mar 4, 1798; bpt. Apr 13, 1799; dau. of
    Apollonia Helmeling
HELMLING, Jacob; bpt. Jul 21, 1799; 18 months; son of Anthony &
    Mary

BAPTISMS

HELMLING, John; bpt. Jul 21, 1799; 2 yrs, 9 months old; son of Anthony & Mary
HEMELIN, Magdalen; bn. Nov 14, 1795; bpt. Nov 15, 1795; dau. of Joseph & Abigail
HENCKER, Juliana; bn. Aug 3, 1792; bpt. Sep 15, 1793; dau. of John & Elizabeth
HENDRICH, Paul; bn. May 29, 1785; bpt. Jun 4, 1785; sps. Sara Boyde
HENINGER, Mary; bpt. Jul 1, 1787; 6 weeks; sps. Mary Bentheim
HENNEGER, Catharine; bn. Jun 13, 1791; bpt. Jul 24, 1791; dau. of John & Elizabeth
HENNEGHER, Catharine; bn. Sep 26, 1789; bpt. Sep 27, 1789; dau. of John & Elizabeth
HENNEGHER, David; bn. Sep 26, 1789; bpt. Sep 27, 1789; son of John & Elizabeth
HENNING, Elizabeth; bpt. Feb 10, 1786; 10 weeks; sps. Elizabeth Steiger
HENNINGER, David; bn. Sep 15, 1795; bpt. Oct 18, 1795; son of John & Elizabeth
HENRICKS, Mary; bn. Jan 19, 1791; bpt. Jan 30, 1791; dau. of Absalom & Eleanor
(HENRY), Charlotte; bn. Mar 18, 1790; bpt. Mar 28, 1790; slave of D. Henry
HENRY, Elizabeth; bn. Jan 11, 1792; bpt. Apr 2, 1792; dau. of Hugh & Rosanna
HENRY, Henry; bn. Sep 20, 1789; bpt. Sep 30, 1789; son of Hugh & Rosanna
HENRY, Honor; bpt. Sep 19, 1784; since dead
HENRY, Hugh; bn. Jun 27, 1795; bpt. Jul 11, 1795; son of Hugh (deceased) & Rosanna
HENRY, Jenny; bn. Feb 6, 1784; bpt. Aug 19, 1786; sps. Mary Ann Simson
HENRY, Margaret; bn. May 26, 1786; bpt. May 15, 1787; sps. Daniel Henry & wife
HENRY, Maria; bn. Mar 11, 1790; bpt. Mar 27, 1790; dau. of Daniel & Elizabeth
HENRY, Mary Magdalen; bn. Jan 19, 1798; bpt. Aug 8, 1798; dau. of Susanna Henry
HENRY, Mary Ann; bn. Jul 18, 1786; bpt. Aug 26, 1786; sps. Mary Ann Simson
HERMAN, Catharine; bn. Sep 15, 1789; bpt. Sep 20, 1789; dau. of Philip & Elizabeth
HERMANGE, John Baptist; bn. Aug 4, 1785; bpt. Aug 21, 1785; sps. Joseph Bertholin & Magdalen Landry
HERMANGE, Joseph; bn. Jul 26, 1787; bpt. Aug 5, 1787; son of John Antony & Peggy
HERMANGE, Peter; bn. Jan 18, 1792; bpt. Jul 3, 1793; son of Anthony & Margaret
HERMAZE, Lewis; bn. Feb 2, 1790; bpt. Feb 25, 1790; son of Antony & Peggy
HERRING, William; bn. Apr 6, 1799; bpt. Aug 1, 1799; son of William & Mary
HERTZOG, Rebecca; bn. Jun 4, 1799; bpt. Jun 23, 1799; dau. of George & Dorothea

BAPTISMS

HEUISLER, Alexander; bn. Dec 3, 1794; bpt. Jun 20, 1795; son of
    Maximilian & Mary
HEUISLER, Harriot; bn. Jul 22, 1796; bpt. Aug 23, 1796; dau. of
    Maximilian & Mary
HEUISLER, Joseph; bn. Jun 24, 1792; bpt. Aug 7, 1792; son of
    Maximilian & Mary
HEUISLER, Margaret; bn. Jan 18, 1800; bpt. Apr 7, 1800; dau. of
    Maximilian & Mary
HEUSLER, Mary Teresa; bn. Feb 20, 1798; bpt. Apr 9, 1798; dau. of
    Maximilian & Mary
HEYDAN, Mary; bn. Jul 26, 1800; bpt. Aug 13, 1800; dau. of James
    & Elizabeth
HICKLEY, John; bn. Aug 7, 1797; bpt. Aug 13, 1797; son of
    Sebastian & Catharine
HICKLEY, William; bn. May 3, 1799; bpt. May 19, 1799; son of
    Sebastian & Catharine
HICKY, Mary; bn. Jul 31, 1797; bpt. Aug 13, 1797; dau. of Timothy
    & Eleanor
HIERMAN, Elizabeth; bpt. Jan 28, 1787; 2 weeks old; sps. Andrea
    Hierman & Sylvester Sacrenov
HIGGINBOTHAM, Ann; bn. May 20, 1793; bpt. Jul 1, 1793; dau. of
    Arthur & Eleanor
HIGIUS, Peter; bpt. Aug 1, 1790
HILBEET, John; bpt. Nov 21, 1787; 20 months; sps. John Jore & Ann
    Marshan
HILL, Catharine; bpt. Oct 7, 1796; 5 3/4 years old; dau. of
    Samuel & Mary
HILL, James; bn. Mar 20, 1799; bpt. Dec 26, 1800; son of Richard
    & Ann
HILL, Jane; bn. Dec 21, 1789; bpt. Oct 20, 1796; dau. of Samuel
    (deceased) & Mary
HILL, Joanna; bn. Dec 21, 1789; bpt. Oct 20, 1796; dau. of Samuel
    (deceased) & Mary
HILL, John; bn. Nov 9, 1790; bpt. Nov 18, 1790; son of Jonathan &
    Elizabeth
(HILLEN), Abraham; bn. Jun 3, 1799; bpt. Aug 10, 1799; son of
    Minty, slave of Solomon Hillen
HILLEN, Ann; bn. Oct 26, 1793; bpt. Dec 1, 1793; dau. of John &
    Catharine
HILLEN, Elizabeth; bpt. Dec 2, 1787; 2 weeks; sps. Thomas Hillen
    & ---
HILLEN, Jennet; bn. May 29, 1796; bpt. Jul 10, 1796; dau. of
    Thomas & Robinie Kennedy
HILLEN, John; bn. Feb 12, 1795; bpt. Mar 15, 1795; son of John &
    Catharine
HILLEN, Martha; bn. Nov 11, 1789; bpt. Jan 24, 1790; dau. of John
    & Catharine
HILLEN, Sara; bn. Sep 1, 1785; bpt. Sep 17, 1785; sps. William
    Litzinger & Catharine Leary
HILLEN, Thomas; bpt. Aug 7, 1792; 1 week; son of John & Catharine
HILLEN, Thomas; bn. Jul 6, 1798; bpt. Aug 12, 1798; son of Thomas
    & Robinie
HILLENGER, Michael; bn. Sep 10, 1799; bpt. Sep 30, 1799; son of
    Jacob & Christina

BAPTISMS

HILLIS, John; bn. Feb 28, 1799; bpt. Jun 5, 1799; son of Emanuel & Margaret
HILLVERT, John Antony; bpt. Jan 18, 1795; 1 year old; son of John & Barbara
HILLVERT, Mary; bpt. Jan 18, 1795; 4 years old; dau. of John & Barbara
HIMMEL, Bernard; bn. Dec 28, 1800; bpt. Dec 29, 1800; son of Jacob & Catharine
HINES, Denis; bpt. Oct 19, 1788; 1 month; sps. Bridget Murphy
HINES, John; bn. Sep 4, 1784; bpt. Sep 27, 1784; sps. Sara Boyle
HINES, Mary; bn. Oct 10, 1783; bpt. Jan 18, 1784; sps. John Ehrman & Clare Dulian
(HINKS), Elizabeth; bpt. Apr 8, 1798; 3 weeks; dau. of Sarah, slave of Mr. Hinks
(HODGSON), Hannah; bn. Sep 14, 1795; bpt. Sep 22, 1795; dau. of Ralph & Jenny, slave of Robert Hodgson
(HOFFMAN), Lucy; bpt. Nov 16, 1799; 4 months; dau. of Isaac, slave of Esq. Hoffman & Hairs, slave of Luky King
HOGAN, Edmond; bn. Oct 7, 1784; bpt. Nov 14, 1784; sps. John Canon & Mary Worthington
HOGAN, James; bn. Sep 3, 1790; bpt. Oct 3, 1790; son of Edmund & Giles
(HOGAN), Jesse; bpt. Apr 15, 1787; 3 years old; slave of Edmund Hogan; sps. Peter Liner
HOGAN, John; bn. Jan 22, 1787; bpt. Mar 11, 1787; sps. William Collins & Elizabeth Shreagly
HOGAN, Michael; bpt. Jul 8, 1791; 10 months; son of Michael & Mary Herring
HOGAN, Thomas; bn. Nov 3, 1795; bpt. Nov 9, 1795; son of Patric & Mary
(HOGAN), Willy; bpt. Apr 15, 1787; 6 months; slave of Edmund Hogan; sps. Peter Liner
HOGGINS, Ann; bpt. Oct 30, 1787; 5 weeks; sps. Sarah Boyde
HOGGINS, Eleanor; bn. Jan 3, 1797; bpt. Apr 20, 1797; dau. of Richard & Elizabeth
HOGGINS, Elizabeth; bn. Jan 16, 1790; bpt. Aug 10, 1790; dau. of Richard & Elizabeth
HOGGINS, Sarah; bn. May 4, 1799; bpt. Jul 5, 1799; dau. of Richard & Elizabeth
HOGGINS, William; bn. Aug 21, 1786; bpt. Aug 26, 1786; sps. Sara Boyd
HOGGINS, William; bn. Dec 23, 1792; bpt. Jan 27, 1793; son of Richard & Elizabeth
HOLLERAND, Frances; bn. Feb 24, 1793; bpt. Mar 5, 1793; dau. of Elizabeth Cunningham
(HOLLINGSWORTH), Diana; bn. Jan 14, 1800; bpt. Mar 16, 1800; dau. of Tobias, slave of Mr. Jesse Hollingsworth & Isabella, slave of Mr. Evans
(HOLLINGSWORTH), Maria; bn. Sep 30, 1798; bpt. Nov 18, 1798; dau. of Toby, slave of Jesse Hollingsworth & Isabel, slave of William Evans
HOLMES, Eliza; bn. Oct 4, 1795; bpt. Dec 20, 1795; dau. of John & Margaret
HOLMES, Elizabeth; bn. Jun 26, 1796; bpt. Jun 28, 1796; dau. of Anthony & Mary

BAPTISMS

HOLMES, Emmanuel; bn. May 21, 1791; bpt. May 24, 1791; son of
    James & Magdalen
HOLMES, James; bn. Aug 7, 1793; bpt. Sep 1, 1793; son of John &
    Margaret
HOLMES, Joseph; bn. Nov 20, 1793; bpt. Nov 22, 1793; son of James
    & Magdalen
HOLMES, Mary; bn. Nov 20, 1793; bpt. Nov 22, 1793; dau. of James
    & Magdalen
(HOLMES), Mary; bn. Dec 27, 1797; bpt. Jan 14, 1798; dau. of
    Simon & Nelly, slave of John Holmes
HOLMES, Mary Ann; bn. Jul 1, 1798; bpt. May 5, 1799; dau. of
    Anthony & Margaret
(HOLMES), Samuel; bpt. May 24, 1795; 5 weeks; son of Samuel &
    Eleanor, slave of John Holmes
HOLMES, Samuel; bn. Apr 3, 1796; bpt. Apr 17, 1796; son of James
    & Magdalen
HOLSHOUSER, Magdalen; bn. Nov 6, 1789; bpt. Nov 11, 1789; dau. of
    Joseph & Catharine Sweeney
HOOK, Anthony; bn. Jun 1, 1783; bpt. Jun 22, 1783; sps. Francis
    Tiegler & Fanny Tiegler
HOOK, Barbara; bn. Jan 15, 1795; bpt. Feb 8, 1795; dau. of
    Ferdinand & Magdalene
HOOK, Catharine; bn. Jan 30, 1789; bpt. Feb 8, 1789; sps. Michael
    Shilling & Catharine Shilling
HOOK, David; bn. Mar 1, 1791; bpt. Dec 6, 1795; son of Michael &
    Jane
HOOK, Eliza; bn. Dec 6, 1792; bpt. Dec 30, 1792; dau. of
    Ferdinand & Magdalen
HOOK, Elizabeth; bn. May 6, 1790; bpt. May 13, 1790; dau. of John
    & Barbara
HOOK, George; bn. Jun 25, 1799; bpt. Jul 7, 1799; son of
    Ferdinand & Magdalen
HOOK, Henry; bn. Nov 26, 1790; bpt. Dec 5, 1790; son of Ferdinand
    & Magdalen
HOOK, James; bn. Apr 24, 1800; bpt. Apr 28, 1800; son of John &
    Barbara
HOOK, John; bn. Oct 6, 1795; bpt. Nov 8, 1795; son of John &
    Barbara
HOOK, John Anthony; bn. Sep 14, 1793; bpt. Nov 17, 1793; son of
    John & Barbara
HOOK, Joseph; bn. Nov 21, 1792; bpt. Dec 2, 1792; son of Joseph &
    Sara
HOOK, Margaret; bn. Jul 5, 1799; bpt. Aug 6, 1799; dau. of
    William & Sarah
HOOK, Mary; bn. Apr 29, 1793; bpt. Dec 6, 1795; dau. of Michael &
    Jane
HOOK, Mary; bn. Feb 26, 1797; bpt. Apr 17, 1797; dau. of
    Ferdinand & Magdalen
HOOK, Michael; bn. Dec 5, 1788; bpt. Dec 14, 1788; sps. Francis
    Tiegler & Fanny Tiegler
HOOK, Sara; bn. Dec 30, 1788; bpt. Feb 15, 1789; sps. Elizabeth
    Steiger
HOOK, Stephen Bennet; bn. Dec 26, 1797; bpt. Jan 4, 1798; son of
    John & Barbara
(HOOK), Thomas; bpt. Dec 5, 1790; slave of A. Hook

BAPTISMS

HOOKE, Francis; bn. Oct 4, 1796; bpt. Mar 13, 1797; son of Michael & Jane
HOREGHAN, Mary; bpt. Sep 18, 1800; 7 weeks; dau. of Thomas & Ruth
HORN, Joseph; bn. Nov 2, 1796; bpt. Nov 13, 1796; son of Joseph & Catharine
HORNE, William; bn. Apr 20, 1799; bpt. Jan 5, 1800; son of Peter & Eve
HORSEFROSS, John; bn. Jan 30, 1792; bpt. Feb 2, 1792; son of George & Dolly
HOSKINS, William; bn. Jan 27, 1793; bpt. Jan 28, 1793; son of William & Mary Lenet
HOSSEFRATZ, Barbara; bn. Jan 5, 1791; bpt. Jan 6, 1791; dau. of George & Dorothy
HOSSEFRATZ, Catharine; bn. Aug 9, 1797; bpt. Aug 13, 1797; dau. of George & Dorothy
HOSSEFRATZ, George; bn. Aug 19, 1798; bpt. Aug 26, 1798; son of George & Ursula
HOSSEFRATZ, Margaret; bn. Jul 19, 1794; bpt. Jul 20, 1794; dau. of George & Dorothy
HOUCK, John; bn. Sep 19, 1797; bpt. Oct 1, 1797; son of William & Sarah
HOVER, George; bn. Dec 10, 1798; bpt. Jan 13, 1799; son of Ignatius & Rebecca
(HOWARD), Eleanor; bn. Feb 10, 1799; bpt. Mar 24, 1799; dau. of John & Sidney, slave of Col. Howard
(HOWARD), James; bpt. Jun 24, 1792; adult; slave of Col. Howard
HOWARD, Joseph; bn. Mar 2, 1800; bpt. Mar 30, 1800; son of Joseph Ferde & Mary
HOWARD, Susanna; bn. Nov 11, 1799; bpt. Feb 16, 1800; dau. of William & Mary
HOWONON, Lewis; bn. Oct 27, 1796; bpt. Oct 27, 1796; son of Robert & Eleanor
HUBER, Ignatius; bn. Dec 3, 1797; bpt. Dec 3, 1797; son of Ignatius & Rebecca
HUDLER, John; bn. Jul 2, 1793; bpt. Aug 13, 1793; son of John & Rebecca
HUDSON, Ann; bn. Mar 6, 1798; bpt. Apr 9, 1798; dau. of James & Joanna
(HUEL), Sarah; bpt. Aug 10, 1800; 5 months; dau. of Hannah, slave of John Huel
HUGHES, Eleanor; bn. Mar 23, 1783; bpt. Jul 23, 1783; sps. William Beyler & Margaret Hartman
HUGHES, Henry; bn. Jan 1, 1800; bpt. Feb 6, 1800; son of John & Elizabeth
HUGHES, Sarah; bn. Dec 23, 1785; bpt. Jun 26, 1791; dau. of John & Tabitha
HULALIE, Mary Ann; bn. Mar 6, 1796; bpt. May 7, 1797; Mulatto; dau. of Ann Hulalie
HULAN, Philip; bn. Mar 31, 1795; bpt. Apr 10, 1795; son of Philip & Eleanor
(HULLA), Josephine Mary Louisa; bpt. Feb 16, 1794; 2 years old; dau. of Mary Louisa, slave of Mary Jane Sophia Hulla
HULLA, Mary Frances Celestine; bn. Nov 4, 1794; bpt. Jul 10, 1795; dau. of Mary Jane Sophia Hulla

BAPTISMS

HUMPHRES, Ann; bn. Apr 13, 1786; bpt. Apr 30, 1786; sps. Charles Butler & Margaret LaTar
HUMPHRES, Sara; bn. Sep 20, 1787; bpt. Oct 7, 1787; sps. Peggy MacNamara
HUMPHREYS, ; bpt. Aug 8, 1790; 10 weeks; of James & Sara
HUMPHRIES, Elizabeth; bn. Mar 14, 1795; bpt. Jul 14, 1796; dau. of James & Sarah
HUMPHRY, David; bn. Dec 23, 1782; bpt. May 4, 1783; sps. John Logsdom & Mary Logsdom
HUSK, James; bn. Jun 16, 1790; bpt. Oct 24, 1790; son of Samuel & Eleanor
HUSS, Elizabeth; bn. Aug ?, 1785; bpt. May 13, 1787; sps. William Fitzgerald & Mary Bier
HUSS, William; bn. Mar ?, 1784; bpt. May 13, 1787; sps. Timothy Morarty & Eleanor Loney
HUTCHINGS, Nicholas; bpt. Jan 21, 1792; 8 weeks; son of William & Eleanor
HUTCHINSON, Julia Ann; bn. Dec 25, 1794; bpt. Dec 20, 1798; dau. of Thomas & Hester
HUTCHINSON, Mary Elizabeth; bn. Apr 18, 1797; bpt. Dec 20, 1798; dau. of Thomas & Hester
HUTCHINSON, Mary Ann; bn. Feb 17, 1793; bpt. Dec 20, 1798; dau. of Thomas & Hester
HYERMAN, Christina Joseph; bn. Nov 18, 1788; bpt. Nov 23, 1788; sps. John Sheuler & Christina Bergman
HYMMEL, Catharina; bn. Dec 9, 1800; bpt. Dec 11, 1800; dau. of Peter & Mary Ann
IRELAND, Appolina; bn. May 17, 1791; bpt. Feb 10, 1793; dau. of --- & Milly Ireland
IRELAND, Mary; bn. Nov 25, 1789; bpt. Dec 5, 1790; dau. of Appollonia
ISAACS, Ralph; bn. Jan 14, 1798; bpt. Nov 3, 1799; son of Rachel Isaacs
ISABEE, Eleanor; bn. Dec 5, 1800; bpt. Dec 21, 1800; dau. of Francis & Martha
ISABEE, Martha; bpt. Jul 13, 1798; adult, about 17 years
ISABEY, Juliet; bn. Apr 3, 1799; bpt. Apr 28, 1799; son of Francis & Martha
ISNARD, Peter John; bn. Jan 23, 1794; bpt. May 11, 1794; son of John Lewis & Mary Ann Euphrasia Merchand of Port au Prince, St. Domingo
(ISOARD), John; bpt. Jul 24, 1800; son of Saul & --, slave of Mrs. Isoard
ISOARD, Mary Matilda; bn. Jul 17, 1800; bpt. Jul 24, 1800; dau. of Frances Isoard
JACKSON, George St. Clair; bn. Feb 11, 1796; bpt. Mar 13, 1796; son of William & Margaret
JACOBS, Ann; bpt. Feb 19, 1799; 5 months; Mulatto, dau. of Phoebe Jacobs, free Mulatto
JAMES, Plaisant; bpt. Oct 8, 1797; 8 months; son of Betsey James, free Negro
JAMESON, James; bn. Oct 4, 1795; bpt. May 7, 1796; son of William & Eve
(JANNIN), Ann; bpt. May 12, 1794; dau. of Clare, slave of Ann Jannin

BAPTISMS

JEFFERSON, Catharine; bpt. Jan 15, 1796; dau. of William, free
    Negro & Charlotte
JEFFERSON, Charles; bpt. May 21, 1797; 4 1/2 months; Mulatto; son
    of James Jefferson, free Negro & Mary Ann, Mulatto, slave of
    Mr. Starck
JEFFERY, Catharine; bpt. Feb ?, 1786; 7 weeks; sps. Peter Plum
JENKINS, Ann; bn. Jan 2, 1789; bpt. Mar 5, 1789; sps. Stephen
    Knot & Ann Knot
JENKINS, Henry; bpt. Mar 27, 1784; 2 weeks; sps. Solomon Hillen &
    --- Jenkins
JENKINS, Marie; bn. Dec 23, 1798; bpt. Jun 2, 1799; dau. of John
    & Jane
JENKINS, Mary Ann; bn. Jun 14, 1799; bpt. Aug 4, 1799; dau. of
    William & Ann
JENKINS, William; bn. Oct 29, 1795; bpt. Dec 6, 1795; son of
    William & Ann
JERSON, Jeremiah James; bpt. May 4, 1800; 2 months; son of
    William & Mary
JOHNSON, Abraham; bn. Mar 29, 1793; bpt. Jul 29, 1797; son of
    Hannah Johnson
JOHNSON, George; bn. Apr 17, 1792; bpt. Jun 2, 1793; son of
    Joshua & Sarah
JOHNSON, James; bn. Jan 7, 1800; bpt. Apr 10, 1800; son of
    Elizabeth Johnson
(JOHNSON), Jeremiah; bn. Apr 8, 1799; bpt. Dec 26, 1800; son of
    Jeremiah, slave of Mr. Johnson & Elizabeth, slave of Mr.
    Walton
JOHNSON, John; bn. Nov 24, 1786; bpt. Jun 2, 1793; son of Joshua
    & Sarah
(JOHNSON), Lioba; bn. Nov 18, 1800; bpt. Dec 5, 1800; dau. of
    Fanny, slave of Jeremiah Johnson
JOHNSON, Luke; bpt. Jul 20, 1798; 1 year old; son of Daniel & Ann
JOHNSON, Lydia; bn. Oct 18, 1795; bpt. Oct 29, 1795; dau. of John
    Johnson, slave of Simon White & Margaret, slave of Mrs.
    Bijot
JOHNSON, Mary; bn. Jul 13, 1796; bpt. Jul 14, 1796; dau. of John
    & Ann
JOHNSON, Mary; bn. Oct 1, 1796; bpt. Dec 4, 1796; dau. of Joshua
    & Sarah
JOHNSON, Phoebe; bn. Jan 18, 1796; bpt. Jan 20, 1796; dau. of
    Thomas & Mary
JOHNSON, Sarah; bn. Nov 15, 1794; bpt. May 10, 1795; dau. of
    Joshua & Sarah
JOHNSON, Sarah; bpt. Jan 7, 1798; 17 days; dau. of Abraham &
    Ally, free Negroes
(JOHNSON), Susanna; bpt. Mar 16, 1800; 2 years old; dau. of
    Henny, slave of Mr. Johnson
JOHNSON, Thomas; bn. Oct 26, 1793; bpt. Oct 27, 1793; son of
    Thomas & Mary McAllister
JOHNSON, William; bn. May 12, 1799; bpt. Jun 13, 1799; son of
    William & Elizabeth
JOINER, Rebecca; bn. Jan 29, 1791; bpt. May 11, 1794; dau. of
    Joseph & Rebecca
JOLLITZ, Mary; bn. May 29, 1783; bpt. Jun 17, 1783; sps. John
    Baptist Crusan & Susanna Woods

BAPTISMS

JONES, Ann; bpt. Nov 11, 1798; adult
JONES, Ann; bn. Feb 2, 1800; bpt. Apr 13, 1800; dau. of William & Hellen
JONES, Charles; bn. Oct 23, 1794; bpt. Oct 30, 1794; son of William & Eleanor
JONES, Edward; bn. Aug 31, 1795; bpt. Oct 11, 1795; son of Awbreay & Sarah
JONES, Flora Mary; bn. Sep 27, 1794; bpt. Jul 12, 1795; dau. of Peter Delivet & Ann
JONES, John; bn. May 16, 1800; bpt. May 18, 1800; son of Aubreay & Sarah
JONES, Lewisa; bn. Nov 3, 1790; bpt. Dec 8, 1790; dau. of Abram & Sara
JONES, Margaret; bn. Jan 31, 1793; bpt. Mar 17, 1793; dau. of Richard & Catharine
JONES, Maria; bn. Oct 21, 1797; bpt. Dec 24, 1797; dau. of William & Eleanor
JONES, Mary; bn. Jun 16, 1793; bpt. Jul 28, 1793; dau. of Awbray & Sarah
JONES, Mary Ann; bn. Aug 31, 1796; bpt. Jul 11, 1797; dau. of William & Ann
JONES, Sarah; bn. Mar 15, 1798; bpt. Apr 9, 1798; dau. of Aubreay & Sarah
JONES, Susanna; bn. Sep 17, 1792; bpt. Apr 7, 1799; dau. of Susanna Jones
JORDAN, Brigit; bn. Sep 2, 1785; bpt. Sep 11, 1785; sps. Edward Kelly & Mary Vauchey
JORDAN, Catharine; bn. Sep 2, 1785; bpt. Sep 11, 1785; sps. William Lynch & Mary Jordan
JORDAN, Catharine; bpt. Jul 20, 1794; 2 years old; dau. of James & Honor
JORDAN, Eleanor; bn. Mar 12, 1783; bpt. Apr 20, 1783; sps. Hugh Lynch & Winifred Star
JORRE, Mary Catharine; bpt. Dec 15, 1799; 1 month; dau. of James & Frances
(JOSE), Ann Mary; bpt. Jul 11, 1796; 14 months; Mulatto; dau. of Petronilla, slave of Mr. Jose
JOSEPH, Francis Anthony; bn. Dec 12, 1784; bpt. Dec 12, 1784; sps. Fr. Anthony Carrera & Marie Cecilia Herman
JOSEPH, Peter Michael; bn. Dec 12, 1784; bpt. Dec 12, 1784; sps. Fr. Anthony Carrera & Marie Cecilia Herman
(JOULLAIN), Marie Olivette; bpt. Jun 2, 1799; 1 1/2 years old; dau. of Desiree, slave of Mrs. Joullain
(JOURDAIN), John Baptist; bpt. Mar 4, 1798; 6 weeks; son of Mary Joseph, slave of Mr. Jourdain
(JOURDAN), Noel; bpt. Feb 26, 1797; 2 months; son of Mary Joseph, slave of Madame Jourdan
JOYCE, John; bn. Jan 20, 1800; bpt. Mar 13, 1800; son of Polly Joyce
JOYCE, John; bn. Aug 11, 1800; bpt. Aug 14, 1800; son of Patrick & Catharine
JRVIN, John Francis Regis; bn. Nov 3, 1799; bpt. Nov 24, 1799; son of James & Mary
(JUDAH), Louise; bpt. Sep 19, 1796; 3 years old; dau. of Mary Joseph, slave of Mrs. Judah

BAPTISMS

(JULIET), Ann Martha; bn. Jan 10, 1796; bpt. Sep 10, 1796; dau. of Colinette, slave of Mrs. Juliet, widow
(JUNCA), Angelique; bpt. Oct 27, 1799; 3 weeks; dau. of Sanite, slave of Mr. Junca
KEAN, Rachel; bn. Dec 29, 1798; bpt. Feb 17, 1799; dau. of James Kean, free Mulatto & Sarah slave of Mr. Zachrie
KEARNS, Charles; bn. Feb 9, 1793; bpt. Mar 15, 1795; son of Charles & Hannah
KEARNS, Elizabeth; bn. May 23, 1797; bpt. May 28, 1797; dau. of Charles & Hannah
KEARNS, Henry; bn. Sep 24, 1793; bpt. Oct 20, 1793; son of Charles & Hannah
(KEENER), Sophia; bpt. Nov 29, 1797; 2 months; Mulatto; dau. of Ruth, slave of Mr. Keener
KEENS, Elizabeth; bn. Sep 14, 1799; bpt. Jun 7, 1800; dau. of Joseph & Ann
KEENS, John; bn. Aug 10, 1795; bpt. Sep 8, 1795; son of Joseph & Ann
KEENS, Joseph; bn. Feb 2, 1793; bpt. Mar 2, 1793; son of John & Elizabeth
KEENS, Mary; bn. Sep 24, 1793; bpt. Oct 15, 1793; dau. of Joseph & Ann Darrell
KEHOE, Elizabeth Harriette; bn. Feb 2, 1789; bpt. Mar 8, 1789; sps. Susanna Burgess
KEITH, Mary; bn. Sep 4, 1786; bpt. Jul 14, 1787; sps. John Harkin & Elizabeth Harkin
KEITH, Sara; bpt. Jul 14, 1787; adult
KELLENBERGER, Charlotte; bn. Dec 20, 1800; bpt. Dec 25, 1800; dau. of George & Elizabeth
KELLENBERGER, George; bn. Jun 26, 1797; bpt. Jul 2, 1797; son of George & Elizabeth
KELLENBERGER, John; bn. Jan 29, 1796; bpt. Feb 2, 1796; son of George & Elizabeth
KELLENBERGER, Mariana Henrietta; bn. Feb 5, 1799; bpt. Feb 10, 1799; dau. of George & Elizabeth
KELLER, Elizabeth; bn. Dec 10, 1783; bpt. Dec 26, 1783; sps. Henry Tomalty & Elizabeth Tomalty
KELLER, Francis Odilia; bn. Feb 3, 1787; bpt. Feb 11, 1787; sps. Francis Foldweiler & Odilia Haise
KELLER, John; bpt. Jul 27, 1784; 9 weeks; sps. John Keller & Hanna Keller
KELLER, Maria Teresia; bn. Jan 5, 1783; bpt. Jan 15, 1783; sps. John Keller & Hannah Keller
KELLY, Catharine; bn. Oct 6, 1786; bpt. May 13, 1792; dau. of Patrick & Jemima Gormly
KELLY, Catharine; bpt. Dec 15, 1799; 9 months; dau. of Patric & Leonora
KELLY, Daniel; bn. May 10, 1788; bpt. Jun 15, 1788; sps. Kitty Murphy
KELLY, Elizabeth; bpt. Feb 20, 1787; 2 weeks; sps. John Ryan & Amelia Peggers
KELLY, Elizabeth; bn. Jul 26, 1799; bpt. Aug 11, 1799; dau. of Thomas & Honor
KELLY, Elizabeth; bn. Oct 26, 1799; bpt. Nov 27, 1799; dau. of John & Ann

BAPTISMS

(KELLY), Harriot; bpt. Jul 8, 1798; 4 years old; dau. of Clare, slave of Mr. Kelly
KELLY, Helen; bn. Jan 5, 1794; bpt. Jul 19, 1795; dau. of John & Ann
KELLY, Henry; bn. Mar 15, 1799; bpt. Mar 21, 1799; son of Thomas & Caroline
KELLY, James; bn. Mar 1, 1799; bpt. Mar 8, 1799; son of James & Sarah
KELLY, John; bpt. Aug 13, 1789; 1 month; son of Thomas & Susanna
KELLY, John; bn. Nov 17, 1796; bpt. Nov 19, 1796; son of Patrick & Eleanor
KELLY, John; bn. Feb 27, 1797; bpt. Apr 30, 1797; son of John & Ann
KELLY, Margaret; bpt. Nov 11, 1787; 7 weeks; sps. Timothy Hannafin & Joanna Henry
KELLY, Mary; bn. Jul 2, 1791; bpt. Aug 14, 1791; dau. of John & Ann
KELLY, Rosanna; bn. Nov 16, 1799; bpt. Nov 21, 1799; dau. of Patrick & Jane
KELLY, William; bn. Dec 19, 1794; bpt. Jul 12, 1795; son of William & Mary
KELLY, William; bn. Feb 9, 1796; bpt. Feb 14, 1796; son of Andrew & Phoebe
KELSER, Jacob; bn. Nov 24, 1790; bpt. Dec 12, 1790; son of George & Ann
KELSER, Mary; bn. Jan 16, 1789; bpt. Jan 25, 1789; sps. Henry Deale & Mary Deale
KELSER, Philip Jacob; bn. Aug 3, 1787; bpt. Aug 12, 1787; sps. Philip Stayler & Katy Stayler
KELTY, William; bn. Jan 4, 1797; bpt. Feb 26, 1797; son of Cornelius & Ann
KELZER, Jacob; bn. Dec 19, 1793; bpt. Dec 27, 1793; son of George & Ann
KENADAY, Catharine; bpt. Oct 31, 1785; 4 years old; sps. Eleanor Alexander
KENNEDY, James; bn. Jan 3, 1800; bpt. Jan 5, 1800; son of James & Sarah
KENNEDY, Sarah; bpt. Oct 11, 1795; 14 months; dau. of Laurence & Mary
KENNELY, Mary Ann; bn. Oct 12, 1800; bpt. Oct 26, 1800; dau. of Timothy & Bridget
KETCH, Peter; bn. Oct 8, 1799; bpt. Dec 29, 1799; son of Peter & Catharine
KILLION, Andrew; bn. Jul 25, 1796; bpt. Mar 26, 1797; son of Jacob & Mary
KILTY, Elizabeth; bn. Apr 4, 1797; bpt. Jul 23, 1797; dau. of Hugh & Bridget
KILTY, Elizabeth; bn. Oct 28, 1798; bpt. Mar 10, 1799; dau. of Edward & Ann
KIN, Catharine; bpt. Oct 13, 1796; 5 weeks; dau. of Mary Kin
KING, Catharine; bn. Jul 14, 1797; bpt. Jul 24, 1797; dau. of Joseph & Ann
KING, Margaret; bn. Sep 24, 1797; bpt. Oct 8, 1797; dau. of David & Honor

BAPTISMS

KING, Richard; bn. Jun 11, 1799; bpt. Jun 20, 1799; son of David & Honor
KING, William; bn. Apr 9, 1797; bpt. Aug 7, 1797; son of Sarah King
KIRBY, Jane; bn. Apr 23, 1798; bpt. Jul 9, 1798; dau. of William & Jaqnet Fontanier
KIRBY, John; bn. Feb 24, 1795; bpt. Jul 9, 1798; son of William & Jaqnet Fontanier
KIRK, Felix; bn. Apr 1, 1789; bpt. May 5, 1789; sps. Daniel Henry & Elizabeth Henry
KIRK, George; bn. Sep 28, 1796; bpt. Oct 2, 1796; son of Felix & Susanna
KIRK, John; bpt. Jul 6, 1788; 14 months; sps. Hugh & Rosanna Henry
KIRK, Sarah Maria; bn. Mar 22, 1798; bpt. Apr 19, 1798; dau. of Felix & Susanna
KIRK, William; bn. May 25, 1796; bpt. Oct 9, 1796; son of Peter & Eleanor
KIRWAN, Eleanor; bn. Sep 20, 1788; bpt. Sep 21, 1788; sps. William Digges & --- Blake
KIRWAN, Mary; bn. Nov 25, 1786; bpt. Dec 6, 1786; sps. Nicholas Sewall & Mrs. Digges
(KIRWAN), Peter; bpt. Jan 27, 1788; about 12 years old; sps. Nace
KIRWAN, Richard; bn. Nov 19, 1789; bpt. Nov 24, 1789; son of John & Mary
KISLAR, John; bn. Apr 27, 1799; bpt. May 4, 1799; son of John & Catharine
KITTY, James; bn. Jul 2, 1787; bpt. Jul 5, 1787; sps. Joseph Puent & Eleanor Cafry
KLEIN, Antony; bn. Feb 1, 1791; bpt. May 29, 1791; son of Antony & Elizabeth
KLEIN, George; bn. Dec 9, 1788; bpt. Dec 14, 1788; sps. George Rozensteel & Susanna Rozensteel
KNIGHT, George; bn. Jan 15, 1798; bpt. Jan 28, 1798; son of Benjamin & Margaret
KNIGHT, James; bn. Nov 17, 1795; bpt. Jan 10, 1796; son of Benjamin & Mary
KNIGHT, John; bn. Apr 16, 1788; bpt. May 11, 1788; sps. Anthony Hook & Catharine Erwin
KNIGHT, John; bn. Jan 21, 1793; bpt. Feb 25, 1793; son of Benjamin & Margaret
KNIGHT, Margaret; bn. Nov 6, 1790; bpt. Dec 5, 1790; dau. of Benjamin & Margaret
KNIGHT, Polly; bn. Mar 12, 1786; bpt. Apr 17, 1786; sps. Anthony Hook & Elizabeth Shregly
KNIGHT, Rebecca; bpt. Oct 7, 1800; dau. of Benjamin & Margaret
KORNPROPTS, Mary Elizabeth; bn. Jun 5, 1798; bpt. Sep 14, 1798; dau. of Ignatius & Catharine
KRAUSS, Catharine; bn. Sep 19, 1787; bpt. Sep 23, 1787; sps. William Boyler & Catharine Geissler
KUENTZ, Francis; bpt. Aug 2, 1789; 3 weeks; son of Nicholas & Margaret
L'ENGLE, John James; bn. Sep 9, 1795; bpt. Dec 21, 1795; son of John & Susanna Guilmain

BAPTISMS

L'ENGLE, Peter; bn. Sep 9, 1795; bpt. Dec 21, 1795; son of John &
    Susanna Guilmain
(L'HOUMEAU), Charlotte Elizabeth; bn. Jan 26, 1797; bpt. Mar 12,
    1797; dau. of Juliet, slave of Mary Magdalen L'Houmeau
(L'HOUMEAU), Jane Margaret; bn. Jun 21, 1798; bpt. Aug 2, 1798;
    dau. of Lisette, slave of Miss Mary Magdalen Sanite
    L'Houmeau; child declared free
LABONDE, Cornelius; bn. Jun 21, 1796; bpt. Jun 26, 1796; son of
    Joseph & Johanna
LABORDE, Gabriel; bn. Jun 3, 1794; bpt. Jun 21, 1794; son of
    Bernard & Mary Modeste Landry
LABORDE, Maria Julia; bn. Feb 5, 1785; bpt. Feb 10, 1785; sps.
    Gabriel LaBorde & Mary LaBorde
LABORDE, Peter Bernard; bn. Jan 5, 1798; bpt. Feb 17, 1798; son
    of Bernard & Modest
LACHARIC, Ann; bn. Sep 20, 1788; bpt. Nov 13, 1788; dau. of
    Stephen & Ann
LACHARIE, Amelia Benedicta; bn. Jun 13, 1790; bpt. Jul 25, 1790;
    dau. of Stephen & Ann
LACHARIE, James Waters; bn. Mar 11, 1797; bpt. Apr 11, 1797; son
    of Stephen & Ann
LACHARIE, Louisa Caroline Adelaide; bn. Apr 21, 1795; bpt. May
    20, 1795; dau. of Stephen & Ann
LACHARIE, Rose Eleanor Elizabeth; bn. Aug 29, 1798; bpt. Oct 6,
    1798; dau. of Stephen & Ann
(LACHARIE), William; bn. Aug 10, 1798; bpt. Sep 16, 1798; son of
    Polly, Mulatto slave of Mr. Lacharie
(LACHERE), Mary Catharine; bpt. Sep 2, 1798; 10 months; dau. of
    Margaret, slave of Mr. Lachere
(LACHERE), Rosette; bpt. Sep 2, 1798; 4 1/2 years; dau. of
    Margaret, slave of Mr. Lachere
(LACOMBE), John Charles; bn. Jul 29, 1793; bpt. Sep 12, 1793; son
    of Magdalen, a Mulatto slave of Mrs. Lacombe
(LACOMBE), Mary Jane; bpt. May 4, 1794; dau. of Rona, slave of
    Mr. LaCombe
(LADLACE), Augustine; bn. Aug 24, 1797; bpt. Dec 10, 1797;
    Mulatto; son of Taire, slave of Mr. Ladlace
LAEHY, Rebecca; bn. Feb 19, 1795; bpt. Apr 12, 1795; dau. of John
    & Esther
(LAFARGE), John Peter; bpt. Apr 10, 1796; 18 months; son of
    Marinette, slave of Madam LaFarge, widow Asselin, St.
    Domingo
LAFARNE, Mary Jane; bn. Jan 7, 1784; bpt. Feb 4, 1784; sps.
    Michael Nicholas & Mary Jane Nicholas
LAFITE, Dominic; bn. Jul 19, 1791; bpt. Jul 20, 1793; son of
    Dominic & Rose Dubruil; born at Cape Francois
LAFITON, Anthony; bn. Jul 25, 1793; bpt. May 11, 1794; son of
    John & Mary Catharine Duplan
LAFREITE, John Baptist; bn. Jan 1, 1784; bpt. Jan 20, 1784; sps.
    John Baptist Gay & Magdalene Shields
LAKE, Mary; bn. Jun 1, 1794; bpt. Sep 9, 1794; dau. of Michael &
    Sarah
(LALANE), Mary; bpt. Sep 14, 1794; dau. of Mary of St Domingo,
    slave of Mrs. LaLane

BAPTISMS

(LALANNE), Augustine; bpt. Apr 5, 1795; son of Rosine, slave of Mr. LaLanne
LALANNE, Elizabeth Genvieve Bernard; bn. May 27, 1794; bpt. May 31, 1795; dau. of John (deceased), merchant of St. Domingo & Magdalen Aimee Rivery
(LALANNE), Genevieve; bn. Sep 22, 1795; bpt. Feb 8, 1796; Mulattoe; dau. of Nanine, slave of Mrs. Lalanne of St. Domingo
LALLY, James; bn. Feb 8, 1791; bpt. Mar 24, 1791; son of John & Joanna
LAMB, Michael; bpt. Apr 29, 1798; 1 month; son of John & Mary
LAMBERT, Cecilia Elizabeth; bn. Nov 21, 1794; bpt. Apr 22, 1795; dau. of Ceicly Euprhrosyna Lambert, free Mulatress of St. Domingo
LAMBERT, Edward; bpt. Oct 26, 1800; son of Maurice & Mary
LAMBERT, Julia; bn. Mar 18, 1794; bpt. Mar 23, 1794; dau. of Lewis & Frances
LANCEFIELD, John; bn. Mar 26, 1799; bpt. Jun 2, 1799; son of George & Mary
LANDERS, Andrew; bn. Feb 27, 1796; bpt. Apr 17, 1796; son of Peter & Lydia
LANDERS, John; bn. Oct 31, 1796; bpt. Nov 8, 1796; son of William (deceased) & Elizabeth
LANDERS, Lydia; bn. Apr 23, 1800; bpt. Jun 8, 1800; dau. of Peter & Lydia
LANDERS, Peter; bn. Aug 10, 1797; bpt. Nov 12, 1797; son of Peter & Lydia
LANDRY, Harriot; bn. Jul 18, 1788; bpt. Jul 20, 1788; sps. Gaspar Cenas & Mary Coulon
LANDRY, Margaret; bn. Feb 1, 1793; bpt. Feb 16, 1793; dau. of George & Magdalene
LANDRY, Pierre George; bn. Apr 23, 1795; bpt. Jun 7, 1795; son of George & Magdelaine Dain
(LANDRY), Richard; bn. Aug 18, 1798; bpt. Aug 19, 1798; son of Sarah, slave of George Landry
LANDRY, Rosalie; bn. Mar 23, 1785; bpt. Apr 1, 1785; sps. John Dorin & Mary DuPuis
LANDY, Henry; bpt. Sep ?, 1799; 7 weeks; son of Alexander & Anne Harding
LANE, Ann; bn. Apr 25, 1796; bpt. May 22, 1796; dau. of James & Elizabeth
LANGUEDY, Mary; bn. Apr 26, 1799; bpt. May 1, 1799; dau. of Hugh & Margaret
(LANNY), John Peter; bpt. Mar 25, 1799; 18 years; slave of Lewis Lenny
LANOIR, Mary Josephe; bn. Apr 7, 1790; bpt. Jun 16, 1790; dau. of August & Mary Catharine
LAPLAGNE, Francois; bn. Jul 22, 1793; bpt. Aug 26, 1793; son of John of Cape Francis & Anglique Christine LaMotte
(LAPLAINE), Augustine; bpt. Nov 10, 1799; 5 weeks; son of Marie, slave of Mr. Laplaine
LAPOULE, Genevieve Elizabeth; bpt. Aug 17, 1798; 1 year old; dau. of Elizabeth LaPoule, Mulatto
(LAPRAGUE), Peter; bpt. Apr 24, 1799; 15 years old

BAPTISMS

LARHENS, Lloyd; bn. Feb 24, 1796; bpt. Apr 3, 1796; son of
    William Larhens, free Mulatto & Ann, Mulatto slave of Luke
    Tiernan
LARKINS, John; bpt. Sep 25, 1797; 2 months; son of Peter & Clare,
    free Mulattoes
LARNER, Ann; bn. Jun 12, 1794; bpt. Sep 7, 1794; dau. of Matthew
    & Mary
LASALLE, Antoine; bn. Dec 26, 1792; bpt. Oct 20, 1793; son of
    Guillanme & Jean Marie Huve
LASALLE, Henrietta Emilia; bn. Mar 5, 1795; bpt. Sep 18, 1796;
    dau. of William & Mary Huve
LASHFORD, Sarah; bn. Mar 19, 1797; bpt. May 14, 1797; dau. of
    Daniel & Catharine
LASHFORD, Thomas; bn. Mar 16, 1795; bpt. Jul 23, 1795; son of
    Daniel & Catharine
LATAR, Charles; bn. Mar 17, 1791; bpt. Apr 17, 1791; son of
    Laurence & Peggy
LATAR, Elizabeth; bpt. Jan 7, 1789; 2 months; sps. Peter Gold &
    Peggy Mongee
LATAR, Mary; bn. Jun 13, 1786; bpt. Oct 2, 1786; sps. Joseph
    Fellen & Rosanna Williams
LATAR, Peter; bn. Mar 4, 1784; bpt. Apr 6, 1784; sps. John Levant
    & Mary Celestin
LATCHFORD, Ann; bn. Jan 27, 1799; bpt. May 19, 1799; dau. of
    Daniel & Catharine
LATOLLE, John Baptist Michael; bn. Jan 14, 1794; bpt. Feb 17,
    1794; son of John Baptist & Mary Joseph Faulean
LATOUCHE, Angeliques Maria; bn. Dec 7, 1788; bpt. Mar 17, 1789;
    sps. Jean Jacques Giosian & Mary Treakle
LATOUCHE, James Williams; bn. Dec 30, 1790; bpt. Mar 23, 1791;
    son of James Williams & Elizabeth
LATOUCHE, Teresia Maria Magdalena; bn. Jan 11, 1793; bpt. Jan 20,
    1793; dau. of Mr. & Elizabeth
LATOURANDAIS, Emilie; bn. Jul 28, 1799; bpt. Oct 24, 1799; dau.
    of Joseph Auguste & Mary Frances Ducas
(LAUMONT), Therese Etienne; bn. Jul ?, 1794; bpt. Jun 6, 1795;
    dau. of Genvieve, slave of Madam Laumont
(LAUNAY), Mary Magdalen; bpt. Sep 15, 1799; 1 month; dau. of
    Venus, slave of Mr. Launay
LAURENCE, Ann; bn. Feb 8, 1792; bpt. Mar 4, 1792; dau. of
    Ferdinand & Elizabeth
LAURENCE, Catharine; bn. Jan 3, 1786; bpt. Jan 8, 1786; sps.
    Ferdinand & Catharine Laurence
LAURENCE, Cornelius; bn. Feb 16, 1798; bpt. Mar 2, 1798; son of
    Wendel & Ann
LAURENCE, Elizabeth; bn. Jan 4, 1786; bpt. Jan 23, 1786; sps.
    Henry & Elizabeth Tomalty
LAURENCE, Jacob; bn. Feb 19, 1790; bpt. Feb 21, 1790; son of
    Jacob & Sara
LAURENCE, Jacob; bn. Dec 7, 1797; bpt. Feb 11, 1798; son of
    Ferdinand & Elizabeth
LAURENCE, James; bpt. Jan 23, 1799; 4 weeks; son of Maria
    Laurence
LAURENCE, John; bn. Nov 28, 1786; bpt. Dec 17, 1786; sps. John
    Sharp & Catharine Krauss

BAPTISMS

LAURENCE, John; bn. Jan 22, 1794; bpt. Feb 2, 1794; son of Wintel & Margaret
LAURENCE, Joseph; bn. Mar 6, 1785; bpt. Apr 17, 1785; sps. George Tunasly
LAURENCE, Joseph; bn. Sep 19, 1789; bpt. Sep 20, 1789; son of Vendel & Margaret
LAURENCE, Joseph; bn. Sep 25, 1794; bpt. Sep 28, 1794; son of Ferdinand & Elizabeth
LAURENCE, Joseph; bn. Jun 13, 1795; bpt. Jun 21, 1795; son of Peter & Ann
LAURENCE, Joseph; bn. Jun 17, 1799; bpt. Jul 14, 1799; son of Jacob & Sarah
LAURENCE, Margaret; bn. May 7, 1790; bpt. May 13, 1790; dau. of Ferdinand & Elizabeth
LAURENCE, Margaret; bn. Oct 28, 1796; bpt. Nov 27, 1796; dau. of Jacob & Sarah
LAURENCE, Mary; bn. Jun 10, 1788; bpt. Jun 29, 1788; sps. John Sheuler & Christina Bergman
LAURENCE, Mary; bn. Jan 4, 1795; bpt. Jan 11, 1795; dau. of Jacob & Sarah
LAURENCE, Nancy; bn. Jun 22, 1792; bpt. Jun 24, 1792; dau. of Jacob & Sarah
LAURENCE, Rachel; bn. Jan 18, 1800; bpt. Sep 28, 1800; dau. of Wendel & Ann
LAURENCE, Thomas; bn. Sep 24, 1792; bpt. Sep 30, 1792; son of Vendel & Margaret
LAURENCE, Vendel; bn. Nov 2, 1783; bpt. Nov 30, 1783; sps. Vendel Laurence & Eve Smith
LAVIGNE, Cassandra; bn. Apr 16, 1796; bpt. Jun 30, 1796; dau. of Augustine & Cassandra Andrews
LAVIGNE, Margaret; bn. Dec 2, 1794; bpt. Jun 30, 1796; dau. of Augustine & Cassandra Andrews
LAVIL, Peter; bn. Sep 15, 1799; bpt. Sep 21, 1799; son of Michael & Mary
(LAW), Mary Louisa; bpt. Mar 25, 1798; Mulatto; dau. of Dalila, slave of Mr. James Law
LAWRENCE, John; bn. Mar 13, 1786; bpt. Dec 18, 1788; sps. Francis Vintry
LAYBRIGHT, William; bn. Dec 23, 1791; bpt. Jun 17, 1792; son of William & Mary
LAZERE, Ann; bn. Mar 13, 1793; bpt. Jun 17, 1793; dau. of Laurence & Margaret
LEARMAN, John Joseph; bn. Jun 8, 1790; bpt. Aug 27, 1790; son of Roman Joseph & Elizabeth
LEARY, Cornelius; bn. Jan 11, 1788; bpt. Aug 24, 1788; sps. Daniel Leary & Mary Leeson
LEARY, John; bn. Feb 8, 1784; bpt. Jul 17, 1785; sps. John & Mary Stokes
LEARY, Mary; bn. Aug 9, 1791; bpt. Aug 28, 1791; dau. of Daniel & Mary
LEARY, Robert; bn. Mar 22, 1785; bpt. Sep 22, 1785; sps. James Power & Mary Hayes
LEARY, Rosa; bn. Mar 5, 1787; bpt. Aug 2, 1787; dau. of Peter & Mary

BAPTISMS

LEARY, William; bn. Nov 27, 1783; bpt. Dec 7, 1783; sps. James
    Flagerty & Mary Flagerty
LEBASTARD, Amand Mary; bn. Jun ?, 1800; bpt. Sep 21, 1800; son of
    John Lewis & Mary Catharine Hubert of Diocese of Bayeux,
    Normandy
LEBASTARD, Edward Hypolite; bn. Mar 30, 1798; bpt. May 4, 1799;
    son of John Lewis & Mary Catharine Hubert
LEBASTARD, Lewis German Mary; bn. Feb 1, 1790; bpt. Nov 7, 1795;
    son of John Lewis of Bayeux, France & Mary Catharine Hubert
(LEBASTARD), Lewis Alexander; bn. Aug 20, 1797; bpt. Sep 10,
    1797; son of Ann, slave of Mr. LeBastard
LEBASTARD, Mary Josephine; bn. Jun 24, 1795; bpt. Nov 7, 1795;
    dau. of John Lewis & Mary Catharine Hubert
(LEBASTARD), Rosiere; bpt. Jan 5, 1800; Mulatto; 2 weeks; son of
    Anne, slave of Mr. LeBastard
(LEBATARD), John William; bpt. May 17, 1795; 1 month; son of Ann,
    slave of Mr. LeBatard
(LEBATARD), Noel; bpt. May 6, 1794; son of Anne, slave of Mr.
    LeBatard
(LEBLANC), Hyacyhte; bpt. Aug 19, 1798; 3 months; dau. of Mary
    Frances, slave of Mr. LeBlanc
(LEBON), Francis; bpt. Jul 8, 1796; 14 months; son of Mirande,
    slave of Miss LeBon
(LEBON), Mary Teresa; bpt. Mar 25, 1799; 2 weeks; Mulatto; dau.
    of Corarie, slave of Miss LeBon
(LECERC), Ann; bn. Dec 24, 1794; bpt. Aug 16, 1795; dau. of
    Agatha, slave of Mr. LeCerc of St. Domingo
(LECLAIR), Aglae; bpt. May 12, 1798; 2 months; Mulatto; dau. of
    Catharine, slave of Mrs. LeClair
(LECLERC), Calistus; bpt. Jan 8, 1799; 1 month; declared born
    free; son of Rosette, Mulatress slave of Mr. LeClerc
(LECLERC), Francis; bn. Dec 17, 1796; bpt. Dec 29, 1796; Mulatto;
    son of Rose, slave of Mr. LeClerc
LECOQ, Ann; bn. Apr 9, 1791; bpt. May 1, 1794; dau. of John &
    Charlotte Chantreau
(LECOQ), Ann; bpt. May 1, 1794; dau. of Zemire, slave of Mr.
    LeCoq
LECOQ, Frances Florence; bn. Dec 21, 1794; bpt. Jun 28, 1797;
    dau. of John & Charlotte Chantreau
LECOQ, Francis Frederic; bn. Jun 6, 1799; bpt. Nov 10, 1799; son
    of John & Charlotte Chantreau
LECOQ, John Baptist; bn. Jul 4, 1793; bpt. May 1, 1794; son of
    John & Charlotte Chantreau, born at sea
(LECOQ), John Peter; bpt. Aug 28, 1796; 1 month; son of Lemir,
    slave of Mr. LeCoq
LECOQ, Margaret Virginie; bn. Mar 25, 1798; bpt. May 6, 1798;
    dau. of John & Charlotte Chantrau
LEE, Eleanor; bn. Apr 15, 1787; bpt. Feb 23, 1793; dau. of
    Michael & Elizabeth
LEE, Elizabeth; bn. Sep 22, 1782; bpt. Oct 16, 1785; sps. Thomas
    Hillen & Catharine Leary
(LEE), Emily; bpt. Mar 4, 1798; 2 months; dau. of Mary, slave of
    Thomas Lee
LEE, George; bpt. Oct 2, 1800; son of Matthew & Elizabeth
LEE, Henry; bpt. Oct 2, 1800; 5 years; son of Matthew & Elizabeth

BAPTISMS

LEE, Jacob; bn. Oct 16, 1800; bpt. Nov 23, 1800; son of Henry & Elizabeth
LEE, John; bn. Jan 31, 1786; bpt. Feb 23, 1793; son of Michael & Elizabeth
LEE, Michael; bn. Oct 19, 1780; bpt. Oct 16, 1785; sps. Garret Dalton & Hanna Reed
LEE, Richard John; bpt. Mar 24, 1789; about 24 years old; sps. John Lynch
LEE, Sarah; bpt. Sep 10, 1793; 14 months; dau. of John & Sarah
LEE, Sarah; bn. Jul 25, 1792; bpt. Oct 27, 1793; dau. of John & Sarah
LEE, Thomas; bn. Sep 6, 1792; bpt. Feb 23, 1793; son of Michael & Elizabeth
LEESON, John; bn. May 12, 1788; bpt. May 30, 1788; sps. Ha---
LEESON, Mary Ann; bpt. May 17, 1795; 2 months; dau. of Francis & Catharine
LEFEBURE, Lewis Edward Henry; bn. Dec 21, 1796; bpt. May 18, 1797; son of John Mary & Catharine Faurie
LEFEBURE, Louise Marguerite Francoise Danice; bn. Jan 14, 1797; bpt. Jun 17, 1798; dau. of James Francis & Margaret Cheneau
LEFEURE, Mary Frances; bpt. Aug 13, 1796; 20 months; dau. of Eugenie LeFeure, free Mulatto
LEFLET, Alexander; bn. Dec 27, 1799; bpt. Apr 20, 1800; son of Peter & Mary Rosalia Perrot
LEFLET, Honoratius Augustus; bn. Oct 10, 1798; bpt. Apr 20, 1800; son of Peter & Mary Rosalia Perrot
LEFLET, Peter Gabriel Aristides; bn. Nov 21, 1794; bpt. Sep 13, 1795; son of Peter & Mary Rosalia Pirot
LEGRAND, Augustus; bn. Jan 4, 1800; bpt. May 8, 1800; son of Samuel & Eleanor
LEGRAND, Caroline; bn. Apr 25, 1798; bpt. Sep 16, 1798; dau. of Samuel & Mary
LEHOUX, Antoine Louis Charles Carroll; bn. Oct 19, 1793; bpt. Oct 20, 1793; son of Louis Denis of Cape Francois & Agnes Sophie DePrunes
LEIGHY, Margaret; bn. Jun 29, 1797; bpt. Aug 9, 1797; dau. of John & Esther
LELAND, Sarah; bn. Aug 25, 1799; bpt. Dec 24, 1799; dau. of Francis & Mary
LELICONE, Charles Antony Mary; bn. Nov 12, 1790; bpt. Sep 18, 1794; son of Charles & Victoire d'Abbeville
LENAGHAN, Eleanor; bn. Feb 27, 1794; bpt. May 11, 1794; dau. of Charles & Sarah
LENAGHAN, John; bn. May 6, 1791; bpt. Jul 3, 1791; son of Charles & Sara
LENEGHAN, Elizabeth; bn. Apr 22, 1796; bpt. Feb 12, 1797; dau. of Charles & Sarah
LENEGHAN, Frances; bn. Jun 1, 1800; bpt. Sep 7, 1800; dau. of Charles & Sarah Leneghan
LENEGHAN, Rebecca; bn. Mar 23, 1798; bpt. Sep 8, 1800; dau. of Charles & Sarah Leneghan
LEONARD, Rosanna; bn. Dec 9, 1790; bpt. Apr 24, 1791; dau. of James & Ann
(LEQUIN), Margaret Celie; bpt. Mar 26, 1796; 16 years old; Mulatto; slave of Mr. Lequin of St. Domingo

BAPTISMS

(LEQUIN), Mary Rose; bpt. Sep 8, 1793; dau. of Sophia, slave of Mr. LeQuin
LEREMAIN, Lewis Joseph; bn. Aug 4, 1793; bpt. Sep 22, 1793; son of Joseph & Elizabeth
LERET, Ann Louisa Beeston; bn. Nov 17, 1796; bpt. Nov 21, 1796; dau. of Peter & Rebecca
LERET, Elizabeth; bn. Oct 27, 1792; bpt. Oct 28, 1792; dau. of Peter & Rebecca
LERET, Louisa Josephine; bn. Aug 6, 1798; bpt. Aug 7, 1798; dau. of Peter & Rebecca
LERET, Mary; bn. Dec 18, 1788; bpt. Dec 18, 1788; dau. of Peter & Rebecca
LERET, Rebecca; bn. Nov 16, 1787; bpt. Nov 17, 1787; sps. Bernard LaBoode & Margaret Compario
LERET, Rebecca; bn. Nov 10, 1794; bpt. Nov 12, 1794; dau. of Peter & Rebecca
(LERET), Robert; bn. Apr 22, 1800; bpt. Apr 28, 1800; Mulatto; son of Catharine, slave of Mr. Leret
LERET, William; bn. Dec 2, 1790; bpt. Dec 5, 1790; son of Peter & Rebecca Leist
(LESPALIERES), John; bn. Oct 29, 1795; bpt. Feb 8, 1796; son of Susanna, slave of Mr. LesPalieres of St. Domingo
LET, Elizabeth; bpt. Jul 20, 1800; dau. of John Christopher & Mary
LEVANT, Sally; bn. Dec 19, 1788; bpt. Jan 24, 1789; sps. Charles Bondrau & Betsy Kennedy
(LEVELINGE), George Felix; bpt. May 9, 1795; 6 months; son of Pelagie, slave of Mlle. Levelinge
LEVILLAIN, John; bn. Aug 21, 1797; bpt. Sep 24, 1797; son of Michael & Catharine
LEVY, Mary; bn. Jul 18, 1795; bpt. Aug 17, 1795; dau. of Winifred Levy
LEWIS, John Mary Petit; bn. Dec 26, 1796; bpt. Aug 28, 1797; son of Claire Lewis, Mulatto, St. Domingo
LEWIS, Joseph; bpt. Jul 15, 1798; 5 months; son of Abraham & Milly, free Mulattoes
LIAUTAND, Sophie; bn. Apr 10, 1800; bpt. Jul 12, 1800; dau. of Claude & Jean Catharine Brule
LICARDI, John Baptist; bn. Sep 22, 1795; bpt. Oct 11, 1795; son of John Baptist, a Genoese & Rachel
LIDDLE, John; bn. Apr 6, 1799; bpt. Apr 7, 1799; son of John & Catharine
LIDDLE, Michael; bn. Feb 19, 1797; bpt. Feb 23, 1797; son of John & Catharine
LIEGFRIET, John; bn. Aug 31, 1789; bpt. Sep 13, 1789; son of George & Gertrude
(LIEUR), St. Cyr; bpt. Apr 27, 1794; son of Mary Clare, slave of Mrs. Lieur
LIHAULT, Joseph; bn. Mar 22, 1785; bpt. Mar 4, 1795; born at Cp. Francois, St. Domingo
LIMES, Margaret; bn. Feb 17, 1788; bpt. Feb 25, 1788; sps. William Hook & Betsy Babin
LINEER, Rose; bn. May 14, 1785; bpt. May 15, 1785; sps. Patrick Reyly & Pricilla Bicker

BAPTISMS

LINER, Ann; bn. Feb 10, 1787; bpt. Apr 15, 1787; sps. Timothy
    Duffy & Katy Kelly
LINER, Elizabeth; bn. Mar 9, 1789; bpt. May 30, 1789; dau. of
    Peter & Barbara
LINER, James; bn. Aug 20, 1791; bpt. Oct 2, 1791; son of Peter &
    Barbara
LINER, Margaret; bn. Sep 22, 1797; bpt. Dec 3, 1797; dau. of
    Peter & Barbara
LINER, Sarah; bn. Apr 3, 1795; bpt. May 3, 1795; dau. of Peter &
    Barbara
LINES, Michael; bn. Sep 3, 1796; bpt. Oct 9, 1796; son of John &
    Joanna
LIOT, Francoise Parfaite Angelique; bn. May 14, 1799; bpt. Aug 6,
    1800; dau. of Francis Benjamin & Mary Frances Charlotte
    Mehul
LITSINGER, John Mabury; bpt. Aug 23, 1799; 2 years, 8 months old;
    son of George & Elizabeth
LITSINGER, Stephen; bpt. Aug 23, 1799; 1 year, 8 months old; son
    of George & Elizabeth
(LITZENGER), Abigail; bpt. Oct 9, 1791; adult
LITZENGER, Dorothea; bpt. Oct 10, 1786; 6 months; sps. James
    Collins & Catharine Leary
LITZENGER, Eliza; bn. Feb 19, 1793; bpt. May 19, 1793; dau. of
    William & ---
LITZENGER, John; bn. Nov 18, 1783; bpt. Nov 30, 1783; sps. John
    Hillen & Elizabeth Freigle
LITZENGER, Mary; bn. Nov 20, 1788; bpt. Jan 1, 1789; sps. Mark
    Morres & Mary Miller
LITZENGER, Peter; bn. Apr 10, 1791; bpt. Jun 5, 1791; son of
    George & Elizabeth
LITZINGER, John; bn. Dec 22, 1795; bpt. Mar 27, 1796; son of
    William & Elizabeth
LITZINGER, Thomas; bn. Jun 4, 1794; bpt. Jul 9, 1794; son of
    George & Elizabeth
LITZINGER, William; bn. Jul 26, 1783; bpt. Aug 3, 1783; sps.
    William Litzinger & Eva Smith
LIVERS, Arnold Aloysius; bn. Jun 2, 1800; bpt. Jun 12, 1800; son
    of Arnold & Mary
LIVERS, Catharine; bn. Apr 29, 1793; bpt. May 5, 1793; dau. of
    Arnold & Mary
LIVERS, Catharine Charlotte; bn. Mar 21, 1799; bpt. Mar 25, 1799;
    dau. of Arnold & Mary
LIVERS, Elizabeth; bn. Sep 1, 1790; bpt. Sep 3, 1790; dau. of
    Arnold & Mary
(LIVERS), Juliana; bn. May 3, 1800; bpt. May 25, 1800; Mulatto;
    dau. of Mima, Mulatto slave of Arnold Livers
LIVERS, Mary; bn. Aug 10, 1797; bpt. Aug 21, 1797; dau. of Arnold
    & Mary Livers
(LIVERS), Mily; bn. Oct 17, 1796; bpt. Oct 23, 1796; dau. of
    Jemima, slave of Arnold Livers
LIVERS, Richard; bn. Aug 22, 1795; bpt. Sep 6, 1795; son of
    Arnold & Mary; sps. Elizabeth McSherry
LIVINGSHINE, Paul Bartholomy Hhym; bpt. Aug 24, 1794; 23 years
    last March; heretofore Jewish

BAPTISMS

LLOYD, Eliza; bn. Oct 23, 1799; bpt. Oct 31, 1799; dau. of
    Richard & Esther
LLOYD, Mary; bn. Feb 5, 1797; bpt. Apr 23, 1797; dau. of Richard
    & Hesther
LLOYD, Sarah; bn. May 26, 1795; bpt. Oct 11, 1795; dau. of
    Richard & Esther
LLOYD, William John; bn. Dec 31, 1799; bpt. Jan 5, 1800; son of
    William & Elizabeth
LOGAN, Andrew; bn. Sep 3, 1798; bpt. Sep 9, 1798; son of
    Cornelius & Mary
LOGAN, John; bn. Jun 24, 1797; bpt. Jun 25, 1797; son of
    Cornelius & Mary
LOGAN, Thomas; bn. Jul 16, 1800; bpt. Jul 28, 1800; son of
    Cornelius & Mary
LOGSDEN, Caleb; bn. Mar 9, 1797; bpt. Jun 5, 1797; son of Job &
    Patience
LOGSDON, Elizabeth; bn. Sep ?, 1794; bpt. Dec 4, 1795; dau. of
    Job & Patience
LOGSDON, Margaret; bn. Oct 28, 1799; bpt. Apr 8, 1800; dau. of
    John & Patience
LOGSDON, Maria; bn. Oct 23, 1792; bpt. Nov 11, 1792; dau. of Job
    & Patiens
LONG, Elizabeth; bn. Jun 19, 1797; bpt. Jul 10, 1797; dau. of
    Thomas & Elizabeth
(LONG), John; bn. Dec 25, 1795; bpt. Apr 17, 1797; Mulatto; son
    of Henny, slave of Mr. Long
LONG, Margaret; bpt. Jul 25, 1794; 10 years old
LONG, Mary; bn. Jul 9, 1794; bpt. Jul 9, 1794; dau. of Thomas &
    Mary
LONG, Mary; bn. Jul 14, 1796; bpt. Jul 14, 1796; dau. of Thomas &
    Elizabeth
LONG, Thomas; bn. Apr 18, 1800; bpt. Apr 22, 1800; son of Thomas
    & Elizabeth
LOUIGA, Francisca Magdalena; bn. Apr 20, 1786; bpt. Apr 21, 1786;
    sps. Anthony Miller & Magdalen Foldweiler
(LOURZAC), Rose; bpt. Oct 27, 1799; 2 months; dau. of Elizabeth,
    slave of Mr. Lourzac
LOVET, John; bn. Oct 31, 1796; bpt. Jul 4, 1797; son of John &
    Ann
LOW, Ann; bpt. Oct 19, 1794; 4 years old; dau. of William & ?,
    both deceased
LOWMAN, John; bn. Feb 14, 1797; bpt. Mar 21, 1797; son of John &
    Mary
LOWMAN, William; bn. Mar 29, 1795; bpt. May 17, 1795; son of John
    & Mary
LUCAS, Francis; bn. Feb 14, 1794; bpt. Feb 16, 1794; son of
    Francis & Elizabeth
LUCAS, Magdalen; bn. Apr 16, 1785; bpt. Apr 18, 1785; sps. James
    Power & Magdalen Saplin
LUGEOL, Joseph; bn. Oct 8, 1797; bpt. May 29, 1798; son of Hilary
    & Ann Lacy Monchet
LUPKY, Ann Catharine; bn. Sep 21, 1799; bpt. Sep 29, 1799; dau.
    of Henry & --
LUSHERAN, Magdalen Angelic; bn. May 11, 1785; bpt. May 15, 1785;
    sps. Mark Morres & Magdalen Sapin

BAPTISMS

LUSHERAN, Margaret; bn. Mar 9, 1783; bpt. Mar 9, 1783; sps. Simon Deagle & Magdalen Babin
LUSUM, John; bn. Feb 27, 1788; bpt. Sep 17, 1788; sps. Eleanor Brien
LUTZ, Joseph; bn. May 6, 1791; bpt. May 8, 1791; son of Valentin & Mary
LUTZ, Valentine; bn. Jan 2, 1790; bpt. Jan 3, 1790; son of Valentine & Mary Appollonia
LYNCH, Benjamin; bn. Jan 20, 1789; bpt. Nov 8, 1789; son of Hugh & Rebecca
LYNCH, Catharine; bn. Jul 24, 1796; bpt. Aug 21, 1796; dau. of Hugh & Rebecca
LYNCH, Daniel; bpt. Jun 4, 1786; 3 weeks; sps. Richard & Ann Burke
LYNCH, George; bn. Feb 25, 1799; bpt. Apr 23, 1799; son of Hugh & Rebecca
LYNCH, Hugh; bn. Jan 17, 1788; bpt. Feb 3, 1788; sps. Philip Downy & Gainy
LYNCH, James; bn. Jan 25, 1799; bpt. Mar 5, 1799; son of John & Patience
LYNCH, James; bn. Jan 21, 1800; bpt. Mar 18, 1800; son of Patrick & Elizabeth
LYNCH, James Owings; bn. Sep 27, 1800; bpt. Nov 2, 1800; son of John & Patience
LYNCH, John; bn. Jul 10, 1785; bpt. Oct 2, 1785; sps. Matthias Downy & Brigit Ragan
LYNCH, John; bn. Nov 19, 1793; bpt. Dec 8, 1793; son of John & Patience
LYNCH, Mary; bn. Dec 12, 1791; bpt. Jan 7, 1792; dau. of John & Patience
LYNCH, Mathias; bn. Apr 28, 1787; bpt. May 27, 1787; sps. John Cole & Catharine Lynch
LYNCH, Nancy; bn. Oct 14, 1786; bpt. Mar 25, 1787; sps. Bernard Lynch & Jane McGuire
LYNCH, Patrick; bn. Nov 13, 1797; bpt. Nov 26, 1797; son of Edward & Mary
LYNCH, Rachael; bn. Mar 16, 1794; bpt. Aug 18, 1794; dau. of Hugh & Rebecca
LYNCH, Rebecca; bn. Oct 7, 1791; bpt. Aug 12, 1792; dau. of Hugh & Rebecca
LYNCH, Thomas; bn. Dec 30, 1796; bpt. Jan 4, 1797; son of John & Patience
LYONS, John; bn. Nov 27, 1798; bpt. Aug 8, 1799; son of Bartholomew & Sarah
LYONS, Thomas; bn. Feb 5, 1798; bpt. Feb 18, 1798; son of Mortagh & Alice
M'CARRETI, John; bn. Sep 7, 1794; bpt. Oct 12, 1794; son of Jeremiah & Anna Williamson
MACKIE, Augustus Alexander; bn. Mar 1, 1797; bpt. Apr 23, 1797; son of Alexander & Margaret
MACKIE, Francis; bn. Jul 30, 1798; bpt. Aug 2, 1798; son of Hugh & Sarah
MACKIE, Isabella; bpt. Apr 15, 1800; 4 months; dau. of John & Sarah

BAPTISMS

MACKIE, Margaret; bn. Aug 24, 1796; bpt. Aug 29, 1796; dau. of
    Hugh & Sarah
MACKY, Elizabeth; bn. Dec 26, 1790; bpt. Dec 28, 1790; dau. of
    John & Elizabeth
MACKY, John; bn. Dec 12, 1788; bpt. Dec 21, 1788; sps. Richard
    Fitzgerald
MACNAMARA, Eleanor; bn. Jul 27, 1794; bpt. Aug 25, 1794; dau. of
    Matthew & Anne
MACNAMARA, John; bpt. Sep 1, 1799; 5 months; son of Thomas & Mary
MADAGIN, John; bn. Mar 12, 1797; bpt. May 28, 1797; son of Thomas
    & Mary
MADDEN, Ann; bn. Apr 12, 1784; bpt. Jun 18, 1785; sps. Richard
    Brien & Margaret Sinson
MADDEN, Catharine; bn. Feb 18, 1799; bpt. Mar 31, 1799; dau. of
    Thomas & Mary
MADDEN, Charles; bn. Nov 26, 1783; bpt. Nov 30, 1783; sps.
    Salvator Lacan & Rose Richards
MADDEN, Elizabeth; bn. Feb 17, 1796; bpt. Apr 24, 1796; dau. of
    John & Elizabeth
MADDEN, John; bn. Jan 21, 1780; bpt. Jun 18, 1785; sps. Richard
    Brien & Margaret Sinson
MADDEN, John; bn. Aug 22, 1789; bpt. Sep 20, 1789; son of Matthew
    & Brigit
MADDEN, Mary; bn. Mar 15, 1791; bpt. Apr 25, 1791; dau. of
    Matthew & Brigit
MADDEN, Peggy; bn. Jul 6, 1782; bpt. Jun 18, 1785; sps. Richard
    Brien & Margaret Sinson
MADIGAN, Sarah; bn. Oct 19, 1795; bpt. Dec 6, 1795; dau. of
    Thomas & Mary
MAGAN, Thomas; bn. Oct 26, 1799; bpt. Oct 27, 1799; son of
    Matthew & Ann
MAGRATH, Stephen; bn. Dec 26, 1797; bpt. Jan 8, 1798; son of
    James & Catharine Cumming
MAGUIRE, Catharine; bpt. Aug 25, 1799; 2 weeks; dau. of Roger &
    Eleanor
MAGUIRE, John; bn. Feb 17, 1797; bpt. Feb 26, 1797; son of Roger
    & Eleanor
MAHONY, Charles; bpt. Nov 16, 1800; 9 months; son of James &
    Teresa, free Mulattoes
MAHONY, William; bn. Mar 8, 1782; bpt. Oct 17, 1790; son of
    William & Catharine
MAKIS, William; bn. Apr 26, 1798; bpt. May 13, 1798; son of
    Judith Makis
MALLIGAN, Margaret; bn. Oct 7, 1796; bpt. Oct 16, 1796; dau. of
    Michael & Mary
MALVILLE, Francois Joseph; bn. May 16, 1793; bpt. Aug 11, 1793;
    son of Joseph & Catharine Descontes
MANLY, Ann; bpt. Jul 4, 1791; 6 weeks; dau. of John & Peggy Dealy
(MANSUY), John Lewis; bn. May 23, 1796; bpt. Jun 22, 1796; son of
    Lanite, slave of Mrs Mansuy, widow
MANUEL, Hanna; bn. Nov 4, 1785; bpt. May 7, 1786; sps. Nancy Cler
MANUEL, James; bn. Nov 4, 1785; bpt. May 7, 1786; sps. Lambeth
    Godey
MAR, Mary Anne; bn. Oct 31, 1793; bpt. Jul 21, 1794; dau. of
    Robert & Margaret

BAPTISMS

MARA, Brigit; bpt. Dec 21, 1792; 13 months; dau. of Robert & Margaret
(MARAS), Josephine; bpt. Mar 25, 1798; dau. of Zayre, slave of Madam Maras
MARGOLLE, Sarah; bn. Feb 11, 1793; bpt. Feb 21, 1793; dau. of John Baptist & Ann Mary
(MARIE), Catharine Elizabeth; bpt. Jun 5, 1799; 2 years old; Mulatto; dau. of Petronille, slave of Joseph Marie
MARR, Margaret; bpt. Oct 5, 1788; 1 month; sps. John Harrigan & Norry Reraden
MARSHALL, Catharina; bn. Dec 18, 1797; bpt. Dec 19, 1797; dau. of Joseph & Christina
MARTIACO, Clara Amelia; bn. Jan 10, 1800; bpt. Feb 16, 1800; dau. of John & Mary
MARTIACQ, Ann Linette; bn. Nov 4, 1798; bpt. Apr 11, 1799; dau. of John & Mary
MARTIN, Catharine; bn. Feb 24, 1794; bpt. Feb 14, 1795; dau. of Robert & Mary
(MARTIN), Christopher Lloyd; bn. May 7, 1798; bpt. Jul 21, 1799; son of Luke & Cassia, slave of Luther Martin, Esq.
(MARTIN), David; bpt. Apr 30, 1797; 7 months; son of Sanders, slave of Luther Martin
MARTIN, Elizabeth; bn. Feb 4, 1790; bpt. Feb 21, 1790; dau. of Robert & Mary
MARTIN, Francis; bpt. May 6, 1799; 2 weeks; son of Mary Martin
MARTIN, James; bn. Jun 15, 1791; bpt. Jul 24, 1791; son of Benjamin & Debra (a Negro)
MARTIN, Jane; bn. Nov 25, 1797; bpt. Mar 7, 1798; dau. of Robert & Margaret
MARTIN, John; bn. Apr 14, 1797; bpt. Apr 26, 1797; son of Thomas & Mary
MARTIN, John Baptist Theodore; bn. Nov 7, 1784; bpt. Nov 28, 1784; sps. John Baptist Feller & Mary Babin
MARTIN, John Baptist; bn. Apr 20, 1795; bpt. Apr 29, 1797; son of John Joseph & Mary Ann Villard
(MARTIN), Julia Ann; bn. Aug 1, 1797; bpt. Aug 19, 1797; dau. of Thomas, slave of Luther Martin & Lydia, slave of Eleanor Browning
(MARTIN), Lucy; bn. Oct 16, 1799; bpt. Feb 26, 1800; dau. of Luke & Cossa, slave of Luther Martin
MARTIN, Margaret; bpt. Nov 16, 1788; 4 weeks; dau. of William & Margaret
MARTIN, Mary; bn. Jul 27, 1787; bpt. Aug 26, 1787; sps. Mark Morres & Margaret Wells
MARTIN, Mary; bn. Jun 10, 1791; bpt. Jun 12, 1791; dau. of Guilliaume & Mary Margaret
MARTIN, Mary Rosalia; bn. Sep 21, 1793; bpt. Apr 5, 1794; dau. of William & Mary Margaret Lejeune, nat. of France
MARTIN, Rachel; bpt. Apr 16, 1796; adult
MARTIN, Sara; bn. May 1, 1784; bpt. May 16, 1784; sps. Samuel Miller & Modest Ross
MARTIN, William; bn. May 1, 1784; bpt. Aug 30, 1784; sps. Susanna Jones
(MARTON), Regis; bpt. Mar 19, 1797; 18 months; free Mulatto; son of Rosette, Mulatto, slave of Miss Marton

BAPTISMS

(MARTON), Ursula; bn. Apr 5, 1798; bpt. May 6, 1798; dau. of
    Rosette, slave of Miss Marton
MASHAU, Mary Ann; bn. Mar 24, 1799; bpt. Mar 31, 1799; dau. of
    Joseph & Christina
MATHIAS, George; bn. Jan 20, 1792; bpt. Dec 7, 1794; son of John
    & Elizabeth Haupt
MATHIAS, Mary; bn. Feb 19, 1794; bpt. Dec 7, 1794; dau. of John &
    Elizabeth Haupt
MATTHEWS, Elizabeth; bn. Mar ?, 1797; bpt. Apr 30, 1797; dau. of
    Samuel & Sina
MATTHEWS, Jane; bpt. Apr 14, 1800; 3 years old; dau. of Edward
    Matthews, free Negro & Mary, slave of Mr. Otto
MATTISON, Aaron; bn. Feb 15, 1793; bpt. Feb 20, 1794; son of
    James & Sarah
MATTISON, Ann; bn. Oct 27, 1794; bpt. Jan 27, 1795; dau. of James
    & Sarah
MAY, Elizabeth; bpt. Jul 13, 1788; 9 weeks; sps. Catharine
    McGrath
MAY, Honor; bn. Mar 31, 1790; bpt. May 23, 1790; dau. of Joseph &
    Catharine
MAYEL, Ann; bn. Mar 22, 1800; bpt. May 10, 1800; dau. of Joseph
    Anthony & Margaret
MAYERS, Mathildis; bn. Nov 19, 1800; bpt. Nov 30, 1800; son of
    Nicholas & Mary
MCADOUGH, Margaret; bn. Aug ?, 1791; bpt. Aug 7, 1791; dau. of
    William & Mary Conden
MCALLISTER, Alexander; bn. May 12, 1797; bpt. May 18, 1797; son
    of Charles & Elizabeth
MCALLISTER, Honor; bn. Jun 8, 1793; bpt. Aug 3, 1793; dau. of
    James & Margarite
MCALLISTER, John; bn. Apr 17, 1799; bpt. Apr 21, 1799; son of
    Charles & Elizabeth
MCBRIERTY, John; bn. Jun 15, 1794; bpt. Jul 13, 1794; son of
    Patrick & Margaret
MCCABE, Catharine; bn. Feb 26, 1793; bpt. Mar 17, 1795; dau. of
    Thomas & Sarah
MCCALLISTER, James; bn. Oct 6, 1791; bpt. Oct 13, 1791; son of
    James & Margaret
MCCAMMEL, Rose; bn. Sep 4, 1796; bpt. Sep 10, 1796; dau. of
    Patrick & ----
MCCAN, Ann; bpt. Mar 29, 1791; adult
MCCAN, John; bn. May 9, 1790; bpt. Jun 6, 1790; son of John &
    Nancy Hagen
MCCAN, John; bn. Jul 22, 1790; bpt. Jul 10, 1791; son of Patrick
    & Abigail
MCCAN, William; bn. Aug 31, 1791; bpt. Nov 6, 1791; son of John &
    Ann
MCCARROLL, Francis; bn. Jul 23, 1795; bpt. Aug 2, 1795; son of
    Francis & Bridget
MCCARTHY, Catharine John Baptist; bn. Dec 28, 1798; bpt. Jan 13,
    1799; dau. of John & Eleanor
MCCARTY, ; bpt. Aug 30, 1789
MCCARTY, Ann; bpt. Jan 26, 1800; 2 months; dau. of Darby & Ann
MCCARTY, Catharine; bn. Aug 2, 1785; bpt. Jun 4, 1786; sps. James
    & Mary Power

BAPTISMS

MCCARTY, Catharine; bpt. Jan 26, 1800; 3 years old; dau. of Darby & Ann
MCCARTY, Eleanor; bn. Oct 8, 1790; bpt. Jan 23, 1791; dau. of Daniel & Susanna
MCCARTY, Eleanor; bpt. Aug 12, 1798; 1 month; dau. of Michael & Eleanor
MCCARTY, Elizabeth; bn. Feb 2, 1789; bpt. Jul 5, 1789; dau. of Daniel & Susanna
MCCARTY, Hannah; bn. Jul 29, 1791; bpt. Aug 23, 1791; dau. of Darly & Nancy
MCCARTY, James; bn. Mar 12, 1783; bpt. Mar 30, 1783; sps. Margaret Murry
MCCARTY, Jane; bn. May 1, 1792; bpt. Oct 7, 1792; dau. of John & Eleanor
MCCARTY, Mary; bpt. Mar 27, 1785; 6 weeks; sps. Sara Boyle
MCCARTY, Mary; bn. Apr 25, 1787; bpt. Aug 12, 1787; sps. Darby McCarty & Mary Hayes
MCCARTY, Mary; bn. Mar 2, 1793; bpt. May 26, 1793; dau. of Darby & Ann
MCCARTY, Patrick; bn. Nov 6, 1799; bpt. Apr 13, 1800; son of Patrick & Sarah
MCCARTY, Rosanna; bn. Apr 6, 1784; bpt. Aug 25, 1784; sps. Margaret Hartman
MCCASKEY, Jane; bn. Jun 3, 1789; bpt. Oct 18, 1789; dau. of Samuel & Mary
MCCAUSLAND, Emily Jane; bpt. Oct 25, 1798; 3 years old; dau. of Marcus & Mary
MCCLAIN, Jeremia; bn. Jun 4, 1787; bpt. Jun 24, 1792; son of James & Mary Evans
MCCLAUD, Daniel; bn. Aug 20, 1789; bpt. Aug 23, 1789; son of Archibald & Sara
MCCLAUD, Mary; bn. Jan 1, 1788; bpt. Jan 1, 1788; sps. --- McMullan & Mary Warring
MCCLOSKY, Sarah; bpt. Jul 15, 1796; 10 months; dau. of Daniel & Margaret
MCCONNELL, Rebecca Eliza; bn. Oct 3, 1800; bpt. Oct 19, 1800; dau. of John & Sarah
MCCONNOR, Ann; bpt. Jul 4, 1797; 12 years old; dau. of John & Elizabeth
MCCORT, William; bn. Jul 2, 1782; bpt. Dec 27, 1782; sps. Francis Smith & Mary Smith
MCCOY, Abraham; bn. Jan 6, 1788; bpt. Apr 14, 1789; sps. Luke
MCCOY, Ann; bn. Aug 6, 1794; bpt. Apr 5, 1795; dau. of Abraham & Elizabeth, free Mulattoes
MCCOY, Harriet; bn. Nov 3, 1790; bpt. Mar 11, 1792; Mulatto; dau. of Abram & Betsy
MCCUBBIN, Hannah; bn. Oct 8, 1798; bpt. Jan 18, 1799; dau. of James & Lydia
MCCUBBIN, William Beeston; bn. Apr 22, 1796; bpt. Jun 29, 1796; son of James & Lydia
MCDANIEL, Alexander; bn. Jan 28, 1788; bpt. Oct 11, 1789; son of Francis & Rachael
MCDANIEL, Alexander; bn. Oct 26, 1797; bpt. Oct 27, 1797; son of Bernard & Jane

BAPTISMS

MCDANIEL, Daniel; bn. Jun 27, 1784; bpt. Aug 22, 1784; sps. George Scot & Catharine Leary
MCDANIEL, Francis; bn. May 28, 1787; bpt. Aug 7, 1787; son of Edward & Ann
MCDANIEL, Jane; bn. Jan 20, 1800; bpt. Jan 30, 1800; dau. of Barney & Jane
MCDANIEL, Rachael; bn. Jul 5, 1791; bpt. Oct 28, 1792; dau. of Francis & Rachael
MCDANIEL, William; bn. Dec 30, 1796; bpt. Jun 5, 1797; son of Francis & Rachel
MCDERMOT, Anne; bn. Aug 21, 1791; bpt. Nov 20, 1791; dau. of Thomas & Henrietta
MCDERMOT, Catharine; bn. Feb 25, 1789; bpt. Apr 26, 1789; sps. John Bready & Mary Farrel
MCDERMOTT, James; bn. Dec 10, 1794; bpt. Jan 4, 1795; son of James & Lydia
MCDERMOTT, John; bn. May 21, 1797; bpt. Jul 9, 1797; son of Thomas & Esther
MCDONALD, Jane; bn. Jul 21, 1796; bpt. Jul 27, 1796; dau. of Bernard & Jane
MCDONALD, John Hamilton; bn. Feb 16, 1793; bpt. May 20, 1793; son of Francis & Rachael
MCDONNEL, Brigit; bn. Apr 18, 1785; bpt. May 15, 1785; sps. Norbert Conway & Elizabeth Shiagly
MCDONNEL, John; bn. Feb 14, 1793; bpt. Mar 12, 1793; son of Edward & Nancy
MCDONNEL, Mary; bn. Oct 7, 1783; bpt. Oct 10, 1783; sps. Patrick Sullivan & Charity Hammer
MCDONNEL, Nancy; bn. Feb 14, 1793; bpt. Mar 12, 1793; dau. of Edward & Nancy
MCELDERICK, Nancy; bn. Apr 7, 1783; bpt. Jul 21, 1783; sps. Ann Harrison
(MCELDERY), Ann; bpt. Jan 5, 1800; 1 month; dau. of Thomas & Mary, slave of Mr. McEldery
(MCELDERY), Henrietta; bn. Apr 10, 1799; bpt. Apr 21, 1799; dau. of Moses & Grace, slave of Thomas McEldery
(MCELDERY), Mary; bpt. Dec 25, 1796; 3 weeks; dau. of Moses & Grace, slave of Thomas McEldery
MCELHINEY, William Jones; bn. Nov 15, 1798; bpt. Dec 9, 1798; son of Michael & Cassandra
MCELLERY, Elizabeth; bn. Dec 26, 1795; bpt. Jan 1, 1796; dau. of William & Elizabeth
MCELLERY, John; bn. Nov 21, 1794; bpt. Dec 21, 1794; son of William & Elizabeth
MCELLERY, William; bn. Jun 27, 1797; bpt. Jul 8, 1797; son of William & Elizabeth
MCEWING, Caroline; bn. Nov 21, 1798; bpt. Dec 17, 1798; dau. of Owen & Elizabeth
MCEWING, Mary Magdalen; bn. Sep 26, 1797; bpt. Oct 3, 1797; dau. of Owen & Elizabeth
MCFARLEN, ; bn. Sep 29, 1793; bpt. Oct 20, 1793; child of Michael & Margaret
MCFARLEN, Daniel; bn. Mar 31, 1795; bpt. May 3, 1795; son of Michael & Margaret

BAPTISMS

MCFARLIN, Peter; bn. Sep ?, 1785; bpt. Sep 29, 1785; sps. James Toole & Mrs. Fretter
MCGARVEN, Mary; bn. Oct 26, 1800; bpt. Nov 2, 1800; dau. of Emmanuel & Elizabeth
MCGEE, Alfred; bn. Sep 19, 1794; bpt. Dec 13, 1795; son of Elizabeth McGee
MCGILL, Dennis; bn. Nov 3, 1797; bpt. Nov 19, 1797; son of Charles & Margaret
MCGILL, George; bn. Jul 27, 1788; bpt. Aug 3, 1788; sps. James Power & Mary Power
MCGILL, John; bn. Sep 18, 1789; bpt. Oct 5, 1789; son of Richard & Peggy
MCGILL, Margaret; bn. Dec 13, 1792; bpt. Dec 23, 1792; dau. of Charles & Margaret LaTar
MCGILL, Sarah; bn. Sep 22, 1784; bpt. Sep 27, 1784; sps. James Cretin & Catharine Green
MCGONAGHAN, Hugh; bn. Sep 22, 1800; bpt. Nov 12, 1800; son of Daniel & Mary
MCGRATH, Ann; bn. Feb 24, 1793; bpt. Mar 25, 1793; dau. of Michael & Ann
MCGRATH, Elizabeth; bn. Apr 27, 1800; bpt. Aug 1, 1800; dau. of Mary McGrath
MCGROGAN, Ann; bn. Nov 28, 1795; bpt. Jul 11, 1796; dau. of Patrick & Charlotte
MCGUIRE, Henry; bn. Jun 19, 1788; bpt. Oct 6, 1790; son of Thomas & Mary
MCGUIRE, Thomas; bpt. Mar 22, 1787; 8 months; sps. Thomas Hillen & Katy Logue
MCGUIRE, Thomas Long; bn. Dec 15, 1782; bpt. Dec 29, 1782; sps. James Conner & Eleanor Walsh
MCHENRY, Dennis; bn. Oct 18, 1800; bpt. Oct 21, 1800; son of Dennis & Mary
MCHENRY, Grace; bn. Aug 6, 1795; bpt. Aug 12, 1795; dau. of Dennis & Mary
MCHENRY, Hugh; bn. Dec 12, 1798; bpt. Dec 14, 1798; son of Dennis & Mary
MCHENRY, Mary; bn. Dec 12, 1796; bpt. Dec 15, 1796; dau. of Dennis & Mary
MCHUGH, Margaret; bn. Jun 12, 1797; bpt. Dec 26, 1797; dau. of Cornelius & Bridget
MCHUGH, Margaret; bn. Jan 4, 1800; bpt. Feb 11, 1800; dau. of Thomas & Sibylla
MCHUGH, Mary; bpt. Aug 6, 1800; 5 months; dau. of Cornelius & Bridget
MCKEAN, Charles; bn. Oct 8, 1799; bpt. Oct 27, 1799; son of James & Elizabeth
MCKEE, Elizabeth; bn. Mar 9, 1789; bpt. Apr 12, 1789; sps. Elizabeth Fitzgerald
MCKENNA, David; bn. Feb 23, 1793; bpt. Mar 17, 1793; son of James & Rosanna
MCKENNA, James; bn. Aug 31, 1799; bpt. Sep 29, 1799; son of James & Jane
MCKINLEY, John; bn. Jun 27, 1797; bpt. Jun 29, 1797; son of Cornelius & Mary

BAPTISMS

MCKINLEY, Margaret; bn. Nov 17, 1795; bpt. Nov 19, 1795; dau. of Neale & Margaret
MCKINLEY, Mary; bn. Apr 9, 1799; bpt. Apr 14, 1799; dau. of Cornelius & Margaret
MCLANE, William; bn. Sep 16, 1799; bpt. Sep 18, 1799; son of Roger & Eleanor
MCLAUGHLIN, Mary; bn. Jan 18, 1800; bpt. Feb 21, 1800; dau. of James & Mary
MCLEAN, Thomas; bn. Oct 30, 1797; bpt. Nov 2, 1797; son of Roger & Eleanor
MCMAHON, Catharine; bpt. Jul 28, 1799; dau. of Michael & Margaret
MCMAHON, John; bpt. Apr 30, 1786; 3 months; sps. John Terean & wife
MCMAHON, Michael; bn. Jan 13, 1797; bpt. Jan 14, 1797; son of James & Bridget
MCMAHON, Thomas; bn. Mar 1, 1797; bpt. Mar 14, 1797; son of Thomas & Mary
MCMANUS, Catharine; bn. May 26, 1798; bpt. May 28, 1798; dau. of Owen & Mary
MCMANUS, James; bn. May 16, 1800; bpt. May 25, 1800; son of Cormick & Margaret
MCMANUS, John; bn. Sep 11, 1799; bpt. Oct 2, 1799; son of Owen & Mary
MCMECHEN, John; bn. Sep 18, 1799; bpt. Oct 13, 1799; son of Margaret McMechen
MCMECHEN, Margaret; bn. Mar 17, 1798; bpt. Jan 21, 1799; dau. of James & Bridget
MCMURRY, Ann; bn. Dec 3, 1788; bpt. Sep 13, 1789; dau. of John & Catharine
MCNAMARA, Francis; bn. Jan 7, 1795; bpt. Jan 21, 1795; son of Thomas & Mary
MCNAMARA, Margaret; bn. Dec 26, 1797; bpt. Jan 14, 1798; dau. of Thomas & Mary
MCNAMARA, Mary; bn. Jun 14, 1793; bpt. Aug 18, 1793; dau. of Thomas & Mary O'Neill
MCNAMARA, Mary Ann; bn. Apr 6, 1796; bpt. May 16, 1796; dau. of Thomas & Mary
MCNAMARA, Thomas; bn. Dec 10, 1791; bpt. Aug 18, 1793; son of Thomas & Mary
MCNEWIS, Margaret; bn. Nov 23, 1800; bpt. Dec 8, 1800; dau. of Charles & Margaret
MCSHERRY, Catharine; bn. Feb 26, 1791; bpt. Mar 1, 1791; dau. of Patrick & Elizabeth
MCSHERRY, Rose; bn. Jul 3, 1788; bpt. Sep 12, 1788; sps. John Rogen & Elizabeth Watson
MEGY, Ann Rosalia; bn. Feb 18, 1796; bpt. Feb 19, 1796; dau. of John Peter Andrew & Mary Louisa LaPeire
MEGY, Margaret Rosalie Aimable; bn. Jan 24, 1797; bpt. Mar 19, 1797; dau. of John Peter Andrew & Mary Louise Lapeire
MEGY, Mary Lucia Virginia; bn. Dec 27, 1793; bpt. May 11, 1794; born at sea in sight of Cp. Henry; dau. of John Peter Andrew & Mary Louisa Lapeire of Port au Prince, St. Domingo
MEINS, Anne Maria; bn. Oct 17, 1798; bpt. Nov 4, 1798; dau. of Marcus & Catharine

BAPTISMS

MELLY, Mary; bn. Jun 3, 1798; bpt. Jul 26, 1798; dau. of John & Mary
MELON, Edward; bn. Mar 29, 1793; bpt. Oct 27, 1793; son of John & Elizabeth
MELONE, James; bn. Dec 24, 1797; bpt. Jan 20, 1799; son of Alexander & Mary
MELONY, John; bn. Mar 25, 1786; bpt. Oct 2, 1791; son of James & Polly
MELONY, Thomas; bn. Jul 6, 1800; bpt. Jul 17, 1800; son of James & Catharine
MELOY, Sally; bn. Nov 18, 1787; bpt. Nov 21, 1787; sps. Ann Pickett
MELY, Margaret; bn. Apr 15, 1797; bpt. Apr 18, 1797; dau. of John & Mary
MENICH, ; bn. Feb 10, 1790; bpt. Feb 28, 1790; of Baltazar & Barbara
(MERGIER), Elizabeth; bpt. Sep 8, 1793; 3 years old; dau. of Louisa, slave of Mrs. Mergier
MERRICK, James; bn. May 31, 1791; bpt. Jul 30, 1791; son of William & Catharine
MERRICK, Lewisa; bn. Oct 15, 1789; bpt. Nov 15, 1789; dau. of William & Catharine Dusman
MERRYGEN, Dennis; bpt. Nov 15, 1789; 2 months; son of John & Katy
MERY, Barbara; bn. Jun 28, 1798; bpt. Jul 29, 1798; dau. of Frederick & Eve
MERY, Jacob; bn. Jul 8, 1795; bpt. Jul 19, 1795; son of Fred & Eve
MERY, John; bn. Jul 8, 1795; bpt. Jul 19, 1795; son of Fred & Eve
MERY, Susanna; bn. Nov 9, 1796; bpt. May 7, 1797; dau. of Frederic & Eve
MEYERS, Mary; bn. Nov 28, 1794; bpt. Dec 7, 1794; dau. of Patrick & Ann
MEYERS, Nicholas; bpt. Mar 7, 1799; 4 months; son of Nicholas & Mary
MEYLER, John; bn. Jan 24, 1792; bpt. Oct 14, 1792; son of Christopher & Fanny
MICHEL, John Baptist; bn. Dec 18, 1795; bpt. Jan 8, 1796; son of Joseph & Sophia
MICHEL, John Peter; bn. Apr 5, 1783; bpt. Apr 7, 1783; sps. Lewis Roads & Mary Cecilia Ehrman
MICHEL, Joseph; bn. Nov 20, 1793; bpt. Dec 12, 1793; son of Joseph Andrew & Ann Henrietta Bonnet
MICHEL, Louisa Felicity; bn. Feb 7, 1800; bpt. Dec 26, 1800; dau. of Lazare & Adelaide
MICHEL, Mary; bn. May 31, 1789; bpt. Jun 23, 1789; dau. of Peter & Barbara
MICKS, James; bn. Feb 2, 1795; bpt. Feb 5, 1795; son of William & Lydia
MILBURN, Mary Susanna; bn. Sep 8, 1786; bpt. Jul 4, 1787; sps. Ann Wilson
(MILHAU), Louis Felix; bpt. Jan 6, 1800; 6 months; son of Susanne, slave of Mr. Milhau
MILHAU, Maria Louise Cecile; bn. Oct 24, 1799; bpt. Jan 6, 1800; dau. of Michael & Marie Pierre Josephine Elizabeth Justine Grenon

BAPTISMS

MILL, Anthony; bn. May 19, 1797; bpt. Oct 23, 1797; son of
    Margaret Mill
(MILLEAU), John Just; bpt. May 25, 1794; son of Therese, slave of
    Mrs. Milleau
MILLEN, William; bn. Mar 24, 1785; bpt. Apr 17, 1785; sps.
    Christopher Brien & Mary Catral
MILLER, Catharine; bn. Jun 1, 1791; bpt. Jun 2, 1791; dau. of
    Antony & Odilia
MILLER, Charles Joseph; bn. Mar 26, 1795; bpt. Apr 10, 1795; son
    of Henry & Ann
MILLER, Francis Anthony; bn. Sep 6, 1785; bpt. Sep 11, 1785; sps.
    Francis Foldweiler & Catharine Smith
MILLER, Henry; bpt. Jun 7, 1794; adult; son of John & Mary
MILLER, Jacob; bn. Nov 8, 1787; bpt. Nov 18, 1787; sps. Jacob
    Krauss & Dolly Krauss
MILLER, James; bn. Mar 13, 1787; bpt. Apr 8, 1787; sps. Michael
    Shreagh & Mary Cecil
MILLER, John; bn. Jun 13, 1784; bpt. Jun 20, 1784; sps. Nicholas
    Plichard & Elizabeth Sheargly
MILLER, John; bpt. Apr 17, 1800; son of Elizabeth Miller
MILLER, Joseph; bn. Jul 22, 1789; bpt. Jul 26, 1789; son of
    Antony & Adilia
MILLER, Peter; bn. Jun 14, 1797; bpt. Jul 9, 1797; son of Henry &
    Ann
MILLER, Sophia; bn. Jan 29, 1800; bpt. Jun 14, 1800; dau. of
    Christian & Margaret
MILTON, Ruth; bpt. Nov 19, 1796; adult
(MIMIE), Ann Louisa; bpt. Sep 25, 1796; dau. of Lulimme, slave of
    Mrs. Mimie
(MIMIE), George; bpt. May 27, 1798; 4 months; son of Teline,
    slave of Mlle. Mimie
(MIMIE), Mary; bpt. May 14, 1797; 2 months; dau. of Victoire,
    slave of Mademoiselle Mimie
(MIMY), Rosette; bpt. Jul 3, 1796; 6 months; dau. of Teresa,
    slave of Miss Mimy
MINE, Elizabeth; bn. Jul 23, 1795; bpt. Jul 29, 1795; dau. of
    Mark & Catharine
MINSON, Gabriel; bn. Jul 16, 1796; bpt. Jul 25, 1796; son of
    Gabriel & Margaret
(MIOU), Mary; bpt. Sep 4, 1796; 3 months; dau. of Rose, slave of
    Mr. Miou
MITCHEL, Mary; bn. Apr 2, 1785; bpt. Apr 17, 1785; sps. Jeremia
    Mahan & Mary McDonnel
MITCHELL, Elizabeth; bn. Feb 19, 1798; bpt. Apr 29, 1798; dau. of
    Francis J. & Sarah
MITHAU, John Francis Gregory Tiburie; bn. Aug 17, 1796; bpt. Oct
    7, 1796; son of Michael & Mary Elizabeth Grenon
MODEST, Mary; bn. Sep 13, 1786; bpt. Sep 16, 1786; sps. Charles
    Bernard & Margaret Wells
(MOGY), Mary Louisa; bpt. Mar 12, 1797; 3 months; dau. of Mary,
    slave of Mr. Mogy
(MOISSONNIER), Mary Eliza; bpt. Oct 13, 1799; dau. of Eugenie,
    slave of Mr. Moissonnier
MOLIER, Henry; bn. Jun 18, 1798; bpt. Jul 18, 1799; son of Henry
    & Elizabeth

BAPTISMS

MOLIER, Joachime; bn. Jan 6, 1800; bpt. Aug 16, 1800; dau. of
    Henry & Elizabeth Lanville
(MOLIER), Joseph; bpt. Jun 2, 1799; 1 year, 4 months old; son of
    Marie, slave of Mr. Molier
MOLIER, Martha; bn. Oct 11, 1796; bpt. Nov 26, 1796; dau. of
    Henry & Elizabeth Lanille
(MOLIER), Peter; bpt. Mar 24, 1799; 2 months; son of Judith,
    slave of Mr. Molier
MOLONEY, Margaret; bn. Feb 7, 1796; bpt. Apr 10, 1796; dau. of
    James & Eve
MOLONEY, Michael; bn. Jan 7, 1794; bpt. Apr 27, 1794; son of
    James & Hebe
MOLOWNY, John; bn. Nov 22, 1798; bpt. Nov 28, 1798; son of Judith
    Molowny
MONET, Mary Louisa Martha Antoinette; bn. Nov 10, 1797; bpt. Jun
    11, 1798; dau. of Mathias & Mary Louise Mallet
MONIER, Ann; bn. Jul 7, 1797; bpt. Jul 9, 1797; dau. of Eleazer &
    Mary
(MONSIGNIAC), John Baptist; bpt. Mar 26, 1797; 6 weeks; son of
    Dauphine, slave of Monsigniac
MOODY, William; bn. Jan 15, 1800; bpt. Feb 17, 1800; son of
    William & Elizabeth
MOONEY, John; bn. Apr 5, 1799; bpt. Apr 28, 1799; son of William
    & Mary
(MOORE), Eliza; bn. Oct 6, 1798; bpt. Oct 20, 1799; dau. of
    Simon, slave of Dr. Moore & Sarah, slave of Miss Levy
MOORE, Elizabeth; bpt. Aug 18, 1799; 6 months; dau. of Matthew &
    --
(MOORE), George; bn. Feb 15, 1800; bpt. May 4, 1800; son of
    Milly, slave of Mary Ann Moore
MOORE, John; bn. Oct 6, 1798; bpt. Oct 21, 1798; son of John &
    Catharine
MOORE, Mary Ann; bn. Jul 24, 1800; bpt. Nov 2, 1800; dau. of
    Ignatius & Mary Ann
MOORE, Matthew; bn. Mar 18, 1794; bpt. Nov 6, 1794; son of
    Patrick & Ann
MOORE, William; bn. Oct 15, 1795; bpt. Nov 3, 1795; son of
    Ignatius & Mary Ann
MORAN, Thomas; bpt. Dec 1, 1799; 3 weeks; son of Paul & Priscilla
MOREHEAD, James; bn. Dec 12, 1798; bpt. Jan 11, 1799; son of
    Thomas & Sarah
(MOREL), Augustin; bn. Sep 20, 1798; bpt. Sep 23, 1798; son of
    Belise, slave of Mr. Morel
(MOREL), John Charles; bpt. Feb 10, 1799; 3 months; son of
    Hortense, slave of Mr. Morel
(MOREL), Lewis Claudius; bpt. May 16, 1797; 7 months; son of Mary
    Louisa, slave of Mrs. Morel
(MOREL), Mary; bpt. Aug 21, 1796; 2 months; dau. of Hortensia,
    slave of Mrs. Morel
(MOREL), Mary Antoinette; bpt. May 16, 1797; 2 1/2 months; dau.
    of Mary Claudine, slave of Mrs. Morel
MOREN, ; bn. Nov 30, 1791; bpt. Mar 24, 1792; of John & Eleanor
MOREN, Fanny; bn. Feb 1, 1784; bpt. Apr 4, 1784; sps. James Green
MOREN, Mary; bn. Feb 1, 1784; bpt. Apr 4, 1784; sps. James Green

BAPTISMS

MOREN, Patrick; bn. Sep 8, 1788; bpt. Sep 14, 1788; sps. Anthony Cunningham

MORENCI, Joseph; bn. Dec 18, 1785; bpt. Jul 3, 1786; sps. Lewis Byrand & Nancy Pluchand

MORGAN, Mary; bn. Oct 14, 1799; bpt. Nov 11, 1799; dau. of Philip & Rosanna

MORGAN, Nancy; bpt. Jun 6, 1786; 8 weeks; sps. Hugh Bahon & Katy Staab

(MORIN), Mary Frances; bn. Apr 3, 1798; bpt. Apr 24, 1798; dau. of Mary Joseph, slave of Mr. Morin

MORRIS, Gerard; bn. Aug 22, 1794; bpt. Aug 31, 1794

MORRISON, Ann; bn. Sep 25, 1798; bpt. Oct 28, 1798; dau. of Patrick & Priscilla

MORRISON, James; bpt. Sep 25, 1791; 5 weeks; son of James & Elizabeth

MORRISON, Lydia; bn. Apr 21, 1797; bpt. May 21, 1797; dau. of Patrick & Priscilla

MORRISON, Margaret; bn. Aug 22, 1800; bpt. Nov 2, 1800; dau. of Patrick & Priscilla

MOUCHET, Mary Frances; bn. Oct 27, 1796; bpt. Nov 9, 1796; dau. of Henry & Mary Jane Calmard of Cp. Francais

MOUCHET, Mary Helen Frances; bn. Apr 20, 1798; bpt. Apr 30, 1799; dau. of Henry & Mary Jane Calmard

(MOUCHET), Peter; bpt. Nov 9, 1796; 11 months; son of Desiree, slave of Mr. Mouchet

MOULIN, John Baptist; bn. May 23, 1795; bpt. Jul 30, 1795; son of John Baptist & Louise Guerchois of Normandy

MOUREL, Peter Joseph; bn. May 28, 1794; bpt. Jul 17, 1794; son of Joseph & Josephine Lerot

MOURIES, Catharine Antoinette; bn. Oct 10, 1796; bpt. Nov 8, 1796; dau. of J. & Mathurine Frances

MOURIES, Josphina Mary; bn. Mar 4, 1795; bpt. Apr 22, 1795; dau. of Joseph & Frances

MOURIES, Rene; bn. Sep 18, 1793; bpt. Oct 19, 1793; son of Antoine & Petronille Domergue

MUININGH, George William; bn. Jan 1, 1788; bpt. Feb 8, 1789; sps. George Knoephlier

MULLAN, Elizabeth; bn. Feb 25, 1792; bpt. Mar 18, 1792; dau. of Patrick & Sarah

MULLAN, Jonathan; bn. Nov 2, 1797; bpt. Nov 27, 1797; son of Patrick & Sarah

MULLAN, Margaret; bn. Mar 19, 1800; bpt. Apr 6, 1800; dau. of Henry & Susan

MULLAN, Maria; bn. Jul 11, 1793; bpt. Aug 11, 1793; dau. of Patrick & Sarah

MULLAN, Peter; bpt. Sep 17, 1797; 5 weeks; born at sea; son of Owen & Honor

MULLAN, Sarah Cassia; bn. Aug 7, 1795; bpt. Sep 6, 1795; dau. of Patrick & Sarah

MULLAN, William; bn. Oct 26, 1783; bpt. Apr 4, 1784; son of Patrick & Sarah; sps. Henry Tomalty & Elizabeth Tomalty

MULLANPHY, Eliza; bn. Nov 14, 1792; bpt. Dec 2, 1792

MULLANPHY, Mary; bn. Oct 11, 1795; bpt. Oct 27, 1795; dau. of John & Elizabeth

BAPTISMS

MULLEN, Catharine; bn. May 28, 1785; bpt. Jul 3, 1785; sps. Andrew Green & Mary Green
MULLEN, John; bn. Feb 10, 1790; bpt. Feb 21, 1790; son of Patrick & Sara
MULLEN, Mary; bn. Aug 4, 1787; bpt. Sep 2, 1787; sps. Thomas Hillen & ---
MUNSEL, Maria; bn. Sep 5, 1798; bpt. Sep 23, 1798; dau. of Gabriel & Maria
MURPHY, Bridget; bn. Jul 30, 1793; bpt. Aug 4, 1793; dau. of James & Christina
MURPHY, Bridget; bpt. Sep 24, 1799; dau. of Nelly Murphy
MURPHY, Christina; bn. Oct 20, 1796; bpt. Oct 20, 1796; dau. of James & Christina
MURPHY, Daniel; bn. Nov 28, 1792; bpt. Aug 9, 1795; son of Jeremiah & Ann
MURPHY, Elizabeth; bn. Jan 22, 1790; bpt. Feb 7, 1790; dau. of Patrick & Eleanor
MURPHY, Henry; bpt. Feb 24, 1795; 2 months; son of Jeremiah & Ann
MURPHY, James; bpt. Sep 1, 1799; 1 week; son of James & Christina
MURPHY, John Robert; bn. Jun 6, 1794; bpt. Jul 27, 1794; son of Patric & Susanna
MURPHY, Mary; bn. Dec ?, 1791; bpt. Apr 10, 1792; dau. of Patrick & Susanna
MURPHY, Mary Magdalen; bn. Mar 5, 1792; bpt. Apr 22, 1792; dau. of James & Christina
MURPHY, Mary; bn. Mar 15, 1795; bpt. Mar 18, 1795; dau. of James & Christina
MURPHY, Mary; bpt. Oct 7, 1797; dau. of John & Joanna, both deceased; sps. Anthony Foulks & Bridget Lynch
MURPHY, Mary; bn. Apr 8, 1798; bpt. Oct 8, 1798; dau. of William & Mary
MURPHY, Philip James; bn. May 11, 1788; bpt. Jun 6, 1788; sps. Susanna Burgess
MURRAY, Ann; bn. May 10, 1795; bpt. Jul 5, 1795; dau. of James & Mary
MURRAY, Catharine; bn. Jul 22, 1797; bpt. Aug 7, 1797; dau. of James & Mary
MURRAY, Cornelius; bn. Apr 7, 1798; bpt. Apr 22, 1798; son of John & Elizabeth
MURRAY, John; bn. Apr 7, 1798; bpt. Jun 17, 1798; son of John & Elizabeth
MURRAY, Joseph; bn. Dec 16, 1799; bpt. Apr 21, 1800; son of James & Mary
MURRAY, Mary Ann; bn. Jul 22, 1800; bpt. Aug 3, 1800; dau. of Charles & Catharine
MURRY, Jane; bn. Jan 15, 1793; bpt. Feb 24, 1793; dau. of James & ---
MURRY, Julia; bn. Sep 13, 1785; bpt. Sep 20, 1785; sps. George Landry & Peggy Hermange
MYERS, Lucy; bn. Jul 19, 1797; bpt. Aug 6, 1797; dau. of Joseph & Catharine
MYERS, Maria; bn. Jun 21, 1799; bpt. Nov 28, 1799; dau. of Joseph & Catharine
MYERS, Michael; bn. Mar 30, 1796; bpt. Jul 17, 1796; son of John & Elizabeth

BAPTISMS

MYLAR, James; bn. Dec ?, 1795; bpt. Jun 26, 1796; son of
    Christopher & Frances
MYLER, Mary; bn. Oct 27, 1793; bpt. Dec 29, 1793; dau. of
    Christopher & Anne
NAGLE, James; bn. Apr 7, 1798; bpt. May 27, 1798; son of Edward &
    Margaret
(NAGOT), Milly; bn. Sep 9, 1796; bpt. Sep 11, 1796; dau. of
    Elizabeth, slave of Rev. Mr. Nagot
NAILER, George; bpt. May 6, 1787; 8 1/2 months; sps. Jeremia
    Conner & Rose Kelly
NANAN, Catharine; bn. Feb 18, 1798; bpt. Mar 18, 1798; dau. of
    Edward & Mary
(NANTE), Elizabeth; bpt. Sep 19, 1793; about 8 years old; slave
    of Mrs. Nante
NARY, Louisa; bn. Apr 6, 1791; bpt. Feb 6, 1792; dau. of Peter &
    Mary
NASH, Latitia; bpt. Oct 12, 1790; 6 weeks old; dau. of John & Ann
(NAU), Ann; bpt. May 18, 1795; 18 months; dau. of Catharine,
    slave of Mr. Nau
NAU, Jeanne Julie; bn. Sep 23, 1796; bpt. Aug 16, 1797; dau. of
    John Baptist & Mary Louisa Beyrac
(NAU), Mary Louisa; bpt. May 18, 1795; 14 years old; nat. of
    Africa; slave of Mr. Nau of St. Domingo
NAU, Rene Pierre Clement; bn. Mar 24, 1794; bpt. May 1, 1794; son
    of John Baptist & Mary Louise Beyrac
NEALE, Catharine; bn. Feb 26, 1783; bpt. Apr 6, 1783; sps. John
    Teigler & Judith Mitchel
NEALE, Elizabeth; bn. May 7, 1800; bpt. May 18, 1800; dau. of
    Edward & Elizabeth
NEALE, Fanny; bn. Jun 13, 1786; bpt. Oct 22, 1786; sps. Jacob
    Laurence & Mary Matthews
NEALE, Henrietta; bn. Apr 20, 1791; bpt. Jun 19, 1791; dau. of
    --- & Peggy Neale
NEALE, Henry; bpt. Sep 17, 1799; 6 weeks; son of Nancy Neale
NEALE, Jane Catharine; bn. Mar 24, 1798; bpt. Apr 5, 1798; dau.
    of Edward & Elizabeth
NEALE, Jeremia; bn. Sep 2, 1784; bpt. May 16, 1785; sps. Peter
    Litzmyer & wife
NEALE, John; bpt. Nov 1, 1790; about 13 years old; son of Doctor
    Neale & ---
NEALE, William Thompson; bn. Nov 10, 1796; bpt. Dec 13, 1796; son
    of Edward & Elizabeth
NEARY, Peter; bn. Aug 9, 1792; bpt. Sep 2, 1792; son of Peter &
    Mary; sps. George Rozensteel, Jr. & Margaret Poiet
NEGOTIANT, Jean Francois Joseph, Jacques; bn. Apr 29, 1793; bpt.
    Oct 22, 1793; son of Jean Baille & Marie Magdaline Arnal
    DeRoche
NEIGHBORS, John Lloyd; bn. Mar 25, 1795; bpt. Apr 12, 1795; son
    of Henry & Ann
NEIGHBOUR, James Robert; bn. Mar 17, 1797; bpt. Apr 21, 1797; son
    of Henry & Ann
NEIGHBOURS, Sarah; bn. Jul 7, 1799; bpt. Aug 12, 1799; dau. of
    Henry & Ann
NEIL, John; bn. Dec 27, 1795; bpt. Jan 5, 1796; son of Mary Neil

BAPTISMS

NEISSON, Maria Ann Desire Sophie; bn. May 24, 1785; bpt. May 25, 1785; dau. of Joseph & Martha LaCage
NELSON, William; bn. Mar 12, 1786; bpt. Mar 26, 1786; sps. William Stone & Mary Deale
NESBIT, Ann; bpt. Mar 2, 1800; 5 years old; dau. of William & Helen, free Negroes
NEUCOMER, Henry; bn. Mar 28, 1798; bpt. Apr 29, 1798; son of John & Margaret
NEUHOF, George Frederic; bpt. Mar 25, 1794; son of Nicholas & Mary Eve
NEUHOFF, Jacob; bn. Sep 16, 1795; bpt. Oct 30, 1795; son of Nicholas & Eve
NEUHOFF, Mary Ann; bn. Jul 30, 1798; bpt. Oct 12, 1798; dau. of Nicholas & Eve
NEWBURY, Catharine; bn. Feb 17, 1799; bpt. Mar 28, 1799; dau. of John & Mary
NEWCOMER, Mary; bn. Dec 29, 1799; bpt. Feb 18, 1800; dau. of John & Margaret
NEWLAN, John; bn. Dec 19, 1794; bpt. Mar 1, 1795; son of Edward & Grace
NEWNHAM, James; bn. Jun 15, 1793; bpt. Jun 26, 1793; son of Edward & Grace
(NEYRON), Josephina; bn. Aug 10, 1795; bpt. Sep 9, 1795; dau. of Solange, slave of Madam Neyron of St. Domingo & August
NICHOLSON, Catharine; bpt. Oct 11, 1789; 8 weeks; dau. of William & Joanna
NICHOLSON, Margaret; bn. Aug 3, 1783; bpt. Aug 10, 1783; sps. George M. C. & Honor Matters
NICHOLSON, William; bpt. Dec 16, 1787; 4 months; sps. James Dealy & Eleanor Lynch
NOCH, Thomas; bn. Mar 3, 1795; bpt. Apr 12, 1795; son of William & Brigitte
(NOGERIES), John Noel; bpt. Apr 26, 1794
NOLEY, John; bn. Aug 17, 1796; bpt. Aug 1, 1797; Mulatto; son of Caroline Noley
NOONAN, James; bn. Mar 29, 1799; bpt. Mar 31, 1799; son of Patrick & Judith
NOONAN, Margaret; bn. Aug 13, 1799; bpt. Sep 8, 1799; dau. of Edward & Mary
NORRIS, Lucy Ann; bn. Dec 7, 1799; bpt. Apr 7, 1800; dau. of Joseph & Ann
NOUVEL, Melonie; bn. Feb 5, 1796; bpt. May 15, 1796; dau. of Peter John & Mary Ann Prodeau
NOUVEL, Michael; bn. Aug 26, 1794; bpt. Sep 21, 1794; son of Peter John & Ann
NOUVELLE, Margaret; bn. Mar 8, 1783; bpt. Mar 9, 1783; sps. Peter Blossom & Margaret Gold
NOUVELLE, Peter; bn. Apr 1, 1786; bpt. Apr 10, 1786; sps. John Vitry & Mary Purry
NOWLAN, Mary; bn. Jun 13, 1793; bpt. Sep 1, 1793; dau. of William & Eleanor
NOWLAND, John; bn. Feb 25, 1795; bpt. Mar 6, 1796; son of William & Eleanor
NOWLAND, Matilda; bn. Dec 7, 1796; bpt. Aug 1, 1797; dau. of James & Honor

BAPTISMS

NOWLAND, William; bn. Mar 21, 1794; bpt. Aug 4, 1796; son of
   James & Honor
NOWNEN, Michael; bpt. Jul 11, 1790; 6 weeks; son of Edward & ---
NUCCOMER, Sarah; bn. Feb 6, 1794; bpt. Feb 7, 1794; dau. of John
   & Margaret
NUECOMER, John Fowler; bn. Jan 22, 1796; bpt. Feb 13, 1796; son
   of John & Margaret
NURSER, Catharine; bn. Jul 10, 1791; bpt. Jul 12, 1791; dau. of
   Sebastian & Barbara
NURSER, George; bn. Oct 15, 1788; bpt. Oct 19, 1788; sps. Jacob
   Weiman & Mary Duffy
NURSER, Jacob; bn. Feb 1, 1787; bpt. Feb 2, 1787; sps. Jacob
   Nurser & Elizabeth
NURSER, Jacob; bn. Feb 18, 1790; bpt. Feb 21, 1790; son of Jacob
   & Elizabeth
NURSER, John; bn. Apr 15, 1786; bpt. Apr 23, 1786; sps. John
   Walter & Peggy Dieffedolf
NURSER, Joseph; bn. Nov 1, 1793; bpt. Nov 3, 1793; son of
   Sebastian & Barbara
NURSER, Mary; bn. Jul 15, 1790; bpt. Jul 18, 1790; dau. of
   Sebastian & Barbara
NUSSEAR, Jesse; bn. Dec 30, 1795; bpt. Jan 2, 1796; son of
   Sebastian & Barbara
NUSSEAR, Mary; bn. Apr 8, 1799; bpt. Apr 14, 1799; dau. of
   Sebastian & Barbara
O'BRIAN, William; bn. Jul 21, 1794; bpt. Aug 17, 1794; son of
   Michael & Margaret
O'BRIEN, Ann; bn. Mar 5, 1795; bpt. Mar 17, 1795; dau. of Charles
   & Martha
O'BRIEN, Ann; bn. Apr 27, 1797; bpt. May 25, 1797; dau. of
   Michael & Dorothy
O'BRIEN, Catharine; bn. Feb 15, 1796; bpt. Apr 10, 1797; dau. of
   John & Hannah
O'BRIEN, Charles Henry; bpt. Oct 9, 1800; son of Charles & Martha
O'BRIEN, Eleanor; bpt. Oct 3, 1790; 6 years old; dau. of Daniel &
   Mary
O'BRIEN, Elizabeth; bn. Dec 30, 1796; bpt. Jan 15, 1797; dau. of
   Charles & Martha
O'BRIEN, Frances; bn. Mar 14, 1799; bpt. Apr 21, 1799; dau. of
   Charles & Martha
O'BRIEN, John; bn. May 25, 1792; bpt. Jun 14, 1792; son of James
   & Dorothy
O'BRIEN, John; bn. Aug 12, 1794; bpt. Sep 25, 1794; son of John &
   Hannah
(O'BRIEN), John; bpt. Apr 9, 1798; son of Rebecca, slave of
   Charles O'Brien
O'BRIEN, Joseph; bn. May 2, 1799; bpt. May 20, 1799; son of
   Michael & Margaret
O'BRIEN, Mary; bn. Oct 29, 1797; bpt. Nov 10, 1797; dau. of
   Michael & Margaret
O'BRIEN, Michael; bn. Jun 10, 1796; bpt. Jun 19, 1796; son of
   Michael & Margaret
(O'BRIEN), Peter; bn. Oct 27, 1799; bpt. Nov 24, 1799; Mulatto;
   son of Rebecca, slave of Charles O'Brien

BAPTISMS

(O'BRIEN), Rosetta; bpt. Sep 1, 1793; 4 months; dau. of Rachel, slave of Mr. Charles O'Brien
O'BRIEN, William; bn. Jul 3, 1785; bpt. Jul 7, 1785; sps. John Hegthrop & Sara Boyde
O'BRIEN, William; bn. Apr 1, 1795; bpt. Nov 30, 1795; son of Margaret O'Brien
O'BRIENNE, James; bn. Nov 4, 1794; bpt. Dec 28, 1794; son of James & Dorothee
O'CONNOR, Margaret; bn. Jan 16, 1799; bpt. Mar 31, 1799; dau. of Thomas & Mary
O'CONNOR, Susanna; bn. Mar 10, 1799; bpt. Mar 13, 1799; dau. of Michael & Catharine
O'DONOVAN, John; bn. Aug 22, 1796; bpt. Sep 15, 1796; son of Bartholomew & Sarah
O'HAGAN, Sarah; bn. Dec 29, 1793; bpt. Jan 5, 1794; dau. of Charles & Sarah
O'HARA, Eleanor; bn. Aug 7, 1797; bpt. Aug 22, 1797; dau. of Matthew & Mary
O'HARA, John; bn. Aug 18, 1795; bpt. Aug 23, 1795; son of Matthew & Mary
O'KEEFFE, Cornelius; bn. Aug 12, 1796; bpt. Aug 15, 1796; son of Patrick & Mary O'Keeffe
O'KIEF, Mary; bn. Sep 5, 1797; bpt. Aug 9, 1798; dau. of Patrick & Mary
O'MARA, William; bn. Dec 31, 1797; bpt. Mar 20, 1798; son of Patric & Villany
O'NEALE, Constantine Benjamin Francis; bn. Mar 1, 1800; bpt. Apr 6, 1800; son of Henry & Elizabeth Eleanor
O'NEALE, Joseph; bn. Feb 1, 1793; bpt. Feb 24, 1793; son of William & Mary
O'NEALE, Mary; bn. Mar 2, 1786; bpt. Mar 16, 1787; sps. John German & Mary Ann Chaplain
O'NEILL, Bernard; bn. Apr 17, 1798; bpt. Apr 27, 1798; son of Bernard & Margaret
O'NEILL, Eleanor; bn. Jan 10, 1797; bpt. Feb 19, 1797; dau. of Bernard & Margaret
O'NEILL, Elizabeth; bpt. Apr 4, 1795; 16 months; dau. of John & Elizabeth
O'NEILL, Elizabeth Eleanor; bpt. Jan 31, 1800; 19 years old;
O'NEILL, James Mansfield; bn. Nov 17, 1800; bpt. Nov 19, 1800; son of Daniel & Prudence
O'NEILL, Jane; bn. Nov 9, 1790; bpt. Jul 28, 1793; dau. of John & Alice
O'NEILL, John; bn. Jun 12, 1787; bpt. Jul 28, 1793; son of John & Alice
O'NEILL, John; bn. Apr 29, 1795; bpt. Aug 15, 1795; son of John & Mary
(O'NEILL), Maria; bn. Jan 23, 1799; bpt. Feb 19, 1799; dau. of Grace, slave of Capt. O'Neill
O'NEILL, Mary; bn. May 31, 1789; bpt. Jul 28, 1793; dau. of John & Alice
(O'NEILL), Mary; bpt. Jan 4, 1799; 13 years old; slave of Capt. O'Neill
O'NEILL, Mary Ann; bn. Jan 12, 1800; bpt. Jan 12, 1800; dau. of Felix & Rosanna

BAPTISMS

O'NEILL, Susanna; bn. Nov 17, 1800; bpt. Nov 19, 1800; dau. of
    Daniel & Prudence
O'RAGAN, Michael; bpt. May 26, 1799; 20 days; son of Michael &
    Mary O'Brien
O'ROURKE, Ann; bn. May 4, 1792; bpt. Jun 30, 1794; born in
    Nantes, France; dau. of Patrick & Mary Angelica Renee de
    Deteaux
(O'ROURKE), William; bn. Jun 24, 1797; bpt. Jul 27, 1797; son of
    Lucy, Mulatto slave of Mr. O'Rourke
OATS, Sophia; bn. Oct 24, 1795; bpt. Jan 21, 1796; dau. of
    William & Mary, both non-Catholic
OCOIN, Lewis; bn. Sep 22, 1784; bpt. Sep 17, 1785; sps. Joseph
    Fougue & Mrs. Gutterau
ODOIN, Joseph Andre; bn. Mar 25, 1788; bpt. Aug 3, 1788; sps.
    Andre Simon & Joseph Landry
OFFERT, Charles; bn. Oct 13, 1788; bpt. Oct 19, 1788; sps. James
    Power & Mary Wedge
OFFERT, Sara; bn. May 28, 1791; bpt. Jun 8, 1791; dau. of Charles
    & Rosy
(OLIVER), Ann; bpt. Jun 9, 1793; adult
OPHOLT, Samuel; bn. Dec 28, 1797; bpt. Jan 14, 1798; son of
    Charles & Rose
ORBAN, George Henry; bn. Jan 9, 1794; bpt. Jan 26, 1794; son of
    Henry & Catharine
ORBAN, John; bn. Apr 5, 1789; bpt. Apr 12, 1789; sps. John Hook &
    Elizabeth Clemens
ORBAN, Mary; bn. Aug 2, 1792; bpt. Aug 12, 1792; dau. of Henry &
    Katy
ORBAN, Sophia; bn. Apr 21, 1790; bpt. May 9, 1790; dau. of Henry
    & Catharine
ORMAN, Louise; bn. Jul 24, 1798; bpt. Oct 27, 1799; dau. of John
    & Margaret
ORMSBY, Unity; bpt. Jul 13, 1798; about 15 years
OTTOWAY, Nicholas; bn. Oct 29, 1785; bpt. May 7, 1786; sps. James
    Wilson & Fanny Martin
OTTOWAY, Samuel; bn. Nov 6, 1777; bpt. May 7, 1786; sps. James &
    Martha O'Brien
OTWA, Victoire Julia; bn. Mar 25, 1791; bpt. Nov 7, 1791; dau. of
    Lewis & Julia
OZA, Stephen; bn. Oct 4, 1796; bpt. Jun 11, 1797; son of Ann Mary
    Oza of Martinico
PAGEZ, Theodore Lewis Martin; bn. May 29, 1797; bpt. Jul 9, 1797;
    son of John Baptist & Mary
(PALLON), Mary Peter; bn. Jul ?, 1795; bpt. Sep 23, 1795; dau. of
    Mary Lewis, Mulatress, slave of Mr. Pallon of St. Domingo
PAOLI, Maria Philippina; bn. Oct 23, 1798; bpt. Oct 28, 1798;
    dau. of John & Joanna
PART, Dorothy; bn. May 9, 1788; bpt. May 25, 1788; sps. Joseph
    Laurence & Dorothy Laurence
(PARTRIDGE), Clarissa; bpt. Mar 12, 1795; 7 1/2 years old; slave
    of John Partridge
PARTRIDGE, Elizabeth Brown; bn. Aug 18, 1800; bpt. Sep 7, 1800;
    dau. of Job & --
PASCAULT, Aime' John; bn. Jun 6, 1793; bpt. Jun 30, 1793; dau. of
    Lewis & Mary

BAPTISMS

PASCAULT, Charles Lewis; bn. Sep 1, 1790; bpt. Sep 12, 1790; son
  of Lewis & Mary
PASCAULT, Eleanora C.; bn. Jun 30, 1799; bpt. Sep 25, 1799; dau.
  of Lewis & Magdalen
PASCAULT, Joseph Nicholas; bn. Aug 31, 1787; bpt. Sep 17, 1787;
  sps. Joseph Bonnehose
(PASCAULT), Maria; bn. May 17, 1796; bpt. Jun 19, 1796; dau. of
  Betsy, slave of Mr. Lewis Pascault
PASCAULT, Thomas Felix; bn. Feb 22, 1795; bpt. Mar 10, 1795; son
  of Lewis & Mary Ann
PASCAULT, William Peter; bn. Dec 29, 1796; bpt. Mar 12, 1797; son
  of Lewis & Mary Magdalen
PASEAULT, Euphrasia Eliza; bn. Apr 8, 1786; bpt. May 1, 1786;
  sps. LeChevalier D'Amour & Euphrasia DeMonlos
PATERSON, Mary; bpt. Sep 18, 1789; 5 weeks; dau. of James & Joanna
PATERSON, Mary Ann; bpt. Sep 18, 1789; 8 weeks; dau. of William &
  Ann
PAULAIN, John; bn. Feb 2, 1794; bpt. Aug 8, 1794; son of Anne
  Paulain, a French woman who left her child with the nurse
PAULI, Daniel; bn. Mar 1, 1800; bpt. Mar 4, 1800; son of John &
  Joanna
PAYETTE, John; bn. Aug 27, 1791; bpt. Feb 6, 1792; son of John
  Baptist & Margaret; sps. Richard Bambaut & Fanny Dashiel
PEARSON, Joseph; bn. Oct 28, 1799; bpt. Nov 9, 1799; son of
  Daniel & Sarah
PECK, Barbara; bn. Aug 27, 1791; bpt. Sep 4, 1791; dau. of John &
  Eleanor Piper
PECK, John; bn. Mar 20, 1793; bpt. Mar 31, 1793; son of John &
  Eleanor Pifer
PECOTIERE, Anne Francois Brutres Gautier; bn. Jan 12, 1794; bpt.
  May 5, 1794; son of Germain Gautier & Mary Frances Maraine
PELAGE, Mary Jane; bpt. Oct 29, 1796; 9 years old; born in
  Plaisance, St. Domingo; Mulatto; dau. of Mary Clare
  Genevieve Pelage
PENDEGRASS, Catharine; bn. May 8, 1799; bpt. May 26, 1799; dau.
  of Robert & Ruth
PENDERGRAST, John; bn. Jan 29, 1798; bpt. Mar 6, 1798; son of
  Robert & Ruth
PERAD, John; bn. Aug 16, 1799; bpt. Oct 13, 1799; son of John &
  Catharine
PERIER, Elizabeth; bpt. Dec 17, 1800; dau. of Francis Firman &
  Mary Frances Berquier
PERIER, Francis Augustin; bn. Jul 11, 1797; bpt. May 26, 1798;
  son of Peter & Ann
PERIER, Mary Frances; bn. Jul 5, 1796; bpt. Oct 17, 1796; dau. of
  Peter & Mary Agnes
PERIER, Victor Marin; bn. Jul 11, 1797; bpt. Jan 13, 1798; son of
  Francois Firmin & Belle Marie Francoise Berquier
(PERIGAND), Mary Louisa; bpt. Jul 11, 1796; 6 months; dau. of
  Nannette, slave of Nelly Perigand
PERRIER, Peter Edward; bn. May 21, 1799; bpt. Mar 31, 1800; son
  of Peter & Ann
PERRY, John; bn. Jan 24, 1797; bpt. Feb 8, 1797; son of Martha
  Perry

BAPTISMS

PERTING, Ann; bn. Jan 17, 1798; bpt. Jan 28, 1798; dau. of Peter & Mary
PETERS, Joseph; bn. Oct 5, 1792; bpt. Apr 10, 1793; son of Henry & Catharine
PFIFER, Francis Anthony; bn. Apr 9, 1799; bpt. Jul 7, 1799; son of Nicholas & Mary
PFIFER, Julia; bn. Jun 3, 1793; bpt. Jun 30, 1793; dau. of John & Susanna
PHEIFER, Maria Odilia; bpt. Sep 5, 1790; 10 weeks; dau. of John & Susanna
(PHILIPPE), John Baptist; bpt. Apr 9, 1797; 1 month; son of Tempe, slave of Mrs. Philippe
PHILIPPIER, Mary Magdalen Tabitha; bn. Nov 27, 1798; bpt. Dec 3, 1798; dau. of Joseph & Esther
PHILIPS, Henry George; bn. Apr 15, 1794; bpt. May 25, 1794; son of Jacob & Mary
PHILIPS, John Andrew; bn. Feb 5, 1792; bpt. Mar 19, 1792; son of Jacob & Mary
PHILIPS, Margaret; bn. Jun 7, 1796; bpt. Jul 31, 1796; dau. of Jacob & Mary
PHILLIPPE, Lewis Gonzaga; bn. Apr 27, 1796; bpt. May 14, 1796; son of Stephen & Mary Frances
PIAMOSET, Charles Elias; bn. May 6, 1799; bpt. Jul 11, 1799; Mulatto; son of Ann Piamoset, free Mulatress
PICOT, Anna Henrietta; bn. Sep 28, 1792; bpt. Sep 12, 1793; dau. of Henry Francis Mary & Magdalen Charlotte Desiree Lunel
PICOT, Magdalene Emilia; bn. Aug 23, 1788; bpt. Jan 13, 1794; dau. of Henry Francis Mary & Magdalene Charlotte Desiree Lunel
PIEDMONT, Antoni Cheri; bn. Jul 1, 1791; bpt. Jun 23, 1794; son of Anna Piedmont, free Mulatress
PIEDMONT, Francis Frederick; bn. Dec 11, 1793; bpt. Jun 23, 1794; son of Anna Piedmont, free Mulatress
PIEDMONT, John; bn. May 20, 1797; bpt. Jun 24, 1797; son of Ann Piedmont of Cp. Francais
PIEMONT, Mary Magdalen; bn. Oct 29, 1795; bpt. Mar 27, 1796; dau. of Ann Piemont, Mulatress of St. Domingo
PIERCY, Ruth; bn. Dec 8, 1797; bpt. Jul 21, 1799; dau. of Daniel & Ruth
PILCH, Charlotte; bn. Nov 29, 1796; bpt. Oct 31, 1800; dau. of James & Elizabeth
PINDA, Magelaine; bpt. Nov 11, 1793; Negro; dau. of Laura, Mulatress
PISE, Peter Lewis; bn. Aug 10, 1799; bpt. Aug 24, 1799; son of Lewis of Turin & Margaret of Philadelphia
PLACIDE, Paul August; bn. Jun 8, 1799; bpt. Jul 3, 1799; son of Paul & Louisa
PLACIDE, Simon Henry; bn. Oct 24, 1800; bpt. Nov 30, 1800; son of Paul & Louisa
PLUM, John; bn. May 12, 1784; bpt. May 23, 1784; sps. John Harly & Betsey Beaver
PLUM, Peter; bn. Mar 11, 1786; bpt. Mar 12, 1786; sps. John & Mary Ehrman
PLUMMER, Ann; bn. Oct 13, 1789; bpt. Jun 5, 1791; dau. of John & Ann

BAPTISMS

PLUMMER, Eleanor; bn. Jul 12, 1784; bpt. Nov 13, 1785; sps. Priscilla Harrison
PLUMMER, John; bn. Mar 9, 1783; bpt. Mar 17, 1784; sps. Edward Digges & Margaret Brook
PLUMMER, Lewis; bn. Jan 26, 1785; bpt. Aug 5, 1787; son of John & Ann
PLUSHAND, Ann Lewis; bn. Oct 20, 1792; bpt. Nov 6, 1792; dau. of Nicholas & Ann Turin
POER, Thomas; bn. Mar 22, 1786; bpt. Jun 10, 1787; sps. Peter Leiner & Mary Duffy
(POIRIER), Francis Anthony; bpt. Jan 4, 1795; 12 years old; slave of Elizabeth Poirier
POLY, Henry Philips; bn. Jun 8, 1798; bpt. Aug 5, 1798; son of Jacob & Mary
POMPONEAU, Francis; bn. May 2, 1794; bpt. Sep 21, 1794; son of John & Mary Fiette
PONTBRUILLET, Teresa Augustina; bn. Sep 25, 1795; bpt. Jan 9, 1796; dau. of -- Robigny
PONTIER, Mary Frances; bn. Jul 6, 1796; bpt. Aug 29, 1796; dau. of Anthony, nat. of Alais in Languedoc & Mary Catharine Duplan of St. Domingo
PONTIER, Ursule; bn. Sep 15, 1799; bpt. Apr 16, 1800; dau. of Anthony & Mary Catharine Duplan; born in Port au Prince, St. Domingo
POOLE, Elizabeth; bn. Jul 12, 1800; bpt. Jul 16, 1800; dau. of Ann Poole
POOLI, Anna Christina; bn. Jun 15, 1797; bpt. Jun 18, 1797; dau. of John & Joanna
POOR, Mary; bn. Jun 14, 1794; bpt. Jun 29, 1794; dau. of Ned & Eleanor
PORE, William; bn. Mar 4, 1788; bpt. May 17, 1788; sps. Timothy Duffy & Ann Drake
PORTIER, Elizabeth; bn. Oct 8, 1795; bpt. Nov 3, 1795; dau. of Lewis & Catharine
(POUPET), John Baptist; bpt. Sep 8, 1793; Mulatto; son of Adelaide, slave of Mr. Poupet of Cape Francais
POWEL, George; bpt. Sep 5, 1786; 5 weeks; sps. Mary Hayes
POWER, Ann; bpt. Aug 30, 1789;
POWER, Ann; bn. Feb 29, 1796; bpt. Mar 13, 1796; dau. of James & Mary
POWER, Catharine; bn. Aug 9, 1787; bpt. Aug 17, 1788; sps. Daniel Foley & Elizabeth Jacobs
POWER, Catharine; bn. Sep 21, 1799; bpt. Oct 21, 1799; dau. of James & Mary
POWER, James; bn. Apr 15, 1795; bpt. May 17, 1795; son of Thomas & Sarah
POWER, James; bn. Feb 13, 1798; bpt. Mar 25, 1798; son of James & Mary
POWER, John; bn. Apr 5, 1790; bpt. May 23, 1790; son of Thomas & Sara
POWER, Joseph; bn. Oct 24, 1792; bpt. Nov 18, 1792; son of James & Mary
POWER, Mary; bn. Sep 28, 1785; bpt. Oct 2, 1785; sps. Moses Walsh & Nance Gochee

BAPTISMS

POWER, Mary; bn. Feb 18, 1793; bpt. Mar 10, 1793; dau. of John & Maria
POWER, Nancy; bpt. Jul 26, 1789; 4 months, 3 days; dau. of Patrick & Peggy
POWER, Peter; bn. Apr 8, 1798; bpt. May 6, 1798; son of Thomas & Sarah
POWER, Samuel; bn. Sep 25, 1791; bpt. Oct 1, 1791; son of James & Mary
POWER, Sarah; bn. Dec 29, 1792; bpt. Jan 27, 1793; dau. of Thomas & Sarah
POWER, Thomas; bpt. Sep 16, 1787; 6 weeks; sps. Daniel McCarty & Mary Celestin
POWER, Thomas; bn. Dec 19, 1790; bpt. Jul 10, 1791; son of Patrick & Peggy
POWER, Thomas; bn. Feb 29, 1796; bpt. Mar 13, 1796; son of James & Mary
(POWERS), Rose; bpt. Sep 19, 1789; about 7 years old; born in N. Carolina; slave of William Powers
PRENDGAST, Mary; bn. Aug 28, 1796; bpt. Sep 1, 1796; dau. of Robert & Ruth
PRESNEHAM, Elizabeth; bn. Jul 17, 1792; bpt. Aug 17, 1792; dau. of James & Eleanor
PRESTON, Anthony; bn. Jan 23, 1796; bpt. Feb 21, 1796; son of Thomas & Margaret
PRIESTMAN, Thomas; bn. Jan 3, 1795; bpt. Jan 11, 1795; son of Thomas & Margaret Maloney
PRINCESS, John James; bn. Jul 14, 1797; bpt. Dec 23, 1797; Mulatto; son of Elizabeth Princess, free French Negro
PROVOST, Julian Charles; bn. Jan 21, 1794; bpt. Mar 24, 1794; son of Julian & Magdalene Josphine Caroline dela Fayettier
PRUDHOMME, Marie Celestine Georgette; bn. Sep 1, 1793; bpt. Oct 19, 1793; dau. of Jean & Jeanne Etiennette Trehou
PURRY, John Joseph; bn. Jul 8, 1783; bpt. Aug 11, 1783; sps. John Levant & Genoveva Melanson
PURSLEY, Mary; bn. May 17, 1784; bpt. May 23, 1784; sps. Richard Daugherty & Eleanor Foy
(PURVIANE), Henrietta; bn. Oct 4, 1799; bpt. Nov 17, 1799; dau. of Nathaniel, Mulatto slave of Mr. Purviane & Juliet, Mulatto slave of Mr. Caton
QUEEN, Mary Angelique; bpt. Nov 30, 1800; 2 months; Mulatto; dau. of Fanny Queen
QUIGLEY, John; bn. Dec 4, 1795; bpt. Jan 11, 1796; son of William & Susanna
QUIN, Catharine; bpt. Oct 19, 1794; 1 month; dau. of David & Mary
QUINLAN, Elizabeth; bn. Oct 7, 1799; bpt. Oct 7, 1799; dau. of Patric & Mary
QUINLAN, Jane; bn. Aug 3, 1795; bpt. Aug 3, 1795; dau. of Edmond & Jane
QUINLAN, Stephen; bn. Dec 26, 1797; bpt. Jun 17, 1798; son of Edmund & Jane
QUINLIN, Ann; bn. Nov 15, 1788; bpt. Dec 25, 1788; sps. Reddy Barry & Susanna Burgess
QUINLIN, Marquis Patrick; bn. Aug 26, 1791; bpt. Sep 11, 1791; son of William & Mary

BAPTISMS

QUINLIN, Mary; bn. Oct 23, 1793; bpt. Dec 25, 1793; dau. of William & Mary
QUINLIN, Robert; bn. Mar 16, 1792; bpt. Nov 15, 1792; son of Edmond & Jane
QUINLIN, Sara; bn. Mar 5, 1791; bpt. Mar 5, 1791; dau. of Edmund & Jane
QUINN, John; bn. Aug 15, 1797; bpt. Aug 17, 1797; son of David & Mary
QULOHERY, John; bn. Oct 22, 1795; bpt. Nov 29, 1795; son of John & Catharine
RAGAN, John; bn. Nov 1, 1799; bpt. Mar 2, 1800; son of John & Ann
RAGAN, Joseph; bpt. Dec 6, 1799; 2 weeks; son of Hannah Ragan
RAGAN, Margaret; bn. Sep 11, 1798; bpt. Sep 30, 1798; dau. of Philip & Mary
RAGEN, Mary; bn. Dec 12, 1794; bpt. Dec 21, 1794; dau. of John & Jane
RAMSAY, John; bpt. Nov 27, 1800; 10 months; son of William & Brigit
RAMSAY, Sarah; bn. Mar 28, 1797; bpt. Apr 4, 1797; dau. of William & Bridget
RAMSAY, William; bn. Oct 29, 1795; bpt. Nov 12, 1795; son of William & Brigit
RANCKAR, Cornelius Romanus; bn. Feb 28, 1800; bpt. Mar 11, 1800; son of John Henry & Christina
RAREDON, John; bn. Apr 9, 1790; bpt. May 2, 1790; son of Patrick & Ann
RAVEN, Helen; bn. Aug 22, 1795; bpt. Sep 3, 1795; dau. of Margaret Raven
READY, James; bpt. Sep 5, 1789; 5 weeks; son of James & Nelly
REARY, John Henry Christian; bn. Aug 26, 1800; bpt. Sep 14, 1800; son of Andrew & Elizabeth
REARY, Juliana; bn. Aug 26, 1800; bpt. Sep 14, 1800; dau. of Andrew & Elizabeth
(REDON), Mary; bn. Aug 13, 1797; bpt. Feb 6, 1798; dau. of Jeanne, Mulatto slave of Mrs. Redon
REED, Daniel; bn. Mar 14, 1782; bpt. Jun 15, 1797; son of Daniel & Susanna
REED, Hanna; bn. Jul 15, 1792; bpt. Jan 13, 1793; dau. of James & Eleanor
REED, James; bn. Feb 19, 1791; bpt. Feb 21, 1791; son of James & Nelly
REEVES, Elizabeth; bn. Feb 24, 1796; bpt. Mar 20, 1796; dau. of William & Abigail
REEVES, Eunice; bpt. Feb 18, 1798; 6 weeks; dau. of William & Appolonia
REEVES, William; bn. Nov 29, 1799; bpt. Mar 30, 1800; son of William & Apollonia
REGAN, James; bpt. May 12, 1796; 4 weeks; son of Hannah Regan
REGAN, William; bn. Nov 21, 1795; bpt. Dec 2, 1795; son of Philip & Mary
REILLY, John; bn. Nov 24, 1797; bpt. Nov 24, 1797; son of John & Mary
REILLY, Stephen; bpt. Nov 25, 1798; 5 weeks; son of John & Mary
REILY, Katy; bn. Apr 14, 1787; bpt. Apr 29, 1787; sps. Anthony Hook & Katy Erwin

BAPTISMS

REINHAULT, Michael; bn. Oct 31, 1796; bpt. Jan 9, 1799; son of
    Joseph & Mary
REINHAULT, Sarah; bn. Dec 4, 1798; bpt. Jan 9, 1799; dau. of
    Joseph & Mary
REINHOLT, Elizabeth; bn. Nov 16, 1793; bpt. Dec 29, 1793; dau. of
    Joseph & Mary
REINHOLT, Joseph; bn. Mar 21, 1799; bpt. Mar 25, 1799; son of
    Sebastian & Juliana
RENAUD, Margaret Elizabeth; bn. Jun 25, 1797; bpt. Mar 18, 1798;
    dau. of John & Irene
RENAUDET, Mary Caroline Victor; bn. Nov 30, 1794; bpt. Jan 14,
    1795; dau. of Peter Abraham & Ann Gautrot
RENELDE, Peter Charles; bn. Nov 20, 1793; bpt. Feb 28, 1795; son
    of Peter & Ann
RENOUS, Andrew John Baptist; bn. Oct 29, 1796; bpt. Dec 25, 1796;
    son of John Baptist & Desdimona
RENOUS, Mary Ann; bn. Sep 10, 1799; bpt. Oct 2, 1799; dau. of
    John & Testimonia
RENOUS, Stephen George; bn. Jan 25, 1795; bpt. Mar 8, 1795; son
    of John Baptist & Destimony Mintz
(REPOLD), Mary; bpt. Aug 19, 1798; 5 months; dau. of Frank &
    Martha, slave of Mr. Repold
REUTER, Catharine; bn. May 26, 1796; bpt. Jun 12, 1796; dau. of
    Abraham & Catharine
REUTER, John; bn. Nov 25, 1797; bpt. Jan 21, 1798; son of Abraham
    & Catharine
REUTER, Peter; bn. Sep 30, 1799; bpt. Oct 20, 1799; son of
    Abraham & Catharine
REY, Ann Sebastian; bn. Apr 21, 1797; bpt. Jun 8, 1797; dau. of
    Joseph Charles & Elizabeth
REYLY, James; bpt. Feb 6, 1788; 3 months; sps. Nelly Reyly
REYNOLDS, James; bn. May 29, 1782; bpt. May 4, 1789; sps. Mary
    Murphy
RICHARD, Elizabeth Frances Susanna; bn. Nov 14, 1797; bpt. Jun
    12, 1798; dau. of Francis & Mary
RICHARD, Mary; bn. Oct 25, 1795; bpt. Dec 27, 1795; dau. of
    Robert Richard, slave & Diana, slave of James Long
RICHARDS, Bridget; bn. Jun 6, 1796; bpt. Jul 19, 1796; dau. of
    Edward & Margaret
RICHARDS, Elizabeth; bn. Nov 12, 1783; bpt. Nov 13, 1783; sps.
    Joseph Bertholin & Elizabeth Lucas
RICHARDS, John; bn. Sep 10, 1797; bpt. Nov 1, 1797; son of Samuel
    & Elizabeth
RICHARDS, Joseph; bn. Apr 11, 1800; bpt. May 10, 1800; son of
    John & Ann
RICHARDS, Mary; bn. Feb 19, 1795; bpt. May 24, 1795; dau. of
    Edward & Margaret
RICHARDS, Mary Ann; bn. Dec 27, 1799; bpt. Mar 30, 1800; dau. of
    Joseph & Mary
RICHARDSON, Charles Dickinson; bn. Jan 9, 1799; bpt. May 10,
    1799; son of William & Elizabeth
(RICHARDSON), Daniel; bn. Feb 24, 1799; bpt. May 10, 1799; son of
    Lydia, slave of William Richardson
RICHARDSON, Eleanor; bn. Mar 11, 1800; bpt. Apr 21, 1800; dau. of
    Mary Richardson

BAPTISMS

RICHARDSON, Henry Dickenson; bn. Aug 25, 1797; bpt. Aug 28, 1797; son of William & Elizabeth
RICHARDSON, John; bn. Jun 19, 1798; bpt. Jul 9, 1798; son of Mary Richardson
RICHARDSON, Mary; bn. May 18, 1800; bpt. Sep 1, 1800; dau. of William & Elizabeth
RICHARDSON, William; bn. Aug 25, 1797; bpt. Aug 28, 1797; son of William & Elizabeth
RICHTER, Elizabeth; bn. Sep 20, 1800; bpt. Sep 25, 1800; dau. of Joseph & Catharine
RICKER, Margaret; bn. Dec 4, 1784; bpt. May 15, 1785; sps. Benjamin Ellot & Mary Handling
(RIDGELEY), John; bpt. Jul 12, 1795; 4 months; son of Lidia Viara, slave of Widow Ridgeley
RILEY, Catharine; bn. Mar 13, 1796; bpt. Mar 27, 1796; dau. of John & Mary
RILEY, Catharine; bn. Apr 5, 1797; bpt. May 7, 1797; dau. of John & Mary
RILEY, John; bn. Mar ?, 1792; bpt. Oct 11, 1795; son of John & Polly
RILEY, Philip; bn. Jun 13, 1794; bpt. Jun 29, 1794; son of John & Mary
RILOUX, Martha Riuline; bn. Feb 18, 1795; bpt. Apr 23, 1795; dau. of Peter & Louisa Sophie Belleville
RINGROSE, Catharine; bpt. Oct 30, 1791; 5 months, 1 week; dau. of Aron & Honor, Protestants
RIO, Mary Catharine; bn. Sep 14, 1798; bpt. Sep 8, 1799; dau. of Peter & Mary
RIVIERE, Elizabeth; bn. Jun 25, 1793; bpt. Sep 28, 1793; dau. of Claude & Elizabeth Toison; sps. Francis & Elizabeth D'Ance Moissonnier
ROACH, Daniel; bn. Jun 14, 1791; bpt. Aug 7, 1791; son of George & Catharine
ROACH, James; bn. Feb 4, 1788; bpt. May 1, 1791; son of John & Margaret
ROACH, James; bn. Sep 27, 1794; bpt. Sep 27, 1794; son of James & Eleanor
ROACH, John; bn. Aug 2, 1785; bpt. Sep 3, 1786; sps. John Staab & Elizabeth Staab
ROACH, Mary; bn. Oct 26, 1795; bpt. Dec 6, 1795; dau. of James & Eleanor
ROACH, Mary Ann; bn. Nov 17, 1782; bpt. May 17, 1783; sps. George Joseph Demanche & Mary Ann Demanche
ROACH, Philip; bn. Aug 29, 1790; bpt. May 1, 1791; son of John & Margaret
ROACH, Sarah; bn. Mar 20, 1794; bpt. Mar 30, 1794; dau. of George & Catharine
ROAN/STOKES, Emily; bn. Dec 29, 1793; bpt. Jan 26, 1794; dau. of John Roan & Elizabeth Stokes
ROBERT, Peter; bn. Jan 17, 1797; bpt. Feb 25, 1797; son of James & Henriette Fier des Bras
ROBERT, Sophia Maria; bn. Jun 8, 1794; bpt. Sep 21, 1794; dau. of James & Veronica
ROBERTS, Eleanor; bn. Nov 11, 1797; bpt. Nov 22, 1797; dau. of James & Elizabeth

BAPTISMS

ROBERTS, Mary Ann; bn. Feb 14, 1795; bpt. Mar 11, 1795; dau. of
    James & Elizabeth
ROBINSON, William; bn. Aug 12, 1799; bpt. Sep 6, 1799; Mulatto;
    son of Jane Robinson, free Negro
ROBISON, Samuel; bn. Jun 27, 1796; bpt. Jul 18, 1796; son of Jane
    Robison
ROCHE, Ann; bn. Aug 15, 1799; bpt. Sep 15, 1799; dau. of John &
    Margaret
ROCHE, Elizabeth; bn. Oct 5, 1796; bpt. Apr 9, 1798; dau. of John
    & Margaret
(ROCHE), Francis; bpt. Oct 25, 1796; 3 weeks; son of Flora, slave
    of Michael Roche, child declared free
RODDY, Barny; bn. Sep 28, 1785; bpt. Sep 30, 1785; sps. Patrick
    Walsh & Catharine Green
RODDY, Catharine; bpt. Feb 15, 1788; 2 weeks; sps. Hugh Henry &
    Rosanne Henry
RODDY, Eleanor; bn. Feb 6, 1794; bpt. Feb 9, 1794; dau. of
    Patrick & Eleanor
RODDY, Eleanor; bn. Jun 26, 1795; bpt. Jul 12, 1795; dau. of
    Patrick & Eleanor
RODDY, Hugh; bn. May 28, 1791; bpt. Jun 19, 1791; son of Patrick
    & Eleanor
RODDY, John; bpt. Dec 14, 1789; 6 weeks; son of Patrick & Eleanor
RODDY, Patrick Brison; bn. Oct 10, 1796; bpt. Oct 15, 1796; son
    of Patrick & Eleanor
RODDY, Patrick Henry; bn. Jul 4, 1798; bpt. Jul 5, 1798; son of
    Patrick & Eleanor
RODDY, Samuel; bpt. Dec 2, 1786; son of Patrick & Eleanor Roddy;
    sps. Patrick & Jane McMullen
RODDY, William; bn. Jul 28, 1792; bpt. Sep 2, 1792; son of
    Patrick & Eleanor
ROERDEN, John; bn. Jul 9, 1791; bpt. Aug 18, 1794; son of William
    & Rachael
ROERDEN, Patrick; bn. Mar 26, 1794; bpt. Aug 18, 1794; son of
    William & Rachael
ROGERS, George; bn. Jul 15, 1791; bpt. Jul 23, 1791; son of Gy &
    Peggy
(ROGERS), John; bpt. May 22, 1791; 7 weeks; slave of Ben Rogers
ROGERS, John; bpt. Jan 5, 1798; adult
ROGERS, Margaret; bpt. Jun 10, 1787; 16 months; sps. Margaret
    Poiety
ROGERS, Peter; bn. Jul 12, 1800; bpt. Jul 29, 1800; son of John &
    Catharine
ROGERS, Thomas; bpt. Jul 28, 1784; 1 week; sps. John Nitiz
ROGERS, William; bn. Apr ?, 1789; bpt. Aug 1, 1790; son of
    Patrick & Agnes
(ROMANET), Anthony; bpt. Nov 1, 1795; 1 month; son of Ann, slave
    of Mrs. Romanet, St Domingo
RONAN, Charlotte; bpt. Feb 19, 1795; 14 years old; dau. of Dennis
    & Hannah
RONAN, Margaret; bpt. Feb 18, 1795; 5 years old; dau. of Dennis &
    Hannah
RONAN, Mary; bpt. Feb 15, 1795; 9 years old; dau. of Dennis &
    Hannah

BAPTISMS

RONEY, Joseph; bn. Aug 5, 1794; bpt. Aug 10, 1794; son of Dennis & Hannah
RONSO, Anthony; bn. May 2, 1798; bpt. May 22, 1798; son of Andrew & Rachel
RONSO, Henry; bpt. Sep 2, 1800; son of Andrew & Rachel
RONSO, John; bn. Aug 27, 1796; bpt. Sep 5, 1796; son of Andrew & Rachel
RONSO, Michael; bn. Mar 9, 1795; bpt. Mar 11, 1795; son of Andrew & Rachel
ROOKE, John; bn. Oct 4, 1798; bpt. May 7, 1799; son of John & Ann
(ROSARD), Edward; bn. Mar 15, 1798; bpt. May 6, 1798; Mulatto; son of Helen, slave of Ann Mary Rosard
ROSE, Elizabeth; bpt. Jun 29, 1800; 2 months; dau. of Primmer & Margaret, free Negroes
ROSENSTEEL, Charles Lazarus; bn. Mar 26, 1800; bpt. Apr 6, 1800; son of George & Barbara
ROSENSTEEL, Samuel; bn. Sep 5, 1798; bpt. Sep 16, 1798; son of George & Susanna
ROSENSTEEL, Sarah; bn. Oct 18, 1795; bpt. Nov 1, 1795; dau. of George & Susanna
ROSENSTEEL, William; bn. Sep 22, 1798; bpt. Sep 30, 1798; son of George, Jr. & Barbara
ROSEY, Margaret; bn. Nov 26, 1783; bpt. Dec 7, 1783; sps. Vincent Campell & Mary Ann Milleret
ROSS, Mary Catharine; bn. Jan 16, 1789; bpt. Jan 24, 1789; sps. Sally Boyde
ROTCH, George; bn. Jan 28, 1799; bpt. Mar 17, 1799; son of George & Catharine
ROTCH, Thomas Dudley; bn. Apr 15, 1796; bpt. May 8, 1796; son of George & Catharine
ROUND, Charlotte Holland; bpt. Sep 4, 1794; adult
(ROUSSELLE), John Baptist; bpt. May 27, 1798; 1 1/2 months; son of Athanasia, slave of Mimie Rousselle
ROWAN, John; bn. Oct 27, 1796; bpt. Nov 6, 1796; son of John & Elizabeth
ROZENSTEEL, Henry; bn. Jun 29, 1792; bpt. Aug 7, 1792; son of George & Susanna
ROZENSTEEL, Jacob; bn. Dec 20, 1789; bpt. Jan 10, 1790; son of George & Susanna
ROZENSTEEL, Michael; bn. Feb 4, 1788; bpt. Feb 10, 1788; sps. Vendel Keller & wife
RUPPERT, John; bn. May 17, 1794; bpt. May 25, 1794; son of Jacob & Bridget
RUSSEL, John Holmes; bpt. Oct 20, 1799; 6 weeks; son of Samuel & Sarah
RUSSELL, George; bn. Jul 31, 1794; bpt. May 10, 1796; son of Elizabeth Russell
RUSSELL, Mary; bpt. Mar 18, 1787; 13 weeks; sps. James Mullen
RUTTER, Thomas; bpt. Dec 16, 1799; 7 months; son of Moses & Elizabeth
RYAN, Catharine; bpt. Sep 16, 1793; about 5 years old; dau. of Edward & Sarah
RYAN, Eleanor; bn. Nov 27, 1795; bpt. Dec 5, 1795; dau. of Michael & Jane

BAPTISMS

RYAN, Elizabeth; bn. Dec 1, 1786; bpt. Jun 22, 1787; sps. James Green
RYAN, James; bn. Jan 1, 1788; bpt. Jan 28, 1788; sps. Jane Flattery
RYAN, Latitia; bn. Feb 11, 1783; bpt. May 2, 1783; sps. Ann Harrison
RYAN, Margaret; bn. Nov 30, 1794; bpt. Dec 2, 1794; dau. of Michael & Juliet
RYLAND, Elizabeth; bn. Jan 12, 1799; bpt. Apr 21, 1799; dau. of John & Sarah
RYND, James; bn. Feb 4, 1797; bpt. Apr 20, 1798; son of Brian & Mary
RYND, Mary Ann; bn. Aug 28, 1794; bpt. Mar 27, 1796; dau. of Bryan & Mary
SABLE, Michael; bn. May 11, 1796; bpt. Apr 21, 1797; son of John & Catharine
SALVAN, Mary Louise; bn. Nov 3, 1796; bpt. Mar 19, 1797; dau. of Joseph Lewis & Jane Lucy Deshayes
SANDERSON, Elizabeth; bn. Dec 7, 1797; bpt. Jan 31, 1798; dau. of Daniel & Elizabeth
(SANGASSIS), Louisa; bpt. Dec 8, 1794; adult; son of Peter Sangassis of St. Domingo
SANITE, Jeanne; bpt. Mar 24, 1797; 18 years old; born in parish of St. Peter, Arch. of St. Domingo
SAP, Anna Marie; bn. Jul 23, 1799; bpt. Jul 30, 1799; dau. of George & Mary
SAP, Regina; bn. Jul 23, 1799; bpt. Jul 30, 1799; dau. of George & Mary
SAVAGE, Elizabeth; bn. Mar 6, 1797; bpt. May 28, 1797; dau. of Patrick & Elizabeth
SAVAGE, John; bn. Oct 15, 1783; bpt. Nov 30, 1783; sps. Richard Fitzgerald & Judith Fitzgerald
SAVAGE, John; bn. Sep 9, 1799; bpt. Nov 10, 1799; son of Patrick & Elizabeth
SAVINGTON, Jacob; bn. Mar 8, 1790; bpt. Mar 24, 1790; son of Jacob & Mary Gallagher
SCHIER, Anthony Benjamin; bn. Jul 24, 1794; bpt. Aug 3, 1794; son of Sarah Schier
SCOT, William; bn. Oct 15, 1790; bpt. Dec 12, 1790; son of John & Ann
SCOT, William; bn. Jul 26, 1795; bpt. Aug 30, 1795; son of William & Julia
SCOTT, Ann; bn. Jul 25, 1796; bpt. Aug 27, 1796; dau. of Michael & Elizabeth
SCOTT, Elizabeth; bn. Jan 1, 1796; bpt. Mar 27, 1796; dau. of James & Susanna
SCOTT, Elizabeth; bn. Sep 25, 1798; bpt. Oct 8, 1798; dau. of Michael & Elizabeth
SCULLY, Jane; bpt. Aug 5, 1799; 9 months; dau. of James & Darkey
SELMAN, John; bpt. Jul 27, 1788; 8 months; son of Wedge & Judy Landres; sps. Ann Patterson
SELMAN, Peter; bpt. Mar 29, 1797; adult
SERJENT, Francis; bn. Dec 2, 1795; bpt. Dec 13, 1795; son of John & Ruth

BAPTISMS

SERJENT, Philip Nicholas; bn. Jul 26, 1794; bpt. Aug 4, 1794; son of John & Ruth
(SEVELINGE), Mary Frances; bn. Jul 19, 1796; bpt. Jul 25, 1796; free Negro; dau. of Pelagie, slave of Miss Sevelinge
SHANNEL, Daniel; bn. Nov 15, 1790; bpt. Nov 21, 1790; son of Timothy & Norris
SHANNING, Elizabeth; bn. Mar 3, 1785; bpt. Aug 1, 1785; sps. Elizabeth Lawson
SHARP, James; bn. Mar 28, 1798; bpt. Apr 17, 1798; son of Mary Sharp
SHARROCK, Elizabeth Atlantic; bn. Aug 9, 1793; bpt. Dec 18, 1793; born on Atlantic Ocean; dau. of William & Elizabeth
SHEA, Dennis; bn. Aug 28, 1793; bpt. Sep 10, 1793; son of John & Mary
SHEA, John; bn. Oct 30, 1791; bpt. Nov 13, 1791; son of John & Mary
SHEANY, Ann; bn. Jun 3, 1788; bpt. Jun 15, 1788; sps. Thomas Muller & Peggy Sheany
SHEELER, Catharine; bn. May 1, 1792; bpt. May 6, 1792; dau. of John & Elizabeth
SHEHAN, Mary; bn. May 4, 1797; bpt. Jan 15, 1798; dau. of Simon & Jane
SHEIDER, Antony; bn. Jun 8, 1786; bpt. Jun 11, 1786; sps. Anthony & Catharine Bergman
SHEPHERD, Eleanor; bn. Apr 5, 1790; bpt. Jun 13, 1790; dau. of John & Eleanor
SHEPHERD, Henry; bn. Jan 11, 1794; bpt. Jan 17, 1794; son of John & Eleanor
SHEPHERD, John; bpt. Aug 14, 1789; 14 months; son of John & Nelly
SHEREDIN, Peggy; bn. Dec 24, 1788; bpt. Jul 31, 1791; dau. of Patrick & Peggy
(SHERLOCK), William; bpt. Sep 29, 1799; 2 months; son of David, slave of Mr. Sherlock & Nelly, slave of Mrs. Diggs
SHERRET, Charlotte; bn. Oct 14, 1786; bpt. Jul 10, 1788; sps. John Kirwan
SHERRET, Harriet; bpt. Sep 21, 1788; a few weeks old; sps. Francis Snowden
SHERRET, Joseph; bpt. May 6, 1792; 2 months; son of William & Teresia
SHEULER, Mary; bn. Jun 27, 1787; bpt. Jul 8, 1787; sps. Anthony Bergman & Elizabeth Laurence
SHEULER, Mary Christina; bn. Mar 6, 1789; bpt. Mar 15, 1789; sps. Anthony Bergman & Christina Bergman
SHICK, Julia; bn. May 3, 1793; bpt. May 19, 1793; dau. of Peter & Peggy
SHILLING, Catharine; bn. Jun 26, 1787; bpt. Jul 8, 1787; sps. Joseph Sindall & Catharine Geissler
SHILLING, Catharine; bn. May 2, 1795; bpt. May 14, 1795; dau. of Tobias & Catharine
SHILLING, Christina; bn. Aug 30, 1792; bpt. Sep 2, 1792; dau. of Tobias & Catharine
SHILLING, Elizabeth; bn. Apr 2, 1785; bpt. Apr 10, 1785; sps. John Steiger & Elizabeth Steiger
SHILLING, Eve; bn. Jun 16, 1789; bpt. Jul 19, 1789; dau. of Michael & Catharine

BAPTISMS

SHILLING, Joseph; bn. Oct 7, 1789; bpt. Oct 11, 1789; son of Tobias & Catharine
SHILLING, Mary; bn. Jul 16, 1791; bpt. Jul 24, 1791; dau. of Michael & Catharine
SHILLING, Michael; bn. Oct 20, 1798; bpt. Nov 11, 1798; son of Tobias & Catharine
SHILLING, Philip; bn. May 30, 1783; bpt. Jun 8, 1783; sps. William Begler & Mary Wyster
SHINEFLEW, Joseph; bn. Feb 13, 1800; bpt. Mar 13, 1800; son of Conrad & Elizabeth
SHINEFREW, William; bn. May 2, 1798; bpt. Jun 3, 1798; son of Conrad & Elizabeth
SHINNEY, Alexander; bn. Nov 1, 1796; bpt. Mar 5, 1797; son of John & Elizabeth
SHINNEY, Susanna Harriot; bn. Dec 14, 1797; bpt. May 13, 1798; dau. of John & Elizabeth
SHIPLEY, Mary Smith; bn. Jan 12, 1791; bpt. Apr 17, 1791; dau. of Reason & Eleanor
SHIRK, Elizabeth; bn. Jun 10, 1797; bpt. Jun 25, 1797; dau. of Peter & Margaret
SHIRK, Margaret; bn. Nov 30, 1795; bpt. Dec 13, 1795; dau. of Peter & Mary
SHORB, Catharine; bn. Nov 7, 1799; bpt. Nov 10, 1799; dau. of Jacob & Barbara
SHORB, Elizabeth; bn. Jun 14, 1799; bpt. Jun 16, 1799; dau. of John & Catharine
SHORB, Elizabeth; bpt. May 4, 1800; 4 days; dau. of Andres & Juliana
SHORB, John; bn. Jun 11, 1793; bpt. Jun 16, 1793; son of John & Catharine
SHORP, Adam; bn. Jun 22, 1797; bpt. Jul 2, 1797; son of John & Catharine
SHORP, Anthony; bn. Aug 27, 1795; bpt. Aug 30, 1795; son of John & Catharine
SHORP, Dorothea; bn. Jun 12, 1787; bpt. Jun 17, 1787; sps. Joseph Laurence & Dorothea Laurence
SHORP, Jacob; bn. Jun 22, 1788; bpt. Jun 29, 1788; sps. Jacob Shorp & Barbara Krauss
SHORP, James; bpt. Apr 18, 1798; 7 weeks; son of John & Catharine
SHORP, Margaret; bn. Aug 11, 1791; bpt. Aug 14, 1791; dau. of John & Catharine
SHORP, Mary; bn. Jun 6, 1789; bpt. Jun 14, 1789; dau. of John & Katy
SHRECK, John; bpt. Oct 5, 1788; 16 days; sps. John Krauss & Mary Shrieck
SHRECK, Mary Catharine; bpt. Jan 14, 1787; 5 weeks old; sps. Christopher Crosley & Catharine Krauss
SHRECK, Philip; bpt. Apr 10, 1791; 3 weeks; son of Diderich & Peggy
SHRECK, Sarah; bpt. Jan 6, 1793; 7 weeks; dau. of Diderick & Margaret
SHRECK, William; bn. Mar 29, 1795; bpt. Jul 19, 1795; son of Diderich & Margaret
SHREECK, Susanna; bn. Jul 22, 1798; bpt. Oct 28, 1798; dau. of Diderich & Margaret

BAPTISMS

SHREIDER, John; bn. May 22, 1788; bpt. May 25, 1788; sps. John Eisler & Mary Eisler
SHROEDER, William; bpt. Nov 22, 1797; 4 weeks; son of Hannah Shroeder
SICKFRIET, George; bn. Dec ?, 1787; bpt. Dec 26, 1787; sps. Joseph Bergman & Catharine Bergman
SIEKFRET, George; bn. Jan 19, 1797; bpt. Jan 22, 1797; son of George & Gertrude
SIMES, Barbara; bn. Jan 21, 1786; bpt. Jan 29, 1786; sps. Nicholas Perry & Magdalen Landry
SIMMON, James; bn. Nov 14, 1799; bpt. Dec 25, 1799; son of James & Mary
SIMON, Henrietta Josephine Sophie; bn. May 14, 1800; bpt. Jun 8, 1800; dau. of Joseph & Sophie Margaritte
(SIMONET), Charles; bpt. Jan 5, 1800; 2 months; son of Nicolle, slave of Mr. Simonet
(SIMONET), John Michael; bpt. Mar 31, 1799; 1 month; son of Charlotte, slave of Mr. Simonet
(SIMONET), Mary Louisa; bpt. Oct 1, 1797; 2 1/2 years old; dau. of Charlotte, slave of Mr. Simonet
(SIMONNET), Antoinette; bpt. Apr 5, 1798; 18 months; dau. of Nicolle, slave of Mr. Simonnet
SIMONNET, Joachim; bn. Dec 12, 1796; bpt. Apr 5, 1798; son of Joachim & Terese Piron
SINDALL, Elizabeth; bn. Mar 5, 1789; bpt. Mar 8, 1789; sps. William Hook & Elizabeth Harmon
SINDALL, Joseph; bn. Dec 4, 1790; bpt. Dec 12, 1790; son of Joseph & Mary
SINDALL, Mary; bn. Mar 1, 1786; bpt. Mar 6, 1786; sps. Joseph Sindall & Mary Bertheim
(SLUBEY), Elizabeth; bpt. Mar 19, 1797; 3 months; Mulatto; dau. of William & Rachel, slave of Mr. Nicholas Slubey
SMALL, Anastasia; bn. Jul 29, 1792; bpt. Aug 26, 1792; dau. of James & Anastasia
SMALL, Eleanor; bn. Jan 26, 1791; bpt. Jan 27, 1791; dau. of James & Ann
SMALL, Susanna; bpt. Sep 8, 1795; 15 months; dau. of James & Anastasia
SMITH, Abraham; bn. Sep 8, 1794; bpt. Nov 28, 1794; son of Abraham & Eleanor
SMITH, Andrew; bn. Apr 22, 1799; bpt. Apr 22, 1799; son of James & Mary
SMITH, Ann; bn. Jul 3, 1795; bpt. Aug 2, 1795; dau. of Isaac & Elizabeth
SMITH, Brien; bpt. Feb 5, 1786; about 12 weeks; sps. Christopher Fleming & Mary Redstone
SMITH, Catharine; bn. May 29, 1796; bpt. Jun 12, 1796; dau. of Eve Smith
SMITH, Daniel; bn. Jun 13, 1791; bpt. Jul 24, 1791; son of Isaac & Elizabeth
SMITH, Fanny; bn. Jan 9, 1792; bpt. Jan 13, 1793; dau. of Rosanna Bowen
(SMITH), George; bn. Dec 24, 1798; bpt. Aug 4, 1799; Mulatto; son of Robert & Rachel, slave of Isaac Smith

BAPTISMS

SMITH, Joanna; bn. Jun 7, 1800; bpt. Aug 6, 1800; dau. of James & Mary
SMITH, Mary; bn. Jun 3, 1793; bpt. Jun 8, 1793; dau. of Robert & Eleanor
(SMITH), Mary Frances; bpt. Apr 20, 1800; 5 months; Mulatto; dau. of Amy, slave of Thorogood Smith
SMITH, Nicholas Cornelius; bn. Aug 15, 1784; bpt. Aug 22, 1784; sps. Cornelius Hagherty & Susan Hagherty
SMITH, Samuel Abraham; bn. Jun 10, 1799; bpt. Oct 20, 1799; son of Sam & Susan, free Negroes
SMITH, Sara; bn. May 26, 1789; bpt. Apr 5, 1790; dau. of Isaac & Elizabeth
SMITH, Thomas; bn. Mar 13, 1793; bpt. Apr 6, 1794; son of Isaac & Elizabeth
SMITH, William; bpt. Nov 17, 1793; 6 months; son of Isaac & ---
SMOTHERS, Thomas; bn. Nov 2, 1792; bpt. May 12, 1793; son of Henry & Mary
SNEYDER, Peter; bn. Oct 19, 1787; bpt. Oct 19, 1787; sps. Peter Litzenger & Catharine Geissler
SNOWDEN, Henry; bn. May 14, 1788; bpt. Jun 17, 1788; sps. Mary Snowden
(SNOWDEN), Rachael; bn. Mar 31, 1794; bpt. May 4, 1794; dau. of Jacob & Mary, slave of Mr. Snowden
SNOWDEN, Thomas; bn. Mar 25, 1785; bpt. Aug 28, 1785; sps. Thomas Fanning & Ann Gutterau
SONFORT, Anna Marie; bn. Mar 13, 1800; bpt. Mar 16, 1800; dau. of Nicholas & Catharine
SOP, Catharine; bn. Sep 4, 1790; bpt. Sep 6, 1790; dau. of John & Sara
SOP, James Valiant; bpt. Apr 14, 1792; son of John & Betty
SOP, William; bn. Jan 7, 1787; bpt. Feb 20, 1787; sps. James Dealy & Catharine Dorney
(SOPHIA), Frances Jane; bn. Jul 8, 1797; bpt. Sep 25, 1797; Mulatto; dau. of Genevieve Louise, slave of Mary Jane Sophia
(SOUBIRA), Mary; bpt. Oct 15, 1797; 2 weeks; dau. of Victoire, slave of Julie Soubira
(SOUBIRA), Mary Joseph; bpt. Mar 25, 1799; 1 month; dau. of Victoire, slave of Mr. Soubira
SOUCRI, Elizabeth; bn. Jul 5, 1787; bpt. Jul 6, 1787; sps. Lewis Barbarin & Eve Elgut
SOUTHERN, James; bn. Jan 2, 1796; bpt. Jan 24, 1796; son of James & Eleanor
SPALDING, Harriot; bn. Oct 17, 1796; bpt. Oct 24, 1796; dau. of William & Mary
SPALDING, Maria; bn. Jun 3, 1794; bpt. Jul 1, 1794; dau. of William & Mary
SPARROW, Peggy; bpt. Sep 16, 1787; 1 month; sps. Robert Marcus & Fanny Marcus
SPELLARD, William; bn. Jan 5, 1798; bpt. Jan 14, 1798; son of Mathias & Winifred
SPENCE, Sarah; bn. Feb 15, 1791; bpt. Jul 24, 1791; dau. of George & Elizabeth Pierson
SPENCER, Mary; bpt. May 31, 1795; 5 weeks; dau. of John & Henrietta, free Mulattoes

BAPTISMS

SPICER, Ann; bn. Dec 16, 1797; bpt. Feb 18, 1798; dau. of John & Harriot
ST. CLAIR, Ann; bn. Mar 13, 1797; bpt. May 28, 1797; dau. of George & Celia Ann
ST. MARTIN, Alexius George Mary; bn. Aug 14, 1797; bpt. Feb 6, 1798; son of Peter James Joseph & Margaret Louisa Josephine Leyritz, St. Domingo
ST. MARTIN, George Peter Lewis; bn. May 15, 1799; bpt. May 29, 1799; son of Peter James Joseph & Mary Louise Josephine DeLeyritz
STAAB, John; bn. Jul 6, 1783; bpt. Jul 9, 1783; sps. George Rozensteel & Susanna Rozensteel
STAELER, Elizabeth; bn. Dec 28, 1795; bpt. Dec 28, 1795; dau. of Philip & Catharine
STAILER, Elizabeth; bn. Dec 30, 1798; bpt. Feb 3, 1799; dau. of Philip & Catharine
STAILER, John; bn. Jan 31, 1791; bpt. Feb 27, 1791; son of Philip & Catharine
STAIR, Nicholas; bn. Mar 31, 1785; bpt. Apr 18, 1785; sps. John Kelly & Sara Boyle
STAR, Susanna; bn. Mar 14, 1787; bpt. Apr 1, 1787; sps. John Kelly & Jane Flattery
STARR, James; bn. Oct 28, 1789; bpt. Nov 22, 1789; son of Obedia & Winny
STAUB, Anna Margareta; bn. Dec 10, 1790; bpt. Dec 13, 1790; dau. of Philip & Catharine
STAYLER, Philip Jacob; bpt. Nov 8, 1788; 4 weeks; son of Philip & Katy
STAZLER, Henry; bn. Jan 18, 1793; bpt. Feb 24, 1793; son of Philip & Catharine
STEARE, Maria; bn. Apr 20, 1800; bpt. May 18, 1800; dau. of John & Rachel
STEER, Frances; bn. Feb 23, 1796; bpt. Feb 28, 1796; dau. of John & Rachel
STEER, George; bn. Apr 23, 1798; bpt. May 6, 1798; son of John & Rachel
STEIGER, Charles; bn. Jul 9, 1793; bpt. Jul 21, 1793; son of John & Elizabeth
(STEIGER), Eleanor; bn. Sep 8, 1799; bpt. Nov 1, 1799; Mulatto; dau. of Rachel, slave of John Steiger
STEIGER, Elizabeth; bn. Jun 7, 1795; bpt. Jun 20, 1795; dau. of John & Elizabeth
STEIGER, George; bn. Jun 17, 1787; bpt. Jun 24, 1787; sps. George Rozensteel & Susanna Rozensteel
STEIGER, George; bn. Aug 19, 1789; bpt. Aug 23, 1789; son of John & Elizabeth
STEIGER, George; bn. Aug 2, 1794; bpt. Aug 15, 1794; son of Tobias & Mary
STEIGER, Henry; bn. Oct 13, 1791; bpt. Oct 30, 1791; son of John & Elizabeth
STEIGER, James; bn. Mar 31, 1784; bpt. Apr 6, 1784; sps. Matthias Baker & Teresia Baker
STEIGER, John; bn. Jul 26, 1787; bpt. Aug 5, 1787; son of John & Elizabeth

BAPTISMS

STEIGER, John; bn. Nov 14, 1797; bpt. Dec 31, 1797; son of John & Elizabeth
STEIGER, Joseph; bn. Jul 1, 1785; bpt. Jul 3, 1785; sps. Joseph Imdalf & Katy Steiger
STEIGER, Mary Magdalen; bn. Apr 1, 1796; bpt. May 8, 1796; dau. of Mathias & Mary Magdalen
STEIGER, Mathais; bn. Dec 22, 1799; bpt. Mar 2, 1800; son of John & Elizabeth
STEIGER, Matilda; bn. Sep 2, 1796; bpt. Sep 25, 1796; dau. of John & Elizabeth
STEIGER, Sarah; bn. Jun 13, 1800; bpt. Jun 22, 1800; dau. of Jacob & Catharine
STEINMETZ, William; bn. May 8, 1799; bpt. May 23, 1799; son of Michael & Mary Ann
STELLER, George; bn. Feb 15, 1792; bpt. Feb 15, 1792; son of Philip & Catharine
(STENSON), Alexius; bpt. Oct 16, 1797; 10 days; son of Hannah Harris, slave of Mr. Stenson
STENSON, Archibald; bn. Feb 27, 1785; bpt. Mar 27, 1785; sps. Mark Morres & Susanna Morres
STENSON, Elizabeth; bn. Mar 2, 1795; bpt. Mar 22, 1795; dau. of William & Elizabeth
(STENSON), Henry; bn. Nov 29, 1793; bpt. Nov 30, 1794; son of Emaus, free Mulatto & Ann, slave of Mr. William Stenson
STENSON, James; bn. Aug 20, 1792; bpt. Aug 24, 1794; son of William & Elizabeth
STENSON, John; bn. Aug 3, 1786; bpt. Sep 3, 1786; sps. John Sharp & Dolly Gross
STENSON, Margaret; bn. Dec 25, 1789; bpt. May 22, 1792; dau. of William & Elizabeth
STENSON, Mary; bn. May 3, 1788; bpt. May 13, 1788; sps. Barbara ---
(STENSON), William; bn. Jun ?, 1792; bpt. Nov 11, 1792
STEPHENSON, John; bn. Feb 13, 1787; bpt. Feb 20, 1787; sps. George Kelly & Abagail Strickland
(STERLING), Edward; bpt. Sep 14, 1794; Mulatto son of Harry & Nelly, slave of Mr. Sterling
(STERLING), Edward; bn. Feb 20, 1797; bpt. Apr 17, 1797; Mulatto; son of Phoebe, slave of Mr. Sterling
(STERLING), Louisa; bpt. Jul 27, 1800; 4 months; dau. of Laurence & Nelly, slave of Mr. Sterling
STEWART, George; bn. Sep 11, 1798; bpt. Jan 22, 1799; son of Jane Stewart
STILLER, Catharine; bn. Feb 24, 1786; bpt. Feb 26, 1786; sps. Henry Deale & Magdalen Deale
STILLINGER, Michael; bn. Jul 21, 1798; bpt. Jul 21, 1798; son of Jacob & Christina
(STIRLING), Eliza; bn. Jun 16, 1799; bpt. Aug 4, 1799; dau. of James & Eve, slave of Mr. Stirling
(STIRLING), John; bpt. Dec 17, 1797; son of Laurence, Negro & Nelly, Mulatto slave of Mr. Stirling
STRATTAN, Obediah; bn. Nov 1, 1798; bpt. Apr 14, 1799; son of William & Mary
STREIDER, Mary; bn. Dec 22, 1790; bpt. Dec 26, 1790; dau. of Joseph & Catharine

BAPTISMS

STRICKER, Magdalen; bn. Aug 3, 1787; bpt. Sep 23, 1787; sps.
    William Fouss & Catharine Fouss
STRIDER, Jacob; bn. Apr 30, 1798; bpt. May 6, 1798; son of
    Catharine Strider
STRIKE, Nicholas; bn. Oct 29, 1797; bpt. Nov 9, 1797; son of
    Nicholas & Margaret
STRIKE, William; bn. Oct 28, 1794; bpt. Nov 11, 1794; son of
    Nicholas & Helen
STRUMPH, Daniel; bn. May 5, 1788; bpt. Aug 24, 1788; sps. Joseph
    Sindall & wife
(STUPUY), Francis; bpt. Jun 10, 1798; 8 months; son of Susanne,
    slave of Peter Stupuy
(STUPUY), John Peter; bpt. Apr 22, 1798; infant slave of Peter
    Stupuy
SUFFREN, Catharine; bpt. May 17, 1795; 6 weeks; dau. of Ann
    Suffren
SULLIVAN, Daniel; bn. Sep 9, 1794; bpt. Sep 20, 1794; son of
    Daniel Colvin & Helen Sullivan
SULLIVAN, Francis Marhal; bpt. Jan 20, 1794; 8 months old; son of
    John & Eleanor
SULLIVAN, Mary; bn. Jun 15, 1793; bpt. Jul 7, 1793; dau. of Jane
    Sullivan
SULLIVAN, Thomas James; bn. May 29, 1793; bpt. Sep 4, 1794; son
    of Paul James & Maria
SUSMAN, Honor; bn. Oct 2, 1787; bpt. Dec 9, 1787; sps. James
    Jordan & Molly Howard
SWARTZ, John; bn. May 15, 1791; bpt. May 22, 1791; son of John &
    Barbara
SWEENEY, Elizabeth; bn. May 12, 1792; bpt. Sep 2, 1792; dau. of
    Hugh of Hook's Town & Priscilla
SWEENEY, George; bn. Apr 10, 1789; bpt. Apr 28, 1789; sps. George
    Sweeny & Isabella Jordan
SWEENEY, Nathaniel; bn. Jun 22, 1792; bpt. Oct 29, 1792; son of
    Hugh & Mary
SWEENY, Alexander; bn. Jul 6, 1798; bpt. Jul 7, 1799; son of
    James & Eleanor
SWEENY, Ann; bpt. Jun 18, 1799; 2 1/2 years old; dau. of Margaret
    Sweeny
SWEENY, Hugh; bn. Jun 4, 1795; bpt. Jun 7, 1795; son of Hugh &
    Mary
SWEENY, Hugh Gabriel; bn. Jan 22, 1791; bpt. Jan 30, 1791; son of
    Hugh & Mary
SWEENY, John; bn. Mar 31, 1796; bpt. Apr 24, 1796; son of Hugh &
    Priscilla
SWEENY, Mary; bn. May 7, 1789; bpt. Dec 26, 1790; dau. of Hugh &
    Priscilla
SWEENY, Sarah Teresa; bn. Jan 28, 1794; bpt. Mar 11, 1794; dau.
    of Hugh & Mary
SWEENY, Thomas; bpt. Sep 13, 1797; son of Edward & Elizabeth
SWORDS, Thomas; bn. Feb 24, 1783; bpt. Jul 20, 1783; sps. William
    Murphy & Mary Sullivan
(TABAYANT), Mary Ursula; bpt. May 13, 1798; 3 1/2 months;
    Mulatto; dau. of Julie, slave of Mr. Tabayant
TANNER, Anna Pamilia; bpt. Oct 20, 1798; 6 months, 13 days old;
    dau. of Pierce Lacey & Pamilia

BAPTISMS

TANNER, James; bn. Aug 26, 1795; bpt. Feb 16, 1796; son of Pierce & Pamelia
TANNER, Louisa; bn. Dec 30, 1796; bpt. Mar 20, 1797; dau. of Pierce L. & Pamphilia
TANNER, Michael Tiernan; bn. Oct 30, 1799; bpt. Jan 5, 1800; son of Pierce Lacy & Pamelia
TAUFF, John; bn. Feb 22, 1787; bpt. Apr 1, 1787; sps. Richard Fitzgerald
TAYLOR, Ambrose; bn. Jun 26, 1783; bpt. Jul 4, 1783; sps. Peter Michel & wife
TAYLOR, Ann; bn. Mar 24, 1787; bpt. Mar 30, 1787; sps. Robert Conway & Barbara Nickel
TAYLOR, Catharine; bn. Jul 9, 1796; bpt. Jan 24, 1798; dau. of Henry & Mary
TAYLOR, Elizabeth; bn. Sep 26, 1784; bpt. Dec 5, 1784; sps. James King & Elizabeth Flin
TAYLOR, George; bn. Feb 16, 1797; bpt. Mar 19, 1797; son of Philip & Catharine
TAYLOR, Sara; bn. May 20, 1788; bpt. Jun 8, 1788; sps. Daniel O'Brien & Mary Box
TAYLOR, Susanna; bn. Jun 9, 1798; bpt. Aug 10, 1798; dau. of Henry & Mary
TAYLOR, William; bn. Jan 11, 1787; bpt. Jul 9, 1787; sps. Jane Farnworth
(TESEK), Ann Marthe; bpt. Jul 29, 1798; 2 months; dau. of Louise, slave of Mr. Tesek
TEUCAS, Sophia; bn. May 1, 1792; bpt. Aug 26, 1792; dau. of Lewis & Maria Sisky
TEYRL, William; bn. Apr 10, 1792; bpt. Jul 29, 1792; son of James & Sarah
THEBAUDIERES, Peter Leon; bn. Jun 24, 1788; bpt. Sep 23, 1793; son of Joseph & Anne Mary Matthews of Port de Paix, St. Domingo
THIEMAN, Maria Isabella; bpt. Dec 28, 1796; 4 years; dau. of William & Ann
THOMAS, Marie Adelle; bn. Jul 2, 1795; bpt. Sep 10, 1795; dau. of John Lewis & Mary Catharine Conrad
THOMAS, Mary Teresa; bn. Dec 25, 1793; bpt. Sep 10, 1796; dau. of Paul & Mary Catharine Bardon Monglar
THOMAS, Robert; bn. Oct 6, 1800; bpt. Dec 21, 1800; son of Nathaniel & Monica
THOMAS, Sarah; bn. May 11, 1796; bpt. May 15, 1796; dau. of Ann Thomas
THOMPSON, Ann; bn. May 2, 1797; bpt. Sep 3, 1797; dau. of Garret & Martha
THOMPSON, Clare; bn. Sep 29, 1798; bpt. Sep 29, 1798; dau. of Josias & Jane
THOMPSON, Elizabeth; bpt. Sep 25, 1796; 1 month; dau. of Sarah Thompson
(THOMPSON), Elizabeth; bn. Nov ?, 1797; bpt. Jan 14, 1798; dau. of James, slave of Mr. Thompson & Elizabeth, Negro
THOMPSON, Mary Ann; bn. Feb 17, 1789; bpt. Oct 11, 1789; dau. of Zacheria & Eleanor
THORNBURG, Sara; bpt. Oct 10, 1786; 4 weeks; sps. Joseph Hook & Magdalen Bush

BAPTISMS

THORNSBURY, Thomas; bn. Jun 18, 1789; bpt. Jun 21, 1789; son of Robert & ---
THORPS, Ann; bn. May 14, 1776; bpt. May 7, 1795; dau. of Thomas & Ann
TIEGLER, Andrew; bn. Dec 31, 1798; bpt. Feb 21, 1799; son of Francis & Frances
TIEGLER, Barbara; bn. Apr 7, 1792; bpt. Apr 25, 1792; dau. of Francis & Fanny
TIEGLER, Francis; bn. Dec 31, 1796; bpt. Jan 26, 1797; son of Francis & Frances
TIEGLER, George; bpt. Sep 13, 1787; sps. George Rozensteel & Susanna Rozensteel
TIEGLER, Joseph; bn. Jan 8, 1790; bpt. Jan 27, 1790; son of Francis & Francisca
TIERNAN, Ann Sarah; bn. Oct 15, 1799; bpt. Nov 24, 1799; dau. of Luke & Ann
TIERNAN, Charles; bn. Nov 3, 1797; bpt. Dec 17, 1797; son of Luke & Ann
(TIERNAN), Eliza; bn. Dec 14, 1798; bpt. Jan 20, 1799; dau. of Nanny, Mulatto slave of Mr. Tiernan
TIERNAN, Luke; bpt. Dec 30, 1800; son of Luke & Ann
TIERNAN, Rebecca; bn. Dec 11, 1795; bpt. Feb 20, 1796; dau. of Luke & Ann
TIMMONS, John; bn. Jan 18, 1785; bpt. Dec 2, 1785; sps. Margaret Diffedall
TIMON, Rose; bn. Oct 5, 1800; bpt. Oct 9, 1800; dau. of James & Eleanor
TOBIN, David; bpt. Oct 13, 1799; 1 week; son of John & Jane
TOOLE, James; bn. Nov 4, 1790; bpt. Nov 15, 1790; son of James & Susanna
TOOLE, Kitty; bn. Dec 18, 1787; bpt. Jun 7, 1788; sps. Daniel Boyle & Mary Cammel
TOOMY, Mary; bn. Aug 1, 1790; bpt. Sep 27, 1790; dau. of Daniel & Sara
TOPP, Mary; bn. Nov 26, 1796; bpt. Feb 1, 1797; dau. of Henry & Rachel
TOUCAS, Anna Maria; bn. Oct 10, 1788; bpt. Nov 4, 1788; dau. of Honore Lewis & Mary L'Estaing; sps. Jean Lacques Grosjean & Anne LeRoi Davis
TOUCAS, Josephe Eustasia Maria; bn. Dec 24, 1789; bpt. Jan 19, 1790; son of Lewis & Maria
TOURANJEAU, Alexandrine Petrinolle; bn. Aug 28, 1798; bpt. Oct 6, 1798; dau. of Louise Elizabeth Touranjeau, Mulatress of St. Domingo
(TOUYA), Maria; bn. Nov 23, 1794; bpt. Jan 1, 1975; dau. of Jesse, slave of Mr. Touya & Susan, slave of Mr. Charles Ghequiere
TOWEL, Daniel; bn. Dec 24, 1786; bpt. Mar 12, 1787; sps. Zacharia Collins
TOWEL, Lacheria; bn. Mar 22, 1788; bpt. Oct 29, 1788; sps. John Collins & Elizabeth Collins
TOWEL, Nancy; bpt. Aug 24, 1787; 16 days; sps. Pierce Jacques Collier & Peggy LaBatte
TOWEL, Richard; bn. Mar 23, 1790; bpt. Aug 12, 1791; son of Thomas & Mary

BAPTISMS

TOWEL, Thomas; bn. Feb 5, 1784; bpt. Jul 17, 1785; sps. Augustin Delatte
TOWNSEND, Rachel; bn. Nov 22, 1796; bpt. Jun 24, 1797; dau. of Josias & Jane
TOY, Ann; bn. Apr 9, 1800; bpt. May 5, 1800; dau. of John & Mary
TRAINER, James; bn. Jul 11, 1793; bpt. Sep 6, 1795; son of Terreme & Temperance
TRAINER, Margaret; bn. Nov 21, 1797; bpt. Feb 5, 1798; dau. of Terence & Temperance
TRAINER, Mary; bn. Dec 11, 1790; bpt. Feb 5, 1798; dau. of Terence & Temperance
TRANER, Thomas; bn. Feb 20, 1796; bpt. Aug 15, 1797; son of Terence & Temperance
TRAVIS, Louisa; bpt. Jul 7, 1799; 4 weeks; dau. of George & Mary Ann
TRAYNER, Price; bn. Mar 27, 1800; bpt. Apr 13, 1800; son of Terrence & Temperance
TREANER, Mary; bn. Nov 8, 1782; bpt. Dec 25, 1782; sps. Thomas Rutledge & Mary Smith
TRENTON, Antony; bn. Aug 9, 1786; bpt. Oct 9, 1786; sps. Peter Lolo & Elizabeth Deagle
TRENTON, John; bn. Feb 7, 1784; bpt. Apr 7, 1784; sps. Peter Leary & Margaret Gold
TREPANIER, Ann; bn. Sep 20, 1794; bpt. Nov 2, 1794; dau. of Augustine & Ann
TROUT, Catharine; bn. Jul 20, 1791; bpt. Aug 28, 1791; dau. of George & Barbara
TROUVE, Mary Teresa; bn. Feb 2, 1792; bpt. Aug 5, 1795; dau. of Peter & Mary Louisa Boy
TRUELY, Henrietta; bn. May 27, 1796; bpt. Jul 23, 1796; dau. of Richard Truely, free Negro; formerly slave of John & Henrietta Moale
TULLY, Matthew; bn. May 23, 1783; bpt. Jul 14, 1783; sps. James Ryan & Brigit McCan
TURENNE, Ann; bn. Jan 2, 1797; bpt. May 27, 1797; dau. of John & Mary Benillant; born in Philadelphia
TURENNE, Ann; bn. Dec 1, 1797; bpt. May 16, 1798; dau. of John & Mary Benillant
TURENNE, John; bn. Jun 2, 1799; bpt. May 8, 1800; son of John & Mary
TURNEL, Isidore William; bn. Mar 9, 1798; bpt. Mar 23, 1798; son of Lydia Turnel
TURNER, Ann; bpt. Apr 3, 1797; 8 years old; dau. of William & Martha
TURNER, George; bn. Jan 13, 1792; bpt. Apr 8, 1792; son of Samuel & Mary
TURNER, John; bn. Jan 11, 1784; bpt. Mar 3, 1784; sps. Timothy Herrin & Eleanor Kid
TURNER, William Brooks; bn. Nov 15, 1789; bpt. Feb 21, 1790; son of Samuel & ---
(TUZA), Augustine; bpt. Oct 12, 1800; 6 months; son of Mary Magdalen, slave of Mr. Tuza--
TYSON, John; bn. Apr 26, 1797; bpt. Apr 30, 1797; son of Henry & Sabina

BAPTISMS

TYSON, Mary Anna Agnes; bn. Aug 17, 1798; bpt. Aug 23, 1798; dau.
    of Henry & Sabina Maria Stricker
USHER, James; bn. Jan 27, 1800; bpt. Apr 13, 1800; son of James &
    Catharine
VALLETTE, Arsemius; bn. Sep 21, 1795; bpt. Dec 19, 1795; son of
    Charles Francis & Jane
VALLETTE, Jeanne Eugenie; bn. Jan 6, 1800; bpt. May 5, 1800; dau.
    of Charles Francis & Jeanne Baque
VALLETTE, John James Augustus; bn. Jul 2, 1798; bpt. Jul 28,
    1798; son of Charles & Jane Baque
VALLETTE, Mary Louisa; bn. Nov 24, 1796; bpt. May 11, 1797; dau.
    of Charles & Jane
VANDERHERCHEN, Francis; bn. Feb 28, 1794; bpt. Mar 13, 1794; son
    of Andrew of Namur & Augustine Bernardine Mortier of Dunkirk
(VAVADENOU), Genevieve; bpt. Feb 7, 1797; 2 months; dau. of
    Julie, slave of Mr. Vavadenou
VEAL, Elenora; bn. Apr 28, 1796; bpt. May 10, 1796; dau. of
    Pierce & Mary
VEAL, Joanna; bn. Jul 30, 1796; bpt. Aug 1, 1796; dau. of
    Nicholas & Catharine
VEAL, Nicholas; bn. Apr 30, 1798; bpt. May 1, 1798; son of
    Nicholas (deceased) & Catharine
VEAL, Pierce Alphonse; bn. Mar 26, 1798; bpt. Jul 26, 1798; son
    of Pierce & Mary
VENNY, Hugh; bn. Jul 12, 1793; bpt. Nov 3, 1793; son of Hugh &
    Margaret
VILLAIN, Michael; bn. Dec 21, 1795; bpt. Jan 30, 1796; son of
    Michael & Catharine
(VILLAR), Lewis; bn. Apr 25, 1797; bpt. Jun 5, 1797; son of
    Jenny, slave of Elizabeth Villar
VILLARD, Rosalie Virginie; bn. Oct 3, 1797; bpt. Jan 23, 1798;
    dau. of Elizabeth Villard, St. Domingo
VINER, Ann; bn. Jan 14, 1785; bpt. Jan 20, 1785; sps. Joseph
    Pebotete & Mary Pinchard
VINEY, John Baptist; bpt. Aug 3, 1788; about 2 months; sps. John
    Baron & Mary Celestin
VINTRY, Francis; bn. Mar 5, 1790; bpt. Mar 21, 1790; son of
    Francis & ---
(VOUARD), Mary Joseph; bpt. Feb 5, 1797; 3 months; dau. of Mary
    Catharine, slave of Mr. Vouard
(VOYARD), John Francis; bpt. Mar 28, 1796; 20 years old; French
    Negro slave of Mr. Voyard of St. Domingo
(VRAIGNAND), Joseph Maryland; bpt. Jul 11, 1796; 13 months;
    Mulatto; son of Rosina, slave of Mr. Vraignand
VRIGNAU, Ann Mary; bn. Jul 5, 1796; bpt. Aug 13, 1796; dau. of
    Nicholas & Michin Mary
WAGERS, Francis; bpt. Sep 7, 1791; adult; conditional
WALKER, Elizabeth; bn. Jul 29, 1797; bpt. Aug 3, 1797; dau. of
    Robert & Sarah
WALKER, John Dennis; bn. Oct 31, 1798; bpt. Nov 16, 1798; son of
    Robert & Sarah
WALKER, Mary; bn. Apr 10, 1794; bpt. Apr 11, 1794; dau. of Robert
    & Sarah
WALKER, Robert; bn. Sep 29, 1800; bpt. Oct 9, 1800; son of Robert
    & Sarah

BAPTISMS

WALLACE/CASEY, Mary; bn. Oct 20, 1793; bpt. Nov 24, 1793; dau. of
    Robert Wallace & Elizabeth Casey
WALSH, Andrew; bn. Apr 2, 1789; bpt. Mar 24, 1790; son of Edmund
    & Hanna
(WALSH), Anna; bn. Oct 30, 1793; bpt. Dec 15, 1793; dau. of
    Flora, slave of Robert Walsh
WALSH, Brigit; bn. Jan 18, 1792; bpt. Jan 21, 1792; dau. of
    Martin & Sally
(WALSH), Charlotte; bn. Mar 28, 1784; bpt. Sep 28, 1784; slave of
    William Walsh; sps. Robert Walsh & Elizabeth Walsh
WALSH, Edmund; bn. Dec 28, 1783; bpt. Nov 7, 1784; sps. Richard
    Burke & Catharine Hook
WALSH, Edward Carrere; bn. Nov 28, 1798; bpt. Jan 4, 1799; son of
    Robert & Elizabeth
WALSH, Eleanor; bn. Aug 27, 1791; bpt. Jun 24, 1792; dau. of
    Pierce & Mary
WALSH, Eleanor; bpt. Jul 29, 1798; 4 months; dau. of Maurice &
    Elizabeth
WALSH, Elizabeth; bn. Jan 26, 1787; bpt. Mar 7, 1787; sps.
    Charles Sewall & Mary Walsh
WALSH, Elizabeth; bpt. Mar 30, 1796; 23 years old; dau. of James
    & Ann
WALSH, Francis; bn. May ?, 1788; bpt. May 22, 1788; son of Robert
    & Elizabeth; sps. Thomas Russel & Elizabeth Clements
WALSH, Francis William; bpt. Apr 16, 1795; son of Robert &
    Elizabeth
WALSH, Hugh; bn. Dec 5, 1798; bpt. Dec 20, 1798; son of Thomas &
    Bridget
WALSH, Ignatius; bn. Nov 1, 1791; bpt. Dec 23, 1791; son of
    Robert & Elizabeth
WALSH, James; bn. Sep 20, 1785; bpt. Sep 22, 1785; sps.
    Archbishop Carroll & Winefrida Deady
WALSH, James; bpt. Jul 2, 1786; 12 weeks; sps. William Collins &
    Betsy Williams
WALSH, James; bn. Oct 19, 1789; bpt. Oct 19, 1789; son of Thomas
    & Mary
WALSH, James; bn. Oct 16, 1793; bpt. Oct 18, 1793; son of Robert
    & Elizabeth
WALSH, Jeremiah; bn. Mar 26, 1798; bpt. Aug 26, 1798; son of
    Pierce & Mary
WALSH, John; bn. Sep 12, 1790; bpt. Oct 21, 1790; son of Robert &
    Elizabeth
WALSH, John; bpt. Sep 3, 1793; 9 weeks; son of Richard & Eleanor
WALSH, John; bn. Aug 25, 1793; bpt. Apr 20, 1794; son of Pierce &
    Mary
WALSH, Joseph; bn. Mar 6, 1777; bpt. May 15, 1791; son of Edward
    & ---
WALSH, Louisa; bn. Apr 2, 1797; bpt. Jul 10, 1797; dau. of Joseph
    & Polly
WALSH, Margaret; bn. Aug 12, 1791; bpt. Dec 18, 1791; dau. of
    Edmund (now dead) & Hannah
WALSH, Mary; bn. Jul 27, 1792; bpt. Aug 8, 1792; dau. of Edward &
    Catharine
WALSH, Mary Ann; bn. Oct 7, 1799; bpt. Nov 3, 1799; dau. of
    Maurice & Elizabeth

BAPTISMS

WALSH, Patrick William; bn. Nov 26, 1783; bpt. Jan 18, 1784; sps.
    Patrick Walsh & Elizabeth Walsh
WALSH, Pierce; bn. Dec 2, 1788; bpt. Jun 1, 1789; son of Pierce &
    Mary
WALSH, Robert; bn. Aug 30, 1784; bpt. Sep 28, 1784; sps. John
    Kirnan & Henrietta Williamson
WALSH, Walter; bn. Jan 1, 1796; bpt. Jan 4, 1796; son of Pierce &
    Mary
WALTER, Catharine; bn. May 18, 1797; bpt. Jun 4, 1797; dau. of
    Peter & Margaret
WALTER, David; bn. Apr 25, 1796; bpt. May 1, 1796; son of
    Nicholas & Ann Mary
WALTER, Elizabeth; bn. Dec 15, 1790; bpt. Dec 25, 1790; dau. of
    John & Elizabeth
WALTER, Jacob; bn. Sep 21, 1792; bpt. Sep 23, 1792; son of John &
    Elizabeth
WALTER, Magdalen; bpt. Jan 23, 1786; 2 weeks; sps. John &
    Elizabeth
WALTER, Magdalen; bn. Feb 25, 1788; bpt. Mar 10, 1788; sps.
    George Rozensteel & Elizabeth Steiger
WALTER, Margaret; bn. Aug 2, 1793; bpt. Sep 1, 1793; dau. of
    Peter & Margaret
WALTER, Peter; bn. Mar 8, 1794; bpt. Mar 30, 1794; son of
    Nicholas & Ann Mary
WALTER, Peter; bn. Aug 11, 1795; bpt. Aug 15, 1795; son of John &
    Elizabeth
WALTER, Peter; bn. Sep 2, 1795; bpt. Sep 2, 1795; son of Peter &
    Marguerite
WALTER, Peter; bn. Nov 17, 1799; bpt. Dec 15, 1799; son of Peter
    & Margaret
WALTER, Tersia; bn. Jan 31, 1791; bpt. Feb 5, 1791; dau. of Peter
    & Margaret
(WALTERS), Mary; bn. Dec 25, 1794; bpt. Jun 7, 1795; dau. of
    Sarah, slave of Mr. James Walters
WALTON, Elizabeth Eleanora; bn. Jun 11, 1797; bpt. Oct 29, 1797;
    dau. of John & Barbara
WALTON, Elizabeth; bn. Oct 24, 1797; bpt. Apr 15, 1798; dau. of
    Charlton Alexander & Sarah
WALTON, John; bpt. Apr 10, 1798; 3 1/2 years old; son of Charlton
    Alexander & Sarah
WALTON, Maria; bn. Feb 26, 1795; bpt. Mar 15, 1795; dau. of John
    & Barbara
WALTON, Mary; bn. Feb 18, 1800; bpt. Apr 20, 1800; dau. of John &
    Barbara
WALTON, Samuel; bn. Nov 3, 1795; bpt. Apr 15, 1798; son of
    Charlton Alexander & Sarah
WALTON, Sarah; bpt. Apr 29, 1800; 3 months; dau. of Charleton &
    Sarah
(WANTE), Achilles; bpt. Aug 24, 1800; 7 months; son of Julie,
    slave of Mr. Wante
WANTE, Ann Felicity; bn. Apr 6, 1799; bpt. Aug 14, 1799; dau. of
    Charles Stephen Peter & Rose DuBreuil
(WANTE), Felicity Adelaide; bpt. Jun 3, 1798; 4 months; dau. of
    Julie Chloe, slave of Mr. Wante

BAPTISMS

WANTE, Teresa Rose; bn. May 7, 1797; bpt. Aug 30, 1797; dau. of Charles Stephen Peter & Mary Rose DuBrauil
WARD, John; bn. Mar 12, 1796; bpt. Jun 26, 1796; son of John & Rachel
WARNER, Mary Ann; bpt. Sep 7, 1800; dau. of Joseph & Sophia
WATKINS, John; bn. Jul 29, 1797; bpt. Aug 12, 1797; son of Joshua & Mary
WATKINS, Rebecca; bn. Aug 12, 1798; bpt. Sep 9, 1798; dau. of Joshua & Mary
WATS, Mary; bn. Sep 8, 1788; bpt. Oct 13, 1788; sps. William Boylan & Catharine Shilling
WATSON, Samuel; bn. Feb 26, 1786; bpt. Mar 26, 1786; sps. Patrick Matthews & Mary Reed
WATTS, Elizabeth; bpt. Jul 10, 1791; born a month ago; dau. of John & Catharine
WATTS, Elizabeth; bpt. Feb 10, 1799; 4 months; dau. of Thomas & Elizabeth
WEAKS, Elizabeth Ann; bn. Apr 16, 1781; bpt. Dec 2, 1783; sps. Ann Nash
WEAVER, Elizabeth; bn. May 14, 1795; bpt. Jun 13, 1795; dau. of Gaspar & Elizabeth
WEAVER, George Frederic; bn. Apr 16, 1790; bpt. Apr 24, 1790; son of Gaspar & Elizabeth
WEAVER, John; bn. May 29, 1796; bpt. Jun 5, 1796; son of Jacob & Elizabeth
WEAVER, Joseph; bn. Apr 15, 1800; bpt. May 31, 1800; son of Gaspar & Elizabeth
WEAVER, Margaret; bn. Oct 20, 1783; bpt. Oct 22, 1783; sps. Matthias Baker & wife
WEAVER, William; bn. Nov 17, 1797; bpt. Dec 11, 1797; son of Gaspar & Elizabeth
WEB, Margaret; bpt. Jun 24, 1787; 3 months; sps. John Ryan & Elizabeth Penston
WEDDERSTRAND, John Carroll; bn. Sep 2, 1799; bpt. May 21, 1800; son of Thomas & Mary Charlotte
WEDERSTRANDT, Thomas; bn. Aug 2, 1797; bpt. Aug 9, 1797; son of Thomas & Mary
WEDGE, Mary; bn. Sep 19, 1794; bpt. Sep 21, 1794; dau. of Joseph & ?
WEDGE, Samuel; bn. Aug 24, 1799; bpt. Sep 29, 1799; son of Simon & Margaret
WEDGE, Sarah; bn. Dec 24, 1799; bpt. Jan 27, 1800; dau. of Joseph & Mary; sps. Samuel Chameau & Ann Caldron
WEEKS, John; bn. Aug 31, 1795; bpt. Oct 18, 1795; son of William & Ann
WEETES, Mary; bpt. Oct 6, 1793; dau. of William & Ann Blackford
WEEVER, Anna Catherina; bn. Jan 1, 1788; bpt. Jan 22, 1788; sps. John Keller & Anna Catharina Keller
WEEVER, John; bn. Jan 28, 1786; bpt. Feb 6, 1786; sps. John Sleigh
WEEVER, Mary; bn. Mar 30, 1792; bpt. Apr 7, 1792; dau. of Jasper & Elizabeth
WEINTNY, George Jack; bn. Feb 15, 1786; bpt. Apr 16, 1786; sps. George Homegers & Catharine Komeirs

BAPTISMS

WEISS, Catharine; bn. Jul 25, 1797; bpt. Jul 31, 1797; dau. of Michael & Catharine
WEISS, Felix; bn. Apr 12, 1798; bpt. Apr 22, 1798; son of Felix & Barbara
WEISS, Felix; bn. Mar 3, 1800; bpt. Mar 9, 1800; son of Felix & Barbara
WEISS, George; bn. Jun 28, 1793; bpt. Jul 3, 1793; son of Felix & Barbara
WEISS, John; bn. Apr 8, 1797; bpt. Apr 17, 1797; son of Felix & Barbara
WEISS, Teresa; bn. Jan 17, 1800; bpt. Feb 2, 1800; dau. of Michael & Catharine
WELLS, Alexander; bn. Feb 24, 1783; bpt. Mar 10, 1783; sps. Joseph Gold & Mary White
WELLS, Ann; bn. Dec 28, 1788; bpt. Apr 26, 1789; sps. William Jenkins & Margaret Gold
WELLS, Cyprian; bn. Sep 17, 1790; bpt. Dec 10, 1790; son of Francis Cyprian & Peggy
WELLS, Harriot; bn. Jul 2, 1798; bpt. Jul 9, 1798; dau. of Cyprian & Margaret
WELLS, John Francis; bn. Aug 27, 1795; bpt. Nov 8, 1795; son of Cyprian & Margaret
WELLS, Margaret; bn. Jan 4, 1785; bpt. Mar 6, 1785; sps. Thomas Jenkins & Ann Wells
WELLS, Sarah Mary Antoniette; bn. Sep 16, 1793; bpt. Nov 10, 1793; dau. of Cyprian & Margaret
WELLS, Thomas William; bn. Nov 18, 1786; bpt. Apr 4, 1787; sps. William Paule & Peggy Mongee
WELSH, Catharine; bn. Dec 1, 1790; bpt. Dec 11, 1790; dau. of Edward & Catharine
WELSH, Mary; bn. Mar 13, 1789; bpt. Apr 5, 1789; sps. Robert Conway & Jane Conway
WELSH, Richard; bn. Jul 3, 1792; bpt. Aug 26, 1792; son of Thomas & Mary
WEST, Susanna; bpt. Jun 28, 1796; 13 years old; dau. of Luke & Sarah
WESTRUM, Andrew; bn. Oct 4, 1787; bpt. Nov 18, 1787; sps. Francis Vintry & Ann Gertrude
WEYMAN, Mary Ann; bn. Feb 17, 1795; bpt. Apr 5, 1795; dau. of Jacob & Hester
WHEELER, Benjamin; bn. Oct 15, 1785; bpt. Jan 25, 1786; sps. Lydia Sanders
WHEELER, Elizabeth Christina; bn. Mar 20, 1797; bpt. Mar 30, 1797; dau. of Leon & Theresa
WHEELER, Francis Benjamin; bn. Aug 12, 1799; bpt. Sep 11, 1799; son of Leonard & Teresa
WHEELER, Jacob; bn. Nov 8, 1792; bpt. Nov 26, 1792; son of Jacob & Ann
WHEELER, Louisa Catharine; bn. Mar 14, 1797; bpt. Apr 20, 1797; dau. of Harriot
WHEELER, Sarah; bn. Nov 30, 1783; bpt. Jan 4, 1784; sps. Thomas Wheeler & Clare Wheeler
WHELAN, Catharine; bn. Nov ?, 1780; bpt. Apr 24, 1790; dau. of Richard & Elenor Burns

BAPTISMS

WHELAN, Frances; bn. Mar 31, 1794; bpt. Jul 18, 1797; dau. of
    Mary Whelan
WHELAN, John; bn. Apr 20, 1783; bpt. Aug 14, 1783; sps. Francis
    Anthony DeFerrera Merrara & Nancy Power
WHELAN, Mary; bn. Jun 5, 1797; bpt. Jun 25, 1797; dau. of
    Jonathan & Mary
WHELAN, Mary; bn. Jun 23, 1800; bpt. Jun 27, 1800; dau. of John &
    Mary
WHELAN, Patrick; bn. Mar 1, 1799; bpt. Mar 10, 1799; son of
    Jonathan & Mary
WHELAN, Walter; bn. May 15, 1797; bpt. Aug 13, 1799; son of
    Daniel & Mary
WHITE, Anthony; bn. Sep 3, 1798; bpt. Sep 16, 1798; son of Lewis
    & Catharine
WHITE, Catharine; bn. Aug 31, 1786; bpt. Sep 17, 1786; sps.
    Cyprian Wells & Margaret Wells
(WHITE), Charles; bpt. Apr 10, 1787; 5 weeks; slave of Joe White;
    sps. Antony Diderich & Polly Babin
WHITE, Cornelius; bn. Feb 27, 1792; bpt. Mar 1, 1792; son of
    Simon & Jenny
WHITE, George; bn. Jan 6, 1783; bpt. Jan 16, 1783; sps. Hermange
    & Mary Purry
(WHITE), James; bpt. Oct 4, 1786; 4 weeks; slave of Joe White;
    sps. Polly White
WHITE, Jane; bn. Oct 2, 1790; bpt. Oct 17, 1790; dau. of Simon &
    Jane
(WHITE), John; bn. Apr 30, 1788; bpt. May 14, 1788; slave of
    Capt. Jos. White; sps. Mary Gutteran
WHITE, John; bn. Jun 18, 1800; bpt. Jul 13, 1800; son of James &
    Honor
WHITE, Joseph; bn. Dec 3, 1788; bpt. Dec 16, 1788; sps. Thomas
    Jenkins & Mary White
WHITE, Laurence; bn. Apr 23, 1787; bpt. Aug 11, 1787; sps. Mary
    Jubel
WHITE, Margaret; bn. Oct 4, 1794; bpt. Oct 12, 1794; dau. of
    Joseph & Margaret; sps. Matthew Deigre & Elizabeth Chameau
WHITE, Peter; bn. Aug 31, 1786; bpt. Sep 15, 1786; sps. Simon
    Deagle & Elizabeth Deagle
WHITE, Rachael; bn. Dec 1, 1784; bpt. Oct 2, 1785; sps. Stephen
    Lynch & Mary Freeman
WHITE, Rachel Maria; bn. Dec 10, 1793; bpt. Jan 26, 1794; dau. of
    Simon & Jane
WHITE, Simon Bijau; bn. Oct 16, 1783; bpt. Dec 29, 1783; sps.
    Paul Bijau & Margaret Goto
WHITE, Stephen; bn. Jan 14, 1785; bpt. Jan 30, 1785; sps. Simon
    Deagle & Margaret Gold
(WHITE), Susanna; bn. Aug 31, 1790; bpt. Sep 19, 1790; slave of
    Joseph White
WHITE, William; bn. Nov 5, 1790; bpt. Nov 7, 1790; son of Joseph
    & Margaret
WHITE, William; bn. Sep 13, 1795; bpt. Oct 18, 1795; son of Simon
    & Jane; sps. Bishop Carroll & Mary Wells, widow
WHITE, William Henry; bn. Apr 22, 1798; bpt. Apr 30, 1798; son of
    Simon & Jane

BAPTISMS

WHITEFIELD, Jacob; bn. Apr 10, 1789; bpt. May 30, 1789; son of
    Philip & Mary
WICKS, Richard; bn. Mar 1, 1800; bpt. Mar 6, 1800; son of John &
    Mary
WIEMAN, Henry; bn. Oct 8, 1800; bpt. Nov 30, 1800; son of
    Matthias & Elizabeth
WILDE, Ann; bn. May 5, 1800; bpt. Jun 1, 1800; dau. of Richard &
    Mary
WILDE, John; bn. Mar 20, 1798; bpt. Apr 4, 1798; son of Richard &
    Mary
WILL, John; bn. Oct 22, 1793; bpt. Nov 26, 1793; son of
    Christopher & Rosanna
WILL, Margaret; bn. Feb 8, 1789; bpt. Feb 15, 1789; sps. Peter
    Walter & Margaret Walter
WILLIAM, Magdalene; bn. Jan 29, 1794; bpt. Mar 23, 1794; dau. of
    Nicholas & Catharine Harvey
WILLIAMS, Catharine; bpt. Feb 19, 1799; 1 year old; Mulatto; dau.
    of Esther Williams, free Multress & John, slave of Mrs.
    Flanagan
WILLIAMS, Elizabeth; bn. Nov 14, 1784; bpt. Nov 28, 1784; sps.
    Peter Blossom & Elizabeth Williams
WILLIAMS, Jennet; bn. Jul 10, 1795; bpt. Jul 16, 1795; dau. of
    John & Jennet
WILLIAMS, John; bn. Dec 21, 1788; bpt. Mar 12, 1789; sps. Mary
    DeLisle
WILLIAMS, John; bpt. Aug 10, 1800; son of Esther Williams, free
    Negro
WILLIAMS, John Baptist; bn. Aug 6, 1797; bpt. Sep 17, 1797; son
    of Charlotte Williams
WILLIAMS, Lucy; bpt. Aug 30, 1789
WILLIAMS, Mary; bn. Oct 25, 1790; bpt. Apr 19, 1791; dau. of
    James & Mary
WILLIAMS, William; bn. Jan 23, 1793; bpt. Feb 9, 1793; son of
    John & Jenette
WILLIAMSON, Catherine; bn. Feb 10, 1783; bpt. Mar 2, 1783; sps.
    William Fousse & Catherine Fousse
WILLIAMSON, Charles Alexander; bn. Jun 2, 1800; bpt. Aug 4, 1800;
    son of David & Juliet
WILLIAMSON, Emily Sophia; bn. Apr 9, 1799; bpt. May 6, 1799; dau.
    of David & Juliet
WILLIAMSON, Henrietta Maria; bn. Jul 7, 1790; bpt. Jul 8, 1790;
    dau. of David & Henrietta
(WILLIAMSON), Henry; bpt. Sep 19, 1799; 4 years old; son of Harry
    & Mira, slave of D. Williamson
WILLIAMSON, James; bn. May 9, 1786; bpt. Jul 14, 1786; sps. James
    Neale & Winifred Deady
WILLIAMSON, John; bpt. Jul 3, 1784; 3,4 weeks; sps. John Kirnan &
    Elizabeth Clemens
(WILLIAMSON), John Lexington; bn. Apr 13, 1799; bpt. Sep 19,
    1799; son of Harry & Mira, slave of D. Williamson
WILLIAMSON, Juliana; bn. Dec 25, 1796; bpt. Jan 22, 1797; dau. of
    David & Juliet
WILLIAMSON, Rachael Frances; bn. Oct 21, 1793; bpt. Nov 3, 1793;
    dau. of David & Henrietta

BAPTISMS

(WILLIAMSON), Rachel; bpt. Sep 19, 1799; 2 years old; dau. of
    Harry & Mira, slave of D. Williamson
WILLIS, Mary; bpt. Sep 17, 1786; 1 month; sps. Nicholas Pluchard
    & Mary Pluchard
WILLS, Penelope; bn. Jul 10, 1796; bpt. Jul 21, 1799; dau. of
    Luke & Eleanor
WILLSON, Herbert; bn. Aug 12, 1795; bpt. Aug 16, 1795; son of
    David & Ann
WILLSON, John Francis; bn. Dec 3, 1797; bpt. Apr 1, 1798; son of
    David & Ann
WILLSON, Stephen Partridge; bn. Jun 5, 1799; bpt. Aug 11, 1799;
    son of David & Ann
WILLY, Charlotte Terese; bn. Dec 24, 1796; bpt. Jul 23, 1797;
    dau. of Joseph & Sarah
WILSON, Elsy; bn. May ?, 1790; bpt. Feb 6, 1791; Negro
WILSON, George; bpt. Nov 9, 1800; son of James & Catharine
WILSON, Margaret; bn. Mar 12, 1793; bpt. Mar 24, 1793; dau. of
    John & Ann
WILSON, William Brown; bn. Jun 16, 1799; bpt. Jul 22, 1799; son
    of Mary Wilson, Mulatress
WINELER, John Jacob; bpt. Nov 27, 1785; 8 weeks; sps. Jacob
    Weismiller & Catharine Bob
WININGER, Ludwick; bn. Jun 25, 1788; bpt. Jun 29, 1788; sps.
    Lewis Porter & Catharine Porter
WININGTEN, Catharine; bn. Dec 27, 1784; bpt. Jan 6, 1785; sps.
    Joseph Sheiden & Catharine Sheiden
WINKLER, George Philip; bpt. Sep 21, 1788; 3 months; sps. John
    Pop & Catharine Pop
WINN, Christopher; bn. Mar 10, 1796; bpt. Sep 10, 1797; son of
    Christopher & Margaret
WINN, Eleanor; bn. Sep 21, 1798; bpt. Oct 28, 1798; dau. of
    Christopher & Margaret
WINN, Lewisa; bn. Jan 24, 1791; bpt. Feb 6, 1791; dau. of
    Christopher & Margaret
WINSTED, Elizabeth; bn. May 1, 1797; bpt. Aug 20, 1797; dau. of
    Charles & Ann
WINSTED, Mary; bn. Jun 23, 1796; bpt. Nov 6, 1796; dau. of
    Elizabeth Winsted
WINTERS, Mary; bpt. Mar 9, 1800; 3 years old, dau. of Rebecca
    Winters, free Negro
WISE, Felix; bn. Sep 2, 1798; bpt. Sep 16, 1798; son of Michael &
    Catharine
WISE, William; bn. Jan 18, 1798; bpt. May 1, 1798; son of Wiliam
    & Rachel
WITENFIELD, Mary Ann; bn. Jun 25, 1783; bpt. Sep 4, 1783; sps.
    Joseph Meyer & Judith
WITHERHOLD, John; bn. Mar 25, 1794; bpt. Mar 26, 1794; son of
    John Mathais & Juliana Witherhold
WOGAN, Denis; bn. Dec 1, 1798; bpt. Jan 13, 1799; son of John &
    Eleanor
WOLFENDEN, George; bn. Dec 19, 1789; bpt. Jun 30, 1790; son of
    Beauchamp & Mary Otway
WOLLS, John; bpt. Jul 4, 1784; 3 weeks; sps. Vincent Champel &
    Peggy Grainger
WOODS, Thomas; bpt. Apr 17, 1793; adult

BAPTISMS

WORINGTON, Elizabeth; bn. Feb 13, 1794; bpt. Feb 20, 1794; dau. of Henry & Mary
WORTHINGTON, Henry; bn. Feb 17, 1783; bpt. Mar 21, 1784; sps. Henry Phillips & Mary Phillips
WORTHINGTON, John; bn. Aug 13, 1789; bpt. Aug 16, 1789; son of Henry & Mary
WRIGHT, Ann; bpt. Jan 1, 1793; 7 weeks; dau. of Alexander & Christina
WRIGHT, Robert; bn. ?, 1777; bpt. Sep 26, 1790; sps. John Ehrmond & wife
WYEMAN, Barbara; bn. Mar 11, 1796; bpt. Jul 31, 1796; dau. of Jacob & Hesther
WYN, Joseph; bn. Sep 7, 1788; bpt. Sep 21, 1788; sps. Peter Gold & Polly White
WYNN, Daniel Stephen; bn. Apr 12, 1793; bpt. May 5, 1793; son of Christopher & Margaret
WYSE, John; bn. Mar 18, 1795; bpt. Jun 17, 1795; son of William & Rachel
YANTS, George; bn. Sep 19, 1798; bpt. Sep 28, 1798; son of George & Mary
YANTS, Susanna; bn. Dec 2, 1793; bpt. Sep 4, 1795; dau. of George & Mary
YANTZ, William; bn. May 15, 1796; bpt. May 24, 1796; son of George & Mary
YAW, Mary Magdalen; bpt. Dec 11, 1787; 5 years old; sps. Renaldus Pinault & Ann Butler
YERBY, Francis Marie; bn. Apr 18, 1800; bpt. Apr 27, 1800; dau. of William & Elizabeth
YERBY, Margaret Mary Ann; bn. May 20, 1799; bpt. Jun 9, 1799; dau. of William & Elizabeth
YERMAN, Stephen; bn. Jun 2, 1784; bpt. Jun 7, 1784; sps. Estenne Ross & Rosaly Mangee
YONS, Catharine; bn. Jun 9, 1779; bpt. Nov 28, 1783; sps. John Casey & Mary Moring
YOUNG, Elizabeth; bpt. May 18, 1793; about 13 years old; conditional; dau. of John & Elizabeth
YOUNG, John William Stenson; bn. Aug 29, 1796; bpt. Nov 28, 1796; son of John (deceased) & Penelope
YOUNG, Mary; bn. Nov 6, 1792; bpt. Dec 26, 1792; dau. of Nicholas & Mary
YOUNG, Milly; bn. Jan ?, 1788; bpt. Oct 19, 1788; Negro; sps. Milly
YOUNG, Rebecca; bn. Feb 13, 1796; bpt. May 8, 1796; dau. of William & Frances
YOUNGER, Elizabeth; bn. Apr 16, 1784; bpt. Apr 17, 1784; sps. John Giban & Elizabeth Sreigly
YOUNGER, Francis; bn. Aug 22, 1785; bpt. Sep 11, 1785; sps. Francis Duluc & Mary Purry
ZACHARIE, Stephen; bn. Jun 14, 1792; bpt. Aug 7, 1792; son of Stephen & Anne
ZEPHINE, John Charles; bpt. Sep 24, 1793; son of Charles & Mary Agnes
ZIEGLER, Elizabeth; bn. Jul 22, 1794; bpt. Aug 24, 1794; dau. of Francis & Frances

BAPTISMS

ZIEGLER, John; bn. Jun 15, 1785; bpt. Jun 26, 1785; sps. Antony
    Hook & wife
ZIMMER, Nicholas; bn. Jul 17, 1799; bpt. Jul 26, 1799; son of
    Henry & Gertrude
ZIMMERMANN, Mary; bpt. Jun 14, 1795; 6 years old; dau. of
    Catharine Zimmermann

MARRIAGES BY GROOM

Alexius to Henrietta, Nov 30, 1799; 1. Bishop Carroll's Negro
    servant; 2. free Mulatto woman
Caleb to Rose, Jun 1, 1788
Hector to Marie Louise, Dec 28, 1799; both Negroes
Jean Jacques to Mary Agnes, Apr 26, 1800; both Negroes
Leonard to Bett, by license, Dec 26, 1786
Ned to Sarah, Apr 22, 1792
Phil to Clare, Jun 10, 1792
ADAMS, James to Margaret SHENEY, by license, May 28, 1800; 1.
    nat. of Ireland; 2. widow Shirk
ADAMS, James to Agnes BUTLER, by banns, Dec 21, 1800; both
    Negroes
ADONIS, Charles to Elizabeth LACHENAL, by license, Jul 16, 1799;
    free Mulattoes of St. Domingo
ALLAERT, James to Ann QUEDAN, by license, Oct 28, 1798
ALLAIN, Lewis to Ann BOISSON, by license, Oct 29, 1796; 1. son of
    Thomas & Jane Roboutet of Bordeaux; 2. dau. of Thomas &
    Adelaide Cornu, nat. of Cp. Francais
ALLEN, Patrick to Elizabeth DOYLE, by banns, Apr 19, 1790
AMI, Francis to Ann TILLARD, by license, Aug 16, 1795; 1. nat. of
    Lyons, France; 2. born in Acadia
AMIE, John Baptist Joseph Amable to Helen Frances Toullain DUPUY,
    by license, Jun 27, 1797; 1. son of John Baptist Joseph &
    Margaret Louise Julie Chambeiron; nat. of Brignoles;
    physician; 2. dau. of Peter Francis Toullain & Margaret
    Susanna Monchet; nat. of Plaisance, St. Domingo
ANDERSON, William to Kitty PATTERSON, by license, Jun 25, 1790
ANTHONY, James to Magdalen PINDARE, Feb 8, 1796; French free
    Negroes from St. Domingo
APHOLD, George Nicholas to Mary MARTIN, by banns, Feb 13, 1796;
    1. nat. of Germany; 2. nat. of Pennsylvania
ARAUGHTY, Laurence to Mary LEWIS, by license, Jul 8, 1800; 1.
    nat. of Ireland; 2. nat. of Pennsylvania; of Balto. Co.
(ARIEU), John Francis to Mary Magdalen, Jul 24, 1796; 1. free
    Negro from St. Domingo, formerly a slave of Mr. Gabriel
    Arieu, planter St. Domingo; 2. free Negro, formerly
    belonging to said, John Francis, her actual husband
ARMAND, Francis to Margaret LEBAT, by license, Jul 3, 1794; 1.
    nat. of LaRochelle, France; 2. widow
ARMOUR, David to Mary HILLEN, by license, May 14, 1793; 1.
    non-Catholic
BACONAIS, Lewis Francis Mary to Constance Agatha ASSAILLY, by
    license, Jun 26, 1798
BADET, John Baptist to Jane Frances CARRERE, by license, May 21,
    1794; 1. nat. of L'Artibonite Is., San Domingo; 2. nat. of
    Bordeaux; widow of Mr. Copela
BAINER, William to Elizabeth STEIGER, by license, Apr 25, 1793
BAKER, Joseph to Magdalen FULWEILER, by license, Jan 30, 1800; 1.
    widower; 2. widow
BARICKMAN, Anthony to Christina BAKER, by license, Jun 12, 1784
BAROUX, James Michael to Mary DEAGLE, by license, Nov 16, 1793;
    1. nat. of Arras
BARRY, Redmond to Johanna HANNECY, by license, Dec 27, 1790

MARRIAGES BY GROOM

BAUDUY, Louis Alexander Amelie to Victoire Agathe Marguerite
    DARNAUD, by license, Apr 15, 1799; 1. son of John Baptist &
    Helene Curon; nat. of St. Domingo; 2. dau. of Stephen &
    Martha Mary Frances Laulaigne; nat. of St. Domingo
BAYLOR, William to Mary WYSTER, by banns, Jun 10, 1783
BEAUDU, William to Mary Ann HUBON, by license, Aug 2, 1796; 1.
    nat. of Bordeaux; 2. nat. of Martinico
BEAUMEZ, Bon Albert Briois to Sarah Lyons FLUKER, by license, Mar
    22, 1796
BEAUPRE, Lewis Nan to Victoire BARDAN, by license, Oct 14, 1795;
    1. son of Lewis Nan Rochefort, counsellor of the King, &
    Mary Bouchereau; 2. dau. of Jon Baptist & Frances Collette
    Lamonie
BECK, John to Anna MILLER, by license, Dec 6, 1794; natives of
    Germany
(BEESTON), Ignatius to Catharine (NAGOT), May 26, 1795; 1. slave
    of Rev. Beeston; 2. slave of Rev. Nagot
BEGNALL, Michael to Ann CROMWELL, by license, Jun 21, 1798
BELLEVILLE, Lewis to Mary Ann FAURE, Feb 7, 1800; 1. Captain
BENER, Henry to Elizabeth HEIMLIN, by banns, Dec 1, 1793
BENILLANT, Stephen to Clare Theresa PISSARD, by license, Feb 22,
    1796; 1. son of Peter & Ann LeCroix; nat. of Cp. Francois,
    St. Domingo; 2. nat. of Marseilles, France; widow Argentel,
    dau. of Raimond & Catharine Chailan
BENTHEIM, Frederic to Mary STEIGER, by banns, Aug 2, 1783
BENTLEY, Michael to Eleanor CATON, by license, Oct 9, 1796;
    natives of Ireland
BERGMAN, Joseph to Catherine STEIGER, by banns, Nov 28, 1786
BERMAN, Matthew to Ann DULIAR, by license, Nov 25, 1783
BERNARD, Charles to Mary WHITE, Dec 4, 1784
BERNETT, Jacob to Mary THOMPSON, by license, Dec 1, 1793
BERRY, John to Mary SPENCE, by banns, Jul 25, 1791
BERTHOLIN, Joseph to Eve ELCON, by license, Jun 11, 1791
BERTRAND, John Peter to Victoire Sophie VATMEL, by license, Feb
    17, 1795; 1. son of Peter Lewis & Mary Martha Poupel; born
    at St. Germain du Montivillers, diocese of Rouen; 2. dau. of
    Lewis & Angelica Godefray, born at Havre de Grace, France
BIDOT, John Peter to Peggy TONEREY, by license, Mar 26, 1788
BIRMINGHAM, James to Ruth WILSON, by license, Aug 6, 1799; 1.
    widower; 2. widow
BISHOP, Richard to Elizabeth YOUNG, by license, Oct 19, 1796; 1.
    mariner; 2. Fells Point
BIZOUARD, Joseph Yves to Reine PATERSON, by license, Aug 25, 1794
BLAIR, John to Catharine CRONAN, by license, Sep 25, 1796;
    natives of Ireland; 1. mariner
BLOSSOM, Peter to Mary Magdalen LEBLANC, by license, Jan 30, 1791
BOISLANDRY, Robert Charles LeGrand to Louisa Frances BUSCAILLE,
    by license, Sep 17, 1796; 1. son of Damien LeGrand &
    Margaret Tassin; nat. of Orleans; widower; 2. dau. of James
    Lewis & Mary Catharine LeGaigneur; nat. of Port du Paix
BONNER, Hugh to Mary SILK, by license, Aug 12, 1796
BORDERIE, Bernard to Elizabeth BULGER, by license, Jan 4, 1794;
    1. merchant of Bordeaux; 2. Montgomery Co., Md.
BORIE, Joseph to Margaret LOCKERMAN, by license, Aug 30, 1794; 1.
    nat. of Point Petre, Is. of Guadaloupe

MARRIAGES BY GROOM

BOUDRAU, Charles to Mary YAU, by banns, Sep 9, 1787
BOURGEOIS, Antony Chapeau to Anna Savon PARCE, by license, Apr 4, 1794; 1. nat. of Conne Province; 2. nat. of St. Heule, diocese of Lisberon, France
BOX, Nicholas to Mary OXFORD, by banns, Oct 14, 1787
BOYLE, William to Mary BURK, by banns, Dec 23, 1787
BOYREAU, John Joseph to Mary MARZIAL, by license, Jun 11, 1792
BRACKMAN, Anthony to Ann HENDERICKS, by license, Sep 8, 1793
BRADBURY, Stephen to Margaret COLGAN, by license, Oct 6, 1798; 1. nat. of Mass.
BRADY, John to Mary MCFEE, by license, Aug 25, 1793
BREARD, Michael Augustus to Sophia Francoise DELORE, by license, Dec 17, 1792
BREIDENBAUGH, John to Anne MORAN, by license, Nov 4, 1798
BREMONT, John to Frances Elizabeth DELESFAURIS, by license, Nov 19, 1793; 1. son of Bernard & Martha Dauhorat; nat. of Rau in Bearn; 2. dau. of John Martin & Radegonde Richer
BROOKS, William to Elizabeth JENNINGS, by license, Jan 24, 1792
BROWN, James to Hannah JAFFRIS, by license, Apr 14, 1793
BROWN, John to Mary ROSENSTEEL, by license, Nov 25, 1798
BROWN, Moses to Mary SNOWDEN, by license, Apr 30, 1797; of Balto. Co.
BROWN, Thomas to Mary COLGAN, by license, Mar 4, 1797
BUCHMAN, George to Barbara FISHER, by license, Mar 28, 1796
BUCHOLTZ, George to Elizabeth BUTCHER, by license, Oct 14, 1798
BUCKLEY, James to Mary LEARY, by license, Jul 1, 1800; natives of Ireland
BUGHEN, Engel to Mary Magdalen HISLIN, by banns, Oct 8, 1793
BUNBURY, M. Simmons to Ann BRIDE, by license, Sep 24, 1795
BURK, John to Mary ROACH, by license, Nov 17, 1784
BURKE, Richard to Catharine GLEESON, by license, Apr 27, 1800; natives of Ireland; 2. widow
BURNS, James to Jane CUMMINS, by license, Jul 28, 1793
BURNS, Simon to Mary KNOWLAN, by license, Jul 15, 1794; natives of Ireland
BUTCHER, Bartholomew to Elizabeth PLUME, by license, Sep 21, 1795
BUTLER, Anthony to Ruth MIDDELTON, Apr 16, 1797; 1. free Negro; 2. free Mulatto
BUTLER, John to Margaret COLEMAN, by banns, Nov 6, 1791
BUTLER, John Holpin to Margaret EVANS, by license, Apr 17, 1792
BUTLER, Walter to Elizabeth FINN, by license, Feb 4, 1786
BYRNE, Columbus John to Margaret HANKEY, Jan 16, 1800; 1. nat. of Ireland; widower; 2. nat. of Maryland
BYRNE, William to Catharine CAREY, by license, May 3, 1800
CABERA, John to Jane MITCHELL, by license, Nov 9, 1794
CAHIL, George to Eleanor MURPHY, by license, Dec 8, 1793; natives of Ireland
CALMAN, Joseph to Mary Martha RENOULLEAU, by license, Jun ??, 1794; 1. nat. of Treves; merchant, Cp. Francois; 2. nat. of San Domingo; dau. of John Baptist Charles and Ann Margaret Patterson
(CAMPBELL), George to Jane REED, Dec 24, 1797; 1. slave of Archibald Campbell; 2. free Negro woman
CAMPBELL, Robert to Catharine RARITY, by license, Sep 18, 1793

MARRIAGES BY GROOM

CANTEGRIL, Lewis to Mary PRUN, by banns, Feb 4, 1794; 1. son of
    John & Jane Lole; 2. dau. of John Baptist & Mary Magdalen
    Berquier
CAREY, Dennis to Margaret DILLON, by license, Sep 10, 1794
CARNAN, Daniel to Mary FREEMAN, by banns, Nov 1, 1786
CARRE, Joseph Mary to Magdalen DESCHAMPS, by license, Oct 27,
    1793; 1. son of Peter & Louisa Haudbois of St. Malo; 2. dau.
    of Lewis & Mary Tibodeau
CARRERE, John to Mary WALSH, by license, Feb 18, 1793
CARRICK, Daniel to Bridget FAHERTY, by license, Oct 1, 1796;
    natives of Ireland
CARROLL, Edward to Mary SULLIVAN, by banns, Aug 2, 1789
CARROLL, Henry Hill to Sarah ROGERS, by license, Nov 10, 1789
CARROLL, Michael to Nancy DRAKE, by license, Aug 26, 1795;
    natives of Ireland
(CARROLL), Samuel to Apollonia, Dec 21, 1793; 1. slave of Rt.
    Rev. Bishop Carroll; 2. free mulatto
CARROLL, Thomas to Rose CRAVEN, by license, Aug 10, 1787
CARROLL, Thomas to Sarah KING, by license, Dec 14, 1797
CARSON, Nathaniel to Eleanor CRESMAN, by license, Mar 5, 1791
CASEY, Robert to Elizabeth DAVIES, by license, Mar 30, 1796
(CATON), James to Clare (CATON), Nov 17, 1799; both belonging to
    Mr. Richard Caton
CATON, Mark to Ann CHERRY, by license, Dec 28, 1799; natives of
    Ireland
CAVAROC, Francis to Mary SEARS, by license, Nov 11, 1793; 1. son
    of John & Catharine Magne; nat. of Tiezac Diocese of
    Auverne; of Cp. Francois, St. Domingo; 2. dau. of James &
    Ann of Annapolis
CAYOL, Antony to Modeste TARDIEU, by license, Oct 7, 1799; 1.
    nat. of Marseilles; 2. nat. of St. Domingo
CEBRON, Olivier to Mary Joanna Foushine TROUVE, by license, May
    5, 1794; lately of San Domingo; 1. parish of Debouches,
    diocese of Nante; 2. from Piffivers, diocese of Orleans
CHAMBERLAIN, Charles to Mary GUTHROW, by license, Jun 21, 1798
CHAMILLON, Joseph to Ann MEADE, Dec 6, 1784
CHANGEUR, Leon to Josephine DeGripiere Monroe MONTALIBOR, by
    license, Jun 30, 1795; 1. son of Peter & Mary Samson of
    Bordeaux, France; 2. dau. of Germain DeGripiere Monroe,
    Order of St. Lewis, Lt. Col., Inf., formerly Commandant for
    the King, St. Domingo at Jeremie, Port au Paix, & Elizabeth
    De Bey
CHAREELE, Peter to Rachel, Feb 10, 1795; 1. free negro; St.
    Domingo; 2. free mulattress; Martinico
(CHASE), Nathaniel to Ann (LEDUC), Dec 2, 1794; 1. slave of
    Samuel Chase
CLARK, Edward to Jemima ADDISON, by license, Apr 8, 1790
CLARK, Patrick to Sarah MITCHELL, by license, Jan 12, 1792
CLARKE, David to Elizabeth CANADY, by license, Jun 13, 1792
CLARKE, Francis to Mary HAGHERTY, by banns, Mar 15, 1795; 1.
    widower; Fifer to Company of Artificers, garrisoned at
    Whetstone Point, Fort near Balto.
CLOHERTY, Patrick to Catharine TAYLOR, by license, Apr 22, 1800;
    1. nat. of Ireland; widower; 2. dau. of Philip & Catharine

MARRIAGES BY GROOM

CLOUGHERTY, Patrick to Honor FAHERTY, by license, Nov 12, 1795; natives of Ireland
COGEN, Dennis to Mary STEWART, by banns, Jul 5, 1795; 1. nat. of Ireland; 2. widow of Robert Stewart, born near Annapolis
COGHLAN, William to Catharine KIRK, by license, Nov 10, 1794; 1. of Washington, D.C.
COLLINS, George to Sarah JOYCE, by license, Nov 30, 1799; 1. widower; 2. widow
COLLINS, John to Mary CARNEY, by license, Jan 27, 1785
COLVIN, Philip to Rosetta Martin DESRAMEAUX, by license, Jan 1, 1793
COMINS, John to Christine GROGEN, by banns, Jan 30, 1785
CONNELLY, Robert to Mary PRESTON, by banns, Jul 10, 1789
CONNER, Arthur to Mary LONEY, by license, Dec 12, 1785
CORBELEY, Nicholas to Hannah KNEASS, by license, Nov 20, 1790
CORBIN, William to Catherine LEARY, by license, Jul 14, 1792
COULON, John Baptist to Mary MANGEE, Dec 12, 1784
COWAN, James to Catharine STRIDER, by license, Apr 30, 1799
COWAN, Thomas to Margaret VENNY, by license, Jul 14, 1796; residents of Fells Point; 1. from Derry in Ireland; non-Catholic; 2. widow
COX, Isaac to Mary BLOSSOM, by license, Jan 12, 1799; 1. sea captain; 2. widow
CRAMER, Edward to Mary BRITT, by license, Aug 31, 1794; natives of Ireland
CRISALL, Peter to Margaret RICHARDS, by license, Oct 6, 1790
CROSILLANT, Joachim to Charlotte ROUND, by license, Sep 4, 1794; 1. nat. of Bordeaux
CULLEN, John to Judith FENIX, by license, Aug 22, 1796; 1. nat. of Ireland; 2. nat. of Germany
CURRAN, James to Mary Ann RODDY, by license, Feb 6, 1800
CURTIS, William to Mary TURINE, by license, Feb 9, 1794
DAILY, James to Catharine KELFOHL, by banns, Jun 22, 1794; natives of Ireland
DALIQUET, John Baptist to Elizabeth MCSHERRY, by license, Sep 22, 1795; 1. nat. of Los Diocese of Auch; lately of St. Domingo; 2. widow of Patrick McSherry, dau. of of Charles & Belinda Clements
DALTON, George to Catharine VENNY, by license, Jan 21, 1798; 1. nat. of Newburyport, Mass.; 2. nat. of Ireland
DANFOSSY, Baltazar Maurice to Catharine Eugenie MORENO, by license, Dec 7, 1797; 1. nat. of Marseilles; lately planter St. Domingo; 2. nat. of Cp Francais
DANNENBERG, Frederick William to Dorothea KOENIG, by license, Apr 16, 1795
DAUGHERTY, Neal to Mary GREEN, by license, Sep 23, 1794; natives of Ireland
DAVIS, Francis to Catherine FITZGERALD, by banns, May 13, 1787
DAVIS, Henry Ferguson to Elizabeth BRITT, by license, Jan 22, 1795; 1. of Boston, Mass.
DAVIS, John to Mary BURDAN, by license, Jun 18, 1795; 1. nat. of Liverpool, Eng.
DAVIS, John to Rosanna MCGINNIS, by license, May 19, 1799
DAVOY, Michael to Ann KNOWLEN, by license, Feb 25, 1786
DAY, Andrew to Bridget COLLINS, by license, Feb 8, 1796

MARRIAGES BY GROOM

DEAGLE, Simon to Elizabeth BOUDVILLE, by license, Jul 9, 1785
DEALE, Jacob to Susanna DOUGHERTY, by license, Nov 15, 1798; of Balto. Co.
DEBEAULIEU, Jacque Simon Poulot to Catherine Mary Elizabeth HAY, by banns, Nov 27, 1794; 1. born at Magny Lepard, diocese of Paris; 2. born at Angouleme, France
DELADEBAT, Auguste Philipe Lasson to Therese ST. AVOYE, May 19, 1794; 1. nat. of Bordeaux; 2. widow of Charles Vallerot
DELAPORTE, Francis Frederic to Elizabeth Herbert COOPER, May 3, 1787
DELAT, Augustine to Frances ROSS, by license, Feb 12, 1786
DELAUNAY, James Anthony to Theresa Charlotte Mary Henrietta LABOURDAIS, by license, Nov 30, 1796; 1. son of late John & Magdalen Gonisseame
DELISLE, John to Mary BLIEZE, by license, Nov 18, 1785
DEMONTI, Joseph Herman to Mary Adelaide CONTANT, by license, Nov 7, 1798; 1. born near Strasbourg in Alsace; 2. nat. of Rouen in Normandy
DEMPSEY, Patric to Elizabeth MCDERMOT, by license, Jan 24, 1796; 1. Anne Arundel Co.; 2. Montgomery Co.
DEMPSEY, Thomas to Eleanor HOY, by license, Jul 11, 1799
DENNY, Neal to Rebecca ANDERSON, by license, Nov 24, 1796
DESAPRADE, John Francis Cabannes to Anne Joseph St. Martin DUFOUREQ, by license, Oct 22, 1798; 1. Knight of order of St. Lewis, Col. Commandant of Artillery & Adjutant General of southern part of St. Domingo; 2. dau. of Simon Joseph St. Martin & Mary Ann Smith, of St. Domingo
DESBORDES, Antony to Mary Clare LeGardeur TILLY, by license, Dec 17, 1795; 1. son of John Mary Landrieve & Mary Gilles Chanssegros DeLery; nat. of Paris; 2. dau. of Stephen Simon LeGardeur & Mary Rose Agnes Lomenie de Marme
DESEZE, John Baptist Alexis Mary to Mary Fortunee Louise BURON, by license, Nov 16, 1793; 1. son of Alexis, Attorney Gen. of the Council, Cp. Francais, St. Domingo & Catharine Rose LaCaze; 2. dau. of Julian & Mary Dasmieres of Ville Franche
DESPAUX, Joseph to Frances DEMANCHE, by license, Sep 10, 1793
DEVALCOURTE, Alexander to Margaret GOTO, by license, Jul 18, 1794; 1. nat. of Paris
DEVICE, John Darch Lovel to Margaret SUMMERS, by license, Nov 9, 1797
DISTANCE, William to Hetty (EVANS), May 31, 1800; 1. free Negro; 2. slave of William Evans
DITTO, Peter to Catharine CONRAD, by license, Oct 18, 1787
DIXON, William to Elizabeth (BERNABEU), Feb 25, 1796; 1. free negro; 2. slave of Mr. John Baptist Bernabeu, Consul of Spain for State of Md.
DIZABEAU, John to Magdalen HOLMES, by license, Apr 21, 1798
DOMBROUSKY, Raymond to Elizabeth MILLER, by banns, Feb 5, 1799
DONALDSON, James to Elizabeth BABINE, by license, Jun 28, 1791
DONOGHUE, Daniel to Bridget KELNAN, by banns, Sep 5, 1790
DOPP, Henry to Rachel MARTIN, by license, Apr 16, 1796; 1. nat. of Germany
DORNEY, John to Jane BLANEY, by license, Sep 25, 1796; born in Harford Co.

MARRIAGES BY GROOM

DORNEY, William to Elizabeth GREEN, by license, Sep 11, 1796; 1. son of John & Martha of Harford Co.; 2. dau. of Edward & Mary
DORSEY, Vachel to Clementine IRELAND, by license, Mar 14, 1786
DOUAT, Peter to Mary Frances, Jan 10, 1794; from Cp Francois; 1. Parish of Margot County of Medoc, Diocese of Bordeaux; 2. St John Baptist du trou, Cp Francois; negro
DOWNEY, Daniel Wilson to Ann BYRON, by banns, May 25, 1794; 2. widow
DOYLE, Nicholas to Ann MCDANIEL, by license, Jun 5, 1794; both Balto. Co.
DRINAN, Thomas to Mary PEMSTON, by license, Jan 6, 1793
DUCATEL, Edmond to Ann Pineau BRUCOURT, by license, May 28, 1795; 1. son of Edmond & Aime Magdalen Lessene; 2. dau. of John & Frances Boissen Pineau
DUCHEMIN, Francis to Margaret MONGEAU, by license, Jan 10, 1793
DUFF, John to Sarah GREEN, by license, Sep 11, 1791
DUFFY, Henry to Mary ROURKE, by license, Aug 3, 1800; natives of Ireland
DUFFY, Owen to Mary WILLIAME, by license, Mar 29, 1788
DUGAN, James to Ann GUTRY, by license, Aug 22, 1789
DULOHANY, John to Catherine FRANKLIN, by license, Apr 30, 1792
(DULONGUEVAL), Lewis John to Melany (DULONGUEVAL), Jun 24, 1795; slave of Mrs. DuLongueval, a French lady from St. Domingo
DUNCAN, William to Brigid RICE, by license, Jan 2, 1794
DUNN, Daniel to Elizabeth PARK, by license, Oct 21, 1798
DUNN, Edward to Mary O'HAGAN, Jun 14, 1794; natives of Ireland
DUNN, John to Eleanor FITZGERALD, by banns, Jul 26, 1790
DUNN, Michael to Mary MCGUIRE, by license, Jul 9, 1788
DUNNAVAN, Pierce to Nellie HARRIS, by license, Jun 20, 1790
DUNPHY, Richard to Mary SMITH, by license, Dec 8, 1799
DUPOIS, Christopher to Mary BRIER, by banns, Jan 19, 1796; 1. nat. of Harve de Grace, France
DURAMIER, Amable Ambrose Herbert to Marie Charlotte Justine TARDIEU, by license, Nov 10, 1800; 1. son of John Peter Nicholas Herbert Demontign, of King's bodyguards & Marie Adelaide LeJaulne; nat. of parish of Lieurai in Normandy; 2. dau. of John Baptist Joseph, parish of St. Lewis of Teremy, St. Domingo & Mary Ann Magdalen O-Coin
DURNEY, James to Ann MINEAHAN, by banns, Jan 22, 1792
DWYER, William to Elizabeth CASEY, by license, Feb 20, 1798; 1. widower; 2. widow
DWYER, William to Eleanor KELLY, by license, Dec 29, 1800; 1. widower; 2. widow
EBBECKE, John Frederick to Catharine FRY, by license, Dec 17, 1797; 1. born Minden, Germany
EDWARDS, Paul to Mary SINDOLPH, by license, Sep 18, 1792
ELMS, Samuel to Margaret DILLON, by license, Jan 5, 1792
ELVES, William to Anne Frances BOURDON, by license, May 12, 1795; 1. nat. of New Jersey; 2. dau. of Peter, formerly president of Supreme Council of Port au Prince, St. Domingo & Ann LeMaitre; born at Port au Prince
ESCAVAILLE, James to Mary HARGROVE, by license, Sep 7, 1799
EVANS, John to Margaret BURKE, by license, Apr 11, 1790

MARRIAGES BY GROOM

FABRE, Lewis Augustin to Henrietta TERRIER, by license, Feb 21, 1795; 1. son of Peter Augustin & Teresa Charlotte Testar; born at Paris; 2. dau. of Lewis & Charlotte Pecoul; widow of John Hermitte
FAGET, John to Catharine ELIE, May 29, 1800; 2. widow Bourges
FAHERTY, Patrick to Maria WHELAN, by license, Oct 4, 1798; natives of Ireland, now residing in Ann Arundel Co.; 2. widow of late Edward Faherty
FARREL, Timothy to Catharine BLAKE, by license, Oct 10, 1793; natives of Ireland
FAUR, Antoine to Janett Ann BROTHERSON, by license, May 19, 1787
FAURIE, Joseph to Ann Francoise Josephine D'ALBAN, by license, Apr 13, 1795; 1. son of Andrew & Petronille Penicand; 2. dau. of John Joseph & Ann Chauvet
FAVIER, John to Mary THOMPSON, by license, Dec 15, 1796
FEIK, Henry to Elizabeth TIETZEN, by license, Dec 26, 1796
FENGEAS, Lewis to Mary Jane Theresa PELLETIER, by banns, Sep 30, 1794; 1. son of Matthew & Magdalen Prat; nat. of Arles, France; 2. dau. of Peter & Mary Theresa Charbonnet Dumas; widow of John Baptist Victor DeBerthe DeRoujere of San Domingo
FENNELL, John to Sarah MILLER, by license, Feb 3, 1799
FERRI, Januarius to Catharine TRUEMAN, by license, Dec 1, 1800; 1. nat. of Naples, Italy; 2. nat. of Ireland
FERRON, John to Elizabeth DELANCO, by license, Feb 24, 1800; free Mulattoes from St. Domingo
FICKE, Herman to Ann CAIN, by license, Dec 3, 1799; 1. nat. of Germany
FIFER, George to Magdalen CONNET, by banns, Jun 24, 1800
FISHER, James to Ann WELLS, by license, May 31, 1787
FITZGERALD, Garrett to Margaret MYERS, by license, Mar 4, 1794; 1. nat. of Ireland
FITZGERALD, Richard to Catherine BUTLER, by banns, Sep 27, 1784
FITZGERALD, Richard to Anne COOPER, by license, Oct 12, 1796; 1. nat. of Ireland; 2. nat. of Virginia
FITZGERALD, Richard to Margaret CURRY, by license, Oct 22, 1798; of Balto. Co.
FITZPATRICK, John to Mary MARHEIM, by banns, Aug 20, 1786
FLAHAVAN, Richard to Catharine BALDWIN, by license, Dec 27, 1799; natives of Ireland; 2. widow
FLAHERTY, Patrick to Catharine CONNER, by license, Sep 8, 1794; natives of Ireland
FLETCHER, William to Melcha BUTTS, by license, Feb 20, 1800
FLEURY, Sebastian to Magdelen SAPEN, by license, Jun 3, 1786
FLIN, Frederic to Mary WRIGHT, by banns, May 17, 1784
FLOYD, Charles to Elizabeth DUNN, by license, Oct 5, 1794; natives of Ireland
FLOYD, Joseph to Catherine LOGUE, by license, Dec 9, 1794; both Co.
FLYNN, John to Margaret RILEY, by license, Mar 2, 1794; natives of Cork, Ireland
FOGERTY, Edward to Judith MEHIN, by license, Oct 30, 1797; natives of Ireland; 1. widower; 2. widow
FOLDWEILDER, Francis to Magdalen WINTZEILER, by banns, Feb 6, 1785

MARRIAGES BY GROOM

FOOSE, John to Augustina RIDDLE, by license, Jun 14, 1796
FOOSE, William to Martha MERIT, by license, Nov 4, 1798; Balto. Co.
FORD, Raymond to Peggy PODDEWANG, by license, May 28, 1784
FORD, William to Jane HOLMES, by license, Aug 11, 1798; natives of Ireland
FOSBENDER, Peter to Hedewig MYER, by banns, Aug 6, 1798
FOSBINDER, Peter to Elizabeth BUTCHER, by license, Dec 30, 1800; 1. widower
FOSSEY, John to Elizabeth MITCHEL, by license, Jan 24, 1798
FOY, Michael to Elizabeth ASPLE, by license, Mar 8, 1787
FRAHER, Edmond to Kitty DILLON, by license, Jul 1, 1800; natives of Ireland
FRIDAY, John to Elizabeth BOUGHAN, by banns, Jan 4, 1791
FULLHART, Jacob to Elizabeth JACOBS, by banns, Nov 8, 1789
GAFFORD, Joseph to Mary YORK, by license, Apr 13, 1800; of Balto. Co.
GALLAGHER, John to Phoebe BAXTLEY, by banns, May 24, 1795
GALLET, John Baptist to Mary CELESTIN, by banns, May 9, 1784
GANTEAUME, James to Elisa CASEY, by license, Sep 4, 1794
GANTEAUME, James to Elizabeth CASEY, by license, Nov 10, 1797; 1. nat. of France; 2. nat. of Ireland
GARLAND, John to Mary Ann LYSTON, by license, Nov 11, 1790
GAULINE, John Baptist to Marie Pauline Justine Betzi LENDER, by license, Nov 22, 1796; 1. son of John Baptist Roch, weigher of town of Marseilles & Ann Armand, nat. of Marseilles, lately planter of Grande Riviere, St. Domingo; 2. dau. of late Dominic & D. Soumillard, lately from Petite Riviere de L'Artbonite, St. Domingo
GAVAN, Matthew to Ann FITZGERALD, by license, Oct 4, 1795; natives of Ireland
GAYNOR, Hugh to Eleanor BURK, by banns, Aug 17, 1788
(GEANTY), John Baptist to Elizabeth, Jan 20, 1798; of St. Domingo; 2. free French Negro woman
GERARD, Peter to Magdalen MAMILLON, by license, Apr 20, 1783
GERBER, Charles to Catherine SMELSER, by license, Mar 13, 1786
GERLACH, John to Mary KEILHOLTZ, by license, Apr 7, 1796
GILBRAITH, John to Hannah CLARKE, by license, Jul 19, 1800
GIRAND, Alexander to Mary RYAN, by license, Oct 29, 1797
GLAVANY, Francis Remy to Elizabeth DECHAMP, by license, May 8, 1791
GLEESON, Morris to Mary MCDANIEL, by banns, May 22, 1788
GLEESON, Roger to Catharine BRYAN, by license, Jun 18, 1797; natives of Ireland; 2. widow
GLOTTUS, Joseph to Catharine HONAUR, by license, Aug 31, 1800
GONET, Marcellin to Louise Catharine PALLON, by license, Jan 2, 1799; 1. son of Sebastian & Magdalen Gravier; nat. of Dauphine; 2. dau. of James & Rose Generes; nat. of St. Domingo
GOODWIN, James to Lilly VINCENT, by license, Jul 15, 1798
GORE, Richard to Lettice MONTGOMERY, by license, Oct 30, 1790
GORE, Richard to Ally LANDILLAND, by license, Nov 8, 1794
GORMAN, Daniel P. to Alice O'DONALD, by license, Oct 25, 1800
GORMLY, Cornelius to Mary O'BRIEN, by license, Sep 18, 1796

MARRIAGES BY GROOM

GOUDAIN, Laurence to Sophia Maria Magdalen DESOBRY, by license, Dec 11, 1799; 1. born at Cp. Francois, eldest son of William & Mary Dupre Mon Troux; 2. dau. of Hilary Joseph & Elizabeth Martin, nat. of Cp. Francois
GOULD, Peter to Mary WHITE, by license, Dec 15, 1791
GOULDING, John to Martha GOULD, by license, Oct 23, 1788
GOULDING, Patrick to Anabella YOUNG, by license, Jun 7, 1794; 2. widow
GOUVERNET, Charles to Margaret WELLS, by license, Nov 28, 1799; 1. born in parish of Tervey Franches Compte
GRACHE, Bartholomew to Mary Ann RICHARDS, by license, Apr 24, 1800; 1. nat. of Genoa
GRANT, John to Jane CUNNINGHAM, by license, Nov 8, 1800
GRAY, John to Mary DWIER, by license, Nov 6, 1796; natives of Ireland
GREEN, Bennett to Anne JONES, by license, Nov 11, 1798
GREEN, Clement to Rebecca TODD, by license, May 8, 1800; 1. son of Benjamin & Elizabeth of Harford Co.
GREEN, James to Elizabeth ADISON, May 8, 1796; negro slaves of Richard Caton
GREEN, Thomas to Ann HARRYMAN, by license, Aug 29, 1795; 1. nat. of Charles Co.; 2. nat. of Arundel Co.
GREGORY, Peter to Mary Louisa (CRENZE), Nov 22, 1795; 1. free negro from St. Domingo; 2. slave of Mrs. Allaire Crenze
GREGORY, William to Ann TANNER, by license, Mar 19, 1796
GREHAN, James to Elizabeth HUNT, by banns, Oct 16, 1788
GRIFFIN, Abraham to Mary MILLER, by license, Aug 11, 1793
GROC, John Anthony to Catherine Mary LEMONNIER, by license, Dec 28, 1794; 2. widow of Charlet Chantrier of San Dominique
GROSS, Lewis to Catharine WISE, by license, Dec 17, 1795; 2. Frederick Co.
GUTHROW, John to Rebecca JOINER, by license, May 20, 1797; 1. widower; 2. widow
HAGAN, Andrew to Ann MCLAUGHLIN, by license, Jun 26, 1800; natives of Ireland
HAGERTY, William to Jenny BARRETT, by license, Apr 23, 1795; natives of Ireland; 2. widow Nicholson
HAILEY, Peter to Margaret LEARY, by license, Nov 28, 1790
HALL, John to Susanna LYNCH, by license, Nov 17, 1795
HALL, John to Juliana TOWNSEND, by license, Feb 7, 1798; 1. mariner; 2. widow
HAMILTON, Livy to Abigail BARRU, by license, Dec 27, 1797; 1. Charles Co.
HAMLIN, Peter to Mary KOALER, by license, Feb 23, 1800
HAMMOND, John to Frances CLIFFORD, by banns, Nov 7, 1790
HANDLEN, Patrick to Jane JAMES, by license, Jul 7, 1798
HANLY, Michael to Mary HANLY, by banns, Jul 21, 1792
HANNA, Andrew to Ann MARA, by license, Jun 21, 1798; 1. printer
HANNAN, James to Elizabeth THOMAS, by license, Jan 17, 1796
HANNAN, John to Margaret TOWERS, by license, Jan 4, 1795
HANNAN, Michael to Jennet WILLIAMS, by license, Apr 4, 1799; 2. widow
HARDEN, John Barton to Ann HUGHES, by license, Feb 25, 1794; both Co.
HARDING, Matthew to Mary DAVIS, by license, Feb 1, 1791

MARRIAGES BY GROOM

HARRISON, John to Elizabeth ROW, by banns, Nov 10, 1799
HARTNELL, James to Ann CARTY, by license, Nov 8, 1788
HARTZHOG, George to Dorothy TEINSNOR, by license, Apr 1, 1797
HASHAN, Josiah to Lucy DAVID, by license, May 26, 1791
HATTIER, Zenny to Magdalen PERDONNE, by license, Oct 31, 1794; 1. son of Edme & Francisca Pleon; nat. of Burgundy Province of France; 2. dau. of Usard & Magdalena Boillon; nat. of Rochelle, France
HAYES, John to Mary LANKSTON, by license, Jul 20, 1796; 1. nat. of Ireland; 2. nat. of Canada
HAYES, Walter C. to Maria Barbara WONDER, by license, Nov 20, 1800
HAYLY, Thomas to Catherine NAWLAN, by banns, Sep 21, 1786
HEALLY, Dennis to Mary HOLLAND, by banns, Nov 3, 1793
HEARN, Anthony to Sarah JENKINS, by license, Nov 18, 1794; 1. nat. of Ireland
HEIMEL, Jacob to Catharine FISHER, by license, May 21, 1798
HENNION, Joseph to Margaret HIONE, Apr 29, 1787
HENRY, Aaron to Minty BUTLER, by banns, Dec 23, 1800; both Negroes
HENRY, Thomas to Monica CARTER, by banns, Nov 24, 1800; both Negroes
HENRY, William to Nancy DUGAN, by license, Jan 21, 1796; natives of Ireland
HERMAN, Philip to Elizabeth HOOK, by license, Oct 20, 1788
HERTHER, Nathan to Catherine DIFFENDOLPH, by license, Sep 5, 1792
HERTZOG, Michael to Margaret BUTCHER, by banns, Apr 27, 1795
HEUISLER, Maximilian to Mary BERNARD, by license, Aug 31, 1791
HEWES, James to Eleanor GREEN, by license, Jan 19, 1789
HEYDEN, James to Elizabeth NUSSEAR, by license, Dec 20, 1798; 2. dau. of Jacob
HIGGENBOTHAM, Arthur to Eleanor WILLSON, by license, Aug 13, 1792
HIGH, Sebastian to Catharine WHITE, by license, Aug 4, 1796
HILLEN, John to Catherine RUSK, by license, Nov 23, 1784
HILLEN, Thomas to Robinie Kennedy MCHAFFIE, by license, Dec 14, 1794; 1. Balto. Co.; 2. Frederick Co.
(HILLENS), Charles to Henny (WALLACE), Nov 9, 1793; 1. slave of Solomon Hillens; 2. slave of John Wallace
HOCK, Frederic to Mary CONRAD, by banns, Jun 4, 1789
HODNETT, John to Mary TESTON, by banns, Nov 20, 1797
HOGAN, Michael to Mary HERRING, Jun 3, 1791
HOLIDAY, Henry to Milly IRELAND, Jan 21, 1796; 1. negro belonging to Mr. Henry Dorsey; 2. mulatto belonging to Col. Rogers
HOLMES, Antony to Margaret REEVES, by license, Jul 7, 1795; 2. widow of George Reeves
HOLMES, James to Magdalen BABIN, by banns, Oct 12, 1790
HOLMES, John to Margaret GERMAINE, by license, Aug 7, 1792
HOOK, Joseph to Sarah JOHNSON, by banns, Jan 25, 1791
HOOKE, John to Sophia HONKO, by license, Apr 20, 1795
HOSSEFRATZ, George to Dolly GROSS, by banns, Feb 1, 1790
HOVER, Ignatius to Rebecca MENTZ, by license, Apr 11, 1797
HOWARD, Edward to Sidith (CRETEN), Dec 26, 1794; of Harford Co.; 2. slave of James Creten
(HOWARD), Jack to Lukey (HOWARD), Dec 18, 1798; slave of Col. John E. Howard

MARRIAGES BY GROOM

HOWARD, William to Mary ROOKE, by license, Feb 18, 1799
HUDSON, James to Joanna MACNAMARA, by license, Sep 8, 1796
HUGHES, John to Elizabeth LABOU, by license, Mar 7, 1799; 1. nat.
    of Virginia, now in garrison at Ft. McHenry
HUGHES, Young Samuel to Ann CULLISON, by license, Nov 15, 1793;
    both Co.
JACKSON, Henry to Clare ANDERSON, by banns, Jul 8, 1792
JENKINS, William to Ann HILLEN, by license, Apr 21, 1793
JENNY, Joseph to Mary CONWAY, by license, Mar 6, 1800; 1.
    Captain; 2. dau. of Robert
JOHNSON, Abraham to Ann BUTLER, Jun 2, 1797; free negroes
JOHNSON, James to Mary Ann Elizabeth, Oct 24, 1799; both Negroes
JOHNSON, Joseph to Julia LACELY, by license, Oct 4, 1794; 2. nat.
    of Ireland
JOHNSON, Peter to Fanny OWINGS, Sep 21, 1791; both mulattoes
JONES, Salsbury to Eleanor LONEY, by license, Apr 28, 1789
JONES, William to Eleanor GREEN, by license, Nov 10, 1793; both
    Co.
JORDAN, James to Honor CALLAHAN, by license, Nov 24, 1791
JORSE, Jack to Frances WAGERMAN, by banns, May 22, 1792
JROINE, James to Mary STEIGER, by license, Feb 18, 1799
KEARNS, Charles to Hannah LONG, by license, Sep 17, 1791
KEATING, Matthew to Elizabeth BARLOW, by license, Apr 14, 1798
(KEENER), Issac to Eleanor BUTLER, Jun 4, 1796; 1. slave of
    Christian Keener; 2. free Negro
KEINAN, Laurence to Polly HALES, by license, Oct 31, 1799
KELLY, John to Sarah DRAYNAN, by license, Feb 22, 1794
KELLY, Patrick to Jane YOUNG, by license, Feb 10, 1799
KENELY, Timothy to Bridget MULLAN, by license, Apr 7, 1799;
    natives of Ireland
KERNS, Joseph to Anna DARRELL, by license, Aug 9, 1792
KEYS, John to Elizabeth DARRELL, by license, Apr 26, 1792
KILLEON, Jacob to Mary NEWMAN, by license, Sep 28, 1795; of
    Frederick Co.
KINTZ, Barney to Elizabeth SHILLING, by license, Jan 12, 1800
KOLLER, Anthony to Maria FIFER, by license, Aug 2, 1794
KRAUSS, John to Catherine HARTMAN, by banns, Oct 23, 1791
L'ENGLE, John to Suzanna GUILMAN, by license, Dec 2, 1793; 1.
    nat. of Ft Dauphin, St Domingo; 2. nat. of Cp Francois, St
    Domingo, Parish of Our Lady
LABATT, John Baptist to Margaret GRANGER, by license, Nov 22,
    1784
LABORDE, Bernard to Modeste LANDRY, by license, May 16, 1784
LABOU, Michael to Catharine KEFFER, by license, May 13, 1800
LAFON, Bernard to Susanna MORIN, by license, Jan 29, 1794; 1.
    nat. of Bayonne, France; 2. widow of Mr. Balfo of San
    Domingo
LAFOREST, Thomas to Hanah SIMMONS, by banns, May 1, 1785
LALOR, James to Ann O'NEALE, by license, Dec 15, 1798; natives of
    Ireland
LANDERKIN, John to Nell BOWSER, by license, Oct 30, 1792
LANDERS, William to Elizabeth TAYLOR, by license, Apr 21, 1796
LANDFORD, Michael to Martha LUCY, by license, Dec 20, 1798;
    natives of Ireland; 2. widow

MARRIAGES BY GROOM

LATOURANDAIE, Joseph to Mary Frances DUCASSE, by license, Oct 23, 1798; from St. Domingo
LATREYTE, John to Marie DESHELDS, by license, Jul 21, 1794
LAURENCE, Wendel to Ann STEELE, by license, Feb 28, 1797
LAVELL, Michael to Mary BOURKE, by license, Oct 25, 1798
LAWLER, David to Ruth CLIFTON, by banns, Oct 18, 1795; 1. widower; 2. widow
LAWRENCE, Vernel to Margaret ROBINSON, by banns, Nov 23, 1788
(LAWSON), Peter to Jane (LAWSON), Nov 20, 1799; slave of Richard Lawson
LAWSON, Robert to Elizabeth MCALLISTER, by license, Feb 12, 1798; natives of Ireland
LAY, Henry to Mary DEAL, by license, Jul 27, 1799
LEARY, Andrew to Mary DEMPSEY, by license, Aug 28, 1796; 2. Anne Arundel Co.
LEARY, Daniel to Mary MCBRIDE, by license, Dec 9, 1790
LEASON, Matthew to Mary JOICE, by license, Oct 7, 1787
LECLAIRE, Lewis Sebastian to Jane Julia Rollin DEMONBOS, by license, Feb 6, 1798; 1. son of Peter & Mary Falher; nat. of Cannes in Britany; surgeon; 2. dau. of Charles Augustus Caesar Rollin & Elizabeth de Toyan
LEE JR., Thomas to Eleanor CROMWELL, by license, Oct ??, 1796; 1. eldest son of Thomas Tim, Esq.; 2. dau. of ? Cromwell, Esq.
LEGUEN, Jacob to Margaret WOODHOUSE, by license, May 13, 1799
LEMOINE, Peter to Elizabeth MONGE, by license, Feb 20, 1798; 1. nat. of France
LENEHAN, Timothy to Mary RYAN, by license, Jun 13, 1798
LET, John to Mary BERONGIER, by license, Aug 25, 1799; 1. born at Ceuta in Provence; 2. widow Nonnier; born at Hieres in Provence, France
LEVINGSTON, Paul Bartholomy Heineman to Lehlia SMITH, by license, Apr 19, 1795
LICK, Peter to Rosanna WILLIS, by banns, Nov 1, 1790
LIDDLE, John to Catharine FOY, by license, May 26, 1796; of Fells Point
LIMES, Barnet to Margaret TURIN, by license, Apr 30, 1785
LINER, Peter to Barbara WHITEMASTERS, by banns, Jan 8, 1786
LITZENGER, Henry to Darcus WARNER, by license, Feb 12, 1786
LITZENGER, William to Elizabeth SHREAGLEY, by license, Jan 31, 1788
LIVERS, Arnold to Polly STANSBURY, by license, Sep 23, 1798; born in Frederick Co.
LLOYD, William to Elizabeth WALTER, by license, Mar 14, 1799; 1. widower; 2. widow
LOGAN, Neil to Mary WHITE, by license, Oct 15, 1796; natives of Ireland
LOGSDON, Job to Patience HELMS, by license, Sep 21, 1790
LONG, Thomas to Elizabeth JOHNSTON, by license, Oct 18, 1792
LOYDE, Robert to Kitty SHAW, by license, Jun 12, 1791
LOYDE, William to Mary WALSH, by banns, Nov 1, 1790
LUTZ, Valentine to Apollonia HEIPERIN, by banns, Oct 29, 1786
LYNCH, Cornelius to Cassandra JOHNS, by license, May 12, 1800; of Balto. Co.
LYNCH, James to Bridget HURLEY, by license, Sep 12, 1795; natives of Ireland

MARRIAGES BY GROOM

LYNCH, Patrick to Elizabeth WALSH, by banns, Dec 24, 1797
LYONS, John to Joanna RAGAN, by license, Jan 24, 1797; natives of Ireland
MACKEY, Hugh to Sarah HENRY, by license, Nov 19, 1795
MACKIE, John to Elizabeth HOLLINGSWORTH, by license, Jul 10, 1787
MACKIN, James to Margaret KELLAGREW, by license, Jul 21, 1800; 1. mariner; 2. nat. of Ireland
MADDEN, John to Elizabeth HOST, by banns, Nov 28, 1790
MAJORS, John to Rachael BACKSTER, by banns, Feb 8, 1789
MALLET, Thomas to Nancy PLUSCHAN, by license, Dec 28, 1790
MALONY, James to Averilla LEAGUE, by license, May 19, 1793
MALONY, James to Catharine VEAL, by license, Dec 9, 1798; 1. widower; 2. widow
MANCHOTE, John to Mary VINEY, by license, Aug 16, 1794; 1. nat. of Bordeaux
MARCH, Andrew to Rebecca STOCK, by license, Nov 23, 1795; of Anne Arundel Co.
MARCHANT, Peter Stephen to Mary Magdalen Martha MALLET, by license, Oct 20, 1798; 1. son of Thomas & Mary Ann Chaille; planter from St. Domingo; 2. dau. of Francis & Mary Jane Yronet; widow Hug
MARGOLLE, John Baptist to Ann Mary OCAIN, by license, Nov 18, 1789
MARTICQ, John to Mary Shammo NERY, by license, Feb 1, 1798
MARTIN, Alexander to Mary GIBSON, by license, Oct 2, 1796; 1. nat. of Virginia
MARTIN, Benjamin to Debora DALTON, by banns, Aug 21, 1791
MASHAN, Joseph to Cristina SWEIGHOFFER, by banns, Oct 20, 1794; natives of Germany
MATTHEWS, Patrick to Elizabeth MATTHEWS, Jul 5, 1790
MAYEL, Joseph Anthony to Margaret DASHIELD, by license, Nov 1, 1798
MCALLISTER, Charles to Elizabeth TRAINER, by license, Jan 21, 1796; natives of Ireland
MCCAN, John to Ann EGAN, Mar 29, 1791; remarried
MCCARTHY, George to Mary COOPER, by license, Nov 30, 1797
MCCARTY, Michael to Helen O'BRIEN, by license, Apr 10, 1796
MCCLAIN, Roger to Elleanor CONNELY, by license, Nov 25, 1795
MCDERMOTT, Henry to Esmy JORDAN, by license, Dec 5, 1797; natives of Ireland
MCDERMOTT, John to Catharine JOYCE, by license, Sep 18, 1797; natives of Ireland
MCDONALD, John to Frances ENGLISH, by banns, Feb 26, 1795; 1. nat. of Harford Co, Md.; 2. nat. of New Jersey; widow
MCDONOGH, John to Bridget CONNELLY, by license, Dec 26, 1799; natives of Ireland
MCDOON, Joseph to Rosanna HUGHS, by license, Oct 5, 1796; natives of Ireland; 2. widow
(MCELDERRY), Moses to Grace (MCELDERRY), Jun 9, 1798; slave of Thomas McElderry
MCFARLIN, Edward to Ann TULL, by license, Dec 18, 1783
MCFARLIN, Michael to Peggy BRAND, by license, Dec 27, 1787
MCGILL, Charles to Margaret LAZAUR, by license, Jun 24, 1786
MCGILL, Richard to Peggy ELSIN, by banns, Jun 29, 1789
MCGOVERN, Emanuel to Elizabeth CHATTEL, by license, Mar 6, 1799

MARRIAGES BY GROOM

MCGRATH, James to Catharine COMMIN, by license, Jan 17, 1798; natives of Ireland
MCGRATH, Michael to Margaret CARROLL, by license, Feb 21, 1792
MCGUIRE, Hugh to Nancy MCECHEN, by license, Jan 8, 1793
MCGUIRE, Roger to Eleanor CASEY, by license, Oct 22, 1795
MCHENRY, Dennis to Mary YOUNG, by license, Oct 7, 1794; 1. nat. of Ireland
MCKENZIE, John to Elizabeth WARNER, by license, Aug 4, 1795
MCKENZIE, Roger to Ann MARTIN, by license, Jul 22, 1793
MCKEWEN, Owen to Elizabeth CRISMAN, by license, Jul 19, 1796
MCKIERNAN, Michael to Mary BOWMAN, by banns, Jan 26, 1793
MCKINLEY, Neale to Margaret KING, by license, Dec 2, 1794
MCKUBBIN, James to Lydia COLLINS, by license, Feb 5, 1795
MCMAHON, Patrick to Nancy BROWN, by license, Sep 12, 1792
MCMEAL, Daniel to Catharine DALTON, by license, Nov 27, 1800; 2. widow
MCMULLEN, Patrick to Jane MCDONOUGH, by license, May 16, 1785
MCMULLEN, Peter to Catherine O'HARA, by banns, Aug 4, 1785
MCNAMARA, John to Judith CLARKE, by license, Mar 29, 1796; of Balto. Co.
MCNAMARA, Matthew to Ann GLASSBY, by license, Jun 15, 1793
MCQUINN, William to Elizabeth RANSFORD, by license, Feb 27, 1797; 1. widower; 2. widow
MCSHERRY, Patrick to Elizabeth CLEMENTS, by license, Apr 11, 1790
MELANCY, John to Catherine TOWEL, by banns, Sep 14, 1786
MERA, Frederic to Mary SNEIDER, by banns, May 20, 1793
MERRICK, Patrick to Ann HAMILTON, by license, Oct 20, 1790
MERRICK, William to Catherine DEASMOND, by license, Sep 4, 1790
MERY, Frederic to Eva ROSENBYKE, by banns, Jul 27, 1794; 2. widow
MILLER, George to Margaret FRAZIER, by license, Oct 12, 1794
MILLER, Henry to Ann FIELDS, by license, Jun 8, 1794; both Co.
MILLER, John to Sarah MCCLOUD, by license, Aug 1, 1791
MILLER, Michael to Elizabeth HARKEN, by license, Jun 4, 1795; 1. son of Donald & Cathrine; 2. dau. of Jacob & Adelaide
MILLER, Samuel to Mary BURK, by license, Aug 2, 1783
MILLERET, Cosme to Mary Ann GRANGER, by license, Apr 20, 1783; from Cp Francois; 1. Parish of Margot County of Medoc, Diocese of Bordeaux; 2. St John Baptist du trou, Cp Francois
MINIERE, John James Joseph to Jane Mary Anne MATHIUS, by license, Sep 26, 1796; natives of Cp. Francois, St. Domingo
MONTOUROY, Lewis Jacynthe to Mary Clare Rabar DEBEAUMALE, by license, Oct 7, 1794
MOONEY, William to Mary SLAYMAKER, by license, Jun 28, 1798
(MOORE), Robert to Clare BUTLER, Apr 30, 1799; 1. slave of David Moore; 2. free Negro woman
MORANCY, Joseph to Ann SPARROW, by banns, Jan 12, 1785
MORE, Patrick to Ann MURRAY, by banns, Jan 24, 1790
MORRES, Mark to Catherine LEARY, by license, Feb 12, 1786
MORRISON, Patrick to Priscilla CONSTABLE, by license, Jul 12, 1796; 2. widow
MULHERN, Bernard to Susanna RANDALL, by license, Jul 30, 1797
MULLAN, Henry to Susan O'BRIEN, by license, Dec 28, 1799; natives of Co. Tyrone
MURPHY, John to Mary HEALY, by license, Jun 6, 1799; natives of Ireland

MARRIAGES BY GROOM

MURPHY, Patrick to Susanna KEARNS, by license, Jun 20, 1790
MURRAY, Francis to Jane HUTTON, by license, Oct 16, 1795
MYERS, Peter Nelson to Elizabeth LAPSTEIN, by license, Dec 11, 1798
MYERS, Philip to Hannah HENLY, by license, Nov 5, 1798; 1. nat. of Germany
NEALE, Edward to Elizabeth MARTIN, by license, Jan 26, 1796
NEIGHBOURS, Henry to Ann KNOTT, by license, Dec 24, 1793; 2. Balto. Co.
NEILL, Michael to Eleanor MCCARTHY, by license, Jun 12, 1799; natives of Ireland
NICOLLE, John Stephen to Mary GLACE, by license, Aug 12, 1799; 1. nat. of Is. of Guadaloupe; 2. nat. of Angouleme, France
NOONAN, Edward to Mary FITZPATRICK, by license, May 11, 1797; natives of Ireland
NORTON, Dennis to Margaret MURPHY, by license, Mar 12, 1797
NORTON, William to Sarah WEST, by license, Apr 20, 1784
NUSSEAR, Jacob, Sr. to Catharine KAPPLER, by license, Mar 26, 1799
O'BRIAN, Joseph D. to Mary FLATTERY, by license, May 15, 1796; 1. widower
O'BRIAN, Patrick to Benea JOHNSON, by license, Aug 15, 1793
O'BRIEN, Charles to Patty COSKERY, by license, Feb 5, 1792
O'BRIEN, John to Hannah WALSH, by banns, Sep 23, 1792
O'BRIEN, Michael to Margaret HOOK, by license, Dec 1, 1791
O'CONNER, Michael to Catharine WALSH, by license, Feb 18, 1798; of Fells Point; 2. widow
O'NEALE, Felix to Rose MORGAN, by license, Oct 9, 1798
O'NEILL, Bernard to Margaret O'BRIAN, by license, Mar 21, 1796; of Fells Point
OFFERT, Charles to Rose RICHARDS, Dec 12, 1784
OLIVER, John to Rachel MACHANIN, by license, Apr 26, 1792
OLLIVE, John Baptist to Louisa THIRON, by license, Oct 12, 1795; 1. nat. of St. Aignan, Brittany; 2. widow Geanty, nat. of Port de Paix, St. Domingo
ORBAN, Henry to Catherine HOCK, by license, Apr 24, 1786
ORT, Conrad to Elizabeth PILLIER, by banns, Apr 10, 1787
OVERTON, John to Mary WEAVER, by license, Jul 23, 1793
PAGEZ, John to Mary BUTTON, by license, Jun 12, 1795; 1. son of Martin & Mary Duhalde, living in France; nat. of Jean de Lux, France; 2. dau. of Oliver (deceased) & Mary Celestine
PASCAL, Paul Francis Victor to Margaret MOREL, by license, May 6, 1796; 1. nat. of LaRochelle, France; 2. nat. of Cp Francais, St. Domingo; widow St. Bris
PASCAULT, Lewis Felix to Mary Ann Magdalen SLY, Dec 22, 1789; 2. in presence of Charles Ghequiene & Richard Ratien - remarried
PECK, John to Eleanor PIPER, by license, Mar 3, 1791
PEDUZI, Peter to Sally SHAW, by license, Sep 5, 1797; 1. nat. of Austrian Lombardy in Italy
PEMPILLION, Thomas to Mary LOVE, by license, Feb 19, 1788
PENNETHO, Joseph to Mary LANDRY, by license, Aug 2, 1783
PERTING, Peter to Mary FIELD, by license, Feb 28, 1797
PETERSON, John to Margaret HOLMES, by license, Apr 15, 1800
PIAT, John Baptist to Peggy CHAMEAU, by license, Sep 20, 1790

MARRIAGES BY GROOM

PIFER, John to Susanna CONEY, by license, Nov 30, 1789
PLACIDE, Paul to Louisa DEVENOIS, by license, Sep 19, 1797; 1.
    nat. of Marseilles, France; 2. nat. of Nismes, France
POLTON, Thomas Ridgely to Sarah BRYAN, by license, Jul 3, 1790
PONSIBY, Thomas to Ann PHILLIPS, by license, Sep 20, 1795
PONTIER, Anthony to Mary Catharine DUPLAN, by license, Feb 19,
    1795; 1. son of Robert Andrew & Mary Teresa Pascal; nat. of
    L'Alais in Longuedoc; 2. dau. of Francis & Charlotte
    DuRoche; nat. of Grande Riviere, St. Domingo; widow
    Lassiteau
POTHAIN, Peter Francis to Sarah JERVIS, by license, Mar 19, 1800;
    of Balto. Co.; 1. lately from St. Domingo
POWER, James to Mary PERVORE, by license, Dec 25, 1784
POWER, Patrick to Margaret GOWEN, by banns, Sep 13, 1788
POWLEY, Daniel to Jane LOGUE, by license, May 25, 1800
PRESTON, Thomas to Margaret CONOLLY, by banns, Sep 7, 1794
PROUIN, Andrew to Mary Anne FOURNACHON, by license, Aug 7, 1792
PRUDHOMME, John Baptist to Mary Glodine BABINEAU, by license, Aug
    14, 1793
(PURVIANCE), Matthew to Juliet (CATON), Jan 8, 1799
QUEEN, Edward to Ann (WELLS), Nov 12, 1797; 1. free Negro; 2.
    slave of Charles Wells
QUINLAN, Edmond to Jane COX, by banns, Jan 30, 1790
QUIRK, Peter to Margaret CHANEY, by license, Jul 10, 1792
RAGAN, Michael to Mary FITZPATRICK, by banns, Feb 4, 1798;
    natives of Ireland
RAMO, Jean to Magdalaine, May 27, 1800; 1. free Mulatto; 2.
    Mulattress
RAPINOT, Michael to Mary Rose PELLERIN, by license, Dec 27, 1796;
    of Balto. Co.; 1. born at Fougeres, parish of St. Leonard,
    Province of Britany, Diocese of Rennes; 2. born Is. of
    Grenada, parish of Our Lady of the Assumption, District of
    Marquis
RARDIN, William to Rachel MILLER, by license, Oct 6, 1792
RAREDON, John to Honor RAREDON, by banns, Aug 10, 1788
REA, William to Mary GARDINER, by license, Nov 5, 1792
REED, Matthew to Elizabeth LUCAS, by license, May 20, 1793; 1.
    Protestant
REEVES, George to Margaret MILLER, by license, Sep 18, 1792
REEVES, William to Abigail GRATE, by license, Apr 23, 1795
REGAIN, Michael to Catharine O'DONNEL, by banns, Jul 17, 1791
REILLY, John to Mary LANDRAGAN, by license, Sep 25, 1797; natives
    of Ireland
RENAUD, John to Ariana FINIGAN, by license, Aug 27, 1796; 1. of
    Petersburgh, Va.; 2. widow
RENAUDET, Peter Abraham to Ann GUTTROW, by license, Nov 17, 1793;
    1. son of Peter & Mary Merlat, parish of Arce in Saintonge;
    2. dau. of Joseph & Ann Tibodeau
RENER, Sebastian to Juliana WITHERHOLT, by license, Dec 15, 1796
RENKER, Henry to Christiana NIESLEM, by license, Apr 4, 1799
REY, Charles to Elizabeth BEAUPRE, by license, Mar 26, 1796; 1.
    nat. of Mont Pellier in Languidor; late from Jeremie, St.
    Domingo
REYNAUD, Francis Regis Benedict to Mary DUBOURG, by license, Apr
    12, 1798; natives of France; 2. widow Carrie

MARRIAGES BY GROOM

RICHARDS, John to Ann MILLS, by license, May 28, 1799
RICHARDS, Joseph to Margaret BERBINE, by license, Jun 3, 1797
ROBINSON, Ephraim to Eve DALE, by license, Dec 19, 1786
ROBINSON, John to Mary BAKER, by license, May 30, 1797; 1. of Chambersburg, Franklin Co., Pa.; 2. dau. of Mathias & Mary
ROGERS, John to Mary BARBINE, by license, Oct 3, 1793
ROSENSTEEL, George, Jr. to Barbara WHITE, by license, Nov 30, 1797
ROSENSTEEL, John to Margaret MYERS, by license, Sep 30, 1798
ROTCH, George to Catharine GREEN, by license, Jul 31, 1790
ROWAN, John to Elizabeth STOKES, by banns, Feb 16, 1794
RUPPER, Jacob to Bridget LYNCH, by banns, Jan 8, 1792
RUSSELL, Samuel to Sarah GERMAN, by license, Feb 13, 1798; 1. nat. of Boston
RYAN, James to Mary PURCELL, by license, Oct 14, 1798; natives of Ireland
SALVAN, Joseph Lewis to Lucy Jane DESHAYES, by license, Dec 19, 1795; 1. nat. of Courbon in Province; 2. nat. of Port au Prince, St. Domingo
SAVAGE, Dennis to Ann MOORE, by license, May 12, 1799; 1. widower; 2. widow
SAVAGE, Peter to Elizabeth KENNEY, by license, Jun 17, 1800; natives of Ireland; 1. widower; 2. widow
SELLMAN, Peter to Elizabeth COLE, by license, Jun 27, 1799; free Mulattoes
SHAY, James to Mary GREEN, by license, Jun 29, 1794; natives of Ireland
SHEA, Daniel to Elizabeth LURDEN, by license, Apr 22, 1786
SHEAN, David to Matto KENOCHEN, by license, Dec 21, 1785
SHILLING, Tobias to Catharine LAWRENCE, by banns, Dec 26, 1787
SHIPLEY, Regin to Eleanor BROOKS, by license, Apr 3, 1790
SHOEMAKER, Ignatius to Louisa SHAFFER, by license, Feb 15, 1795; 1. nat. of Hirsingen, Alsace; 2. nat. of Erhelen, Germany
SHORB, Andrew to Juliana GOLDEN, by license, May 24, 1798
SHORP, John to Catherine GROFE, by banns, Oct 10, 1786
SIEG, Peter to Mary WEISS, by license, Sep 2, 1800
SINDALL, Joseph to Mary HOOKE, by license, Sep 24, 1787
SMALL, James to Ann CRESMAN, by license, May 29, 1789
SPELLARD, Mathias to Winifred GLEESON, by license, Sep 24, 1797
STAAB, Philip to Catherine KRAUSE, by banns, May 9, 1790
STEARE, John to Rachael FIFER, by license, Jun 29, 1794; natives of Germany
STEIGER, Jacob to Catherine TICHNER, by banns, Oct 9, 1786
STEIGER, John to Elizabeth STEPHENSON, by banns, Jun 3, 1783
STEIGER, Mattias to Mary CRISSMAN, by license, Oct 13, 1793
STEWART, James to Eleanor EWING, by license, Dec 25, 1785
STEWART, James to Margaret BRITT, by license, Aug 15, 1793
STILLENGER, Jacob to Christiana LEBOUGH, by license, Feb 28, 1797
STONE, Thomas to Henrietta JENKINS, by license, Jan 29, 1796; 2. widow of John Jenkins, late of Balto. Co.
STRATTON, William to Mary HOWARD, by license, Feb 21, 1797; 1. nat. of Boston; 2. nat. of Ireland
STRENEY, Nicholas to Mary GREEN, by license, May 16, 1788

MARRIAGES BY GROOM

STUPUY, Peter to Susanna Catharine DUHARLAY, by license, Jul 26, 1798; 1. son of John Baptist & Ann Deval; widower of Catharine Chadwick of Conn.; 2. dau. of John Baptist & Barbara Perigo; widow of Bartholomew Camiran
SWEENY, Edward to Elizabeth BLATCHFORD, by license, Oct 1, 1796
SWEENY, Hugh to Priscilla HOOK, by license, Jul 19, 1789
SYLVA, Frances to Catharine O'BRIAN, by license, Nov 30, 1799
TAYLOR, Matthew to Mary SMITH, by license, Oct 20, 1790
THORNBURY, Robert to Magdalen BARBIN, by license, May 25, 1786
TICKLIN, William to Eleanor CRAWLEY, by license, Nov 27, 1795; 1. Protestant
TOOLE, James to Hetty NOBLE, by license, Dec 12, 1786
TOP, John to Sarah CARTY, Jan 4, 1786
TOURNEROCHE, Francis Mary Tsembard to Adeline MORTON, by license, May 17, 1794; 1. baron of St. Marguerite; 2. nat. of England
TROTT, Alexander to Sarah TRAVERSE, by license, May 10, 1788
TSOARD, Joseph to Frances DESCHAMPS, by license, Oct 27, 1793; 1. son of Mark & Rosalia De Fougerer; nat. of Argon; 2. dau. of Lewis & Mary Tibodeau
TULLEN, John to Genevieve MELANSON, by license, May 16, 1784
TYSON, Henry S. to Sabina O'CONNOR, by license, Aug 9, 1796; 1. nat. of England; 2. nat. of Ireland
VANBIBBER, Abraham to Mary YOUNG, by license, Nov 22, 1795; 2. Balto. Co.
VEINTRY, Francis to Susanna BRAND, by banns, Feb 6, 1785
VERLY, George to Elizabeth FREEMAN, by banns, May 6, 1795
VIBERT, Francis to Mary BELANGER, by license, Apr 18, 1796
VILLENEUVE, Lewis to Jeanne Antoinette GROC, by license, Jun 24, 1800; free French Mulattoes
WADE, John to Charlotte ROSSITER, by license, Aug 7, 1800; 1. nat. of Santa Cruce; widower; 2. dau. of Thomas & Charlotte, both deceased
WAGERS, Francis to Patience LOGSDAN, by banns, Sep 7, 1791
WALKER, Robert to Sarah MURPHY, by license, Jul 11, 1793
WALSH, Edward to Catherine CONWAY, by license, Apr 9, 1787
WALSH, Maurice to Elizabeth LEE, by banns, Aug 2, 1795; natives of Ireland
WALSH, Michael to Anna Catharina FASBENDER, by license, Jul 27, 1800; 2. of Balto. Co.
WALSH, Peter to Sarah CANNON, by banns, Jun 19, 1796; natives of Ireland; 2. widow
WALSH, Robert to Elizabeth STEEL, by license, Nov 1, 1783
WALTON, John to Barbara HOOK, by license, Apr 1, 1793
WANTE, Charles Stephen Peter to Mary Rose DEBREUIL, by license, Jul 28, 1796; 1. widower; nat. of Gravelines; son of Charles & Mary Ann Audibert; born in 1756; 2. widow LaFitte; dau. of John Baptist & Felicity Fauche; nat. of Petite Anne, St. Domingo
WATERS, Martin to Dianna HARROMAN, by banns, Mar 5, 1791
WATTS, George to Mary THOMPSON, by banns, May 22, 1791
WEDGE, Joseph to Mary JUBILL, by license, Jan 18, 1787
WHELAN, Bartholomew to Bridget FLAHARTY, by license, Nov 23, 1794; natives of Ireland
WHELAN, Basil to Catharine RIDDELMOSER, by license, Feb 11, 1800
WHELAN, Laurance to Elizabeth WILLIAMS, by license, Nov 30, 1787

MARRIAGES BY GROOM

WHITE, James to Honor KING, by license, Dec 25, 1799; natives of
 Ireland; 2. widow of David King
WHITE, Joseph, Jr. to Rosetta LANDRY, by license, Feb 14, 1799
WIDERSTRAND, Thomas to Mary Charlotte DARINGTON, by license, Dec
 1, 1795
WILHELM, Jacob to Catharine OTTEN, by license, May 22, 1800
WILLIAMS, John to Jannet MALCOM, by license, Oct 13, 1788
WILLIAMS, Joseph to Rose BLOSSOM, by banns, Dec 20, 1783
WILLIAMSON, David to Juliet MULLET, by license, Dec 15, 1795; 1.
 widower; merchant of Balto. 2. nat. of Dixonuyde, Flanders
WILLING, Leonard to Margaret ANDERSON, by license, Nov 9, 1800;
 of Fells Point
WILLSON, David to Ann PARTRIDGE, by license, Apr 29, 1794
WILSON, James to Catharine SHILLING, by license, Dec 8, 1799; 1.
 widower; 2. widow
WIMFET, Charles to Ann CHANEY, by license, Mar 2, 1794; both Co.
WINN, Christopher to Margaret GOULD, by license, Sep 9, 1787
WISE, Felix to Barbara GROSS, by license, Aug 26, 1792
WISE, Michael to Catharine YOUNG, by license, Feb 8, 1796;
 natives of Germany
WYSE, William to Rachel MORRISON, by license, May 29, 1794; 1.
 nat. of Ireland; ship captain
YANDA, John Peter to Margaret Aimee LECLERC, by license, Nov 2,
 1795; 1. son of Joseph, formerly officer, Inf., in service
 of the Emperor; lately from St. Domingo; resident of
 Limoges, & the late Catharine Arenima; 2. dau. of Frances of
 Plaisance & the late Margaret Perigault; widow of Rosier
 Rostaing from Plaisance, St. Domingo
YERBY, William to Elizabeth WHITE, by license, Aug 9, 1798; 1. of
 Virginia
ZACHARIE, Stephen to Ann WATERS, by license, May 12, 1787

MARRIAGES BY BRIDE

Apollonia to Samuel CARROLL
Bett to Leonard
Clare to Phil
Elizabeth to John Baptist GEANTY
Henrietta to Alexius
Magdalaine to Jean RAMO
Marie Louise to Hector
Mary to John Francis ARIEU
Mary Agnes to Jean Jacques
Mary Ann to James JOHNSON
Mary Frances to Peter DOUAT
Rachel to Peter CHAREELE
Rose to Caleb
Sarah to Ned
ADDISON, Jemima to Edward CLARK
ADISON, Elizabeth to James GREEN
ANDERSON, Clare to Henry JACKSON
ANDERSON, Margaret to Leonard WILLING
ANDERSON, Rebecca to Neal DENNY
ASPLE, Elizabeth to Michael FOY
ASSAILLY, Constance to Lewis BACONAIS
BABIN, Magdalen to James HOLMES
BABINE, Elizabeth to James DONALDSON
BABINEAU, Mary Glodine to John Baptist PRUDHOMME
BACKSTER, Rachael to John MAJORS
BAKER, Christina to Anthony BARICKMAN
BAKER, Mary to John ROBINSON
BALDWIN, Catharine to Richard FLAHAVAN
BARBIN, Magdalen to Robert THORNBURY
BARBINE, Mary to John ROGERS
BARDAN, Victoire to Lewis Nan BEAUPRE
BARLOW, Elizabeth to Matthew KEATING
BARRETT, Jenny to William HAGERTY
BARRU, Abigail to Livy HAMILTON
BAXTLEY, Phoebe to John GALLAGHER
BEAUPRE, Elizabeth to Charles REY
BELANGER, Mary to Francis VIBERT
BERBINE, Margaret to Joseph RICHARDS
BERNABEU, Elizabeth to William DIXON
BERNARD, Mary to Maximilian HEUISLER
BERONGIER, Mary to John LET
BLAKE, Catharine to Timothy FARREL
BLANEY, Jane to John DORNEY
BLATCHFORD, Elizabeth to Edward SWEENY
BLIEZE, Mary to John DELISLE
BLOSSOM, Mary to Isaac COX
BLOSSOM, Rose to Joseph WILLIAMS
BOISSON, Ann to Lewis ALLAIN
BOUDVILLE, Elizabeth to Simon DEAGLE
BOUGHAN, Elizabeth to John FRIDAY
BOURDON, Anne Frances to William ELVES
BOURKE, Mary to Michael LAVELL
BOWMAN, Mary to Michael MCKIERNAN
BOWSER, Nell to John LANDERKIN
BRAND, Peggy to Michael MCFARLIN

MARRIAGES BY BRIDE

BRAND, Susanna to Francis VEINTRY
BRIDE, Ann to M. Simmons BUNBURY
BRIER, Mary to Christopher DUPOIS
BRITT, Elizabeth to Henry DAVIS
BRITT, Margaret to James STEWART
BRITT, Mary to Edward CRAMER
BROOKS, Eleanor to Regin SHIPLEY
BROTHERSON, Janett Ann to Antoine FAUR
BROWN, Nancy to Patrick MCMAHON
BRUCOURT, Ann Pineau to Edmond DUCATEL
BRYAN, Catharine to Roger GLEESON
BRYAN, Sarah to Thomas POLTON
BULGER, Elizabeth to Bernard BORDERIE
BURDAN, Mary to John DAVIS
BURK, Eleanor to Hugh GAYNOR
BURK, Mary to Samuel MILLER
BURK, Mary to William BOYLE
BURKE, Margaret to John EVANS
BURON, Mary to John Baptist DESEZE
BUSCAILLE, Louisa to Robert BOISLANDRY
BUTCHER, Elizabeth to George BUCHOLTZ
BUTCHER, Elizabeth to Peter FOSBINDER
BUTCHER, Margaret to Michael HERTZOG
BUTLER, Agnes to James ADAMS
BUTLER, Ann to Abraham JOHNSON
BUTLER, Catherine to Richard FITZGERALD
BUTLER, Clare to Robert MOORE
BUTLER, Eleanor to Issac KEENER
BUTLER, Minty to Aaron HENRY
BUTTON, Mary to John PAGEZ
BUTTS, Melcha to William FLETCHER
BYRON, Ann to Daniel DOWNEY
CAIN, Ann to Herman FICKE
CALLAHAN, Honor to James JORDAN
CANADY, Elizabeth to David CLARKE
CANNON, Sarah to Peter WALSH
CAREY, Catharine to William BYRNE
CARNEY, Mary to John COLLINS
CARRERE, Jane Frances to John Baptist BADET
CARROLL, Margaret to Michael MCGRATH
CARTER, Monica to Thomas HENRY
CARTY, Ann to James HARTNELL
CARTY, Sarah to John TOP
CASEY, Eleanor to Roger MCGUIRE
CASEY, Elisa to James GANTEAUME
CASEY, Elizabeth to James GANTEAUME
CASEY, Elizabeth to William DWYER
CATON, Clare to James CATON
CATON, Eleanor to Michael BENTLEY
CATON, Juliet to Matthew PURVIANCE
CELESTIN, Mary to John Baptist GALLET
CHAMEAU, Peggy to John Baptist PIAT
CHANEY, Ann to Charles WIMFET
CHANEY, Margaret to Peter QUIRK
CHATTEL, Elizabeth to Emanuel MCGOVERN

MARRIAGES BY BRIDE

CHERRY, Ann to Mark CATON
CLARKE, Hannah to John GILBRAITH
CLARKE, Judith to John MCNAMARA
CLEMENTS, Elizabeth to Patrick MCSHERRY
CLIFFORD, Frances to John HAMMOND
CLIFTON, Ruth to David LAWLER
COLE, Elizabeth to Peter SELLMAN
COLEMAN, Margaret to John BUTLER
COLGAN, Margaret to Stephen BRADBURY
COLGAN, Mary to Thomas BROWN
COLLINS, Bridget to Andrew DAY
COLLINS, Lydia to James MCKUBBIN
COMMIN, Catharine to James MCGRATH
CONEY, Susanna to John PIFER
CONNELLY, Bridget to John MCDONOGH
CONNELY, Elleanor to Roger MCCLAIN
CONNER, Catharine to Patrick FLAHERTY
CONNET, Magdalen to George FIFER
CONOLLY, Margaret to Thomas PRESTON
CONRAD, Catharine to Peter DITTO
CONRAD, Mary to Frederic HOCK
CONSTABLE, Priscilla to Patrick MORRISON
CONTANT, Mary to Joseph DEMONTI
CONWAY, Catherine to Edward WALSH
CONWAY, Mary to Joseph JENNY
COOPER, Anne to Richard FITZGERALD
COOPER, Elizabeth to Francis DELAPORTE
COOPER, Mary to George MCCARTHY
COSKERY, Patty to Charles O'BRIEN
COX, Jane to Edmond QUINLAN
CRAVEN, Rose to Thomas CARROLL
CRAWLEY, Eleanor to William TICKLIN
CRENZE, Mary Louisa to Peter GREGORY
CRESMAN, Ann to James SMALL
CRESMAN, Eleanor to Nathaniel CARSON
CRETEN, Sidith to Edward HOWARD
CRISMAN, Elizabeth to Owen MCKEWEN
CRISSMAN, Mary to Mattias STEIGER
CROMWELL, Ann to Michael BEGNALL
CROMWELL, Eleanor to Thomas LEE JR.
CRONAN, Catharine to John BLAIR
CULLISON, Ann to Young Samuel HUGHES
CUMMINS, Jane to James BURNS
CUNNINGHAM, Jane to John GRANT
CURRY, Margaret to Richard FITZGERALD
D'ALBAN, Ann to Joseph FAURIE
DALE, Eve to Ephraim ROBINSON
DALTON, Catharine to Daniel MCMEAL
DALTON, Debora to Benjamin MARTIN
DARINGTON, Mary to Thomas WIDERSTRAND
DARNAUD, Victoire to Louis BAUDUY
DARRELL, Anna to Joseph KERNS
DARRELL, Elizabeth to John KEYS
DASHIELD, Margaret to Joseph MAYEL
DAVID, Lucy to Josiah HASHAN

MARRIAGES BY BRIDE

DAVIES, Elizabeth to Robert CASEY
DAVIS, Mary to Matthew HARDING
DEAGLE, Mary to James BAROUX
DEAL, Mary to Henry LAY
DEASMOND, Catherine to William MERRICK
DEBEAUMALE, Mary Clare to Lewis MONTOUROY
DECHAMP, Elizabeth to Francis Remy GLAVANY
DELANCO, Elizabeth to John FERRON
DELESFAURIS, Frances to John BREMONT
DELORE, Sophia to Michael BREARD
DEMANCHE, Frances to Joseph DESPAUX
DEMONBOS, Jane Julia to Lewis LECLAIRE
DEMPSEY, Mary to Andrew LEARY
DESCHAMPS, Frances to Joseph TSOARD
DESCHAMPS, Magdalen to Joseph Mary CARRE
DESHAYES, Lucy Jane to Joseph Lewis SALVAN
DESHELDS, Marie to John LATREYTE
DESOBRY, Sophia Maria to Laurence GOUDAIN
DESRAMEAUX, Rosetta to Philip COLVIN
DEVENOIS, Louisa to Paul PLACIDE
DIFFENDOLPH, Catherine to Nathan HERTHER
DILLON, Kitty to Edmond FRAHER
DILLON, Margaret to Samuel ELMS
DILLON, Margaret to Dennis CAREY
DOUGHERTY, Susanna to Jacob DEALE
DOYLE, Elizabeth to Patrick ALLEN
DRAKE, Nancy to Michael CARROLL
DUBOURG, Mary to Francis REYNAUD
DUBREUIL, Mary Rose to Charles WANTE
DUCASSE, Mary Frances to Joseph LATOURANDAIE
DUFOUREQ, Anne Joseph to John Francis DESAPRADE
DUGAN, Nancy to William HENRY
DUHARLAY, Susanna to Peter STUPUY
DULIAR, Ann to Matthew BERMAN
DULONGUEVAL, Melany to Lewis John DULONGUEVAL
DUNN, Elizabeth to Charles FLOYD
DUPLAN, Mary to Anthony PONTIER
DUPUY, Helen to John Baptist AMIE
DWIER, Mary to John GRAY
EGAN, Ann to John MCCAN
ELCON, Eve to Joseph BERTHOLIN
ELIE, Catharine to John FAGET
ELSIN, Peggy to Richard MCGILL
ENGLISH, Frances to John MCDONALD
EVANS, Hetty to William DISTANCE
EVANS, Margaret to John Holpin BUTLER
EWING, Eleanor to James STEWART
FAHERTY, Bridget to Daniel CARRICK
FAHERTY, Honor to Patrick CLOUGHERTY
FASBENDER, Anna to Michael WALSH
FAURE, Mary Ann to Lewis BELLEVILLE
FENIX, Judith to John CULLEN
FIELD, Mary to Peter PERTING
FIELDS, Ann to Henry MILLER
FIFER, Maria to Anthony KOLLER

MARRIAGES BY BRIDE

FIFER, Rachael to John STEARE
FINIGAN, Ariana to John RENAUD
FINN, Elizabeth to Walter BUTLER
FISHER, Barbara to George BUCHMAN
FISHER, Catharine to Jacob HEIMEL
FITZGERALD, Ann to Matthew GAVAN
FITZGERALD, Catherine to Francis DAVIS
FITZGERALD, Eleanor to John DUNN
FITZPATRICK, Mary to Edward NOONAN
FITZPATRICK, Mary to Michael RAGAN
FLAHARTY, Bridget to Bartholomew WHELAN
FLATTERY, Mary to Joseph D. O'BRIAN
FLUKER, Sarah Lyons to Bon Albert BEAUMEZ
FOURNACHON, Mary Anne to Andrew PROUIN
FOY, Catharine to John LIDDLE
FRANKLIN, Catherine to John DULOHANY
FRAZIER, Margaret to George MILLER
FREEMAN, Elizabeth to George VERLY
FREEMAN, Mary to Daniel CARNAN
FRY, Catharine to John EBBECKE
FULWEILER, Magdalen to Joseph BAKER
GARDINER, Mary to William REA
GERMAINE, Margaret to John HOLMES
GERMAN, Sarah to Samuel RUSSELL
GIBSON, Mary to Alexander MARTIN
GLACE, Mary to John Stephen NICOLLE
GLASSBY, Ann to Matthew MCNAMARA
GLEESON, Catharine to Richard BURKE
GLEESON, Winifred to Mathias SPELLARD
GOLDEN, Juliana to Andrew SHORB
GOTO, Margaret to Alexander DEVALCOURTE
GOULD, Margaret to Christopher WINN
GOULD, Martha to John GOULDING
GOWEN, Margaret to Patrick POWER
GRANGER, Margaret to John Baptist LABATT
GRANGER, Mary Ann to Cosme MILLERET
GRATE, Abigail to William REEVES
GREEN, Catharine to George ROTCH
GREEN, Eleanor to James HEWES
GREEN, Eleanor to William JONES
GREEN, Elizabeth to William DORNEY
GREEN, Mary to Nicholas STRENEY
GREEN, Mary to James SHAY
GREEN, Mary to Neal DAUGHERTY
GREEN, Sarah to John DUFF
GROC, Jeanne to Lewis VILLENEUVE
GROFE, Catherine to John SHORP
GROGEN, Christine to John COMINS
GROSS, Barbara to Felix WISE
GROSS, Dolly to George HOSSEFRATZ
GUILMAN, Suzanna to John L'ENGLE
GUTHROW, Mary to Charles CHAMBERLAIN
GUTRY, Ann to James DUGAN
GUTTROW, Ann to Peter RENAUDET
HAGHERTY, Mary to Francis CLARKE

MARRIAGES BY BRIDE

HALES, Polly to Laurence KEINAN
HAMILTON, Ann to Patrick MERRICK
HANKEY, Margaret to Columbus BYRNE
HANLY, Mary to Michael HANLY
HANNECY, Johanna to Redmond BARRY
HARGROVE, Mary to James ESCAVAILLE
HARKEN, Elizabeth to Michael MILLER
HARRIS, Nellie to Pierce DUNNAVAN
HARROMAN, Dianna to Martin WATERS
HARRYMAN, Ann to Thomas GREEN
HARTMAN, Catherine to John KRAUSS
HAY, Catherine to Jacque Simon DEBEAULIEU
HEALY, Mary to John MURPHY
HEIMLIN, Elizabeth to Henry BENER
HEIPERIN, Apollonia to Valentine LUTZ
HELMS, Patience to Job LOGSDON
HENDERICKS, Ann to Anthony BRACKMAN
HENLY, Hannah to Philip MYERS
HENRY, Sarah to Hugh MACKEY
HERRING, Mary to Michael HOGAN
HILLEN, Ann to William JENKINS
HILLEN, Mary to David ARMOUR
HIONE, Margaret to Joseph HENNION
HISLIN, Mary to Engel BUGHEN
HOCK, Catherine to Henry ORBAN
HOLLAND, Mary to Dennis HEALLY
HOLLINGSWORTH, Elizabeth to John MACKIE
HOLMES, Jane to William FORD
HOLMES, Magdalen to John DIZABEAU
HOLMES, Margaret to John PETERSON
HONAUR, Catharine to Joseph GLOTTUS
HONKO, Sophia to John HOOKE
HOOK, Barbara to John WALTON
HOOK, Elizabeth to Philip HERMAN
HOOK, Margaret to Michael O'BRIEN
HOOK, Priscilla to Hugh SWEENY
HOOKE, Mary to Joseph SINDALL
HOST, Elizabeth to John MADDEN
HOWARD, Lukey to Jack HOWARD
HOWARD, Mary to William STRATTON
HOY, Eleanor to Thomas DEMPSEY
HUBON, Mary Ann to William BEAUDU
HUGHES, Ann to John Barton HARDEN
HUGHS, Rosanna to Joseph MCDOON
HUNT, Elizabeth to James GREHAN
HURLEY, Bridget to James LYNCH
HUTTON, Jane to Francis MURRAY
IRELAND, Clementine to Vachel DORSEY
IRELAND, Milly to Henry HOLIDAY
JACOBS, Elizabeth to Jacob FULLHART
JAFFRIS, Hannah to James BROWN
JAMES, Jane to Patrick HANDLEN
JENKINS, Henrietta to Thomas STONE
JENKINS, Sarah to Anthony HEARN
JENNINGS, Elizabeth to William BROOKS

MARRIAGES BY BRIDE

JERVIS, Sarah to Peter POTHAIN
JOHNS, Cassandra to Cornelius LYNCH
JOHNSON, Benea to Patrick O'BRIAN
JOHNSON, Sarah to Joseph HOOK
JOHNSTON, Elizabeth to Thomas LONG
JOICE, Mary to Matthew LEASON
JOINER, Rebecca to John GUTHROW
JONES, Anne to Bennett GREEN
JORDAN, Esmy to Henry MCDERMOTT
JOYCE, Catharine to John MCDERMOTT
JOYCE, Sarah to George COLLINS
JUBILL, Mary to Joseph WEDGE
KAPPLER, Catharine to Jacob, Sr. NUSSEAR
KEARNS, Susanna to Patrick MURPHY
KEFFER, Catharine to Michael LABOU
KEILHOLTZ, Mary to John GERLACH
KELFOHL, Catharine to James DAILY
KELLAGREW, Margaret to James MACKIN
KELLY, Eleanor to William DWYER
KELNAN, Bridget to Daniel DONOGHUE
KENNEY, Elizabeth to Peter SAVAGE
KENOCHEN, Matto to David SHEAN
KING, Honor to James WHITE
KING, Margaret to Neale MCKINLEY
KING, Sarah to Thomas CARROLL
KIRK, Catharine to William COGHLAN
KNEASS, Hannah to Nicholas CORBELEY
KNOTT, Ann to Henry NEIGHBOURS
KNOWLAN, Mary to Simon BURNS
KNOWLEN, Ann to Michael DAVOY
KOALER, Mary to Peter HAMLIN
KOENIG, Dorothea to Frederick DANNENBERG
KRAUSE, Catherine to Philip STAAB
LABOU, Elizabeth to John HUGHES
LABOURDAIS, Theresa to James DELAUNAY
LACELY, Julia to Joseph JOHNSON
LACHENAL, Elizabeth to Charles ADONIS
LANDILLAND, Ally to Richard GORE
LANDRAGAN, Mary to John REILLY
LANDRY, Mary to Joseph PENNETHO
LANDRY, Modeste to Bernard LABORDE
LANDRY, Rosetta to Joseph, Jr. WHITE
LANKSTON, Mary to John HAYES
LAPSTEIN, Elizabeth to Peter MYERS
LAWRENCE, Catharine to Tobias SHILLING
LAWSON, Jane to Peter LAWSON
LAZAUR, Margaret to Charles MCGILL
LEAGUE, Averilla to James MALONY
LEARY, Catherine to Mark MORRES
LEARY, Catherine to William CORBIN
LEARY, Margaret to Peter HAILEY
LEARY, Mary to James BUCKLEY
LEBAT, Margaret to Francis ARMAND
LEBLANC, Mary to Peter BLOSSOM
LEBOUGH, Christiana to Jacob STILLENGER

MARRIAGES BY BRIDE

LECLERC, Margaret to John Peter YANDA
LEDUC, Ann to Nathaniel CHASE
LEE, Elizabeth to Maurice WALSH
LEMONNIER, Catherine to John Anthony GROC
LENDER, Marie to John Baptist GAULINE
LEWIS, Mary to Laurence ARAUGHTY
LOCKERMAN, Margaret to Joseph BORIE
LOGSDAN, Patience to Francis WAGERS
LOGUE, Catherine to Joseph FLOYD
LOGUE, Jane to Daniel POWLEY
LONEY, Eleanor to Salsbury JONES
LONEY, Mary to Arthur CONNER
LONG, Hannah to Charles KEARNS
LOVE, Mary to Thomas PEMPILLION
LUCAS, Elizabeth to Matthew REED
LUCY, Martha to Michael LANDFORD
LURDEN, Elizabeth to Daniel SHEA
LYNCH, Bridget to Jacob RUPPER
LYNCH, Susanna to John HALL
LYSTON, Mary Ann to John GARLAND
MACHANIN, Rachel to John OLIVER
MACNAMARA, Joanna to James HUDSON
MALCOM, Jannet to John WILLIAMS
MALLET, Mary to Peter MARCHANT
MAMILLON, Magdalen to Peter GERARD
MANGEE, Mary to John Baptist COULON
MARA, Ann to Andrew HANNA
MARHEIM, Mary to John FITZPATRICK
MARTIN, Ann to Roger MCKENZIE
MARTIN, Elizabeth to Edward NEALE
MARTIN, Mary to George APHOLD
MARTIN, Rachel to Henry DOPP
MARZIAL, Mary to John Joseph BOYREAU
MATHIUS, Jane Mary to John James MINIERE
MATTHEWS, Elizabeth to Patrick MATTHEWS
MCALLISTER, Elizabeth to Robert LAWSON
MCBRIDE, Mary to Daniel LEARY
MCCARTHY, Eleanor to Michael NEILL
MCCLOUD, Sarah to John MILLER
MCDANIEL, Ann to Nicholas DOYLE,
MCDANIEL, Mary to Morris GLEESON
MCDERMOT, Elizabeth to Patric DEMPSEY
MCDONOUGH, Jane to Patrick MCMULLEN
MCECHEN, Nancy to Hugh MCGUIRE
MCELDERRY, Grace to Moses MCELDERRY
MCFEE, Mary to John BRADY
MCGINNIS, Rosanna to John DAVIS
MCGUIRE, Mary to Michael DUNN
MCHAFFIE, Robinie to Thomas HILLEN
MCLAUGHLIN, Ann to Andrew HAGAN
MCSHERRY, Elizabeth to John Baptist DALIQUET
MEADE, Ann to Joseph CHAMILLON
MEHIN, Judith to Edward FOGERTY
MELANSON, Genevieve to John TULLEN
MENTZ, Rebecca to Ignatius HOVER

MARRIAGES BY BRIDE

MERIT, Martha to William FOOSE
MIDDELTON, Ruth to Anthony BUTLER
MILLER, Anna to John BECK
MILLER, Elizabeth to Raymond DOMBROUSKY
MILLER, Margaret to George REEVES
MILLER, Mary to Abraham GRIFFIN
MILLER, Rachel to William RARDIN
MILLER, Sarah to John FENNELL
MILLS, Ann to John RICHARDS
MINEAHAN, Ann to James DURNEY
MITCHEL, Elizabeth to John FOSSEY
MITCHELL, Jane to John CABERA
MITCHELL, Sarah to Patrick CLARK
MONGE, Elizabeth to Peter LEMOINE
MONGEAU, Margaret to Francis DUCHEMIN
MONTALIBOR, Josephine to Leon CHANGEUR
MONTGOMERY, Lettice to Richard GORE
MOORE, Ann to Dennis SAVAGE
MORAN, Anne to John BREIDENBAUGH
MOREL, Margaret to Paul Francis PASCAL
MORENO, Catharine to Baltazar DANFOSSY
MORGAN, Rose to Felix O'NEALE
MORIN, Susanna to Bernard LAFON
MORRISON, Rachel to William WYSE
MORTON, Adeline to Francis TOURNEROCHE
MULLAN, Bridget to Timothy KENELY
MULLET, Juliet to David WILLIAMSON
MURPHY, Eleanor to George CAHIL
MURPHY, Margaret to Dennis NORTON
MURPHY, Sarah to Robert WALKER
MURRAY, Ann to Patrick MORE
MYER, Hedewig to Peter FOSBENDER
MYERS, Margaret to Garrett FITZGERALD
MYERS, Margaret to John ROSENSTEEL
NAGOT, Catharine to Ignatius BEESTON
NAWLAN, Catherine to Thomas HAYLY
NERY, Mary Shammo to John MARTICQ
NEWMAN, Mary to Jacob KILLEON
NIESLEM, Christiana to Henry RENKER
NOBLE, Hetty to James TOOLE
NUSSEAR, Elizabeth to James HEYDEN
O'BRIAN, Catharine to Frances SYLVA
O'BRIAN, Margaret to Bernard O'NEILL
O'BRIEN, Helen to Michael MCCARTY
O'BRIEN, Mary to Cornelius GORMLY
O'BRIEN, Susan to Henry MULLAN
O'CONNOR, Sabina to Henry S. TYSON
O'DONALD, Alice to Daniel P. GORMAN
O'DONNEL, Catharine to Michael REGAIN
O'HAGAN, Mary to Edward DUNN
O'HARA, Catherine to Peter MCMULLEN
O'NEALE, Ann to James LALOR
OCAIN, Ann Mary to John Baptist MARGOLLE
OTTEN, Catharine to Jacob WILHELM
OWINGS, Fanny to Peter JOHNSON

MARRIAGES BY BRIDE

OXFORD, Mary to Nicholas BOX
PALLON, Louise to Marcellin GONET
PARCE, Anna Savon to Antony BOURGEOIS
PARK, Elizabeth to Daniel DUNN
PARTRIDGE, Ann to David WILLSON
PATERSON, Reine to Joseph Yves BIZOUARD
PATTERSON, Kitty to William ANDERSON
PELLERIN, Mary Rose to Michael RAPINOT
PELLETIER, Mary Jane to Lewis FENGEAS
PEMSTON, Mary to Thomas DRINAN
PERDONNE, Magdalen to Zenny HATTIER
PERVORE, Mary to James POWER
PHILLIPS, Ann to Thomas PONSIBY
PILLIER, Elizabeth to Conrad ORT
PINDARE, Magdalen to James ANTHONY
PIPER, Eleanor to John PECK
PISSARD, Clare to Stephen BENILLANT
PLUME, Elizabeth to Bartholomew BUTCHER
PLUSCHAN, Nancy to Thomas MALLET
PODDEWANG, Peggy to Raymond FORD
PRESTON, Mary to Robert CONNELLY
PRUN, Mary to Lewis CANTEGRIL
PURCELL, Mary to James RYAN
QUEDAN, Ann to James ALLAERT
RAGAN, Joanna to John LYONS
RANDALL, Susanna to Bernard MULHERN
RANSFORD, Elizabeth to William MCQUINN
RAREDON, Honor to John RAREDON
RARITY, Catharine to Robert CAMPBELL
REED, Jane to George CAMPBELL
REEVES, Margaret to Antony HOLMES
RENOULLEAU, Mary Martha to Joseph CALMAN
RICE, Brigid to William DUNCAN
RICHARDS, Margaret to Peter CRISALL
RICHARDS, Mary Ann to Bartholomew GRACHE
RICHARDS, Rose to Charles OFFERT
RIDDELMOSER, Catharine to Basil WHELAN
RIDDLE, Augustina to John FOOSE
RILEY, Margaret to John FLYNN
ROACH, Mary to John BURK
ROBINSON, Margaret to Vernel LAWRENCE
RODDY, Mary Ann to James CURRAN
ROGERS, Sarah to Henry Hill CARROLL
ROOKE, Mary to William HOWARD
ROSENBYKE, Eva to Frederic MERY
ROSENSTEEL, Mary to John BROWN
ROSS, Frances to Augustine DELAT
ROSSITER, Charlotte to John WADE
ROUND, Charlotte to Joachim CROSILLANT
ROURKE, Mary to Henry DUFFY
ROW, Elizabeth to John HARRISON
RUSK, Catherine to John HILLEN
RYAN, Mary to Alexander GIRAND
RYAN, Mary to Timothy LENEHAN
SAPEN, Magdelen to Sebastian FLEURY

MARRIAGES BY BRIDE

SEARS, Mary to Francis CAVAROC
SHAFFER, Louisa to Ignatius SHOEMAKER
SHAW, Kitty to Robert LOYDE
SHAW, Sally to Peter PEDUZI
SHENEY, Margaret to James ADAMS
SHILLING, Catharine to James WILSON
SHILLING, Elizabeth to Barney KINTZ
SHREAGLEY, Elizabeth to William LITZENGER
SILK, Mary to Hugh BONNER
SIMMONS, Hanah to Thomas LAFOREST
SINDOLPH, Mary to Paul EDWARDS
SLAYMAKER, Mary to William MOONEY
SLY, Mary Ann to Lewis Felix PASCAULT
SMELSER, Catherine to Charles GERBER
SMITH, Lehlia to Paul LEVINGSTON
SMITH, Mary to Matthew TAYLOR
SMITH, Mary to Richard DUNPHY
SNEIDER, Mary to Frederic MERA
SNOWDEN, Mary to Moses BROWN
SPARROW, Ann to Joseph MORANCY
SPENCE, Mary to John BERRY
ST. AVOYE, Therese to Auguste DELADEBAT
STANSBURY, Polly to Arnold LIVERS
STEEL, Elizabeth to Robert WALSH
STEELE, Ann to Wendel LAURENCE
STEIGER, Catherine to Joseph BERGMAN
STEIGER, Elizabeth to William BAINER
STEIGER, Mary to Frederic BENTHEIM
STEIGER, Mary to James JROINE
STEPHENSON, Elizabeth to John STEIGER
STEWART, Mary to Dennis COGEN
STOCK, Rebecca to Andrew MARCH
STOKES, Elizabeth to John ROWAN
STRIDER, Catharine to James COWAN
SULLIVAN, Mary to Edward CARROLL
SUMMERS, Margaret to John Darch DEVICE
SWEIGHOFFER, Cristina to Joseph MASHAN
TANNER, Ann to William GREGORY
TARDIEU, Marie to Amable DURAMIER
TARDIEU, Modeste to Antony CAYOL
TAYLOR, Catharine to Patrick CLOHERTY
TAYLOR, Elizabeth to William LANDERS
TEINSNOR, Dorothy to George HARTZHOG
TERRIER, Henrietta to Lewis FABRE
TESTON, Mary to John HODNETT
THIRON, Louisa to John Baptist OLLIVE
THOMAS, Elizabeth to James HANNAN
THOMPSON, Mary to George WATTS
THOMPSON, Mary to Jacob BERNETT
THOMPSON, Mary to John FAVIER
TICHNER, Catherine to Jacob STEIGER
TIETZEN, Elizabeth to Henry FEIK
TILLARD, Ann to Francis AMI
TILLY, Mary Clare to Antony DESBORDES
TODD, Rebecca to Clement GREEN

MARRIAGES BY BRIDE

TONEREY, Peggy to John Peter BIDOT
TOWEL, Catherine to John MELANCY
TOWERS, Margaret to John HANNAN
TOWNSEND, Juliana to John HALL
TRAINER, Elizabeth to Charles MCALLISTER
TRAVERSE, Sarah to Alexander TROTT
TROUVE, Mary Joanna to Olivier CEBRON
TRUEMAN, Catharine to Januarius FERRI
TULL, Ann to Edward MCFARLIN
TURIN, Margaret to Barnet LIMES
TURINE, Mary to William CURTIS
VATMEL, Victoire to John Peter BERTRAND
VEAL, Catharine to James MALONY
VENNY, Catharine to George DALTON
VENNY, Margaret to Thomas COWAN
VINCENT, Lilly to James GOODWIN
VINEY, Mary to John MANCHOTE
WAGERMAN, Frances to Jack JORSE
WALLACE, Henny to Charles HILLENS
WALSH, Catharine to Michael O'CONNER
WALSH, Elizabeth to Patrick LYNCH
WALSH, Hannah to John O'BRIEN
WALSH, Mary to William LOYDE
WALSH, Mary to John CARRERE
WALTER, Elizabeth to William LLOYD
WARNER, Darcus to Henry LITZENGER
WARNER, Elizabeth to John MCKENZIE
WATERS, Ann to Stephen ZACHARIE
WEAVER, Mary to John OVERTON
WEISS, Mary to Peter SIEG
WELLS, Ann to James FISHER
WELLS, Ann to Edward QUEEN
WELLS, Margaret to Charles GOUVERNET
WEST, Sarah to William NORTON
WHELAN, Maria to Patrick FAHERTY
WHITE, Barbara to George, Jr. ROSENSTEEL
WHITE, Catharine to Sebastian HIGH
WHITE, Elizabeth to William YERBY
WHITE, Mary to Charles BERNARD
WHITE, Mary to Peter GOULD
WHITE, Mary to Neil LOGAN
WHITEMASTERS, Barbara to Peter LINER
WILLIAME, Mary to Owen DUFFY
WILLIAMS, Elizabeth to Laurance WHELAN
WILLIAMS, Jennet to Michael HANNAN
WILLIS, Rosanna to Peter LICK
WILLSON, Eleanor to Arthur HIGGENBOTHAM
WILSON, Ruth to James BIRMINGHAM
WINTZEILER, Magdalen to Francis FOLDWEILDER
WISE, Catharine to Lewis GROSS
WITHERHOLT, Juliana to Sebastian RENER
WONDER, Maria to Walter C. HAYES
WOODHOUSE, Margaret to Jacob LEGUEN
WRIGHT, Mary to Frederic FLIN
WYSTER, Mary to William BAYLOR

MARRIAGES BY BRIDE

YAU, Mary to Charles BOUDRAU
YORK, Mary to Joseph GAFFORD
YOUNG, Anabella to Patrick GOULDING
YOUNG, Catharine to Michael WISE
YOUNG, Elizabeth to Richard BISHOP
YOUNG, Jane to Patrick KELLY
YOUNG, Mary to Dennis MCHENRY
YOUNG, Mary to Abraham VANBIBBER

BURIALS

Andrew; died Aug 14, 1799; bur. Aug 15, 1799; age - 1 yr.;
    mulatto
Apollonia; died Oct 27, 1798; bur. Oct 28, 1798; wf. of Samuel,
    free negro; free mulatto
Desir; died Sep 12, 1800; bur. Sep 13, 1800; age - 5 yrs.; a
    French mulatto
George; died Aug 2, 1799; bur. Aug 3, 1799; age - 7 mo.; son of
    Mary; child of color
Georgette Augustine; died Nov 22, 1799; bur. Nov 22, 1799;
    mulatto; age - 14 mo.
John Charles; died Jan 11, 1798; bur. Jan 11, 1798; age - 3 mo.;
    son of Mary Jane, an Indian woman
Kate; died Sep 29, 1799; bur. Sep 30, 1799; a free mulatto; died
    at the house of Aubrey Jones
Mary Joseph; died Apr 23, 1799; bur. Apr 24, 1799; age - 6 yrs.;
    a mulatto
Mary Joseph; died Jul 25, 1799; bur. Jul 26, 1799; age - 7 mo.;
    French mulatto
Rosine; died Aug 26, 1798; bur. Aug 27, 1798; French negro woman
Thomas; died Jun 5, 1798; bur. Jun 5, 1798; age - 10 mo.; a
    foundling
Thomas; died May 28, 1800; bur. May 29, 1800; age - 25 yrs.; free
    French negro; small pox
William; bur. Jul 3, 1799
ADOUE, Susanne Julie; died Oct 29, 1799; bur. Oct 30, 1799; age -
    16 mo.; dau. of Peter & Catherine Ester
ALBERT, John; died Mar 4, 1798; bur. Mar 5, 1798; age - 6 wks.
ALLAERT, James; died Mar 23, 1799; bur. Mar 24, 1799
ALLEN, Henry; died Aug 15, 1800; bur. Aug 16, 1800; age - 4 mo.;
    son of Luke & Catherine
ALLEN, James; died Sep 29, 1794; bur. Sep 30, 1794; age - 14 mo.
    9 da.
ALLEN, John; died Jul 31, 1798; bur. Aug 1, 1798; age - 11 mo.;
    son of Patrick & Elizabeth
ALLEN, Mary; died May 1, 1795; bur. May 3, 1795; age - 4 yrs.;
    dau. of Patrick & Elizabeth
ALPS, Lawrence; died Apr 28, 1799; bur. Apr 29, 1799; Italian
ANDERSON, Arthur; died Aug 31, 1796; bur. Sep 1, 1796; age - 7
    mo. 21 da.; son of Thomas & Rebecca
ANDERSON, Rebecca; died Dec 2, 1798; bur. Dec 3, 1798; age - 42
    yrs.; widow of Thomas
ANDERSON, Thomas; died May 10, 1798; bur. May 11, 1798; age - 55
    yrs.
ANDREWS, Mary Ann; died Jul 26, 1799; bur. Jul 27, 1799; age - 2
    mo.; dau. of George & Elizabeth
ANSELE, Nicholas; died Nov 25, 1793; bur. Nov 26, 1793; nat. of
    parish of St. Sauveuir of Montivillier, Diocese of Rouen
ANTHONY, Joseph; died Sep 16, 1798; bur. Sep 16, 1798; age - 30
    yrs.; nat. of Italy
ANTICHAN, Gerard; died Jul 22, 1795; bur. Jul 23, 1795; age - 1
    yr. 6 mo.; son of Anthony & Elizabeth St. Martin
ARMAND, John Peter; died Sep 11, 1796; bur. Sep 12, 1796; age - 1
    mo. 22 da.; son of Francis & Margaret
ARMAND, Margaret; died Sep 13, 1800; bur. Sep 13, 1800; age - 33
    yrs.; wf. of John

BURIALS

ARMAND, Mary; died Jul 31, 1796; bur. Aug 1, 1796; age - 11 da.; dau. of Francis & Margaret

ARMI, Armand; died Jul 26, 197; bur. Jul 27, 1797; age - 1 yr. 3 mo. 21 da.; son of Peter & Sophia

ATRIDGE, Mary; died Jul 23, 1797; bur. Jul 24, 1797; age - 20 yrs.; wf. of James

ATRIDGE, Thomas; died Aug 27, 1795; bur. Aug 27, 1795; age - 16 mo.; son of James & Mary

ATTALIE, Catherine; died Oct 24, 1793; bur. Oct 25, 1793; age - 7 yrs.; nat. of Cape Island, St. Domonique

BABIN, Margaret; died Jan 30, 1794; bur. Jan 31, 1794; nat. of Nova Scotia; advanced age

BADIAN, Catherine; died Jun 19, 1798; bur. Jun 19, 1798; age - 6 yrs.; dau. of Peter & Mary

BADIAN, Elizabeth; died Aug 22, 1800; bur. Aug 23, 1800; age - 13 mo.; dau. of Peter & Mary

BAHON, Stephen; died Feb 7, 1799; bur. Feb 9, 1799; age - 54 yrs.; nat. of Ireland; died of apoplexy

BAKER, Anthony; died Oct 28, 1800; bur. Oct 29, 1800; age - 1 mo.; son of Adam & Mary

BAKER, Elizabeth; died Aug 9, 1800; bur. Aug 10, 1800; age - 9 mo.; dau. of Mathias (deceased) & Magdalen

BAKER, Julia; died Sep 25, 1800; bur. Sep 25, 1800; nat. of Ireland

BAKER, Mathias; died Sep 27, 1799; bur. Sep 29, 1799; age - 54 yrs.

BALL, Ely; died Sep 28, 1797; bur. Sep 28, 1797; age - 5 yrs. 6 mo.

BALLIER, Laurent Charles Pierre; died Nov 2, 1793; bur. Nov 2, 1793; son of Pierre & Marguerette

BARAUX, Mary; died Sep 13, 1800; bur. Sep 13, 1800; age - 28 yrs.; wf. of Michael

BARBARIN, Teresa; died Sep 24, 1796; bur. Sep 25, 1796; age - 6 yrs. 5 mo.; dau. of Louis & Mary

BARBINE, Margaret; died Aug 23, 1796; bur. Aug 23, 1796; age - 14 yrs.

BARDOIS, John Baptist; died Aug 8, 1793; bur. Aug 9, 1793; age - 20 yrs.; nat. of St. Jean de Luc

BARICKMAN, Christina; died Jul 27, 1793; bur. Jul 28, 1793; wf. of Anthony

BARKLEY, Ann; died May 4, 1800; bur. May 5, 1800

BARLEY, John; died Aug 11, 1800; bur. Aug 11, 1800; age - 3 mo.

BARNEY, William Moses; died Aug 16, 1800; bur. Aug 17, 1800; age - 1 mo.; son of Samuel & Eve

BAROUX, Augustina; died Oct 28, 1800; bur. Oct 29, 1800; age - 4 yrs. 8 mo. 2 da.; dau. of James Michael & Mary

BARRATON, John Joseph; died May 11, 1798; bur. May 11, 1798; age - 3 yrs.; son of Justine, a free woman from St Domingo

BARRY, Edward Ward; died Jul 11, 1800; bur. Jul 12, 1800; age - 1 yr.; son of Michael & Elizabeth

BARRY, John; died Jun 29, 1799; bur. Jun 29, 1799; nat. of & lately from Ireland

BARRY, Thomas; died Sep 15, 1793; bur. Sep 15, 1793

BASTARD, John; died Aug 9, 1795; bur. Aug 10, 1795; age - 12 da.; son of John & Louisa

BURIALS

BASTERATE, Frances Schafer; died Mar 13, 1794; bur. Mar 13, 1794; age - 55 yrs.; widow of Mr Basterate of Cape St Francis, St Domingo

BATAILLE, Mary Magdalen Brodin; died Nov 12, 1793; bur. Nov 13, 1793; age - 60 yrs.; widow a 2nd time of Mr Hugh Gabriel Bataille de la Garet, Ancient Commandant of the quarter of Mont Rouis, parish of St Peter Harcahayes, St Domingo

BATILLE, Mary Joseph; died Apr 28, 1798; bur. Apr 29, 1798; age - 23 yrs.; son of Hugh Gabriel Batille, former commanding officer of militia at Larcahaye; planter of St Domingo & of Mary Magdalen Brodine

BATPARO, Michael; died Sep 1, 1798; bur. Sep 1, 1798; age - 30 yrs.; a Spainard

BECK, Helena; died Sep 19, 1794; bur. Sep 20, 1794; wf. of John

BELLEROCHE, John Baptist; died Aug 5, 1795; bur. Aug 5, 1795; age - 4 mo.; son of Rene & Jane Bouchereau

BELNOUX, Marianne; died Sep 22, 1799; bur. Sep 23, 1799; age - 30 yrs.; nat. of Orleans

BENER, Henry; died Aug 28, 1795; bur. Aug 29, 1795; age - 8 da.; son of William & Elizabeth

BENNET, Mary; died Jun 21, 1800; bur. Jun 22, 1800; age - 56 yrs.; wf. of Peter; died at Fells Point

BERGER, Claudia; died Jan 15, 1794; bur. Jan 15, 1794; age - 4 mo.

BERGMAN, Joseph; died May 27, 1797; bur. May 28, 1797; age - 10 yrs.; son of Joseph & Catherine

BERKLEY, Daniel; died Oct 18, 1800; bur. Oct 20, 1800; age - 9 yrs.; son of Elizabeth

BERNABEU, Josepha Joanna Matilda; died Jul 26, 1797; bur. Jul 27,1797; age - 9 mo. 19 da.; dau. of Dr John Baptist, Counsel for Catholic Majesty in Maryland & Donna Marie Bethsabee

BERNABEU, Maria; died Oct 11, 1796; bur. Oct 12, 1796; age - 2 yrs. 6 mo.; dau. of Dr. John Baptist, Consul of his Catholic Majesty at Baltimore & Donna Bethsabee Marie

BERNARD, Jean Joseph; died Oct 4, 1793; nat. of Cape Francis, San Domingo

(BERNARD), Mary; died Oct 21, 1798; bur. Oct 22, 1798; age - 9 yrs.; negro slave of Mary Bernard

BERRY, Mary; died Dec 20, 1796; bur. Dec 22, 1796; age - 6 yrs. 11 mo. 11 da.; dau. of Regis & Harriot

BERRY, Sarah; died Jul 7, 1798; bur. Jul 8, 1798; age - 5 da.; dau. of Regis & Harriot

BERTIN, Jane; died Nov 18, 1793; bur. Nov 19, 1793; age - 4 da.; dau. of James & Ann Chirot; Cape Francois

BERTOULIN, Francis; died Jul 27, 1794; bur. Jul 28, 1794; age - 18 mo.; son of Joseph & Eve

BESSE, Alexander; died Jul 9, 1800; bur. Jul 10, 1800; age - 3 wks.; Claudius & Margaret

BESSIERE, Peter; died Nov 28, 1793; bur. Nov 29, 1793; age - 21 yr.; parish of St. Lewis, Bordeaux; deceased on board the ship Angelique de Bordeaux, Capt. Cherchy

BESSON, Joseph; died Nov 29, 1796; bur. Nov 29, 1796; age - 5 da.; son of Lewis & Ann Boilenne

BURIALS

BLACK, Barbara; died Sep 30, 1800; bur. Sep 30, 1800; age - 41 yrs.; widow of John
BLACK, John; died Sep 23, 1800; bur. Sep 23, 1800; age - 40 yrs.
BLACK, Nicholas; died Aug 26, 1800; bur. Aug 26, 1800; age - 3 yrs.; son of John & Barbara
BLACK, Peter; died Jun 25, 1800; bur. Jun 26, 1800; age - 8 mo.; son of John & Barbara
BLAIR, Edward; died Aug 13, 1799; bur. Aug 14, 1799; age - 14 mo.; son of John & Catherine
BLAKE, Michael; died Jan 4, 1796; bur. Jan 7, 1796; nat. of Ireland
BLOT, Sarah; died Dec 22, 1797; bur. Dec 23, 1797; age - 2 yrs.; dau. of Francis & Margaret
BOARMAN, Benedict Leonard; died Jul 14, 1799; bur. Jul 15, 1799; age - 18 yrs.; son of Charles & Mary of Charles Co.
BOIS TRUVE, Mary Louise; died May 5, 1798; bur. May 7, 1798; age - 39 yrs.; wf. of Peter
BOISLANDRY, Orpheus Arthur; died Oct 28, 1798; bur. Oct 29, 1798; age - 17 mo.; son of Robert Charles Le Grand & Louisa Frances Buscaille
BOLAND, Thomas; died Sep 3, 1800; bur. Sep 3, 1800; age - 26 yrs.
BONER, William; died Sep 6, 1800; bur. Sep 6, 1800
BONN, Barbara Teresia; died Aug 10, 1797; bur. Aug 10, 1797; age - 10 mo.; dau. of Joseph & Ann
BONN, Catherine; died Jun 25, 1799; bur. Jun 25, 1799; age - 3 yrs.; dau. of Phillip & Mary
BORIE, Elizabeth; died Aug 10, 1797; bur. Aug 11, 1797; age - 2 yrs. 1 mo. 2 wks. 4 da.; dau. of Joseph & Margaret
BORIE, Margaret; died Oct 30, 1799; bur. Oct 31, 1799; wf. of Joseph
BOSCH, John; died Jul 11, 1798; bur. Jul 12, 1798; age - 6 yrs.
BOSLEY, (?); died Sep 10, 1797; bur. Sep 10, 1797; wf. of ? Bosley
BOUCHER, Arthur; died Aug 22, 1794; bur. Aug 23, 1794
BOUCHER, Helen; died May 31, 1793; bur. Jun 1, 1793; born diocese of Bordeaux; late from San Domingo
BOUDIN, Henry; died Jun 24, 1796; bur. Jun 25, 1796; age - 1 yr.; son of Richard & Rebecca
BOULAND, Genevieve; died Jan 29, 1794; bur. Jan 30, 1794; age - 24 yrs.; dau. of Louis Oliver, merchant, & Janir Lamere of St. Peter's parish, Besancon, Francheconte
BOUSSEREAU, Ann; died May 1, 1796; bur. May 2, 1796; nat. of Acadia
BOWEN, James; died Jul 13, 1800; bur. Jul 14, 1800; age - 41 yrs.; nat. of Ireland; palsy
BOWEN, Matthew; died Sep 16, 1800; bur. Sep 16, 1800; son of James
BOYD, Sarah; died Sep 5, 1800; bur. Sep 5, 1800; age - 66 yrs.; widow
BOYLE, Bernard; died Jan 17, 1800; bur. Jan 17, 1800; age - 22 yrs.
BRADLEY, John Columbus; died Aug 21, 1799; bur. Aug 22, 1799; age - 9 mo.; son of Thomas & Ann
BRADLEY, William; died Apr 26, 1799; bur. Apr 27, 1799; age - 8 yrs.; son of John

BURIALS

BRADY, Elizabeth; died Oct 9, 1796; bur. Oct 9, 1796; age - 13 da.; dau. of John & Elizabeth
BRADY, James; died Jul 10, 1794; bur. Jul 12, 1794; age - 10 mo. 10 da.; son of John & Elizabeth
BRADY, John; died Mar 14, 1798; bur. Mar 15, 1798; age - 7 yrs.; son of John & Elizabeth
BRADY, Mary; died Sep 11, 1800; bur. Sep 12, 1800; age - 21 yrs.
BRANNICK, Patrick; died Oct 9, 1796; bur. Oct 9, 1796; age - 32 yrs.; nat. of Ireland
BRAY, Susanna; died Sep 26, 1797; bur. Sep 26, 1797; nat. of Ireland; advanced age
BRAZIER, Peter; died Jul 31, 1800; bur. Aug 1, 1800; age - 5 mo.; son of John & Eleanor
BREMONT, Mary; died Sep 29, 1796; bur. Sep 30, 1796; age - 1 yr. 1 mo.; dau. of John & Mary Frances Elizabeth Lesfauries
BRETET, Charles Bruneau; died Aug 25, 1796; bur. Aug 25, 1796; age - 1 yr.; son of Charles Amand & Flore Contant
BRETET, Charles Amand; died Dec 31, 1796; bur. Dec 31, 1796; age - 3 yrs.; son of Charles Amand & Flore Contant
BRIEN, Lawrence; died Sep 11, 1794; bur. Sep 11, 1794; age - 70 yrs.
BRITT, Ann; died Sep 24, 1797; bur. Sep 24, 1797; nat. of Ireland
BRITT, Robert; died Jul 7, 1793; bur. Jul 8, 1793; age - 40 yrs.; died in Fells Point; cause - consumption
BROOK, Henry; died Sep 11, 1796; bur. Sep 12, 1796; age - 1 yr. 5 mo.; son of Henry & Priscilla
BROWN, Catherine; died Aug 3, 1794; bur. Aug 4, 1794; age - 10 da.; dau. of James & Mary
BROWN, James; died Aug 31, 1795; bur. Sep 1, 1795; age - 2 da.; son of James & Mary
BROWN, James; died Dec 15, 1799; bur. Dec 16, 1799
BROWN, Mary; died Sep 19, 1795; bur. Sep 20, 1795; age - 3 mo.; dau. of James & Mary
BROWN, Sarah Williams; died Aug 21, 1796; bur. Aug 22, 1796; age - 20 mo.; dau. of James & Hannah
BROWN, William; died Jul 25, 1799; bur. Jul 26, 1799; negro; age - 7 mo.
BROWNE, James; died Nov 7, 1796; bur. Nov 8, 1796; son of James & Mary; born & died Nov 7, 1796
BROWNE, James; died Apr 15, 1800; bur. Apr 16, 1800; nat. of Ireland
(BROWNING), Lydia; died May 12, 1800; bur. May 12, 1800; negro slave of Mrs Browning; small pox
BRUCOURT, Michael Philip; died Dec 16, 1795; bur. Dec 17, 1795; age - 60 yrs.; planter of Ft. Dauphin at Fend Blanc, St Domingo
BRUSLE, Peter; died Jul 18, 1794; bur. Jul 19, 1794; age - 35 yrs.; nat. of Grand Riviere; planter of Jeremie, St Domingo
BRYAN, Mary; died Oct 31, 1797; bur. Oct 31, 1797; age - 26 yrs.; wf. of John
BUCHEN, John; died Sep 28, 1797; bur. Sep 28, 1797; age - 35 yrs.
BUCHOLTZ, Catharine; died May 23, 1800; bur. May 24, 1800; age - 25 yrs.
BUCHON, Margaret Gramon; died May 11, 1794; bur. May 12, 1794; age - 38 yrs.; inh. of St. Domingo; wf. of John

BURIALS

BUCKEN, Mary; died Apr 6, 1800; bur. Apr 7, 1800; age - 76 yrs.
BUNBURY, Hannah Elizabeth Wentworth; died Aug 15, 1799; bur. Aug 16, 1799; age - 3 mo.; dau. of John & Ann
BURK, Leonard; died Aug 9, 1796; bur. Aug 10, 1796; age - 8 mo.; son of Elizabeth, sl; Daniel & Henry
BURKE, Michael; died Sep 25, 1797; bur. Sep 25, 1797; nat. of Ireland
BURKE, Richard; died Sep 19, 1800; bur. Sep 19, 1800; age - 26 yrs.; nat. of Ireland; hsb. of Catharine
BURNS, John; died Sep 28, 1797; bur. Sep 28, 1797
BUTCHER, Bartholomew; died Jan 4, 1797; bur. Jan 5, 1797; age - 6 mo.; son of Bartholomew & Elizabeth
BUTLER, (?); died Oct 7, 1799; bur. Oct 8, 1799; age - 8 yrs.; a mulatto child
BUTLER, Charles; died Aug 29, 1799; bur. Aug 29, 1799; age - 4 mo.; a negro child
BUTLER, Francis; died Jul 26, 1800; bur. Jul 27, 1800; age - 20 yrs.; free negro
BUTLER, George; died Sep 5, 1796; bur. Sep 6, 1796; age - 19 mo.; son of Joannah, free negro & Henry, slave of Robert Walsh
BUTLER, Henry; died Aug 2, 1799; bur. Aug 3, 1799; age - 3 mo.; son of Nellie
BUTLER, Henry; died Oct 29, 1800; bur. Oct 30, 1800; age - 20 yrs.; son of Benjamin & Ann; free negro
BUTLER, John; died Jan 30, 1794; bur. Feb 2, 1794; age - 30 yrs.; tabacconist at Fells Point; accidentally drowned
BUTLER, John; died Nov 21, 1800; bur. Nov 21, 1800; a free mulatto
BUTLER, Peter; died Jul 12, 1799; bur. Jul 13, 1799; age - 4 yrs.
BYRNE, Eleanor; died Oct 12, 1798; bur. Oct 13, 1798; nat. of Ireland; wf. of John
BYRNE, James; died Oct 12, 1794; bur. Oct 13, 1794; age - 2 yrs.; son of John & Elizabeth
CABROL, John Baptist Joseph; died Aug 16, 1800; bur. Aug 17, 1800; age - 45 yrs.; nat. of Marseilles, France
CALDRON, John Baptist; died Sep 14, 1793; bur. Sep 15, 1793; age - 8 da.; son of Francis & Mary
CALLAGHAN, Denis; died Sep 12, 1797; bur. Sep 12, 1797; age - 28 yrs.
CAMPBELL, Ann; died May 12, 1794; bur. May 13, 1794; age - 2 yrs.; dau. of Robert & Judith
CAMPBELL, Mary Ann; died Oct 28, 1798; bur. Oct 29, 1798; age - 11 mo.; dau. of Matthew & Jane
(CAMPBELL), Peggy; died Apr 25, 1800; bur. Apr 26, 1800; age - 25 yrs.; negro slave of Mr Archibald Campbell
CAMPBELL, Rosanna; died Aug 9, 1797; bur. Aug 9, 1797; age - 9 mo.; dau. of Patrick & Jane
CANNERE, John; died Aug 4, 1797; bur. Aug 5, 1797; age - 2 wks.; son of John & Mary
CAREY, Catherine; died Nov 11, 1800; bur. Nov 12, 1800; age - 1 yr.; dau. of Dennis & Judith
CAREY, Darby; died Nov 23, 1796; bur. Nov 24, 1796; son of Dennis & Margaret; born & died Nov 23, 1796
CAREY, Dennis; died Jul 31, 1795; bur. Aug 1, 1795; age - 16 mo.; son of John & Eleanor

BURIALS

CAREY, Eleanor; died Aug 20, 1800; bur. Aug 21, 1800; age - 29 yrs.; wf. of John
CAREY, James; died Feb 27, 1795; bur. Feb 28, 1795; age - 5 wks.; son of Patrick & Eleanor
CAREY, John; died Aug 25, 1794; bur. Aug 26, 1794; son of Dennis & Margaret
CAREY, John; died Sep 8, 1800; bur. Sep 8, 1800; age - 3 mo.; son of John & Eleanor
CAREY, John; died Sep 13, 1800; bur. Sep 13, 1800; age - 34 yrs.; nat. of Ireland
CAREY, Margaret; died Sep 13, 1797; bur. Sep 14, 1797; nat. of Ireland; wf. of Dennis
CAREY, Timothy; died Aug 24, 1797; bur. Aug 25, 1797; age - 22 yrs.; nat. of Ireland
CAREY, Timothy; died Aug 27, 1800; bur. Aug 27, 1800; age - 3 yrs.; son of John & Eleanor
CARRE, (?); died Sep 10, 1796; bur. Sep 11, 1796; son of Joseph Mary Carre & Magdalen Deschamps; born & died Sept 10, 1796
CARRERE, Teresa; died Oct 4, 1796; bur. Oct 5, 1796; age - 2 yrs.; born Apr 5, 1794; dau. of John, native of Bordeaux, France & Mary of Balto
CARRICK, Richard; died May 7, 1800; bur. May 7, 1800; age - 5 mo.; son of Daniel & Bridget; small pox
CARROLL, David; died Aug 22, 1796; bur. Aug 23, 1796; age - 1 yr.; son of John & Hebe
CARROLL, Mary; died Sep 27, 1797; bur. Sep 28, 1797; age - 32 yrs.; wf. of James of Fells Point
CARROLL, Michael; died May 13, 1798; bur. May 13, 1798; age - 28 yrs.; nat. of Ireland
CARSON, Eleanor; died May 25, 1800; bur. May 26, 1800; age - 32 yrs.; wf. of Nathaniel
CARSON, Juliet; died Apr 22, 1798; bur. Apr 23, 1798; age - 15 mo.; dau. of Nathaniel & Eleanor
CARTY, Bridget; died Jan 6, 1797; bur. Jan 7, 1797; age - 1 mo. 10 da.; dau. of Michael & Eleanor
CARY, John; died Jul 26, 1796; bur. Jul 27, 1796; age - 17 da.; son of John & Eleanor
CASEY, Robert; died Oct 15, 1796; bur. Oct 16, 1796; age - 40 yrs.; nat. of Ireland
CASSAGNE, Peter; died Sep 23, 1797; bur. Sep 23, 1797; age - 18 mo.; son of Sylvester & Mary Fauconet
(CATON), Elizabeth; died May 14, 1799; bur. May 15, 1799; mulatto slave of Richard Caton
CAUSSE, Francis Bartholomew; died Jun 24, 1799; bur. Jun 24, 1799; age - 42 yrs.; born Guilla in Languadve
CAVAROS, Marie; died Mar 2, 1795; bur. Mar 2, 1795; age - 6 mo.; dau. of Francois & Marie
CAZEAUX, Catherine LaPlace; died Aug 22, 1796; bur. Aug 22, 1796; age - 33 yrs.; dau. of Joseph Paschal delaPlace & Catherine Loison; nat. of Reims in Champaigne; wf. of Peter
CEBRON, Ann Frances; died Oct 26, 1796; bur. Oct 27, 1796; age - 15 mo. 4 da.; dau. of Oliver & Mary Jane Trouve
CHABERT, Antoine; died Nov 22, 1793; bur. Nov 23, 1793; age - 49 yrs.; nat. of Toulin; inh. of Jacquezes, parish of Terriere Rouge, St. Domingo

BURIALS

CHAMEAU, Rose; died Oct 28, 1797; bur. Oct 29, 1797; nat. of Nova Scotia; widow
CHAMPAGNE, John Charles; died Dec 20, 1793; bur. Dec 21, 1793; age - 45 yrs.; nat. of Champagne, France; merchant at St. Mark, St. Domingo
CHAMPALBERT, Elizabeth; died Oct 18, 1793; bur. Oct 19, 1793; age - 19 yrs.; wf. of M. Jean Frignot of Fermagh, Surveyor of King, District of Jeremie, St Domingo
CHANCE, Jean Francis; died Nov 2, 1793; bur. Nov 2, 1793; son of Jean & Catherine Provoty
CHANCE, Lawrence; died Apr 4, 1795; bur. Apr 5, 1795; age - 8 mo.; son of John & Catherine Provost
CHANCE, Marie Francois; died Nov 6, 1793; bur. Nov 6, 1793
CHANCHE, Jean Paul; died Oct 18, 1793; bur. Oct 19, 1793; nat. of D'Orthez; inh. of St. Domingo
CHANCHE, Louis Paul; died Aug 16, 1796; bur. Aug 16, 1796; age - 2 yrs. 10 mo.; son of John & Catharine Provost
CHANTREAU, Philip; died Apr 17, 1797; bur. Apr 18, 1797; age - 40 yrs.; nat. of Orleans, France
CHAUVIN, Yvoix; died Sep 8, 1793; bur. Sep 9, 1793; Aux Cayes parish, St Domingo
CHEMINAU, Francis; died Jul 15, 1793; bur. Jul 15, 1793; nat. of France
CHESTREND, Mary; died Oct 3, 1798; bur. Oct 4, 1798; age - 42 yrs.; wf. of David
CHEVALIER, Marie Magdalaine; died Nov 1, 1793; bur. Nov 1, 1793; nat. of Coty; died - 4 AM
CHIRAC, John Baptist; died Jul 28, 1799; bur. Jul 29, 1799; age - 58 yrs.; son of John & Frances Bousse; nat. of Lezoux in Auvergne now Dept du Puy de Dom
CICERON, Felix; died Sep 22, 1795; bur. Sep 22, 1795; age - 20 mo.
CICERON, Francis Cummings; died Mar 1, 1798; bur. Mar 2, 1798; age - 4 mo.; son of Anthony & Mary
CICERON, Zeline; died Jul 2, 1798; bur. Jul 3, 1798; age - 9 mo.; dau. of Anthony & Mary
CLANCY, Elizabeth; died Aug 26, 1800; bur. Aug 27, 1800; age - 5 yrs.; dau. of Patrick & Joanna
CLANCY, Pierce; died Aug 14, 1799; bur. Aug 15, 1799; age - 18 mo.; son of Roger & Lydia
CLARK, (?); died Aug 24, 1800; bur. Aug 25, 1800; age - 3 yrs.; of -- Clark, widow
CLARKE, Mary; died Dec 10, 1794; bur. Dec 11, 1794; age - 16 da.; dau. of William & Susanna
CLARKE, William; died Nov 3, 1797; bur. Nov 4, 1797; age - 2 yrs.; son of David & Elizabeth
CLEMENT, Francois; died Aug 22, 1794; bur. Aug 23, 1794; age - 37 yrs.; nat. of Grandville in Normandy
CLONEY, Mary; died Feb 3, 1797; bur. Feb 4, 1797; age - 24 yrs.; wf. of James
CLOUGHERTY, Honor; died Jan 27, 1799; bur. Jan 27, 1799; age - 25 yrs.; nat. of Ireland; wf. of Patrick
CLOUGHERTY, Honor; died Feb 2, 1800; bur. Feb 3, 1800; age - 10 mo.; dau. of John & Margaret

BURIALS

COADY, John; died Sep 15, 1795; bur. Sep 16, 1795; age - 5 mo.; son of David & Johanna

COBLER, Joseph; died Sep 18, 1798; bur. Sep 19, 1798; age - 53 yrs.; nat. of Germany

COGHLAN, Catherine; died Sep 6, 1797; bur. Sep 7, 1797; nat. of Ireland; widow of William

COKELY, Patrick; died Aug 23, 1794; bur. Aug 24, 1794; nat. of Ireland

COLGAN, Lydia; died Oct 20, 1798; bur. Oct 21, 1798; age - 11 yrs.; dau. of Michael & ?

COLLIN, Peter; died Sep 6, 1797; bur. Sep 7, 1797; age - 34 yrs.; nat. of Ireland

COLLINS, Jerimiah; died Sep 3, 1800; bur. Sep 3, 1800

COLLINS, John; died Sep 1, 1797; bur. Sep 2, 1797; age - 25 yrs.; nat. of Ireland

COLVIN, Philip; died Sep 14, 1796; bur. Sep 15, 1796; age - 25 yrs.; nat. of Ireland

COMPAYNE, Margaret; died Dec 1, 1798; bur. Dec 2, 1798; age - 5 yrs.; born Cape Francis; dau. of John Francis Joseph James, nat. of Languedor & of Margaret Sudre, nat. Plaisance, St Domingo; baptized at Cape Francis; godparents, M/M Sudre, her grandparents

CONBRON, John; died Oct 16, 1797; bur. Oct 16, 1797; age - 4 yrs.; son of William & Catherine Hertzboc

CONDEN, Edward; died Sep 13, 1800; bur. Sep 14, 1800; age - 23 yrs.; nat. of Ireland

CONDEN, John; died Apr 2, 1800; bur. Apr 2, 1800; born & died Apr 2, 1800; privately baptized by the midwife

CONDEN, Mary; died Aug 4, 1799; bur. Aug 5, 1799; age - 1 yr.; dau. of John & Sarah

CONNELLY, Michael; died Oct 4, 1794; bur. Oct 4, 1794; nat. of Ireland

CONNERS, Thomas; died Nov 24, 1797; bur. Nov 25, 1797; age - 42 yrs.; nat. of Ireland; hsb. of Catherine

CONNOR, Patrick; died Sep 17, 1797; bur. Sep 17, 1797; nat. of Ireland

CONNOR, Thomas; died Oct 25, 1800; bur. Oct 26, 1800; age - 30 yrs.; nat. of Ireland

COOK, Honour; died Jan 7, 1796; bur. Jan 9, 1796; wf. of Michael

COONEY, Thomas; died Apr 10, 1796; bur. Apr 11, 1796; nat. of Ireland

COONY, Bartholomew; died Nov 12, 1797; bur. Nov 13, 1797; age - 5 yrs.; son of Thomas (deceased) & Elizabeth

CORBET, Catharine; died Aug 22, 1800; bur. Aug 23, 1800; wf. of William

CORBET, Catherine; died Aug 19, 1800; bur. Aug 20, 1800; age - 3 yrs.; dau. of William & Catherine

CORRIN, Mary Catherine; died Sep 6, 1794; bur. Sep 7, 1794; wf. of Michael

COSKERY, Bennet; died Feb 15, 1800; bur. Feb 16, 1800; age - 2 wks.; son of Bernard & Anastasia

COSKERY, Charles; died Jun 24, 1795; bur. Jun 25, 1795; age - 2 da.; son of Bernard & Anastasia

COSTELLO, Bartholomew; died Sep 10, 1800; bur. Sep 10, 1800; age - 40 yrs.; nat. of Ireland

BURIALS

COTERELLE, Mary; died May 2, 1795; bur. May 3, 1795; age - 28 yrs.; nat. of Plaisame, St. Domingo
COTTER, William; died May 30, 1796; bur. May 31, 1796; age - 29 yrs.; nat. of Prussia
COUTIER, Gabriel; died Jul 22, 1796; bur. Jul 22, 1796; age - 1 yr. 2 mo. 8 wks.; son of John Anthony & Mary Bouvier
COWEN, Catherine; died Oct 22, 1794; bur. Oct 23, 1794; age - 45 yrs.; wf. of John
CRAHELL, Ann; died Sep 5, 1793; bur. Sep 6, 1793; age - 18 mo.; dau. of Will & Susanna
CREAGH, John; died Aug 27, 1800; bur. Aug 27, 1800; age - 30 yrs.; nat. of Ireland
CREAGH, Mary; died Aug 9, 1798; bur. Aug 10, 1798; age - 2 mo.; dau. of John & Mary
CREMER, Robert; died Jul 22, 1796; bur. Jul 23, 1796; age - 1 yr. 12 da.; son of Edward & Mary
CROLLY, Helena; died Oct 4, 1796; bur. Oct 4, 1796; age - 50 yrs.
CUJAS, John Frances; died Dec 12, 1793; bur. Dec 13, 1793; age - 40 yrs.; son of Leonard Cujas of Loutraine, Diocese of Limoges & Marianne Bonnet
CULLADIN, George; died Jan 8, 1796; bur. Jan 8, 1796; age - 4 mo.; son of George & Margaret
CULLIDON, John; died Aug 19, 1797; bur. Aug 20, 1797; age - 10 mo.; son of George & Mary
CUNNINGHAM, Margaret; died Oct 21, 1794; bur. Oct 22, 1794; age - 35 yrs.; wf. of John
CURRAN, Mary; died Oct 5, 1799; bur. Oct 6, 1799; age - 21 yrs.; nat. of Ireland
CURTIS, William; died Sep 3, 1798; bur. Sep 4, 1798; age - 1 wk.; son of William & Mary
CUSICK, John; died Jun 28, 1800; bur. Jun 29, 1800; age - 3 da.; son of John & Mary
CUSICK, William; died Oct 23, 1799; bur. Oct 23, 1799; age - 1 yr. 8 mo.; son of John & Mary
DACOSTA, Bento; died Oct 22, 1793; bur. Oct 23, 1793; age - 65 yrs.; nat. of Portugal; Captain of the St. George
DALIQUET, Ann Louisa; died Mar 13, 1800; bur. Mar 14, 1800; age - 2 mo.; dau. of Mrs D.
DALIQUET, Ann Mary; died Nov 28, 1796; bur. Nov 29, 1796; age - 1 yr.; dau. of John Baptist & Elizabeth
DALY, (?); died Aug 27, 1796; bur. Aug 28, 1796; age - 100 yrs.; nat. of Ireland
DALY, Catherine; died Nov 27, 1793; bur. Nov 29, 1793
DALY, Eleanor; died Aug 2, 1797; bur. Aug 3, 1797; age - 1 wk.; dau. of Timothy & Catherine
DALY, James; died Aug 27, 1800; bur. Aug 27, 1800; age - 25 yrs.; nat. of Ireland
DALY, Patrick; died Jan 23, 1797; bur. Jan 24, 1797; age - 2 mo.; son of Sybil
DANNENBERG, Julia; died Jul 31, 1796; bur. Aug 1, 1796; age - 2 yrs. 8 da.; dau. of Frederick William & Catherine Frey
DARKEY, Ann; died Aug 4, 1798; bur. Aug 5, 1798; age - 35 yrs.; an Indian
(DARNAND), Joseph; died Jan 6, 1800; bur. Jan 7, 1800; negro slave of Mr Darnand

BURIALS

DARNELL, Henry Bennet; died Sep 7, 1793; bur. Sep 8, 1793; died in Balto Co

DAVANNE, Philip; died Aug 5, 1796; bur. Aug 6, 1796; age - 1 yr. 2 wks.; son of John & Lucy

DAVEY, Ann; died Sep 30, 1800; bur. Sep 30, 1800; age - 38 yrs.; wf. of (Capt) Peter

DAVID, Hipolite Amand; died Nov 11, 1799; bur. Nov 12, 1799

DAVIES, Catherine; died Oct 20, 1794; bur. Oct 21, 1794; wf. of Matthew

DAVIES, Elizabeth; died Oct 9, 1796; bur. Oct 10, 1796; age - 7 yrs.; dau. of Peter & Ann

DAVIES, Margaret; died Sep 18, 1797; bur. Sep 18, 1797

DAVIES, Peter; died Oct 10, 1796; bur. Oct 11, 1796; age - 4 yrs.; son of Peter & Ann

DAVIES, Thomas; died Jul 30, 1796; bur. Jul 31, 1796; age - 9 mo.; son of William & Mary

DE LA RUE, Lewis; died Dec 9, 1797; bur. Dec 9, 1797; age - 1 da.; son of Francis & Ann Margaret Zeline Daulede

DE LA RUE, Lewis Francis; died Jan 16, 1798; bur. Jan 17, 1798; age - 7 yrs.; son of Francis Lewis, planter, St Domingo & Ann Margaret Zeline Daulede

DEADY, Francis; died Feb 11, 1795; bur. Feb 11, 1795; age - 3 yrs. 6 mo.; son of Daniel & Winifred

DEAGLE, Charles; died Sep 22, 1800; bur. Sep 23, 1800; age - 14 yrs.; son of (Capt) Simon & Elizabeth

DEAGLE, Hannah; died Dec 3, 1797; bur. Dec 4, 1797; age - 1 mo.; dau. of Simon & Elizabeth

DEAGLE, Margaret; died Jul 29, 1796; bur. Jul 30, 1796; age - 1 yr.; dau. of Simon & Elizabeth

DEAGLE, Matthew; died Jul 30, 1797; bur. Aug 1, 1797

DEAGLE, Simon; died Aug 18, 1799; bur. Aug 19, 1799; age - 1 da.; son of Simon & Elizabeth

DEAL, William; died Oct 10, 1799; bur. Oct 11, 1799; age - 7 da.; son of Jacob Deal, Jr & Susanna

DEALY, James; died Sep 12, 1793; bur. Sep 13, 1793; age - 17 mo.

DEBOURD, Elizabeth; died Oct 7, 1793; bur. Oct 8, 1793; age - 17 yrs.; dau. of Daniel & Rose Grainger

DEBOYSERE, Charles; died Sep 16, 1797; bur. Sep 16, 1797; nat. of Bruges in Flanders

DEBOYSERE, Mary Teresa Caroline; died May 5, 1797; bur. May 6, 1797; age - 19 wks.; dau. of Charles & Mary Teresa

DECHEFFONTAINES, Jonathan Charlotte George; died Jan 10, 1794; bur. Jan 11, 1794; age - 5 da.; dau. of Ambrose Joseph Stephen Mary DePenfentenio, Lt Navy of his Christian Majesty & Mary Henrietta Creuze

DECHEFFONTAINES, Mary Henrietta Creuze; died Feb 12, 1794; bur. Feb 13, 1794; age - 23 yrs.; wf. of Ambrose Joseph Stephen Mary dePenfentenio Chevaliar, Lt, His Majesty's Navy

DEDIOL, John; died Oct 17, 1797; bur. Oct 18, 1797; age - 21 yrs.; sailor, belonging to the Ragusan ship, the Constant

DEFAY, Michael Robert; died Feb 23, 1796; bur. Feb 24, 1796; age - 43 yrs.; nat. of Falaize, lately from Jeremie, St Domingo

DEFLECHIER, John James Dennis Hercules; died Aug 17, 1798; bur. Aug 18, 1798; age - 1 yr. 6 mo.; son of Mary Stephen Mirals & Frances Dusceau

BURIALS

DEGAN, Charles; died Jul 28, 1798; bur. Jul 29, 1798; age - 2 yrs.; son of Catherine

DEGAN, Darby; died Jun 26, 1797; bur. Jun 27, 1797; age - 23 yrs.; accidentally drowned

DELADIBAT, Jeanne Therese St. Avoye; died Jan 28, 1795; bur. Jan 29, 1795; age - 28 yrs.; nat. of St Domingo; wf. of August Phillippe Laffen, Esq.; deceased at Abington

DELAPERRIERE, (?); died Dec 23, 1795; bur. Dec 24, 1795; age - 52 yrs.; nat. of Chamberry, Savoy; surgeon, Petit Goave, St Domingo

DELAPRADE, Ann Joseph St Martin Dufoureq; died Nov 20, 1799; bur. Nov 21, 1799; age - 21 yrs.; dau. of Simon Joseph St Martin Dufoureq & Mary Ann Smith; wf. of John Francis Cabannes, Knight of Order of St Louis, Col Commandant of Artillery & Adj Gen of So. part of St Dominique

DELAPRADE, Marie Ann Sebastian; died Aug 5, 1800; bur. Aug 5, 1800; age - 11 mo.; dau. of John Francis Cabannes, Knight of order St Louis, comdr of Artillery, southern part, St Domingo & Ann Joseph St Martin Dufoureq

DELARUE, Ann Frances; died Oct 22, 1796; bur. Oct 22, 1796; age - 3 yrs. 2 mo. 18 da.; dau. of Francis Lewis & Ann Margaret Teline Daulede

DELAVAU, Louis, Rev. Casar; died Aug 20, 1795; bur. Aug 20, 1795; age - 67 yrs.; nat. of Tours; Priest & Ancient Canon, St. Martin of Tours

DELEZE, Charles; died Mar 30, 1796; bur. Mar 31, 1796; age - 8 mo.; son of Ulalie of St Domingo

DELISLE, Modest; died Sep 12, 1794; bur. Sep 13, 1794; age - 35 yrs.; wf. of John Baptist, M.D.

DELISLE, Sophie Pontier; died Jun 14, 1796; bur. Jun 14, 1796; age - 23 yrs.; born Cape Francis & baptized at Jeremie, St Domingo; wf. of John Baptist Godart

DELMAS, Edmund; died Sep 8, 1798; bur. Sep 9, 1798; age - 14 mo.

(DEMONTALIBER), John Baptist; died Sep 1, 1793; inh. of San Domingo; mulatto slave

DEMONTIS, Mary Marcella Rousslein; died Jun 5, 1795; bur. Jun 6, 1795; age - 27 yrs.

DEMPSEY, Eleanor; died Aug 23, 1800; bur. Aug 24, 1800; age - 2 mo.; dau. of John & Mary

DEMPSEY, James; died May 7, 1798; bur. May 8, 1798; age - 3 yrs.; son of John & Elizabeth

DEMSEN, Diana; died Aug 10, 1793; bur. Aug 10, 1793; age - 5 da.; dau. of John & Elizabeth

DENAHY, Catherine; died Jan 12, 1794; bur. Jan 13, 1794; age - 16 yrs.; nat. of Ireland

DEPLASME, John Claude Joseph Gagnew; died Apr 17, 1790; bur. Apr 18, 1790; age - 36 yrs.; nat. of Poligny, France

DERIVARDI, Mariana Amelia; died Jul 14, 1795; bur. Jul 14, 1795; age - 8 mo.; dau. of James Leopold Ulrich, noble citizen of Berra, Geneva & Mary Antonia, born Vienna, Austria, Countess of Sporck

DEROUAULT, Marias; died Oct 16, 1796; bur. Oct 17, 1796; wf. of Viscount de Rouault of St. Domingo

DESCHAMPS, Magdalen; died Sep 19, 1796; bur. Sep 20, 1796; age - 41 yrs.

BURIALS

DESGRANGES, Paul Francis Leroy D'Hewal; died Dec 17, 1797; bur. Dec 17, 1797; planter from Petit St Louis, St Domingo

DESHIELDS, Francis; died Mar 10, 1795; bur. Mar 11, 1795; age - 48 yrs.

DESHIELDS, Joseph Alexander; died May 22, 1800; bur. May 23, 1800; age - 6 mo.; son of Joseph & Mary

DESHIELDS, Samuel; died Jul 5, 1797; bur. Jul 6, 1797; age - 26 yrs.; son of Lewis & Mary

DESPATE, Bertrand; died Aug 26, 1800; bur. Aug 26, 1800; age - 2 yrs.; son of Joseph & Frances Demanche

DESPERSBASQNES, Marie Adelaide; died Oct 23, 1799; bur. Oct 24, 1799; age - 42 yrs.; free mulatto

DESPOT, Joseph; died May 2, 1797; bur. May 2, 1797; age - 1 yr. 11 mo.; son of Joseph & Frances Demanche

DESROUILLERES, Rene Robin; died Nov 18, 1795; bur. Nov 18, 1795; age - 64 yrs.; planter of Frou Bonbon; parish of St. Lewis, Jeremie Island, St. Domingo

DESSALLES, Elizabeth Asselin; died Aug 4, 1796; bur. Aug 5, 1796; age - 1 yr. 5 mo.; dau. of Charles Asselin & Mary Joseph LaFarge

DEVILLE, Joseph; died Nov 23, 1793; bur. Nov 23, 1793; age - 33 yrs.; nat. of parish of Mardacon in Guiennes, Diocese of Sarlat

DEVINE, Catharine; died Aug 25, 1799; bur. Aug 25, 1799; age - 14 mo.; (Baptized July 17, 1798 by the name of Ferguson)

DIGNOR, Mary; died Oct 7, 1797; bur. Oct 7, 1797

DILLON, Daniel; died Nov 17, 1799; bur. Nov 18, 1799; age - 68 yrs.; nat. of Ireland

DILLON, William; died Sep 22, 1800; bur. Sep 22, 1800; age - 9 yrs.; son of John & Cecily

DISPAN, Margueritte Antoinette; died Feb 3, 1794; bur. Feb 4, 1794; age - 28 yrs.; nat. of Cape Francois, St Domingo; widow of Laurence Boucharlat

DISTANCE, Elizabeth; died Nov 13, 1798; bur. Nov 14, 1798; age - 2 yrs.; dau. of William Distance, free negro & Elizabeth, negro slave of Mr. Bernabeu

DIZABEAU, Ann Margaret; died Jan 6, 1799; bur. Jan 7, 1799; dau. of John & Magdalen

DIZIER, Ann Mary; died May 24, 1794; bur. May 25, 1794; age - 17 yrs.; nat. of St. Domingo; small pox

DONOVAN, Alexander; died Dec 19, 1800; bur. Dec 19, 1800; age - 20 yrs.

DONOVAN, John; died Oct 16, 1796; bur. Oct 17, 1796; age - 8 wks.; son of Bartholomew & Sarah

DOOLAN, John; died Nov 6, 1798; bur. Nov 7, 1798; age - 40 yrs.

DORNEY, Elizabeth; died Sep 3, 1800; bur. Sep 4, 1800; age - 2 yrs.; dau. of John & Jane

DOUCET, Margaret; died Oct 23, 1800; bur. Oct 24, 1800; age - 63 yrs.; widow Dispan

DOUGHERTY, George; died Oct 15, 1797; bur. Oct 15, 1797; nat. of Ireland

DOUGHERTY, Hugh; died Aug 24, 1796; bur. Aug 25, 1796; age - 24 yrs.

DOUGHERTY, Mary; died Oct 9, 1797; bur. Oct 9, 1797

BURIALS

DOUGLAS, Joseph John; died Jul 4, 1800; bur. Jul 5, 1800; age - 3 mo.; son of Cantwell & Ann; small pox
DOWLING, Philippa; died Sep 13, 1800; bur. Sep 14, 1800; age - 28 yrs.; wf. of Dr Dowling of Fells Point
DOWNEY, Matthew; died Feb 28, 1797; bur. Mar 1, 1797; age - 35 yrs.; nat. of Dublin; died at Fells Point
DOYLE, James; died Oct 1, 1797; bur. Oct 1, 1797; age - 28 yrs.
DOYLE, Mary; died Mar 13, 1798; bur. Mar 14, 1798; age - 2 yrs. 6 mo.; dau. of Nicholas & Ann
DRAKE, Francis; died Apr 18, 1795; bur. Apr 19, 1795; age - 50 yrs.
DRAYMAN, Thomas; died Jul 11, 1795; bur. Jul 12, 1795; age - 1 yr. 8 mo.
DRINAN, John; died Jul 25, 1797; bur. Jul 25, 1797; age - 7 mo.; son of Thomas & Mary
DRINAN, Mary; died Oct 1, 1797; bur. Oct 1, 1797; dau. of Simon & Mary; born & died Oct 1, 1797
DRINAN, Mary; died Oct 2, 1797; bur. Oct 3, 1797; nat. of Ireland; wf. of Simon
DRISCOLL, Mary; died Aug 13, 1799; bur. Aug 15, 1799; age - 4 yrs.; dau. of Mark & Mary
DRISKILL, Patrick; died Aug 16, 1798; bur. Aug 17, 1798; age - 15 mo.; son of Clark & Mary
DUBOIS, John Francis Dumenil; died Jan 5, 1794; bur. Jan 6, 1794; age - 33 yrs.; nat. of St. Omer in Artois
DUBOURG, Aloysius Joseph; died Jul 22, 1800; bur. Jul 22, 1800; age - 1 da.; son of Peter Francis St Colombo & Mary Elizabeth De Charette
DUCAS, John Baptist; died Oct 22, 1795; bur. Oct 22, 1795; age - 45 yrs.; nat. of Tarbes in Bigore
DUCATEL, Aimee Adelaide; died Aug 14, 1799; bur. Aug 15, 1799; age - 7 mo.; dau. of Edne & Ann Catherine Pineau
DUCHEMIN, Francis Agustin; died Jan 13, 1795; bur. Jan 14, 1795; age - 8 da.; son of Francis & Margaret
DUCHEMIN, James Joseph; died Dec 5, 1800; bur. Dec 6, 1800; age - 3 mo.; son of Francis & Margaret
DUCHEMIN, Nicholas; died Jan 3, 1796; bur. Jan 4, 1796; age - 1 da.; son of Francis & Margaret
DUFFY, Mary; died Aug 11, 1800; bur. Aug 12, 1800; age - 2 yrs.
DUFFY, Owen; died Aug 17, 1798; bur. Aug 18, 1798; age - 40 yrs.; nat. of Ireland
DUGAN, James; died Jul 19, 1794; bur. Jul 20, 1794; labourer
DULANY, Eleanor; died Aug 19, 1798; bur. Aug 20, 1798; age - 17 mo.; dau. of ? & Bridget
DUMAS, John Gustave; died Feb 2, 1797; bur. Feb 3, 1797; age - 11 mo. 9 da.; son of John & Mary Magdalen Bertan of Cape St. Frances
DUMIRAIL, Joseph Gabriel DeMagallon; died May 25, 1794; bur. May 25, 1794; age - 67 yrs.; born Grenoble, Oct. 1727; inh. of Genaive Island, St Domingo; Knight of Royal Military Order, St Louis; Lt Col French Infantry
DUNLEVY, Andrew; died Sep 1, 1800; bur. Sep 2, 1800; age - 3 yrs.; son of Andrew & Abigale
DUNLEVY, Andrew; died Sep 10, 1800; bur. Sep 10, 1800; nat. of Ireland

BURIALS

DUNN, Edward; died Oct 7, 1800; bur. Oct 7, 1800; age - 9 mo.; son of Daniel & Elizabeth
DUPOIS, Elizabeth; died Aug 4, 1798; bur. Aug 5, 1798; age - 1 yr. 8 mo.; dau. of Christian & Mary
DUPUY, Maurice; died Apr 28, 1798; bur. Apr 28, 1798; age - 3 mo.; son of David & Ann
DURANTAU, (?); bur. Nov 10, 1793; son of Mr. Durantau; inh. of San Domingo
DUWELZ, Julie Joseph; died Nov 10, 1793; bur. Nov 11, 1793; age - 14 mo. 3 da.; dau. of Louis Marie Joseph & Marie Angelique Joseph Louis Lichoux
DUZOBERIL, John Mary; died Jul 22, 1799; bur. Jul 22, 1799; age - 35 yrs.; nat. of Ploermel, France, diocese St Malo; former Lt in Royal Navy of France
DWYER, Ann; died Jul 31, 1795; bur. Aug 1, 1795; age - 48 yrs.; nat. of Ireland; wf. of William
DWYER, Charles; died Sep 11, 1796; bur. Sep 12, 1796; age - 11 mo.; son of John & Margaret
DWYER, Elizabeth; died Sep 4, 1800; bur. Sep 5, 1800; age - 40 yrs.; wf. of William
DWYER, John; died Sep 29, 1797; bur. Sep 30, 1797; nat. of Ireland
DWYER, John; died Sep 7, 1800; bur. Sep 7, 1800; age - 8 yrs.; son of William & Elizabeth
DWYER, Mary; died May 8, 1795; bur. May 9, 1795; age - 2 yrs.; dau. of Edward & Mary
DYER, Andrew; died Dec 30, 1795; bur. Dec 31, 1795; age - 40 yrs.; nat. of Tipperary, Ireland
EDWARD, Bridget; died Oct 8, 1800; bur. Oct 8, 1800; age - 13 yrs.; dau. of James & Mary, both deceased
EDWARD, James; died Oct 2, 1800; bur. Oct 2, 1800; age - 40 yrs.
EDWARD, Mary; died Oct 6, 1800; bur. Oct 7, 1800; age - 40 yrs.; widow of James
EDWARD, Thomas; died Oct 17, 1800; bur. Oct 18, 1800; age - 9 yrs.; son of James & Mary, both deceased
EGAN, Matthew; died Nov 14, 1796; bur. Nov 15, 1796; age - 23 yrs.; nat. of Ireland
EISEL, Philip; died Oct 21, 1799; bur. Oct 22, 1799; age - 7 yrs.; son of John & Mary
ELDER, William; died Aug 22, 1799; bur. Aug 23, 1799; age - 21 yrs.; son of Thomas & Elizabeth
ELWORD, Thomas; died Oct 2, 1799; bur. Oct 3, 1799; nat. of Ireland
ENNIS, Mary; died Jul 12, 1794; bur. Jul 13, 1794; age - 3 yrs. 8 mo. 10 da.
ENWRIGHT, Margaret; died Aug 28, 1799; bur. Aug 29, 1799; age - 29 yrs.; wf. of Thomas
ERSKINE, John; died Jul 2, 1799; bur. Jul 2, 1799; age - 16 yrs.; son of Archibald & Ruth
ERSKINE, Robert; died Jun 11, 1799; bur. Jun 12, 1799; age - 1 da.; son of Edward & Sidney
ESLING, George; died Feb 20, 1800; bur. Feb 21, 1800; age - 6 mo.; son of Paul & Catherine
ESLING, Paul; died Oct 8, 1800; bur. Oct 9, 1800; age - 49 yrs.

BURIALS

ETIENNE, Frederic; died May 11, 1795; bur. May 11, 1795; age - 22 yrs.; son of Frederic, planter, Jeremie & of Bouche; nat. of Jeremie, St. Domingo; merchant at Nantes, France
EVERETT, Margaret; died Oct 21, 1793; bur. Oct 22, 1793; age - 10 da.; dau. of John & Eleanor
EYRY, John; died Oct 14, 1797; bur. Oct 14, 1797
FAIRCHELEN, Lewis; died Sep 21, 1800; bur. Sep 22, 1800; age - 35 yrs.; nat. of Dunfair in Anjou
FALLAN, Charles; died Sep 18, 1800; bur. Sep 19, 1800; age - 30 yrs.; nat. of Ireland
FARLING, Edward; died Sep 12, 1797; bur. Sep 13, 1797
FARRELL, George; died Oct 12, 1797; bur. Oct 13, 1797; age - 40 yrs.; nat. of Ireland
FARRELL, Jane; died Jul 19, 1796; bur. Jul 20, 1796; age - 3 mo. 10 da.; dau. of George & Mary
FARRELL, William; died Feb 26, 1795; bur. Feb 27, 1795; age - 8 mo. 3 wks.; son of George & Mary
FAUCHER, John Charles; died Jul 20, 1797; bur. Jul 21, 1797; age - 11 mo.; son of John, late of Cape Francis & Mary Dupont
FAULKNER, John; died Aug 8, 1800; bur. Aug 8, 1800; age - 9 mo.
FENNEL, Mary Ann; died Sep 12, 1797; bur. Sep 13, 1797; nat. of Ireland; wf. of Edward, a tailor
FENNELL, Sarah; died Sep 12, 1800; bur. Sep 12, 1800; wf. of John
FERRY, Elizabeth Emelie Peyne; died Apr 2, 1798; bur. Apr 6, 1798; age - 2 mo.; dau. of Francis Rene & Frances Elizabeth Montpellier
FINERTY, James; died Feb 27, 1799; bur. Feb 28, 1799; age - 36 yrs.; accidentally drowned
FINIGAN, John; died Dec 18, 1797; bur. Dec 18, 1797; age - 45 yrs.
FISHER, Elizabeth; died May 17, 1795; bur. May 18, 1795; age - 7 yrs. 8 mo.; dau. of Joseph & Magdalen
FISHER, John Baptist Oliver; died Oct 24, 1800; bur. Oct 24, 1800; age - 4 yrs.; son of James & Ann
FISHER, William; died Jun 13, 1800; bur. Jun 14, 1800; age - 8 mo.; son of James & Ann
FITZ-JEFFRAY, Elizabeth; died Jul 27, 1794; bur. Jul 28, 1794
FITZGERALD, Ann; died Aug 18, 1798; bur. Aug 19, 1798; age - 18 mo.; dau. of John & Mary
FITZGERALD, Mary; died Apr 10, 1798; bur. Apr 10, 1798; dau. of Garret & Margaret
FITZGERALD, Robert; died Jul 28, 1800; bur. Jul 29, 1800
FITZPATRICK, Susanna; died Oct 5, 1794; bur. Oct 5, 1794; age - 7 yrs.
FLAHARTY, Mary; died Apr 24, 1798; bur. Apr 25, 1798; age - 46 yrs.; wf. of James
FLAHERTY, Thomas; died Dec 14, 1800; bur. Dec 15, 1800; age - 32 yrs.; nat. of Ireland; accidentally drowned
FLATTERY, Alice; died Nov 21, 1795; bur. Nov 23, 1795; age - 61 yrs.; Widow of John; buried in family burying grounds of late John Ireland, near Charles Carroll's manor in Anne Arundel Co.
FLATTERY, Jane; died Dec 28, 1795; bur. Dec 29, 1795; age - 26 yrs.; dau. of late John & Alice

BURIALS

FLEMING, Larsfield; died May 2, 1798; bur. May 3, 1798; age - 19 da.; son of James & Sarah
FLEMING, Michael; died Dec 8, 1797; bur. Dec 9, 1797; age - 32 yrs.
FLETCHER, Elizabeth; died Jun 27, 1798; bur. Jun 28, 1798; age - 86 yrs.; widow
FLEURY, Mary Magdalen; died Oct 6, 1800; bur. Oct 6, 1800; age - 35 yrs.; widow of Sebastian
FLEURY, Sebastian; died Oct 23, 1796; bur. Oct 24, 1796; age - 34 yrs.
FLINN, John; died Aug 5, 1794; bur. Aug 6, 1794; nat. of Ireland
FLOYD, William John; died Sep 8, 1797; bur. Sep 8, 1797; age - 29 yrs.; nat. of England; Rev., assistant priest St Peter, Baltimore
FLYN, James; died Jan 13, 1797; bur. Jan 14, 1797; nat. of Ireland
FLYNN, John; died May 22, 1799; bur. May 23, 1799
FOLEY, Jeremiah; died Sep 23, 1799; bur. Sep 24, 1799; age - 28 yrs.; nat. of Ireland
FOOS, Catharine; died Dec 18, 1799; bur. Dec 20, 1799; age - 60 yrs.; wf. of William
FORTUNE, James; died Nov 5, 1797; bur. Nov 5, 1797; age - 57 yrs.; nat. of Ireland; Captain
FOSBENDER, John; died Aug 2, 1800; bur. Aug 3, 1800; age - 1 yr. 2 mo. 14 da.; son of Peter & Heldwigis
(FOUQNEAU), George; died Oct 13, 1800; bur. Oct 14, 1800; age - a few months; a mulatto child belonging to Mde Fouqneau
FOX, Samuel Washington; died Jul 18, 1796; bur. Jul 19, 1796; age - 16 mo.; son of Anthony & Sarah
FOX, Sarah; died Sep 14, 1800; bur. Sep 15, 1800; wf. of Anthony
FREEMAN, Thomas; died Nov 8, 1796; bur. Nov 8, 1796; age -2 yrs. 4 mo.; son of Nicholas & Catherine
FREEMAN, Thomas; died Oct 7, 1800; bur. Oct 7, 1800; age - 1 yr.; son of Thomas William & Catharine
FREEMAN, William; died Jan 12, 1797; bur. Jan 13, 1797; age - 11 mo.; son of Nicholas & Catherine
FRIDAY, Charles; died Apr 2, 1800; bur. Apr 3, 1800; age - 2 mo.; son of John & Elizabeth
FRIDAY, Jacob; died Mar 18, 1797; bur. Mar 19, 1797; age - 2 mo. 15 da.; son of John & Elizabeth
FROGGET, Rose; died Sep 24, 1797; bur. Sep 24, 1797
FROST, George; died Nov 15, 1794; bur. Nov 16, 1794
FUDGE, Mary; died Sep 20, 1800; bur. Sep 20, 1800; age - 51 yrs.; widow of John
FULLERTON, James; died Mar 23, 1800; bur. Mar 24, 1800; age - 1 yr.
GANBERT, Francois Honore; died Aug 3, 1793; bur. Aug 4, 1793; nat. of Castres Albigeois
GARTY, William; died Aug 21, 1797; bur. Aug 22, 1797; age - 14 mo.; son of Peter & Eleanor
GARVEN, Ann; died Oct 5, 1800; bur. Oct 6, 1800; wf. of Matthew
GARVEN, Susanna; died Sep 16, 1799; bur. Sep 17, 1799; age - 7 mo.; dau. of Matthew & Ann
GATCHER, Louis; died Sep 17, 1793; bur. Sep 18, 1793; merchant of St. Domingo; died near Baltimore

BURIALS

GAUTIER, Charles; died Oct 18, 1800; bur. Oct 19, 1800; age - 2 yrs.; son of -- & Mary
GAUTIER, Luce; died Apr 20, 1798; bur. Apr 20, 1798; age - 50 yrs.; nat. of St Domingo; widow LaTask
GHERIZZA, Lucas DiNichola; died Sep 8, 1797; bur. Sep 8, 1797; age - 36 yrs.; nat. of Ragusa
GIBSON, Frederic; died Dec 20, 1799; bur. Dec 21, 1799; age - 48 yrs.
GINNISAN, Patrick; died Jun 27, 1795; bur. Jun 28, 1795; age - 50 yrs.
GLEESON, John; died Aug 29, 1800; bur. Aug 29, 1800; age - 10 yrs.; son of Maurice & Mary; small pox
GLEESON, Mary Ann; died Aug 5, 1795; bur. Aug 6, 1795; age - 5 mo.; dau. of James & Catherine
GLEESON, Roger; died Nov 6, 1798; bur. Nov 7, 1798
GLEESON, William; died Oct 12, 1800; bur. Oct 12, 1800; age - 3 yrs.; son of Roger & Catherine
GLIN, Thomas; died Jul 9, 1795; bur. Jul 10, 1795; age - 35 yrs.; nat. of Ireland
GOCHY, Joseph; died Nov 20, 1796; bur. Nov 21, 1796; age - 1 yr. 14 da.; son of Charles & Mary
GODIN, Charles Francis; died Sep 30, 1794; bur. Sep 30, 1794; age - 23 yrs.; nat. of parish of St. Mary, Port-au-Prince, St Domingo
GOLD, Lewis; died Jul 31, 1796; bur. Aug 1, 1796; age - 2 yrs. 7 mo.; son of Paul & Sarah
GONJON, John Baptist; died Jan 12, 1794; bur. Jan 13, 1794; age - 48 yrs.; nat. of Toulouse; Captain of ship LaPurcelle de Bordeaux
GOODWIN, Jane; died Sep 24, 1800; bur. Sep 24, 1800; age - 16 yrs.; wf. of James
GORE, Letitia; died Apr 21, 1794; bur. Apr 22, 1794; age - 56 yrs.; wf. of Richard Gore of Fells Point; last name could be Yore
GOREL, None; died Jan 16, 1794; bur. Jan 16, 1794; age - 24 yrs.; nat. of Mal Etriot in Britany, Diocese of Vannes
GORMBY, James; died Jun 18, 1798; bur. Jun 18, 1798; nat. of Ireland
GORMBY, Sarah; died Feb 11, 1800; bur. Feb 12, 1800; nat. of Ireland; wf. of Owen; advanced age
GORMLY, Owen; died Aug 3, 1800; bur. Aug 4, 1800; age - 94 yrs.; nat. of Ireland
GOSLING, Emilia; died Jan 6, 1798; bur. Jan 7, 1798; age - 1 yr.; dau. of John & Susanna
GOUFFRAN, John Baptist; died Aug 10, 1798; bur. Aug 11, 1798; age - 41 yrs.; nat. of Nantz, France
GOUIRAN, Ann Eleanor; died Nov 29, 1796; bur. Nov 30, 1796; age - 2 mo. 14 da.; dau. of Isadore & Margaret Pierrette Chaillan
GOUIRAN, Henrietta; died Oct 24, 1799; bur. Oct 25, 1799; age - 2 yrs.; dau. of Isidore & Margaret Pierrette Cheylan
GOUIRAN, Virginia Sophie Fanny; died Sep 1, 1795; bur. Sep 1, 1795; age - 11 mo. 8 da.; dau. of Isidere & Margaret Pierrette Chaillan
GOULDING, John; died Sep 28, 1796; bur. Sep 29, 1796; age - 9 da.; son of John & Martha

BURIALS

GRACE, Oliver; died Nov 10, 1794; bur. Nov 11, 1794; late of Annamessic on the Eastern Shore
GRADY, Catherine; died Jul 30, 1794; bur. Jul 31, 1794; age - 30 yrs.; nat. of Co. Kerry, Ireland
GRATE, Nicholas; died Aug 8, 1796; bur. Aug 9, 1796; age - 16 mo.; son of Nicholas & Hannah
GREEN, Benedict; died Nov 26, 1800; bur. Nov 27, 1800; age - 30 yrs.
GREEN, Catharine; died Sep 21, 1800; bur. Sep 21, 1800; age - 50 yrs.; wf. of Bennet
GREEN, Charles; died Sep 6, 1800; bur. Sep 7, 1800; age - 19 yrs.; son of Edward & Mary
GREEN, Eleanor; died Nov 8, 1796; bur. Nov 9, 1796; age - 6 yrs. 4 mo. 4 da.; dau. of Edward & Mary
GREEN, Susanna; died Jul 10, 1794; bur. Jul 11, 1794; age - 42 yrs.; wf. of Thomas
GREGOR, Harriot; died Oct 19, 1797; bur. Oct 20, 1797; age - 3 mo.; dau. of William & Ann
GRELLAND, Mary Frances; died Aug 6, 1797; bur. Aug 6, 1797; age - 1 yr. 6 mo.; dau. of Henry & Antoinette Dollun
GRIFFIN, Catherine; died Mar 4, 1798; bur. Mar 5, 1798; age - 6 mo.; dau. of Mary Griffin
GRIFFIN, Margaret; died Feb 16, 1795; bur. Feb 17, 1795; age - 9 mo.; dau. of Abraham & Mary
GRIFFIN, Thomas; died Jul 12, 1799; bur. Jul 13, 1799; age - 11 mo.; son of Abraham & Mary
GUERDINE, Mary Rose; died Jun 24, 1795; bur. Jun 25, 1795; age - 1 yr.; dau. of Peter & Victoria Baupuy
GUILLANCHAUX, Lewis; died Oct 17, 1797; bur. Oct 17, 1797; age - 35 yrs.; son of Lewis & Mary Roussaux; nat. of Nantes, France
GUILLON, Frances Catherine; died Sep 13, 1793; bur. Sep 13, 1793; born LaRochelle; widow - Brisson; parish Son of Sauveur, died near Balto
GUTTERAN, Ann Bourke; died Mar 9, 1794; bur. Mar 11, 1794; age - 49 yrs.; nat. of Nova Scotia; widow of John
GUYNEMER, Mary Louise; died Sep 1, 1794; bur. Sep 2, 1794; age - 17 mo.; dau. of John Augustine & Mary Foley
GUYTON, Antoinette Gigon; died Feb 20, 1796; bur. Feb 21, 1796; age - 35 yrs.; from St. Domingo
HAGERTY, James; died Apr 3, 1797; bur. Apr 4, 1797; nat. of Ireland
HAGERTY, Luke; died Jun 22, 1798; bur. Jun 23, 1798; age - 2 yrs.; son of Michael & Eleanor
HAGERTY, Matthew; died Aug 22, 1799; bur. Aug 23, 1799; age - 15 mo.; son of Matthew & Ann
HAGERTY, Michael; died Nov 16, 1799; bur. Nov 17, 1799; age - 1 mo.; son of Michael & Eleanor
HAGTHROP, Eleanor; died Sep 10, 1794; bur. Sep 10, 1794; age - 5 yrs.
HAGTHROP, Eleanor; died Jan 30, 1799; bur. Jan 31, 1799; age - 33 yrs.; wf. of Edward
HAILY, Robert; died Jul 1, 1794; bur. Jul 2, 1794; age - 45 yrs.
HALFPENNY, Catherine; died Jan 31, 1798; bur. Feb 1, 1798; age - 45 yrs.; nat. of Ireland; wf. of Patrick

BURIALS

HALL, John; died Apr 12, 1799; bur. Apr 13, 1799; age - 2 da.; son of John & Susanna
(HALL), John; died Jul 23, 1800; bur. Jul 24, 1800; age - 3 yrs.; slave of McCaleb Hall
HALL, Susanna; died Apr 12, 1799; bur. Apr 13, 1799; age - 20 yrs.; wf. of John
HANDOIN, Mary Agathe; died Dec 2, 1793; bur. Dec 3, 1793; surgeon on board the Calypso of Havre
HANNAN, Elizabeth; died Apr 30, 1800; bur. May 1, 1800; age - 66 yrs.; widow
HANNAN, John Hodgkin; died Jul 11, 1796; bur. Jul 12, 1796; age 7 mo. 11 da.; son of John & Margaret
HANNAN, Margaret; died Aug 21, 1797; bur. Aug 22, 1797; age - 24 yrs.; wf. of James
HANNAN, William; died Mar 28, 1798; bur. Mar 29, 1798; age - 11 mo.; son of John & Margaret
HARDICK, Peter; died Nov 1, 1800; bur. Nov 3, 1800; age - 2 yrs. 6 mo.; son of Emericus
HARE, Samuel; died Jul 23, 1797; bur. Jul 23, 1797; age - 10 mo.; son of Patience
HARENT, Mary Magdalene; died May 11, 1794; bur. May 12, 1794; age - 35 yrs.; mulatto from St Domingo
HARKINS, Elizabeth; died Jul 28, 1800; bur. Jul 29, 1800; age - 7 mo.; dau. of Hugh & Barbara
HARMAN, Elizabeth; died Oct 21, 1800; bur. Oct 21, 1800; age - 31 yrs.; wf. of Philip
HARMAN, Mary; died Oct 18, 1797; bur. Oct 18, 1797; age - 90 yrs.; nat. of Ireland
HARMAN, Mary Ann; died Oct 22, 1800; bur. Oct 22, 1800; age - 1 yr. 1 mo. 8 da.; dau. of Philip & Elizabeth (deceased)
HARRIEN, Joseph; died Dec 16, 1795; bur. Dec 17, 1795; age - 5 da.; son of Joseph & Margaret
HARRIETTE, Mary Frances; died Dec 22, 1793; bur. Dec 23, 1793; age - 6 yrs.; born St. Domingo; dau. of John Baptist & Victoire Gerard
HARRIS, William; died Sep 24, 1797; bur. Sep 24, 1797
HARRISON, Ann; died Sep 23, 1797; bur. Sep 24, 1797; age - 85 yrs.; nat. of London
HARRISON, Eleanor; died Sep 18, 1800; bur. Sep 19, 1800; age - 3 yrs.; dau. of Joseph & Eleanor
HARRISON, Joseph; died Oct 28, 1800; bur. Oct 28, 1800; age - 10 da.; son of John & Elizabeth
HARTNELL, John; died Sep 12, 1797; bur. Sep 13, 1797; nat. of Ireland
HARTNETT, Ann; died Feb 27, 1796; bur. Feb 28, 1796; wf. of James
HARWOOD, Rachel; died Dec 8, 1798; bur. Dec 9, 1798; age - 36 yrs.; widow
HASHAM, Lucy; died Dec 25, 1799; bur. Dec 26, 1799; age - 38 yrs.; wf. of Josiah
HASHAM, Susanna; died Sep 21, 1800; bur. Sep 22, 1800; age - 3 yrs.; dau. of Josiah & Lucy
HASSEFRATZ, Catherine; died Aug 27, 1797; bur. Aug 28, 1797; age - 1 mo.; dau. of George & Dorothy
HATCH, George; died Aug 5, 1796; bur. Aug 6, 1796; age - 1 yr. 5 da.; son of John & Margaret

BURIALS

HATCH, John; died Aug 21, 1797; bur. Aug 22, 1797; age - 7 mo.; son of John & Margaret
HAYES, Alexander; died Nov 21, 1799; bur. Nov 22, 1799; age - 2 yrs.; son of Alexander & Elizabeth
HEALY, Henry; died Dec 22, 1794; bur. Dec 23, 1794; age - 13 mo.; son of Dennis & Mary
HEINLEN, Catherine Elizabeth; died Sep 1, 1793; bur. Sep 2, 1793; age - 4 mo.; dau. of Anne Mary
HENNINGER, David; died Jan 16, 1796; bur. Jan 17, 1796; age - 4 mo.; dau. of (sic.) John & Elizabeth
HENRY, Ann; died Apr 10, 1799; bur. Apr 11, 1799; dau. of late Daniel & his wife Elizabeth
HENRY, Hugh; died Mar 17, 1800; bur. Mar 18, 1800; age - 5 yrs.; son of Susanna & late Hugh
(HENRY), Matthew; died Feb 19, 1800; bur. Feb 20, 1800; age - 17 mo.; negro slave of Mrs Elizabeth Henry, widow
HENRY, William; died Jul 22, 1800; bur. Jul 23, 1800
HERMELIN, Margaret; died Oct 4, 1794; bur. Oct 5, 1794; age - 7 da.; dau. of Joseph & Abigail
HERRON, Elizabeth; died Jan 27, 1798; bur. Jan 28, 1798; nat. of Ireland; advanced age
HEUISLER, Philippina; died Oct 14, 1800; bur. Oct 14, 1800; age - 54 yrs.; nat. of Germany; wf. of Anthony
HICKLEY, John; died Jul 14, 1798; bur. Jul 15, 1798; age - 1 yr.; son of Sebastian & Catherine
HILFERTY, Hugh; died Sep 13, 1800; bur. Sep 13, 1800; nat. of Ireland; hsb. of Mary
HOCK, Mary; died Sep 4, 1798; bur. Sep 5, 1798; age - 1 yr. 6 mo.; dau. of Ferdinand & Magdalen
HOGAN, Dennis; died Aug 17, 1796; bur. Aug 18, 1796; age - 3 yrs.; son of Patrick & Mary
HOGAN, Edward; died Mar 12, 1794; bur. Mar 13, 1794; age - 32 yrs.; nat. of Co. Tipperary, Ireland
HOGAN, Matthew; died Feb 25, 1797; bur. Feb 26, 1797; age - 7 yrs.; son of Patrick & Mary
HOGAN, Thomas; died Aug 11, 1796; bur. Aug 11, 1796; age - 9 mo. 8 da.; son of Patrick & Mary
HOGGINS, Eleanor; died Sep 25, 1800; bur. Sep 25, 1800; age - 3 yrs.; dau. of Richard & Elizabeth
HOGGINS, Sarah; died Jul 25, 1799; bur. Jul 25, 1799; age - 3 mo.; dau. of Richard & Elizabeth
HOGGINS, William; died May 18, 1796; bur. May 19, 1796; son of Richard & Elizabeth
HOLLAND, Ann; died Jun 8, 1799; bur. Jun 8, 1799; age - 1 yr.; dau. of Thomas & Margaret
(HOLMES), Eleanor; died Aug 4, 1798; bur. Aug 5, 1798; age - 9 yrs.; dau. of Sam & Nellie, negro slaves of Mr John Holmes
HOLMES, James; died May 30, 1797; bur. May 31, 1797; age - 29 yrs.; of Baltimore
HOLMES, John; died Jul 26, 1794; bur. Jul 27, 1794; son of William & Catherine
HOLMES, John; died Jun 17, 1799; bur. Jun 18, 1799; age - 29 yrs.
HOLMES, Joseph; died Jul 25, 1794; bur. Jul 26, 1794; age - 7 mo.; son of James & Magdalen

BURIALS

HOLMES, Samuel; died Feb 4, 1797; bur. Feb 5, 1797; age - 10 mo.
 1 da.; son of James & Magdalen
HOOK, Anthony; died Jun 7, 1798; bur. Jun 8, 1798; age - 71 yrs.;
 hsb. of Mary
HOOK, Anthony; died Aug 21, 1800; bur. Aug 22, 1800; age - 17
 yrs.; son of Anthony & Mary (both deceased)
HOOK, Barbara; died Aug 8, 1796; bur. Aug 9, 1796; age - 1 yr. 6
 mo. 14 da.; dau. of Ferdinand & Magdalen
HOOK, Bennet; died Sep 9, 1800; bur. Sep 10, 1800; age - 3 yrs.;
 son of John & Barbara
HOOK, George; died Jul 24, 1799; bur. Jul 24, 1799; age - 4 wks.;
 son of Ferdinand & Magdalen
HOOK, George; died Sep 29, 1800; bur. Sep 29, 1800; age - 20
 yrs.; son of Anthony (deceased) & Mary
HOOK, John; died Aug 25, 1800; bur. Aug 25, 1800; hsb. of Barbara
HOOK, John; died Aug 26, 1800; bur. Aug 26, 1800; age - 5 yrs.;
 son of John (deceased Aug 25, 1800) & Barbara
HORN, Joseph; died Nov 14, 1796; bur. Nov 15, 1796; age - 12 da.;
 son of Joseph & Catherine
HORNE, Henry; died Jul 21, 1799; bur. Jul 22, 1799; age - 2 yrs.;
 son of John & Jane
HOVER, Ignatius; died Aug 8, 1798; bur. Aug 9, 1798; age - 8 mo.;
 son of Ignatius & Rebecca
HOWARD, Susanna; died Apr 25, 1800; bur. Apr 27, 1800; age - 5
 1/2 mo.; dau. of William & Mary
HOYL, Dominic; died Oct 27, 1793; bur. Oct 28, 1793; age - 22
 yrs.; nat. of Ireland
HOYT, Elizabeth; died Aug 2, 1800; bur. Aug 3, 1800; age - 4 da.;
 dau. of -- & Elizabeth
HUBON, Oliver; died Nov 26, 1796; bur. Nov 27, 1796; age - 63
 yrs. 6 mo. 10 da.; nat. of Ft. Royal Martinico
HUGHES, James; died Oct 11, 1795; bur. Oct 12, 1795
HUMPHRIES, Elizabeth; died Jul 19, 1796; bur. Jul 20, 1796; age -
 1 yr. 4 mo. 5 da.; dau. of James & Sarah
HUTCHISON, Frances; died Nov 14, 1796; bur. Nov 15, 1796; age -
 44 yrs. 9 mo.
JACQUINOT, Jacques Antoine; died Aug 26, 1795; bur. Aug 26, 1795;
 age - 28 yrs.; nat. of Chardville; inh. of St. Dominque
JADOUIN, Peter; died Jul 26, 1796; bur. Jul 27, 1796; age - 30
 yrs.; nat. of Bordeaux
JALABERT, Anthony Francis; died Sep 26, 1794; bur. Sep 27, 1794;
 born parish of St. Francis, Nantes in Britany
JENKINS, Ann; died Aug 9, 1799; bur. Aug 10, 1799; age - 26 yrs.;
 wf. of William
(JOHNSON), Andrew; died Jul 25, 1800; bur. Jul 26, 1800; age - 1
 yr.; slave of Mr Johnson
JOHNSON, James; died Apr 25, 1800; bur. Apr 26, 1800; age - 3
 mo.; son of Elizabeth
JOHNSON, Joseph; died Jun 21, 1798; bur. Jun 21, 1798; age - 18
 yrs.; free negro
(JOHNSON), Maria; died Oct 26, 1800; bur. Oct 27, 1800; age - 2
 yrs.; slave of Mr Johnson
JOHNSON, Mary; died Nov 1, 1795; bur. Nov 2, 1795; age - 15 mo.;
 dau. of John & Ann

BURIALS

JOHNSON, Sarah; died Oct 21, 1795; bur. Oct 22, 1795; age - 11 mo.; dau. of Joshua & Sarah

JOHNSON, Thomas; died Oct 7, 1795; bur. Oct 8, 1795; age - 2 yrs.; son of Thomas & Mary

JONES, Anastasia; died May 14, 1799; bur. May 15, 1799; age - 12 yrs.; dau. of Aubrey & Sarah

JONES, Charles; died Jul 22, 1796; bur. Jul 22, 1796; age - 1 yr. 9 mo.; son of William & Eleanor

JONES, Elizabeth; died Nov 2, 1794; bur. Nov 3, 1794; age - 8 yrs. 8 mo.; dau. of Aubreay & Sarah

(JONES), Elizabeth; died Mar 20, 1800; bur. Mar 21, 1800; age - 15 yrs.; slave of Mr Aubrey Jones

JONES, Mary; died Sep 10, 1800; bur. Sep 10, 1800; age - 7 yrs.; dau. of Aubrey & Sarah

JONES, Sarah; died Sep 13, 1800; bur. Sep 14, 1800; age - 38 yrs.; wf. of Aubrey

JOURDAN, Joseph; died Oct 29, 1793; bur. Oct 30, 1793; age - 37 yrs.; nat. of Mazorques, Marseilles; inh. of Cape Francis, St Domingo

JOYCE, John; died Mar 15, 1800; bur. Mar 16, 1800; age - 6 mo.

KEAN, Alexander; died Oct 1, 1794; bur. Oct 1, 1794; age - 4 yrs.; son of Hugh & Rose; small pox

KEARNS, Charles; died Apr 17, 1797; bur. Apr 18, 1797; age - 2 yrs.; son of Charles & Hannah

KEARNS, Henry; died Apr 12, 1794; bur. Apr 13, 1794; age - 7 mo.; son of Charles & Hannah

KEEFE, Mary; died Sep 4, 1798; bur. Sep 5, 1798; age - 14 mo.; dau. of Patrick & Mary

KELLER, Vendel; died Sep 13, 1794; bur. Sep 13, 1794

KELLY, Catharine; died Oct 26, 1800; bur. Oct 27, 1800; age - 3 yrs.; dau. of Patrick & Eleanor

KELLY, Catherine; died Oct 2, 1793; bur. Oct 3, 1793

KELLY, Eleanor; died Jan 29, 1798; bur. Jan 30, 1798; age - 4 yrs.; dau. of John & Ann

(KELLY), Harriot; died Jul 8, 1798; bur. Jul 9, 1798; age - 5 yrs.; dau. of Clare, negro slave of Mr Kelly

KELLY, James; died May 5, 1799; bur. May 6, 1799; age - 2 mo.; son of James & Sarah

KELLY, John; died Feb 11, 1795; bur. Feb 12, 1795; age - 17 mo.; born Ireland; son of Andrew & Alice

KELLY, John; died Aug 12, 1800; bur. Aug 13, 1800; age - 4 yrs.; son of Patrick & Eleanor

KELLY, Patrick; died Jun 13, 1794; bur. Jun 15, 1794; age - 37 yrs.; nat. of Ireland

KELLY, Rosa; died Oct 15, 1796; bur. Oct 16, 1796; age - 50 yrs.; nat. of Ireland

KELLY, Rosanna; died Feb 17, 1800; bur. Feb 18, 1800; age - 3 mo.; dau. of Patric & Jane

KELLY, William; died Jul 26, 1796; bur. Jul 27, 1796; age - 5 mo. 17 da.; son of Andrew & Phoebe

KING, David; died Oct 19, 1799; bur. Oct 20, 1799; age - 52 yrs.; nat. of Ireland

KING, Elizabeth; died Sep 22, 1800; bur. Sep 23, 1800; age - 23 yrs.

BURIALS

KING, Richard; died Jun 23, 1799; bur. Jun 24, 1799; age - 12 da.; son of David & Honor
KIRK, George; died Oct 3, 1796; bur. Oct 3, 1796; age - 4 da.; son of Felix & Susanna
KIRWAN, Marie; died Jul 15, 1796; bur. Jul 16, 1796; age - 9 yrs. 7 mo. 9 da.; dau. of John & Mary
KNIGHT, James; died Feb 28, 1797; bur. Mar 1, 1797; age - 16 mo.; son of Benjamin & Margaret
KNOTT, James; died May 10, 1796; bur. May 11, 1796; age - 33 yrs.
KOFFER, John; died Oct 9, 1800; bur. Oct 9, 1800; age - 73 yrs.; nat. of Germany
KOFFER, Mary; died Oct 13, 1800; bur. Oct 13, 1800; age - 60 yrs.; widow of John
LABROUCHE, John Baptist; died Dec 13, 1793; bur. Dec 14, 1793; age - 47 yrs.; son of Bernard Timothy & Mary Magdalene Dessens; nat. of Dax in Gascony; hsb. of Mary Magdalene Berquier
LACLERQUE, John; died Jun 27, 1793; bur. Jun 28, 1793; nat. of Province of Bearn
LACOMBE, Jean Joseph; died Oct 6, 1793; bur. Oct 7, 1793; nat. of Cossade, Diocese of Cahors, France; previously inh. of St Domingo
LACOSTE, Bernard; died Jul 28, 1793; bur. Jul 29, 1793; nat. of parish of St. Valie at Bordeaux
LAFARGE, Marie Elizabeth Ariol; died Feb 11, 1793; bur. Feb 12, 1793; inh. of North Province, San Domingo; wf. of Joseph Louis; Advocate in Parliament
LAFITEAUX, Anthony; died Sep 27, 1796; bur. Sep 27, 1796; age - 3 yrs.; son of J.B. & Mary Catherine Duplan, planter, Grande Riviere, St. Domingo
LAFITEAUX, John; died Oct 19, 1793; bur. Oct 20, 1793; nat. of Bordeaux; inh. of LaGrande Riviere, St Domingo
LAGRAVE, Pierre; died Aug 24, 1793; bur. Aug 25, 1793; age - 51 yrs.; born 6/3/1742; son of Peter & Elizabeth DeMirolpour; baptized at St Catherine of Slusmion & Castelmaie, diocese of Oleran, Bearn at 2 PM
LAMBERT, Cheri; died Apr 23, 1796; bur. Apr 24, 1796; age - 18 mo.; son of Victoire
LAMBERT, Juliana; died Aug 17, 1794; bur. Aug 18, 1794; age - 4 mo.
LAMOTTE, Pierre; died Sep 27, 1793; born Baltimore, Sept 19, 1793; son of Jean & Genevieve Victoire Darnet; inh. of San Domingo
LANAGHAN, John; died Nov 13, 1793; bur. Nov 14, 1793; age - 2 yrs. 6 mo.; son of Charles & Sarah
LANDERS, Andrew; died Jul 30, 1796; bur. Jul 31, 1796; age - 5 mo.; son of Peter & Lydia
LANDERS, William; died Oct 20, 1796; bur. Oct 22, 1796; age - 35 yrs.; nat. of Ireland
LANDRY, Barbara; died Jun 14, 1799; bur. Jun 15, 1799; age - 49 yrs.
LANDSFIELD, John; died Aug 7, 1799; bur. Aug 7, 1799; age - 19 wks.; son of George & Mary
LANIGNE, Cassandra; died Jul 22, 1797; bur. Jul 23, 1797; age - 1 yr. 3 mo.; dau. of Aug & Cassandra Andrews

BURIALS

LAPOULE, Elizabeth; died Aug 17, 1798; bur. Aug 18, 1798; age - 1 yr.; dau. of Elizabeth; child of color
LASALLE, Henrietta Emilia; died Oct 3, 1796; bur. Oct 3, 1796; dau. of William, nat. of Orbaix in Bearn, France & Jane Mary Huve of Baquery in Bigorre
LASHFORD, Sarah; died Nov 19, 1797; bur. Nov 19, 1797; age - 7 mo.; dau. of Daniel & Catharine
LATAPY, Rosalie Flamand; died Jan 7, 1800; bur. Jan 8, 1800; age - 32 yrs.; wf. of Romain (called Brizard), planter of L'Artibone, jurisdiction of St Mark, St Domingo; called Rossignol
(LAURENT), Toussant; died Oct 28, 1793; age - 3 yrs.; negro slave of M. Sequin Laurent
LAVALE, Jean; died Oct 17, 1793; bur. Oct 17, 1793; age - 71 yrs.; nat. of Sempe pays de Labour; Lt. of vessel "L'Indien de Bordeaux"
LAVILLE, Peter; died May 25, 1797; bur. May 25, 1797; age - 89 yrs.; nat. of Bordeaux, parish of St Croix; lately from Cape Francis, St Domingo
LAWRENCE, Jacob; died Jul 23, 1799; bur. Jul 24, 1799; age - 20 mo.; son of Ferdinand & Elizabeth
LAWRENCE, Joseph; died Jan 25, 1797; bur. Jan 26, 1797; age - 53 yrs.; nat. of Germany
LAWRENCE, Margaret; died Mar 27, 1794; bur. Mar 29, 1794; age - 4 yrs.; dau. of Ferdinand & Elizabeth
LAWRENCE, Margaret; died Mar 30, 1796; bur. Apr 3, 1796; age - 24 yrs.; wf. of Wendel
LEARY, Daniel; died May 25, 1797; bur. May 26, 1797; age - 40 yrs.; accidentally drowned
LEBATARD, Marie Louise Josephine; died Feb 1, 1797; bur. Feb 2, 1797; age - 1 yr. 8 mo.; dau. of John Lewis & Jean Catherine Hubert
LEBLANC, Margaret; died Nov 21, 1799; bur. Nov 22, 1799; age - 71 yrs.; nat. of Nova Scotia
(LEBON), Francis; died Jul 13, 1796; bur. Jul 14, 1796; age - 1 yr. 2 mo.; French negro child; slave of Miss LeBon
LEBON, Mary Louisa; died Nov 29, 1795; bur. Nov 30, 1795; age - 50 yrs.; widow of Charles of St. Domingo
LECLERC, Margaret Perigault; died Sep 25, 1795; bur. Sep 25, 1795; age - 43 yrs.; wf. of Francis, planter of Plaisance, St Domingo
LECOQ, John; died Dec 8, 1794; bur. Dec 8, 1794; age - 17 mo.; son of John & Charlotte Chautrot
LECOQ, Mary; died Nov 26, 1794; bur. Nov 27, 1794; age - 4 yrs. 7 mo.; dau. of John & Charlotte Chautrot
LECOQ, Virginia; died Jul 10, 1798; bur. Jul 11, 1798; age - 3 mo.; dau. of John & Charlotte Chantrau
LEE, Michael; died Aug 15, 1799; bur. Aug 15, 1799; age - 54 yrs. 11 mo.; nat. of Ireland
LEE, Sarah; died Sep 7, 1794; bur. Sep 8, 1794; age - 2 yrs. 3 mo.; dau. of John & Sarah
LEE, Sarah; died Sep 12, 1794; bur. Sep 13, 1794; age - 43 yrs.
LEEKS, Rose; died Jan 30, 1795; bur. Jan 31, 1795; age - 39 yrs.
LEFEORE, Mary Francis; died Aug 14, 1796; bur. Aug 15, 1796; age - 1 yr. 8 mo.; dau. of Eugenie, free mulatto

BURIALS

LEGRAND, Caroline; died Aug 5, 1799; bur. Aug 6, 1799; age - 2 yrs.; dau. of Samuel & Eleanor
LEGROS, James; died Jan 16, 1794; bur. Jan 16, 1794; age - 6 mo.; son of Gabriel & Margaret Renandy
LEGUIN, Jacque Ferdinand; died Jun 8, 1795; bur. Jun 9, 1795; son of Jean & Jane Marie Afou; nat. of Cape St. Francis
LEHOUX, Anthony Lewis Charles Carroll; died Nov 26, 1793; bur. Nov 27, 1793; age - 5 wks. 2 da.; son of Louis Dennis, physician at Cape Francois & Agnes Sophia de Prunes
LELAND, Sarah; died Jun 30, 1800; bur. Jul 1, 1800; age - 10 mo.; dau. of Francis & Mary
LEMANGUEN, Mary Jane; died Aug 19, 1799; bur. Aug 19, 1799; age - 61 yrs.; born Croisie in the Bishoprick of Nantes; widow LeRoy
LENDER, Frances; died Aug 13, 1797; bur. Aug 14, 1797; age - 1 yr. 6 mo.; dau. of Elizabeth
LENEGHAN, Charles; died Oct 12, 1800; bur. Oct 13, 1800; age - 28 yrs.; nat. of Ireland
LENEGHAN, Frances; died Oct 4, 1800; bur. Oct 4, 1800; age - 4 mo.; dau. of Charles & Sarah (deceased)
LEONARD, Ann; died Sep 12, 1797; bur. Sep 12, 1797; age - 40 yrs.
LERET, Ann Louisa Beeston; died Oct 16, 1797; bur. Oct 16, 1797; age - 11 mo.; dau. of Peter & Rebecca
LEVACHER, Mary Joanna; died Oct 5, 1794; bur. Oct 6, 1794; age - 36 yrs.; wf. of Mr. Fage
LEWIS, Peter; died Aug 13, 1800; bur. Aug 14, 1800; age - 4 mo.; a negro
LEYDECKER, Catherine; died Jul 20, 1797; bur. Jul 21, 1797; age - 74 yrs.; wf. of Simon
LEYDECKER, Simon; died Feb 15, 1798; bur. Feb 16, 1798; age - 70 yrs.
LIAUTRAND, Sophie; died Aug 5, 1800; bur. Aug 6, 1800; age - 4 mo.; dau. of Claude & Jeanne Catherine Brule
LIHAULT, Peter Francis; died Sep 2, 1800; bur. Sep 2, 1800; age - 39 yrs.; nat. of Honfleur in Normandy
LINEGHAN, Rebecca; died Sep 22, 1800; bur. Sep 23, 1800; age - 3 yrs.; dau. of Charles & Sarah
LINEGHAN, Sarah; died Sep 27, 1800; bur. Sep 28, 1800; age - 29 yrs.; wf. of Charles
LINER, James; died Jan 1, 1800; bur. Jan 2, 1800; age - 9 yrs.; son of Peter & Barbara
LINER, Peter; died Jan 19, 1798; bur. Jan 20, 1798; age - 37 yrs.; nat. of Ireland
LISKY, Anastasia; died Oct 11, 1797; bur. Oct 11, 1797; age - 49 yrs.
LITZENGER, Peter; died Oct 23, 1793; bur. Oct 25, 1793; age - 61 yrs.; nat. of Germany
LITZINGER, Elizabeth; died Nov 26, 1793; bur. Nov 27, 1793; age - 9 mo.; dau. of William & Elizabeth
LITZINGER, Mary; died Sep 29, 1793; bur. Sep 30, 1793; age - 7 yrs.; appendill
(LIVERS), Mily; died Oct 25, 1797; bur. Oct 25, 1797; age - 1 yr.; dau. of Jemina; slave of Arnold Livers
LIVERS, Richard; died May 8, 1796; bur. May 9, 1796; age - 6 mo.; son of Arnold & Mary

BURIALS

LLOYD, Catharine; died Oct 11, 1798; bur. Oct 12, 1798; age - 35 yrs.; wf. of William
LLOYD, Elizabeth; died Nov 8, 1799; bur. Nov 9, 1799; age - 2 wks.; dau. of Richard & Ester
LLOYD, Sarah; died Jun 1, 1796; bur. Jun 2, 1796; age - 17 yrs.; dau. of Richard & Ester
LLOYD, William John; died Mar 10, 1800; bur. Mar 11, 1800; age - 3 mo.; son of William & Elizabeth
LOCKERMAN, Mary; died Mar 11, 1797; bur. Mar 12, 1797; age - 22 yrs.
LOGAN, Andrew; died Nov 16, 1799; bur. Nov 17, 1799; age - 2 yrs.; son of Cornelius & Mary
LOGAN, John; died Jul 16, 1797; bur. Jul 16, 1797; age - 3 wks. 3 da.; son of Cornelius & Mary
LOGSDON, Mary; died Oct 16, 1796; bur. Oct 17, 1796; age - 3 yrs.; born Oct 23, 1792; dau. of Job & Patience
LOMBARD, Thomasine; died Nov 27, 1794; bur. Nov 28, 1794; age - 11 mo.; dau. of Sylvester & Mary Magdalen Clauveau
LONG, Mary; died Nov 5, 1794; bur. Nov 6, 1794; age - 4 mo.; dau. of Thomas & Elizabeth
LOUCAS, James Joseph; died Jun 10, 1793; bur. Jun 11, 1793; born Apr 11, 1743, Marseilles, France
LUCAS, Francis; died Feb 18, 1794; bur. Feb 19, 1794; age - 5 da.; son of Francis & Elizabeth
LUNK, (?); died Nov 21, 1794; bur. Nov 22, 1794
LUPTHY, Catharine; died Sep 26, 1800; bur. Sep 27, 1800; age - 1 yr.; dau. of Henry & Anna
LUSKEROW, Angelica; died Sep 9, 1794; bur. Sep 9, 1794; age - 9 yrs.
LUSKEROW, Margaret; died Sep 11, 1794; bur. Sep 12, 1794; age - 14 yrs.
LUTZ, Valentine; died Jan 23, 1797; bur. Jan 24, 1797
LYNCH, Daniel; died Jul 29, 1799; bur. Jul 31, 1799; age - 23 yrs.; accidentally drowned
LYNCH, John; died Dec 4, 1796; bur. Dec 5, 1796; nat. of Ireland; Major in service of USA
LYNCH, John; died Oct 22, 1797; bur. Oct 22, 1797; nat. of Ireland
LYNCH, Martin; died Sep 14, 1800; bur. Sep 14, 1800; age - 58 yrs.; nat. of Ireland
LYNCH, Mary; died Sep 30, 1800; bur. Sep 30, 1800; age - 55 yrs.; nat. of Ireland; widow of Martin
LYNCH, Michael; died Nov 10, 1793; bur. Nov 10, 1793; age - 25 yrs.; nat. of Ireland
LYNCH, Patrick; died Aug 2, 1798; bur. Aug 4, 1798; age - 10 mo.; son of Edward & Mary
LYONS, John; died Aug 10, 1799; bur. Aug 11, 1799; age - 8 mo.; son of Bartholomew & Sarah
LYONS, Michael; died Sep 20, 1800; bur. Sep 21, 1800; age - 4 yrs.; son of John & Susanna
LYSTON, John; died Sep 12, 1794; bur. Sep 13, 1794
MACKIE, Francis; died Sep 12, 1799; bur. Sep 13, 1799; age - 14 mo.; son of Hugh & Sarah
MACKIE, Hugh; died Nov 3, 1799; bur. Nov 4, 1799

BURIALS

MACLAY, Hamilton; died Sep 1, 1799; bur. Sep 2, 1799; age - 35 yrs.
MACNAMARA, Ann; died Sep 29, 1794; bur. Sep 30, 1794; age - 35 yrs.; wf. of Matthew; could be McNamara
MACNAMARA, Eleanor; died Aug 27, 1794; bur. Aug 27, 1794; age - 6 wks.; dau. of Matthew & Anne
MACNAMARA, Margaret; died Aug 23, 1798; bur. Aug 24, 1798; age - 8 mo.; dau. of Thomas & Mary
MADDEN, Carolina; died Aug 22, 1799; bur. Aug 23, 1799; age - 11 mo.; dau. of Amelia, free mulatto
MAGAN, Thomas; died Jul 16, 1800; bur. Jul 17, 1800; age - 9 mo.; son of Matthew & Ann
MAGUIRE, Catharine; died Aug 19, 1800; bur. Aug 19, 1800; age - 1 yr.; dau. of Roger & Eleanor
MAGUIRE, John; died Jul 18, 1797; bur. Jul 19, 1797; age - 5 mo.; son of Roger & Eleanor
MAGUIRE, Roger; died Sep 28, 1800; bur. Sep 28, 1800
MALONEY, Margaret; died Aug 10, 1797; bur. Aug 11, 1797; age - 1 yr. 6 mo.; dau. of James & Eve
MALONEY, Thomas; died Mar 28, 1795; bur. Mar 29, 1795; age - 3 mo.; son of Margaret
MANVILLE, Thomas Duval; died Jun 4, 1797; bur. Jun 5, 1797; age - 30 yrs.
MARECHAL, Pierre; died Oct 4, 1793; nat. of Moirmontier, France; sailor; son of Michael & Susanne Contuis; died aboard vessel "Les Deux Amis of Nantes", fortified with the sacraments
MARIE, Joseph; died May 30, 1800; bur. May 30, 1800; age - 43 yrs.; born parish of St John, diocese of Marseilles; died near Balto
MARKS, Michael; died Feb 12, 1798; bur. Feb 13, 1798; age - 23 yrs.; nat. of Ireland
MARR, Mary Ann; died Aug 16, 1794; bur. Aug 17, 1794; age - 8 mo.; dau. of Robert & Mary
MARRAST, Rose; died Aug 3, 1796; bur. Aug 4, 1796; age - 20 mo.; dau. of John & Mary Louisa Tolane
MARTIN, Catherine; died Aug 21, 1796; bur. Aug 22, 1796; age - 2 yrs. 6 mo.; dau. of Robert & Mary
MARTIN, Jane; died Jun 20, 1798; bur. Jun 21, 1798; age - 4 mo.; dau. of Robert
MARTIN, John; died Jul 18, 1797; bur. Jul 19, 1797; age - 3 mo.; son of Thomas & Mary
MARTIN, Robert; died Oct 16, 1800; bur. Oct 17, 1800; age - 45 yrs.; nat. of Ireland
MARY, Catharine; died Jul 16, 1798; bur. Jul 17, 1798; age - 6 yrs. 3 mo.; dau. of Bartholomew & Adelade DuHarlay
MASHAN, Catherine; died Dec 23, 1797; bur. Dec 24, 1797; age - 10 da.; dau. of Joseph & Christina
MAUREAU, John Baptist; died Jul 13, 1795; bur. Jul 14, 1795; age - 40 yrs.; planter, St Domingo
MAY, William Dominic; died Oct 2, 1794; bur. Oct 2, 1794; age - 33 yrs.; Catholic priest lately from Ireland; malignant fever
MAZE, John Peter Toussain; died May 6, 1794; bur. May 7, 1794; age - 22 yrs.; nat. of Cape Francis, St Domingo

BURIALS

MCALISTER, Alexander; died May 4, 1798; bur. May 4, 1798; age - 11 mo.; son of Charles & Elizabeth
MCALLISTER, James; died Jan 22, 1796; bur. Jan 23, 1796; age - 40 yrs.
MCCAN, John; died Oct 11, 1795; bur. Oct 12, 1795; cooper of this town
MCCARTY, James; died Nov 19, 1791; bur. Nov 20, 1791; age - 2 yrs.; son of Michael & Eleanor
MCCARTY, Mary; died Oct 30, 1797; bur. Oct 31, 1797; age - 2 yrs. 6 mo.; dau. of Michael & Mary
MCCOY, Rachael; died Oct 31, 1793; bur. Oct 31, 1793; age - 6 mo.; negro dau. of Abraham & Elizabeth (free negroes)
MCDANIEL, (?); died Nov 10, 1794; bur. Nov 12, 1794; age - 19 mo.; dau. of Edward & Ann
MCDANIEL, Rachael; died Oct 27, 1793; bur. Oct 28, 1793; age - 3 yrs.; dau. of Francis & Rachael
MCDERMOTT, Thomas; died Mar 11, 1799; bur. Mar 12, 1799; age - 38 yrs.; nat. of Ireland
MCDEVIT, Neil; died Aug 21, 1800; bur. Aug 21, 1800; nat. of Ireland
MCDONALD, Alexander; died Oct 28, 1797; bur. Oct 29, 1797
MCDONALD, James; died Oct 26, 1799; bur. Oct 27, 1799; nat. of Ireland
MCDONALD, James; died May 5, 1800; bur. May 6, 1800; nat. of Ireland; advanced age
MCDONALD, Jane; died Jul 28, 1796; bur. Jul 29, 1796; age - 7 da.; dau. of Bernard & Jane
MCDONOGH, Thomas; died Nov 5, 1798; bur. Nov 6, 1798
MCEWING, Mary Magdalen; died Jul 9, 1798; bur. Jul 10, 1798; age - 9 mo.; dau. of Owen & Elizabeth
MCFARLEN, Catherine; died Jul 25, 1800; bur. Jul 26, 1800; age - 1 1/2 yrs.; dau. of Michael & Margaret
MCFARLEN, Mary; died Nov 18, 1793; bur. Nov 19, 1793; age - 7 wks.; dau. of Michael & Margaret
MCGEE, Alfred; died Jul 9, 1796; bur. Jul 10, 1796; age - 8 1/2 mo.
MCGILL, Dennis; died Aug 6, 1799; bur. Aug 7, 1799; age - 2 yrs.; son of Charles & Margaret
MCGOVERN, Eleanor; died Aug 27, 1800; bur. Aug 27, 1800; age - 26 yrs.; wf. of James
MCGUIRE, James; died Jul 16, 1796; bur. Jul 17, 1796; age - 50 yrs.
MCILROY, John; died Sep 7, 1796; bur. Sep 8, 1796; age - 1 yr. 10 mo.; son of William & Elizabeth
MCILROY, William; died Aug 9, 1798; bur. Aug 10, 1798; age - 14 mo.; son of William & Elizabeth
MCKINLEY, Margaret; died Nov 22, 1795; bur. Nov 23, 1795; age - 5 da.; dau. of Neale & Margaret
MCKINLEY, Mary; died Aug 10, 1800; bur. Aug 11, 1800; age - 16 mo.; dau. of Neil & Margaret
MCLAUGHLIN, James; died Sep 7, 1800; bur. Sep 7, 1800; nat. of Ireland
MCLAUGHLIN, Mary; died Sep 10, 1800; bur. Sep 11, 1800; age - 8 mo.; dau. of James & Mary
MCMAHON, Jane; died Oct 24, 1795; bur. Oct 25, 1795; wf. of James

BURIALS

MCMAHON, Margaret; died Oct 31, 1800; bur. Nov 1, 1800; age - 24 yrs.; wf. of Michael
MCMAHON, Michael; died Jan 16, 1797; bur. Jan 16, 1797; age - 3 da.; son of James & Bridget
MCMAHON, Thomas; died Jun 23, 1798; bur. Jun 24, 1798; age - 15 mo.; son of Thomas & Mary
MCNAMARA, Ann; died Sep 29, 1794; bur. Sep 30, 1794; age - 35 yrs.; wf. of Matthew
MCNAMARA, Francis; died Aug 12, 1795; bur. Aug 12, 1795; age - 7 mo.; son of Thomas & Mary
MCNAMARA, Margaret; died Aug 11, 1794; bur. Aug 12, 1794; age - 5 yrs.; dau. of Thomas & Mary
MCNAMARA, Mary; died Aug 23, 1794; bur. Aug 23, 1794; dau. of Thomas & Mary
MCNAMARA, Matthew; died Aug 18, 1795; bur. Aug 18, 1795; nat. of Ireland; widower
MCNAMARA, Thomas; died Aug 23, 1794; bur. Aug 23, 1794; son of Thomas & Mary
MCNEVIF, Charles; died May 28, 1800; bur. May 29, 1800; age - 40 yrs.
MCSHERRY, Barnaby; died Aug 15, 1796; bur. Aug 16, 1796; age - 32 yrs.; son of Patrick & Catherine
MERY, Mary; died Dec 12, 1793; bur. Dec 13, 1793
MICHAEL, Augustine; died Aug 21, 1796; bur. Aug 22, 1796; age - 40 yrs.; nat. of Italy
MICHEL, Nicholas Francis Just; died Aug 10, 1795; bur. Aug 10, 1795; age - 53 yrs.; nat. of Fontainbleau, late Notary General, Western part, St Domingo, at Port-au-Prince; deceased at Fells Point
MICKINS, Benjamin; died Nov 17, 1795; bur. Nov 18, 1795
MIFFLIN, Jacob; died Mar 7, 1798; bur. Mar 8, 1798; age - 3 yrs.; son of Elizabeth
MILLAR, Anna Maria; died Jan 12, 1796; bur. Jan 12, 1796; age - 1 da.; dau. of Michael & Elizabeth
MILLER, David; died Aug 31, 1800; bur. Aug 31, 1800; age - 22 yrs.
MILLER, Eve; died Mar 19, 1794; bur. Mar 20, 1794; age - 28 yrs.; wf. of Michael
MILLER, Francis Anthony; died Oct 9, 1797; bur. Oct 10, 1797; nat. of Alsace
MILLER, John; died May 16, 1795; bur. May 17, 1795
MILLER, Madalen; died Feb 22, 1794; bur. Feb 24, 1794; age - 57 yrs.; widow
MILLER, Matthew; died Oct 16, 1795; bur. Oct 17, 1795; age - 16 yrs.; son of Matthew & Mary
MINEHAN, John; died Jul 29, 1800; bur. Jul 30, 1800; age - 16 mo.; son of Martin & Susan
MINIERE, Gustavus; died Aug 31, 1796; bur. Sep 1, 1796; age - 9 mo.
MINSON, Gabriel; died Nov 4, 1797; bur. Nov 5, 1797; age - 1 yr.; son of Gabriel & Margaret
MITCHELL, Patrick; died Aug 20, 1794; bur. Aug 22, 1794; age - 60 yrs.
(MITCHELL), William; died Feb 13, 1800; bur. Feb 14, 1800; age - 15 mo.; negro child belonging to Francis J Mitchell

BURIALS

MOES, Francis Joseph; died Feb 11, 1795; bur. Feb 12, 1795; age - 9 yrs. 10 mo.
MOLIER, Henry; died Aug 17, 1799; bur. Aug 17, 1799; age - 14 mo.; son of Henry & Elizabeth
MOLONEY, Eve; died Sep 8, 1797; bur. Sep 9, 1797; wf. of James
MONNIER, Eleanor; died Apr 7, 1799; bur. Apr 8, 1799; age - 45 yrs.; nat. of Provence
MOODY, William; died Jul 6, 1800; bur. Jul 6, 1800; age - 6 mo.; son of William & Elizabeth
MOORE, John; died Sep 12, 1797; bur. Sep 12, 1797; age - 19 yrs.
MOORE, Joseph; died Apr 19, 1794; bur. Apr 20, 1794; age - 8 wks.; son of William & Catherine
MORIN, Catherine; died Mar 28, 1795; bur. Mar 29, 1795; age - 3 yrs. 6 mo.; dau. of John & Eleanor
MORRIN, Paul; died Aug 31, 1800; bur. Aug 31, 1800; age - 25 yrs.
MORRIS, Mark; died Nov 2, 1799; bur. Nov 3, 1799
MORRISON, Garret; died Sep 20, 1794; bur. Sep 21, 1794; age - 1 mo.
MULLAN, (?); died Jun 7, 1799; bur. Jun 7, 1799; son of Patrick & Sarah; born and died June 7, 1799
MULLAN, Maria; died Aug 11, 1794; bur. Aug 12, 1794; age - 13 mo.; dau. of Patrick & Sarah
MULLANPHY, Elizabeth; died Oct 21, 1795; bur. Oct 22, 1795; age - 3 yrs.; dau. of John & Elizabeth
MULLANPHY, Mary; died Oct 28, 1795; bur. Oct 28, 1795; age - 17 da.; dau. of John & Elizabeth
MULLOY, Arthur; died Feb 18, 1795; bur. Feb 19, 1795; age - 48 yrs.; nat. of Ireland
MULLOY, Mary; died Mar 10, 1795; bur. Mar 11, 1795; age - 43 yrs.
MURPHY, James; died Mar 8, 1800; bur. Mar 9, 1800; age - 7 yrs.; son of James & Christina
MURPHY, John; died Dec 7, 1796; bur. Dec 8, 1796; age - 2 yrs. 9 mo.; son of Patrick & Susanna
MURPHY, John; died Sep 12, 1800; bur. Sep 12, 1800; nat. of Ireland
MURPHY, Mark; died Oct 13, 1799; bur. Oct 14, 1799; age - 28 yrs.; nat. of Ireland
MURPHY, Mary; died Aug 6, 1795; bur. Aug 7, 1795; age - 4 mo.; dau. of James & Christina
MURPHY, Mary; died Sep 5, 1800; bur. Sep 5, 1800; age - 34 yrs.; wf. of John
MURPHY, Patrick; died Oct 15, 1798; bur. Oct 16, 1798; age - 30 yrs.
MURPHY, Thomas; died Jul 26, 1796; bur. Jul 27, 1796; age - 32 yrs.; at Fells Point
MURRAY, Cornelius; died Jun 15, 1798; bur. Jun 16, 1798; age - 2 mo.; son of John & Elizabeth
MURRAY, Henrietta; died Aug 8, 1794; bur. Aug 10, 1794; age - 15 yrs.
MURRAY, John; died Sep 9, 1795; bur. Sep 10, 1795; age - 6 mo.; son of Mary
MURRAY, John; died Jul 20, 1798; bur. Jul 21, 1798; age - 3 1/2 mo.; son of John & Elizabeth
MURRAY, Mary; died Dec 21, 1800; bur. Dec 22, 1800; wf. of James, a printer

BURIALS

MYERS, John; died Jul 29, 1799; bur. Jul 30, 1799; age - 3 yrs.; son of Patrick & Ann
MYLER, John; died Aug 24, 1793; bur. Aug 25, 1793; age - 1 yr. 8 mo.; son of Christopher & Frances
NAU, Rene Peter Clement; died Aug 7, 1795; bur. Aug 7, 1795; age - 18 mo.; dau. of (sic.) John Baptist & Mary Louisa Beyrae
NEALE, Edward; died Sep 11, 1800; bur. Sep 11, 1800; age - 36 yrs.; son of Jer & Jane of St Mary's County
NEALE, John; died Aug 11, 1795; bur. Aug 11, 1795; age - 29 yrs.; nat. of Cork, Ireland
NEIGHBOURS, John Lloyd; died Sep 9, 1796; bur. Sep 10, 1796; age - 17 mo. 15 da.; son of Henry & Ann
NEIGHBOURS, Sarah; died Aug 18, 1800; bur. Aug 19, 1800; age - 13 mo.; dau. of Henry & Ann
NEIL, Agnes; died Nov 4, 1800; bur. Nov 5, 1800; widow of Dennis
NEIL, John; died Oct 12, 1797; bur. Oct 13, 1797; age - 40 yrs.; nat. of Ireland
NEILL, Mary; died Sep 7, 1798; bur. Sep 8, 1798; nat. of Ireland
NEILLE, Dennis; died Mar 9, 1800; bur. Mar 10, 1800; age - 52 yrs.; nat. of Ireland
NEWLAND, Grace; died Jul 29, 1796; bur. Jul 30, 1796; age - 27 yrs.; wf. of Edward
NEZEL, John Baptist Cesar; died May 3, 1794; bur. May 4, 1794; age - 28 yrs.; born Paris, France, parish of St. Sauveur
(NICOLE), Eustace; died Apr 4, 1796; bur. Apr 5, 1796; slave of Mr. Nicole from Guadaloupe
NICOLE, Stephen; died May 5, 1794; bur. May 5, 1794; born Marseilles, France; inh. of Island of Guadaloupe
NOONAN, John; died Sep 13, 1800; bur. Sep 13, 1800; age - 6 yrs.; son of Edward & Mary
NORRIS, Mary; died Sep 5, 1800; bur. Sep 5, 1800; age - 22 yrs.; nat. of Ireland
NOWLAND, Ann; died Aug 24, 1794; bur. Aug 25, 1794; age - 7 yrs. 6 mo. 7 da.
NOWLAND, Ann; died Sep 17, 1797; bur. Sep 17, 1797; nat. of Ireland; wf. of Michael
NOWLAND, John; died Mar 6, 1796; bur. Mar 7, 1796; age - 1 yr.; son of William & Eleanor
NOWLAND, Mary; died Sep 23, 1800; bur. Sep 23, 1800; age - 20 yrs.
NOWLAND, Michael; died Oct 6, 1797; bur. Oct 6, 1797; age - 46 yrs.; nat. of Ireland
NOWLAND, William; died Jun 22, 1800; bur. Jun 23, 1800; age - 3 yrs.; son of William & Eleanor; small pox
NUSSEAR, Dorothea; died Nov 12, 1798; bur. Nov 13, 1798; age - 70 yrs.; wf. of Jacob
O'BRIEN, Dennis; died Aug 28, 1795; bur. Aug 29, 1795; age - 28 yrs.; nat. of Ireland
O'BRIEN, Eleanor; died Oct 20, 1798; bur. Oct 21, 1798; age - 53 yrs.
O'BRIEN, Eleanor; died May 13, 1800; bur. May 13, 1800; age - 35 yrs.
O'BRIEN, Elizabeth; died Jul 26, 1798; bur. Jul 26, 1798; age - 1 yr. 6 mo.; dau. of Charles & Martha

BURIALS

O'BRIEN, Frances; died Dec 25, 1799; bur. Dec 26, 1799; age - 9 mo.; dau. of Charles & Martha
O'BRIEN, Henry; died Aug 15, 1800; bur. Aug 15, 1800; age - 19 yrs.; born Aug 15, 1781 at 11 AM; nat. of Ireland
O'BRIEN, James; died Aug 19, 1795; bur. Aug 20, 1795; age - 30 yrs.; nat. of Ireland & lately from thence
O'BRIEN, John; died Apr 13, 1797; bur. Apr 14, 1797; age - 3 yrs. 6 mo.; son of John & Hannah
O'BRIEN, Joseph; died Jul 21, 1800; bur. Jul 22, 1800; age - 1 yr. 2 mo.; son of Michael & Margaret
O'BRIEN, Mary; died Oct 12, 1793; bur. Oct 12, 1793; age - 11 da.; dau. of Charles & Martha
O'BRIEN, Mary; died Aug 9, 1797; bur. Aug 9, 1797; age - 34 yrs.; nat. of & lately from Ireland; wf. of Patrick
O'BRIEN, Mary; died Jul 7, 1798; bur. Jul 8, 1798; age - 9 mo.; dau. of Michael & Margaret
O'BRIEN, Patrick; died Aug 20, 1797; bur. Aug 21, 1797; nat. of Ireland
O'CONNOR, Charles; died Jun 8, 1799; bur. Jun 9, 1799; age - 48 yrs.; nat. of Ireland
O'CONNOR, Patrick; died May 26, 1794; bur. May 27, 1794; age - 3 yrs.; son of Thomas & Catherine; nat. of Ireland; killed yesterday by being accidentally run over by a cart
O'DOIN, Joseph; died Jul 10, 1800; bur. Jul 11, 1800; age - 12 yrs.; son of Lewis & Julia
O'HARA, John; died Sep 11, 1797; bur. Sep 11, 1797; age - 2 yrs.; son of Matthew & Mary
O'HARA, Mary; died Sep 13, 1797; bur. Sep 13, 1797; nat. of Ireland
O'KEEFFE, Cornelius; died Aug 20, 1796; bur. Aug 20, 1796; age - 8 da.; son of Patrick & Mary
O'KEEFFE, Mary; died Jul 30, 1796; bur. Jul 31, 1796; age - 1 yr.; dau. of Patrick & Mary
O'MARA, William; died Apr 5, 1798; bur. Apr 6, 1798; age - 3 mo.; son of Patrick & Mary
O'NEAL, Felix; died Jan 11, 1800; bur. Jan 13, 1800
(O'NEIL), Maria; died Mar 5, 1799; bur. Mar 6, 1799; age - 6 wks.; a mulatto child, slave of Capt O'Neil
O'NEIL, Mary; died Sep 16, 1798; bur. Sep 17, 1798; age - 13 mo.
O'NEILL, Bernard; died Sep 11, 1797; bur. Sep 11, 1797; hsb. of Margaret
O'NEILL, James Mansfield; died Nov 30, 1800; bur. Nov 30, 1800; son of Daniel & Prudente
O'NEILL, John; died Feb 5, 1799; bur. Feb 6, 1799; died at Fells Point
O'NEILL, Margaret; died Sep 21, 1799; bur. Sep 22, 1799; age - 25 yrs.; widow
O'ROURKE, Nicholas; died Aug 25, 1794; bur. Aug 26, 1794; age - 24 yrs.; son of Patrick Esq & Mary Angelina Renee de Veteana; Captain of Regiment of Walsh, service of His Most Christian Majesty
(O'ROURKE), William; died Jun 4, 1799; bur. Jun 5, 1799; age - 2 yrs.; a French mulatto child, son of a negro slave of Mr O'Rourke

BURIALS

ORMSBY, Catharine; died Jan 29, 1800; bur. Jan 30, 1800; age - 5
    da.; dau. of John & Unity
ORR, Thomas; died Oct 10, 1799; bur. Oct 11, 1799; age - 25 yrs.
OXFORD, James; died Oct 11, 1800; bur. Oct 12, 1800; age - 8
    yrs.; son of Charles & Rose
OXFORD, Rose; died Oct 13, 1800; bur. Oct 14, 1800; age - 50
    yrs.; wf. of Charles
PAINE, John; died Sep 1, 1799; bur. Sep 2, 1799; age - 25 yrs.;
    nat. of Ireland
PAOLIE, Paul Mark; died Nov 2, 1794; bur. Nov 2, 1794; age - 30
    yrs.; hsb. of Mary
PASCAULT, Aime John; died Apr 28, 1795; bur. Apr 29, 1795; age -
    1 yr. 11 mo. 3 wks. 1 da.; son of Louis & Mary
PASCAULT, William Peter; died Aug 4, 1798; bur. Aug 5, 1798; age
    - 19 mo.; son of Lewis & Mary Magdalen
PATAT, John; died Nov 7, 1798; bur. Nov 8, 1798; age - 45 yrs.;
    nat. of France
PAULI, Marcia Philippina; died Oct 17, 1799; bur. Oct 18, 1799;
    age - 1 yr.; dau. of John & Joanna Catherine
PECOTIERE, Ann Frances Brutus Gautier; died Dec 9, 1796; bur. Dec
    10, 1796; age - 2 yrs. 9 mo. 27 da.; dau. of Germaine
    Gautier & Mary Frances Maraine
PELISSOT, John Baptist; died Nov 21, 1793; bur. Nov 22, 1793;
    nat. of Ricey Hautrive near Bar on the Saone
PENDERGAST, John; died Jul 30, 1798; bur. Jul 31, 1798; age - 6
    mo.; son of Robert & Ruth
PENPALLON, Lewis; died Mar 11, 1800; bur. Mar 12, 1800; age - 17
    yrs.; nat. of Male St Nicholas (breakwater - pier)
PEREMONT, John Baptist; died Jun 9, 1800; bur. Jun 10, 1800; age
    - 3 yrs.; son of Ann
PERIER, Mary Frances; died Oct 19, 1797; bur. Oct 19, 1797; age -
    17 mo.; dau. of Peter & Agnes
PERRON, Stephen; died Apr 24, 1795; bur. Apr 25, 1795; age - 38
    yrs.; nat. of LaRochelle
PETEL, Joseph; died Jul 2, 1798; bur. Jul 3, 1798; age - 49 yrs.;
    nat. of Canada
PETERS, Catherine; died May 5, 1797; bur. May 6, 1797; age - 30
    yrs.; widow
PETERS, Henry; died Oct 10, 1793; bur. Oct 11, 1793; shoemaker;
    died at Fells Point
PFIFER, John; died Sep 10, 1797; bur. Sep 10, 1797; son of George
PFIFER, Ursula; died May 3, 1798; bur. May 4, 1798; age - 54
    yrs.; wf. of George
PHILIPS, John; died Jan 31, 1795; bur. Feb 1, 1795
PHILIPS, Margaret; died Aug 19, 1797; bur. Aug 20, 1797; age - 1
    yr.; dau. of Jacob & Mary
PICARD, Peter; died Feb 16, 1798; bur. Feb 17, 1798; age - 34
    yrs.; nat. of Burgundy, France; mariner
PIETTE, Antoine Casmir Joseph; died Dec 26, 1790; bur. Dec 29,
    1790; nat. of Valenciennes, France
PILCH, Charlotte; died Oct 31, 1800; bur. Nov 1, 1800; age - 4
    yrs.; dau. of James & Elizabeth
PINEAU, Jean Marie Nicolas; died Oct 12, 1793; bur. Oct 13, 1793;
    age - 27 yrs.; son of Jean & Marie Francoise Boisson; nat.
    of parish St John Baptist, Ft Dauphin, St Domingo

BURIALS

PINEAU, Marie Francoise Boisson; died Oct 14, 1793; bur. Oct 14, 1793; age - 50 yrs.; nat. of Rochelle Diocese; inh. of Ft. Dauphin, St Domingo; wf. of recently deceased Jean

PLACIDE, Paul Agustus; died Jul 18, 1799; bur. Jul 18, 1799; age - 5 wks.; son of Paul & Louisa

PLUNKETT, Louise Josephine Athanaise; died Jul 14, 1800; bur. Jul 15, 1800; age - 12 yrs.; dau. of Edward & Marie Louise Yeonnet

POIRIER, Peter; died Mar 19, 1796; bur. Mar 20, 1796; age - 66 yrs. 10 mo.; nat. of Acadia

POIRVIER, Margaret; died Feb 5, 1799; bur. Feb 6, 1799; widow; nat. of Nova Scotia

POLY, Henry George; died Sep 24, 1796; bur. Sep 25, 1796; age - 2 yrs. 5 mo. 9 da.; son of Jacob & Mary

POLY (PHILLIPS), Jacob; died Feb 22, 1800; bur. Feb 23, 1800

PONCET, Joseph; died Jan 8, 1797; bur. Jan 9, 1797; age - 2 mo.; son of Louis Joseph & Ann Veneau

PONCET, Lewis; died Mar 7, 1799; bur. Mar 7, 1799; born Mar 6, 1799; son of Lewis & Mary Julia

PONS, Anthony; died Jan 19, 1797; bur. Jan 19, 1797; nat. of Port Mahon, Island of Minorco

POOLE, Ann; died Jun 28, 1798; bur. Jun 29, 1798; age - 11 mo.; dau. of John & Hannah

POOLE, Elizabeth; died Jul 17, 1800; bur. Jul 17, 1800; age - 5 da.

PORTIER, Louis; died Jan 30, 1794; bur. Jan 31, 1794; age - 45 yrs.; nat. of Burgundy, France

POULLET, John Baptist; died May 17, 1793; bur. May 18, 1793; inh. of Cape Francois, St. Domingo

POUPONNEAU, Francis; died Jul 28, 1795; bur. Jul 29, 1795; age - 14 mo.; son of Oliver & Mary Chevalier

POWER, Ann; died Jul 13, 1796; bur. Jul 14, 1796; age - 4 mo. 2 wks.; dau. of James & Mary

POWER, Catherine; died Aug 11, 1800; bur. Aug 12, 1800; age - 11 mo.; dau. of James & Mary

POWER, Thomas; died Aug 26, 1796; bur. Aug 27, 1796; age - 6 mo.; son of James & Mary

POWER, William; died Dec 11, 1793; bur. Dec 11, 1793

(PRENDEVILLE), Anny; died Jan 6, 1799; bur. Jan 7, 1799; mulatto slave of Mr Garret Prendeville

PRESNEHAM, Elizabeth; died Mar 1, 1795; bur. Mar 2, 1795; age - 2 yrs. 7 mo.; dau. of James & Eleanor

PREVOT, Elizabeth; died Nov 20, 1798; bur. Nov 21, 1798; age - 4 yrs.; dau. of John & Mary

PROVOST, Julian Charles; died Sep 20, 1794; bur. Sep 20, 1794; age - 8 mo.; son of Julian & Magdalen Josephine Caroline de la Faychere

QUEEN, Edward; died Feb 23, 1798; bur. Feb 24, 1798; free negro

QUIN, Catherine; died Apr 14, 1795; bur. Apr 15, 1795; age - 7 mo.; dau. of David & Mary

QUIN, John; died Aug 29, 1797; bur. Aug 30, 1797; age - 14 da.; son of David & Mary

QUINLAN, Jane; died Aug 3, 1795; bur. Aug 4, 1795; dau. of Thomas & Jane; born & died August 3, 1795

BURIALS

QUINLAN, Mark; died Oct 20, 1795; bur. Oct 21, 1795; nat. of Ireland
QUINLAN, Stephen; died Jun 30, 1798; bur. Jul 1, 1798; age - 6 mo.; son of Edward & Jane
QUINLIN, Edward; died Feb 20, 1798; bur. Feb 21, 1798; age - 30 yrs.
READ, Hannah; died Aug 24, 1793; bur. Aug 25, 1793; age - 14 mo.; dau. of James & Eleanor
READ, James; died Sep 11, 1793; bur. Sep 12, 1793
REBOUD, Pauline; died Nov 21, 1796; bur. Nov 22, 1796; age - 21 mo.; dau. of James & Louise Sophie
REDON, Mary Louisa; died Mar 4, 1798; bur. Mar 5, 1798; age - 52 yrs.; nat. of St Domingo
REGAN, John; died Jul 27, 1800; bur. Jul 28, 1800; age - 10 mo.; son of John & Ann
REGAN, Margaret; died Aug 10, 1799; bur. Aug 11, 1799; age - 11 mo.; dau. of Philip & Mary
REILLY, John; died Dec 2, 1797; bur. Dec 2, 1797; age - 8 da.; son of John & Mary
REINHAULT, Frances; died Jan 5, 1800; bur. Jan 5, 1800; age - 4 yrs.; dau. of Sebastian & Juliana
RENAUD, Margaret Louisa; died Jul 25, 1798; bur. Jul 26, 1798; age - 14 mo.; dau. of John & Harriot
RENOUS, Andrew John Baptist; died Apr 29, 1797; bur. Apr 30, 1797; age - 5 mo.; son of John Baptist & Desdimona
REUTER, Catherine; died Feb 23, 1797; bur. Feb 24, 1797; age - 9 mo.; dau. of Abraham & Catherine
RHODY, John Albert; died Apr 29, 1798; bur. Apr 30, 1798; age - 20 yrs.; nat. of Curracoa
RICE, Felix; died Sep 20, 1797; bur. Sep 20, 1797; age - 43 yrs.; nat. of Ireland
RICHARD, Elizabeth Frances Susanna; died Jun 6, 1799; bur. Jun 7, 1799; age - 19 mo.; dau. of Francis & Mary
RICHARD, John; died Jan 5, 1796; bur. Jan 6, 1796; age - 48 yrs.; nat. of LaRochelle, France
RICHARDS, Bridget; died Jul 19, 1796; bur. Jul 20, 1796; age - 2 wks.; dau. of Peter & Margaret
RICHARDS, Herman; died Nov 18, 1797; bur. Nov 19, 1797; age - 54 yrs.
RICHARDS, Joseph; died Jun 24, 1800; bur. Jun 25, 1800; age - 2 mo.; son of John & Ann
RICHARDS, Mary; died Jul 13, 1795; bur. Jul 14, 1795; age - 5 mo.; dau. of Edward & Mary
RICHARDS, Mary; died Jul 30, 1800; bur. Jul 31, 1800
RICHARDSON, Henry William Dickinson; died Aug 8, 1798; bur. Aug 9, 1798; age - 1 yr.; son of William & Elizabeth
RICHARDSON, John; died Jul 9, 1798; bur. Jul 9, 1798; age - 3 wks.; son of Mary
RICHARDSON, William Henry Dickinson; died Aug 12, 1798; bur. Aug 13, 1798; age - 1 yr.; son of William & Elizabeth
RIGGS, Mary; died Aug 13, 1799; bur. Aug 14, 1799; dau. of Daniel & Sarah
RILEY, Philip; died Jul 14, 1795; bur. Jul 15, 1795; age - 13 mo.; son of John & Mary

BURIALS

RIVIERA, Elizabeth; died Sep 29, 1793; dau. of Claude & Elizabeth Foison
ROACH, Mary; died Aug 3, 1796; bur. Aug 4, 1796; age - 9 mo.; dau. of James & Eleanor
ROACH, Thomas; died May 7, 1795; bur. May 8, 1795; age - 2 mo.; son of William & Bridget
ROBERT, Peter; died May 23, 1798; bur. May 24, 1798; age - 2 yrs.; son of James & Fiere Debras
ROBERTS, Eleanor; died Jul 28, 1798; bur. Jul 29, 1798; age - 8 mo.; dau. of James & Elizabeth
ROBERTS, Jemima; died Apr 28, 1796; bur. Apr 29, 1796
ROBERTS, Levin; died Dec 3, 1800; bur. Dec 3, 1800
ROBINSON, Mary; died Mar 9, 1796; bur. Mar 11, 1796; age - 55 yrs.
ROCHE, Edward; died Oct 8, 1797; bur. Oct 9, 1797; age - 4 yrs. 3 mo.; son of John & Mary
ROCHET, Joseph Duroche; died Jul 28, 1793; bur. Jul 29, 1793; age - 70 yrs.; nat. of Nantes; time of death 11 PM
RODDY, Eleanor; died May 9, 1794; bur. May 10, 1794; age - 3 mo.; dau. of Patrick & Eleanor
RODDY, Eleanor; died Jul 28, 1795; bur. Jul 29, 1795; age - 1 mo.; dau. of Patrick & Eleanor
RODDY, John; died Feb 14, 1795; bur. Feb 15, 1795; age - 5 yrs.; son of Patrick & Eleanor
RODDY, Patrick Brinson; died Jan 12, 1797; bur. Jan 13, 1797; age - 3 mo.; son of Patrick & Eleanor
RODDY, Patrick; died Jul 24, 1798; bur. Jul 25, 1798; age - 20 da.; son of Patrick & Eleanor
ROGERS, Mary; died Oct 18, 1800; bur. Oct 19, 1800; age - 25 yrs.; wf. of John
ROMAIN, Palmire; died Jul 27, 1793; bur. Jul 28, 1793; age - 6 yrs.; dau. of Arnold & Antoinette Cahuel; from St. Francis
RONE, John; died Mar 13, 1797; bur. Mar 14, 1797; age - 5 mo.; son of John & Elizabeth; nat. of Ireland
RONSEAU, John; died Jan 3, 1798; bur. Jan 4, 1798; age - 17 mo.; son of Andrew & Rachel
RONSO, Anthony; died Sep 5, 1799; bur. Sep 6, 1799; age - 16 mo.; son of Andrew & Rachel
ROSENSTEEL, Samuel; died Dec 23, 1800; bur. Dec 24, 1800; age - 3 yrs.; son of George & Susanna
ROSENSTEEL, William; died Jun 1, 1799; bur. Jun 2, 1799; age - 9 mo.; son of George & Barbara
ROSSINOT, (?); died Jan 21, 1799; bur. Jan 22, 1799; age - 17 da.; son of Michael & Mary Rose Pellerin
RUTLEDGE, Mary; died Nov 14, 1793; bur. Nov 15, 1793; age - 43 yrs.; wf. of Thomas
RUTTER, Thomas; died Jun 20, 1800; bur. Jun 20, 1800; age - 1 yr.; son of Moses & Elizabeth; small pox
RYAN, Eleanor; died Jul 22, 1796; bur. Jul 23, 1796; age - 7 mo. 25 da.; dau. of Michael & Jane
RYAN, James; died Nov 19, 1798; bur. Nov 20, 1798; age - 19 yrs.; nat. of Ireland
RYAN, Margaret; died Jan 30, 1795; bur. Jan 31, 1795; age - 2 mo.; dau. of Michael & Jane

BURIALS

SANDERSON, Elizabeth; died Jan 31, 1799; bur. Feb 1, 1799; age - 14 mo.
SANDFORD, Nicholas; died Jun 27, 1800; bur. Jun 27, 1800; age - 41 yrs.
SAP, James; died Jul 2, 1799; bur. Jul 3, 1799; age - 6 yrs.; son of John & Sarah
SAVAGE, Hester; died Feb 2, 1794; bur. Feb 3, 1794; age - 30 yrs.; wf. of Dennis
SAVAGE, John; died Jul 15, 1800; bur. Jul 16, 1800; age - 2 yrs.; son of Patric & Elizabeth
SCHWARTZ, Elizabeth; died May 14, 1795; bur. May 15, 1795; age - 12 yrs.; dau. of John & Barbara
SCOTT, Luke; died Jan 12, 1796; bur. Jan 13, 1796; age - 50 yrs.
SCOTT, Mary; died Feb 4, 1797; bur. Feb 5, 1797; age - 70 yrs.; nat. of Ireland; widow
SCULLION, George; died Nov 21, 1800; bur. Nov 21, 1800; son of James & Darky
SCULLY, Jane; died Aug 7, 1799; bur. Aug 8, 1799; age - 9 mo.; dau. of James & Darkey
SEGELER, Theobald; died Feb 2, 1795; bur. Feb 3, 1795; nat. of Germany
SENECHAL, Gabriel Alexis; died Oct 1, 1793; dau. of Bonaventure & Marie Catherine Labry; nat. of San Domingo
SERJENT, Francis; died Jun 18, 1796; bur. Jun 19, 1796; age - 6 1/2 mo.; son of John & Ruth
SERJENT, Nicholas; died Jul 24, 1796; bur. Jul 25, 1796; age - 2 yrs.; son of John & Ruth
SHADDOCK, William; died Feb 24, 1798; bur. Feb 25, 1798; age - 4 yrs.
SHARK, Mary Magdalen; died Jun 3, 1794; bur. Jun 4, 1794; age - 10 da.; dau. of Peter & Margaret
SHARP, Anthony; died Aug 11, 1796; bur. Aug 12, 1796; age - 11 mo. 2 wks.; son of John & Catherine
SHAY, James; died Oct 6, 1800; bur. Oct 7, 1800
SHEPHERD, Henry; died Jan 17, 1794; bur. Jan 18, 1794; age - 6 da.; son of John & Eleanor
SHILLING, Christina; died Jul 9, 1794; bur. Jul 10, 1794; age - 1 yr. 11 mo.; dau. of Tobias & Catherine
SHILLING, Michael; died May 21, 1798; bur. May 22, 1798; age - 39 yrs.
SHINEFLEW, (?); died May 12, 1799; bur. May 13, 1799; age - 10 da.; son of Conrad & Elizabeth
SHOEMAKER, Charlotte Magdalen Chevin; died Sep 28, 1794; bur. Sep 29, 1794; age - 34 yrs.; wf. of Ignatius, locksmith
SHRECK, Sarah; died Mar 28, 1799; bur. Mar 29, 1799; age - 6 yrs.; dau. of Diderick & Margaret
SHREEK, Mary; died Nov 5, 1796; bur. Nov 6, 1796; age - 100 yrs.
SIAS, Sarah; died May 23, 1799; bur. May 23, 1799; age - 22 yrs.; dau. of John & Rose
SICKFORT, Gertrude; died Jun 21, 1797; bur. Jun 22, 1797; wf. of George
SIEKFRET, Catharine; died Sep 16, 1797; bur. Sep 16, 1797; age - 13 yrs.; dau. of George
SIEKFRET, George; died Oct 28, 1797; bur. Oct 29, 1797; age - 9 mo.; son of George & Gertrude

BURIALS

SIMON, Maria; died Aug 5, 1799; bur. Aug 6, 1799; age - 8 mo.;
    dau. of Joseph & Wilhelmina
SIMON, William; died Aug 23, 1797; bur. Aug 24, 1797; age - 6
    wks.; son of Joseph & Mina
SINCLAIR, Robert; died Oct 19, 1795; bur. Oct 20, 1795; age - 2
    wks.; son of George & Celia
SMITH, Andrew; died Apr 22, 1799; bur. Apr 23, 1799; son of James
    & Mary; an infant
SMITH, Daniel; died Nov 23, 1794; bur. Nov 24, 1794; age - 2 yrs.
    3 mo.; son of Issac & Elizabeth
SMITH, Eleanor; died May 5, 1799; bur. May 6, 1799; age - 16 mo.;
    dau. of John & Mary
SMITH, Jonathan; died Aug 24, 1798; bur. Aug 25, 1798; age - 22
    yrs.; nat. of Ireland; mariner
SMITH, Mary; died Oct 29, 1793; bur. Oct 30, 1793; age - 4 mo.;
    dau. of Robert & Eleanor
SMITH, Sarah; died Sep 15, 1796; bur. Sep 16, 1796; age - 14 mo.
    12 da.; dau. of Isaac & Elizabeth
SMITH, Thomas; died Nov 26, 1794; bur. Nov 27, 1794; age - 1 yr.;
    son of Issac & Elizabeth
SMITH, William; died Mar 17, 1794; bur. Mar 18, 1794; age - 1
    yr.; son of Isaac & Elizabeth
SOUCOROWITZ, Francis; died Oct 7, 1797; bur. Oct 7, 1797; age -
    30 yrs.; nat. of Ragusa
SPEAR, Jane; died Oct 19, 1795; bur. Oct 20, 1795; age - 3 yrs. 6
    mo.; dau. of John & Eleanor
SPELLARD, William; died Sep 11, 1798; bur. Sep 12, 1798; age - 8
    mo.; son of Mathias & Winifred
SPELLARD, Winifred; died Sep 29, 1798; bur. Sep 30, 1798; age -
    24 yrs.; wf. of Mathias
SPENCER, Edward; died Dec 5, 1796; bur. Dec 6, 1796; age - 32
    yrs.; nat. of Ireland
SPICER, Mary; died May 21, 1798; bur. May 22, 1798; age - 3 yrs.;
    dau. of George & Harriot, free negroes
(ST MARTIN), (?); died Feb 13, 1799; bur. Feb 14, 1799; a negro
    child belonging to Mde St Martin
ST MARTIN, Alexis George Mary; died Sep 6, 1798; bur. Sep 6,
    1798; age - 1 yr.; son of Peter James Joseph of St Domingo &
    Margaret Louisa Josephine Leyritz
ST MARTIN, Peter James Joseph; died Feb 13, 1800; bur. Feb 14,
    1800; age - 42 yrs.; nat. of parish of Torbec, St Domingo
STACLER, Elizabeth; died Dec 28, 1795; bur. Dec 29, 1795; dau. of
    Philip & Catherine; born & died Dec. 28, 1795
STAR, (?); died Jan 21, 1795; bur. Jan 22, 1795; wf. of ? Star
STEIGER, George; died Feb 18, 1795; bur. Feb 19, 1795; age - 6
    mo.; son of Mathis & Mary
STEIGER, Henry; died Oct 11, 1797; bur. Oct 11, 1797; age - 30
    yrs.
STEIGER, John; died Jan 8, 1797; bur. Jan 10, 1797; age - 73 yrs.
STEIGER, Mathias; died Sep 7, 1797; bur. Sep 8, 1797; house
    carpenter
STEINMETZ, Theresa; died Sep 6, 1798; bur. Sep 7, 1798; age - 5
    yrs.; dau. of Gabriel & Barbara
STEINMETZ, William; died Aug 24, 1800; bur. Aug 24, 1800; age -
    14 mo.; son of Michael & Mary

BURIALS

STENSON, Elizabeth; died Aug 24, 1796; bur. Aug 25, 1796; age - 2 yrs.; dau. of William & Elizabeth
STENSON, William; died Jun 12, 1796; bur. Jun 13, 1796; age - 4 yrs. 6 mo.
STEWART, George; died Jul 19, 1800; bur. Jul 20, 1800; age - 1 yr. 10 mo.; dau. of (sic) Jane
STILLINGER, Michael; died Jul 22, 1798; bur. Jul 22, 1798; age - 1 da.; son of Jacob & Christina
STRICKER, Eleanor; died Nov 19, 1794; bur. Nov 20, 1794; wf. of Nicholas
STRIDER, Anthony; died May 16, 1798; bur. May 17, 1798; age - 12 yrs.
STRIDER, Elizabeth; died Jun 9, 1797; bur. Jun 10, 1797; age - 15 yrs.; dau. of Joseph & Catherine
STRIKE, William; died Feb 12, 1795; bur. Feb 13, 1795; age - 3 mo.; son of Nicholas & Eleanor
SUIRE, Edmond; died Dec 11, 1798; bur. Dec 12, 1798; age - 42 yrs.; son of Abraham & ? LaPorte; nat. of parish Aux Cayes, St Domingo
SULLIVAN, Daniel; died Sep 21, 1794; bur. Sep 22, 1794; age - 1 mo.
SULLIVAN, Jeremiah; died Sep 23, 1800; bur. Sep 23, 1800; age - 30 yrs.; nat. of Ireland
SULLIVAN, Timothy; died May 16, 1796; bur. May 17, 1796
SWEENEY, (?); died Nov 12, 1799; bur. Nov 13, 1799; age - 2 yrs.; of Alexander & ?
SWEENY, Ann; died Oct 23, 1794; bur. Oct 23, 1794; dau. of Hugh & Mary
SWEENY, Edward; died Jun 24, 1799; bur. Jun 25, 1799; age - 25 yrs.
SWEENY, Hugh; died Aug 7, 1795; bur. Aug 8, 1795; age - 2 mo.; son of Hugh & Mary
SWEENY, John; died Aug 7, 1798; bur. Aug 8, 1798; age - 3 yrs.; son of Hugh & Priscilla
SYLVA, Mary Ann; died Feb 13, 1799; bur. Feb 14, 1799; wf. of Francis
TARDIEU, Mary Louisa; died Oct 20, 1796; bur. Oct 21, 1796; age - 1 yr. 3 mo.; dau. of John from Jeremie, St Domingo & Josephine Oquam
TAYLOR, (?); died Oct 7, 1799; bur. Oct 8, 1799; age - 10 mo.; a child
TAYLOR, Henry; died Aug 28, 1800; bur. Aug 28, 1800; hsb. of Mary
TAYLOR, Susanna; died Aug 26, 1800; bur. Aug 27, 1800; age - 3 yrs.; dau. of Henry & Mary
TECHLIN, Eleanor; died May 16, 1800; bur. May 17, 1800; age - 26 yrs.; wf. of William
TENAGHAN, John; died Nov 13, 1793; bur. Nov 14, 1793; age - 2 yrs. 6 mo.; son of Charles & Sarah; could be Lenaghan
THOMAS, Ann; died Jul 6, 1796; bur. Jul 7, 1796; age - 8 mo.; dau. of Paul & Mary Catherine Bardon de Monglas
THOMAS, Mary Adelle; died Sep 1, 1796; bur. Sep 1, 1796; age - 1 yr. 2 mo.; dau. of John Lewis & Mary Catherine Conrad
THOMAS, Sarah; died May 21, 1796; bur. May 22, 1796; age - 11 da.; dau. of Ann

BURIALS

THOMPSON, Clara; died Sep 29, 1798; bur. Sep 30, 1798; dau. of
    Josias & Jane; born & died Sept 29, 1798
THOMPSON, Mary; died May 29, 1795; bur. May 30, 1795; age - 31
    yrs.; widow
TIEGLER, Elizabeth; died Jul 12, 1796; bur. Jul 14, 1796; age - 1
    yr. 11 mo. 20 da.; dau. of Francis & Frances
TIMON, John Mathias; died Oct 31, 1800; bur. Nov 1, 1800; age - 9
    mo.; son of James & Frances
TONCAS, John Lewis; died Jan 13, 1798; bur. Jan 14, 1798; age - 1
    yr.; son of Lewis & Mary
TOOLE, Bernard; died Oct 3, 1798; bur. Oct 3, 1798; age - 2 yrs.;
    son of Edward & Elizabeth
TOPP, Mary; died Aug 3, 1797; bur. Aug 4, 1797; age - 8 mo. 8
    da.; dau. of Henry & Mary
TOUCAS, Mary; died Oct 7, 1797; bur. Oct 7, 1797; age - 30 yrs.;
    wf. of Capt Lewis
TOWSEND, Robert; died Jan 21, 1796; bur. Jan 22, 1796; age - 45
    yrs.; of Fells Point
TRACEY, Mary; died Feb 11, 1794; bur. Feb 12, 1794; age - 65
    yrs.; nat. of Ireland; wf. of Usher, carpenter of Fells
    Point; died at Fells Point
TREPANNIER, Ann; died Sep 29, 1800; bur. Sep 30, 1800; age - 46
    yrs.; wf. of Augustine
TREPANNIER, Michael; died Oct 9, 1800; bur. Oct 9, 1800; age - 14
    yrs.; son of Augustine & Ann (deceased)
TREVIN, Rebecca; died Feb 15, 1794; bur. Feb 16, 1794; nat. of
    Nova Scotia; advanced age
TRUELY, Henrietta; died Jul 25, 1796; bur. Jul 26, 1796; age - 2
    mo.; Negro dau. of Richard & Henrietta
TYSON, John; died May 28, 1797; bur. May 28, 1797; age - 1 mo. 2
    da.; son of Henry & Sabina
USHER, James; died Sep 3, 1800; bur. Sep 4, 1800; age - 7 mo.;
    son of James & Catharine
VALETTE, Arsenius Joseph; died Feb 2, 1797; bur. Feb 3, 1797; age
    - 1 yr. 4 mo. 12 da.; son of Charles Francis & Jane Baque
VALETTE, Louisa; died Oct 14, 1797; bur. Oct 15, 1797; age - 10
    mo.; dau. of Charles & Jane Bagne
VEAL, Joanna; died Oct 15, 1797; bur. Oct 15, 1797; age - 1 yr.;
    dau. of Nicholas & Catherine
VEAL, Nicholas; died Sep 8, 1797; bur. Sep 8, 1797; nat. of
    Ireland
VEAL, Nicholas; died Sep 8, 1800; bur. Sep 9, 1800; age - 2 yrs.
    4 mo.; son of Nicholas (deceased) & Catherine Melone,
    formerly Veal
VEAL, Pierce; died Sep 10, 1797; bur. Sep 10, 1797; nat. of
    Ireland
VEAL, Thomas; died Sep 12, 1797; bur. Sep 12, 1797; age - 24
    yrs.; nat. of Ireland
VENNY, Evans; died Sep 23, 1800; bur. Sep 23, 1800; age - 13
    yrs.; son of -- & Margaret (now Cowen)
VERDIER, Jane Merel; died May 20, 1795; bur. May 21, 1795; age -
    58 yrs.; nat. of Lions, France; wf. of John Peter, surgeon
VIDAL, John Lewis; died May 1, 1797; bur. May 2, 1797; age - 43
    yrs.; born Toulous, France; inh. of Southern District, St.
    Domingo

BURIALS

VINCHES, Louis; died Oct 6, 1793; age - 52 yrs.; nat. of parish of Boudon, Diocese of Cahors, France; inh. of bottom plain, Isle of Vache, parish of Torbeck, St Domingo
VINEY, John; died Sep 30, 1794; bur. Oct 1, 1794; son of Thomas & Ann
VININGDER, Catherine; died Sep 24, 1800; bur. Sep 25, 1800; age - 16 yrs.
VINNEY, Patrick; died Sep 16, 1797; bur. Sep 16, 1797
WALKER, Elizabeth; died Oct 29, 1797; bur. Oct 30, 1797; age - 3 mo.; dau. of Robert & Sarah
WALKER, John Dennis; died Dec 29, 1799; bur. Dec 30, 1799; age - 14 mo.; son of Robert & Sarah
WALKER, Mary; died Aug 9, 1797; bur. Aug 10, 1797; age - 3 yrs. 7 mo.; dau. of Robert & Sarah
WALSH, Edward; died Apr 7, 1795; bur. Apr 8, 1795; age - 28 yrs.; nat. of Ireland; deceased at Fells Point
WALSH, Edward Carrere; died Apr 25, 1799; bur. Apr 26, 1799; age - 5 mo.; son of Robert & Elizabeth
WALSH, Eleanor; died Jul 31, 1798; bur. Aug 1, 1798; age - 4 mo.; dau. of Maurice & Elizabeth
WALSH, Francis William; died Apr 22, 1795; bur. Apr 23, 1795; age - 5 wks.; son of Robert & Elizabeth
WALSH, Ignatius; died Sep 20, 1796; bur. Sep 21, 1796; age - 4 yrs. 8 mo. 20 da.; son of Robert & Elizabeth
WALSH, John; died Sep 11, 1794; bur. Sep 12, 1794; age - 15 mo.; son of Richard & Eleanor
WALSH, John; died Aug 21, 1800; bur. Aug 22, 1800; age - 25 yrs.; nat. of Ireland
WALSH, Mary Ann; died Aug 8, 1800; bur. Aug 9, 1800; age - 10 mo.
WALSH, Michael; died Aug 25, 1800; bur. Aug 26, 1800; hsb. of Anna Catharina
WALSH, Patrick; died Aug 12, 1798; bur. Aug 12, 1798; age - 30 yrs.; nat. of Ireland
WALSH, Pierce; died Dec 19, 1799; bur. Dec 20, 1799; age - 1 yr.
WALSH, Walter; died Feb 7, 1798; bur. Feb 7, 1798; age - 2 yrs.; son of Pierce & Mary
WALTER, David; died Jul 5, 1796; bur. Jul 6, 1796; age - 2 mo. 10 da.; son of Nicholas & Ann Mary
WALTER, Elizabeth; died Sep 3, 1800; bur. Sep 3, 1800; age - 10 yrs.; dau. of Lewis & Eve
WALTER, Eve; died Sep 5, 1800; bur. Sep 5, 1800; age - 30 yrs.; wf. Lewis who died the same day
WALTER, John; died Aug 21, 1797; bur. Aug 22, 1797; hsb. of Elizabeth; tailor; inhumanly murdered
WALTER, Lewis; died Sep 5, 1800; bur. Sep 5, 1800; age - 36 yrs.; hsb. of Eve
WALTER, Peter; died Sep 2, 1795; bur. Sep 3, 1795; son of Peter & Margaret; born & died Sept. 2, 1795
WALTER, Peter; died Aug 11, 1797; bur. Aug 12, 1797; age - 2 yrs.; son of John & Elizabeth
WALTON, Maria; died Nov 26, 1800; bur. Nov 27, 1800; age - 5 yrs.; dau. of John & Barbara
WALTON, Sarah; died Apr 30, 1800; bur. May 1, 1800; age - 3 mo.; dau. of Charleton & Sarah

BURIALS

WANTE, Magdalen Felicity Casanbon; died Jan 13, 1795; bur. Jan 14, 1795; age - 42 yrs.; nat. of Brest; wf. of Charles Stephen; deceased near Baltimore

WATKINS, John; died Aug 12, 1797; bur. Aug 13, 1797; age - 2 wks.; son of Joshua & Mary

WATKINS, Rebecca; died Aug 8, 1799; bur. Aug 9, 1799; age - 1 yr.; dau. of Joshua & Mary

WEAVER, Peter; died Jan 13, 1800; bur. Jan 14, 1800; nat. of Germany

WEDGE, Elizabeth; died Jul 16, 1798; bur. Jul 17, 1798; age - 1 yr.; dau. of Joseph & Mary

WEEKS, John; died Oct 17, 1799; bur. Oct 18, 1799; age - 45 yrs.; nat. of Ireland

WEEKS, Richard; died Jun 12, 1800; bur. Jun 12, 1800; age - 3 mo.; son of John & Mary

WEEKS, Thomas; died May 28, 1800; bur. May 29, 1800; age - 2 1/2 yrs.; son of John & Mary

WEISS, Catharine; died Feb 28, 1800; bur. Mar 1, 1800; age - 5 yrs.; dau. of Felix & Barbara

WEISS, George; died Mar 10, 1800; bur. Mar 11, 1800; age - 6 yrs.; son of Felix & Barbara

WEISS, John; died Jul 16, 1797; bur. Jul 17, 1797; age - 3 mo.; son of Felix & Barbara

WELLS, Sarah Mary Antoinette; died Aug 15, 1794; bur. Aug 16, 1794; age - 11 mo.; dau. of Cyporian & Margaret

WHEELER, Aloysius; died May 8, 1796; bur. May 9, 1796; age - 11 mo.; son of Leonard & Teresa

WHEELER, Charles; died Sep 17, 1794; bur. Sep 17, 1794

WHEELER, Jacob; died May 21, 1799; bur. May 22, 1799

WHEELER, Louisa Catharine; died Apr 26, 1798; bur. Apr 27, 1798; age - 14 mo.; dau. of Harriot

WHELAN, Daniel; died Jul 29, 1799; bur. Jul 30, 1799; age - 4 yrs.; son of Daniel & ?

WHELAN, Mary; died Sep 8, 1795; bur. Sep 9, 1795; age - 24 yrs.; nat. of Ireland

WHITE, Elizabeth; died Oct 14, 1800; bur. Oct 14, 1800; wf. of Capt Joseph White, Sr

WHITE, John; died Sep 5, 1800; bur. Sep 6, 1800; age - 3 mo.; son of James & Honor

WHITE, Oliver; died Jun 14, 1799; bur. Jun 14, 1799; age - 70 yrs.; nat. of Acadia

WHITE, William; died Aug 6, 1796; bur. Aug 7, 1796; age - 11 mo.; son of Simon & Jane

WHITE, William; died Jun 23, 1798; bur. Jun 24, 1798; age - 2 mo.; son of Simon & Jane

WILDE, Ann; died Apr 25, 1797; bur. Apr 26, 1797; age - 1 yr. 4 mo.; dau. of Richard & Mary

WILL, Christina; died Nov 9, 1799; bur. Nov 10, 1799

WILL, John; died Sep 22, 1794; bur. Sep 23, 1794; age - 10 mo.

WILLIAMS, Catherine; died May 30, 1799; bur. May 31, 1799; age - 16 mo.; dau. of Ester

WILLIAMS, Jennet; died Aug 6, 1796; bur. Aug 7, 1796; age - 13 mo.; dau. of John & Jennet

WILLIAMS, John Baptist; died Jul 16, 1798; bur. Jul 17, 1798; age - 11 mo.; son of Charlotte

BURIALS

WILLIAMS, William; died Aug 27, 1800; bur. Aug 27, 1800; age - 36 yrs.; nat. of Wales
WILLIAMS, William; died Sep 3, 1800; bur. Sep 3, 1800; age - 7 yrs.; son of John & Jennet
WILLIAMSON, Henrietta; died Dec 26, 1793; bur. Dec 29, 1793; wf. of David, merchant, Baltimore
WILLIAMSON, Rachael Frances; died Oct 15, 1794; bur. Oct 16, 1794; age - 1 yr.; dau. of David & Henrietta
WILLSON, John Francis; died Sep 18, 1798; bur. Sep 19, 1798; age - 10 mo.; son of David & Ann
WILSON, Mary; died Sep 21, 1800; bur. Sep 21, 1800; age - 30 yrs.; wf. of James
WINEMAN, Eleanor; died May 12, 1800; bur. May 13, 1800; wf. of Henry; small pox
WINN, Joseph; died Oct 27, 1794; bur. Oct 28, 1794; age - 5 yrs.; son of Joseph & Margaret
WISE, Catherine; died Jul 24, 1798; bur. Jul 25, 1798; age - 1 yr.; dau. of Michael & Catherine
WORTHY, Rachel; died Apr 29, 1799; bur. Apr 30, 1799; age - 36 yrs.; slave of John Martiacq
WRIGNAUSE, Ann Mary; died Oct 12, 1796; bur. Oct 13, 1796; age - 4 mo.; dau. of Nicholas & Ann Michon
YANDA, Margaret Aimee LeClerc; died Nov 14, 1796; bur. Nov 14, 1796; age - 22 yrs.; dau. of Framcis LeClerc & Margaret Perigault of Plaisance, St. Domingo; wf. of John Peter lately of St. Domingo
YANTS, George; died Sep 30, 1798; bur. Oct 2, 1798; age - 11 da.; son of George & Mary
YANTZ, William; died May 31, 1796; bur. May 31, 1796; age - 2 wks.; son of George & Mary
YERBY, Margaret Mary Ann; died Oct 6, 1800; bur. Oct 6, 1800; age - 2 yrs.; dau. of William & Elizabeth
YORE, Letitia; died Apr 21, 1794; bur. Apr 22, 1794; age - 56 yrs.; wf. of Richard Yore of Fells Point; last name could be Gore
ZIEGLER, Francis; died Oct 24, 1797; bur. Oct 25, 1797; age - 9 mo.; son of Francis & Frances

www.ingramcontent.com/pod-product-compliance
Lightning Source LLC
Chambersburg PA
CBHW062209080426
42734CB00010B/1859